Contents at a Glance

D0523260

CHAPTER 8: Using Multiple Layers to Edit Images PAGE 243

54 Create a New Image Layer

55 Create a Layer Filled with a Color, Gradient, or Pattern

56 Create an Adjustment Layer

57 Erase Part of a Layer

58 Replace a Background with Something Else

59 Move, Resize, Skew, or Distort a Layer or Selection

60 Rotate the Data in a Layer or Selection

61 Mask an Adjustment or Fill Layer

62 Mask an Image Layer

PART III: EDITING IMAGES

CHAPTER 9: Making Quick Corrections to a Photograph PAGE 279

63 About Color Management

64 Install a Color Profile

65 Crop a Portion of an Image

66 Straighten an Image

67 Correct Red Eye

68 Apply a Quick Fix

CHAPTER 10: Retouching Photos with Tools PAGE 307

69 About the Toolbox

70 Create Your Own Brush Tips

71 Select a Color to Work With

72 Draw on a Photo with a Pencil

73 Paint an Area of a Photo with a Brush

74 Paint an Area of a Photo with the Airbrush

75 Fill an Area with a Color or Pattern

76 Fill an Area with a Gradient

77 Draw a Shape

78 Add a Text Caption or Label

79 Add a Backscreen Behind Text

80 Create Metallic Text

81 Create Text That Glows

82 Fill Text with an Image

CHAPTER 11: Repairing and Improving Photographs PAGE 353

83 Remove Specks, Spots, and Scratches

84 Repair Minor Tears

85 Repair Large Holes, Tears, and Missing Portions of a Photo

86 Restore Color and Tone to an Old Photograph

87 Restore Quality to a Scanned Photograph

88 Remove Unwanted Objects from an Image

CHAPTER 12: Correcting Brightness, Contrast, Color, and Sharpness PAGE 375

89 About an Image's Histogram

90 Improve Brightness and Contrast

91 Improve a Dull, Flat Photo

92 Lighten a Subject on a Snowy Background

93 Lighten or Darken Part of an Image

94 Correct Color, Contrast, and Saturation in One Step

95 Adjust Hue and Saturation Manually

96 About Sharpness

97 Sharpen an Image

98 Blur an Image to Remove Noise

99 Blur a Background to Create Depth of Field

PART IV: CHAPTERS ON THE WEB

CHAPTER 13: Blending Pixels Together WEB: 1

100 About Blend Modes

CHAPTER 14: Improving Portraits WEB: 11

101 Create a Soft Focus Effect

102 Remove Wrinkles, Freckles, and Minor Blemishes

103 Whiten Teeth

104 Awaken Tired Eyes

105 Remove Glare from Eyeglasses

CHAPTER 15: Creative Photographs WEB: 29

106 Frame a Photograph

107 Create a Scrapbook Page

108 Create a Panorama

109 "Melt" an Image

110 Create the Illusion of Snow or Rain

111 Simulate a Water Reflection

112 Make a Photograph Look Old

113 Change a Color Photograph to Black and White

114 Make a Photograph Look Like an Oil Painting

115 Turn a Photograph into a Watercolor

116 Make a Photograph Look Like It Was Drawn

117 Make a Photograph Look Like Andy Warhol Painted It

Adobe® Photoshop® Elements 4

Jennifer Fulton
Scott M. Fulton III

SAMS
Teach Yourself

Sams Publishing, 800 East 96th Street, Indianapolis, Indiana 46240 USA

Adobe® Photoshop® Elements 4 in a Snap

International Standard Book Number: 0-672-32850-X

Library of Congress Catalog Card Number: 2005928914

Printed in the United States of America

First Printing: December 2005

08 07 06 05   4 3 2 1

Trademarks

Warning and Disclaimer

Bulk Sales

Sams Publishing offers excellent discounts on this book when ordered in quantity for bulk purchases or special sales. For more information, please contact

> **U.S. Corporate and Government Sales**
>
> 1-800-382-3419
>
> corpsales@pearsontechgroup.com

For sales outside of the United States, please contact

> **International Sales**
>
> international@pearsoned.com

Acquisitions Editor
Betsy Brown

Development Editor
Alice Martina Smith

Managing Editor
Charlotte Clapp

Project Editor
Dan Knott

Indexer
Julie Bess

Technical Editor
Doug Nelson

Publishing Coordinator
Vanessa Evans

Multimedia Developer
Dan Scherf

Book Designer
Gary Adair

Page Layout
Bronkella Publishing

About the Authors

Jennifer Fulton, iVillage's former "Computer Coach," is an experienced computer consultant and trainer with more than 20 years of experience. Jennifer is also the best-selling author of more than 100 computer books written for both the education and retail markets, including *How to Use Dreamweaver and Fireworks, Adobe Photoshop Elements 3 in a Snap, Digital Photography with Photoshop Album in a Snap, Paint Shop Pro 8 in a Snap, Sams Teach Yourself Adobe Photoshop Elements 2 in 24 Hours, Sams Teach Yourself Windows Me in 10 Minutes, How to Use Microsoft Publisher 2000, How to Use Microsoft Office XP, Easy Microsoft Outlook 2000, Sams Teach Yourself Excel 2000 in 10 Minutes, Microsoft Office 2000 Cheat Sheet*, and *The Complete Idiot's Guide to Upgrading and Repairing PCs*.

Scott M. Fulton III is a 22-year veteran technology author, currently featured online at InformIT.com and *Tom's Hardware Guide*. In the 1980s, as "D. F. Scott," he launched one of the world's first online technology news sources for *Computer Shopper* magazine, long before the Internet gave birth to the World Wide Web. In the 1990s, Scott published a dozen books and hundreds of articles, many on the topic of high-level programming. In 1994, just after they married, Scott and Jennifer formed Ingenus, a technology editorial partnership in the Midwest. But their greatest success to date is their daughter, Katerina, who at age eight is in the process of forming an art school, a radio station, and a presidential campaign exploratory committee.

Dedication

To the memory of Betty J. Edwards, whom we all knew as "Aunt Betty," for her service to her country, her dedication to her patients and to her church, and for the tireless love and generosity she gave to her large, extended family, especially her many nieces and nephews. She will be missed beyond measure.

—Scott and Jennifer Fulton

Acknowledgments

Thanks to everyone at Sams for their help and support in getting this book to print, especially Alice Martina Smith, Betsy Brown, and Dan Knott.

Thanks also to wonderful people at Adobe for producing a quality, easy-to-use program and for their support during the writing of this book.

We Want to Hear from You!

As the reader of this book, *you* are our most important critic and commentator. We value your opinion and want to know what we're doing right, what we could do better, what areas you'd like to see us publish in, and any other words of wisdom you're willing to pass our way.

You can email or write me directly to let me know what you did or didn't like about this book—as well as what we can do to make our books stronger.

Please note that I cannot help you with technical problems related to the topic of this book, and that due to the high volume of mail I receive, I might not be able to reply to every message.

When you write, please be sure to include this book's title and author as well as your name and phone or email address. I will carefully review your comments and share them with the author and editors who worked on the book.

Email: graphics@samspublishing.com

Mail: Mark Taber
         Associate Publisher
         Sams Publishing
         800 East 96th Street
         Indianapolis, IN 46240 USA

Reader Services

For more information about this book or another Sams Publishing title, visit our website at www.samspublishing.com. Type the ISBN (excluding hyphens) or the title of a book in the Search field to find the page you're looking for.

Bonus Content on the Web

Visit www.samspublishing.com/title/067232850X, register your book, and download additional information to enhance your Photoshop Elements experience:

- Blend Mode Examples
- Improving Portraits
- Creative Photographs

PART I

Organizing Items in the Catalog

IN THIS PART:

CHAPTER 1	Start Here	3
CHAPTER 2	Importing Items into the Organizer Catalog	29
CHAPTER 3	Organizing and Creating Items	63
CHAPTER 4	Finding Images, Movies, and Audio Files	95

1

Start Here

You might not have discovered it yet, but Photoshop Elements is actually two programs designed to work seamlessly together: the Editor and the Organizer. You use the **Editor** to make changes to digital images, such as brightening and sharpening them. You use the **Organizer** to catalog your images so that you can quickly locate and edit, print, or email them when needed.

▶ KEY TERM

Editor—The portion of Photoshop Elements you use to make changes to images.

Organizer—The portion of Photoshop Elements you use to categorize your collection of graphic images.

Given the recent advancements in the field of digital photography, you might be surprised at how easy it is to take a bad picture. Even when your digital camera is taking pictures in Automatic mode, it might not properly compensate for less-than-favorable lighting conditions, unexpected movement of your subject matter, or poor composition. Luckily, in the digital world of photography, you can correct most mistakes with the help of a **graphics editor** such as the Photoshop Elements Editor.

▶ KEY TERM

Graphics editor—An application that allows you to edit your digital images.

Perhaps you don't use a digital camera; the quality of film photography is often far superior to that of digital images. Unfortunately, when you scan a photo print into a digital file, you often lose the qualities that made the original print superior in the first place—its sharpness, depth of tone, and color. Again, with the aid of graphic editors such as the Photoshop Elements Editor, you can restore the beauty your prints might have lost in translation. In this book, you'll learn everything you need to know about working with digital images, including how to use the Organizer and the Editor to categorize and manipulate them.

The Nature of Digital Photography

If you use a digital camera, you are more likely to print your photos at home rather than have a photo shop print them. Your computer essentially becomes the film lab, making you responsible for the touch-ups and corrections you'd otherwise trust to a lab technician. Don't let this new responsibility overwhelm you. As you'll learn in this book, the *Editor* provides many simple-to-use tools for fixing just about any problem in a digital image. When working with digital images, keep these things in mind:

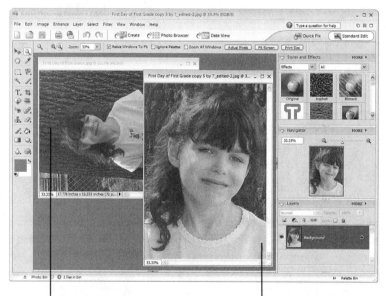

Before Editing, This Image Is Dark and Rotated Incorrectly

After Brightening and Cropping, the Image Is Ready for Printing

With the Editor, you become your own photo lab technician.

- **Film can record more detail than digital media**—To compensate, always take photos at your digital camera's highest *resolution*. Yes, this means you won't be able to store as many photos on the camera's memory card, but the photos you do save will be worth printing.

▶ KEY TERM

Resolution—In digital images, the number of pixels per inch/centimeter. The higher an image's resolution, the more detail it can contain.

▶ TIP

If you're given a choice of formats to use with your digital camera, choose RAW. If your camera doesn't use RAW, choose the TIFF format over JPEG because RAW and TIFF save more photographic detail than JPEG does.

- **Digital photos accumulate quickly**—Early on, you should develop a plan for managing your images, such as importing photos from your camera directly into the Organizer, a process that copies the images to the hard disk, renames them (if desired), and even fixes any red eye (again, if you choose that option). You should then back up these new, original images onto a CD-R, DVD-R, or other high-volume, permanent storage medium. If you select the **Move Files** option when you copy the new images to optical disc, the images are removed from the hard disk (saving space), but you can still review, print, and edit the images from the Organizer.

  Next, in the Organizer, you should review the *thumbnail* of each new image, selecting the best ones to keep and deleting the rest of the image files from the hard disk (if they are still there) and the *catalog*. As you review the images, you can tag those you do keep with special markers that identify their content. These *tags* will help you later locate these images in the catalog. You'll find that the Organizer is uniquely designed to help you with all the stages in this process.

- **Before making changes to your images, save copies of them, but do not edit your original images**—Before beginning to edit images, save them in PSD (Photoshop) format. This format allows you to use all of Photoshop Elements' tools to make your images picture perfect. When you're done editing, resave your images in a universal format such as TIFF or JPEG so they're easier to share and print than your edited PSD versions. Using the Organizer, back up the PSD and TIFF/JPEG versions of your edited images onto a CD-R, a DVD-R, or other storage medium.

- **Printing quality photos requires a printer designed and tested not only for color, but also for use with photo paper**—A photo printer specifically designed for printing photos is a good addition to your computer family if you want to print good-looking photos for albums, scrapbooks, and picture frames at home. As an alternative to buying your own color photo printer, consider a do-it-yourself printing kiosk that lets you insert a CD-R or PhotoCD and print photos on high-quality photo paper. Find a kiosk in your neighborhood (many discount department stores and drug stores have one) and study the instructions so you can save your photos in a compatible format on a compatible medium. For occasional photo printing needs, online services such as Adobe Photoshop Services enable you to upload your photos over the Internet, have them printed on quality stock, and have them delivered to you for reasonable fees.

▶ **NOTE**

For optimum results, use only the photo paper that's compatible with your particular printer. Another consideration when printing photos at home is longevity. Archival inks and papers, though expensive, produce the best results.

- **If you intend to use the Editor to repair images scanned from old prints, invest in a quality scanner with high resolution**—Some premium scanner models include special features such as a film reader for scanning film strips and slides.

What You Should Know About Resolution and Size

A digital image is composed of a series of small points, called *pixels* , of a particular color and brightness. The higher a digital photo's resolution, the more pixels it has per inch, and thus the more detail and clarity it can contain. For example, if a photo of a person's face has a low resolution, the face will lack detail and might lack the nuances that give a person character. The same photo with a higher resolution shows more detail, such as the texture of the skin, some of which can distinguish the mood of the subject. When editing digital images, you must always remember that the resolution you are using directly affects the quality of the final result. The resolution of an image also affects both its onscreen size and its final printed size; more on that in a moment.

How much resolution do you need for a good-looking image? This depends on where the image will be used—displayed onscreen or printed on paper. Onscreen images in a web page, PowerPoint presentation, or Windows desktop background require only low resolutions—between 72 and 120 *pixels per inch (PPI)* to look good. Images you intend to print require higher resolutions to pass muster: typically 300 pixels per inch. PPI is great for describing image resolution, but there's another term you should know: *dots per inch (DPI)*. You can pretty much ignore DPI and concentrate solely on image resolution or *PPI*, and I'll tell you why. Deep in ancient history (months and months ago), printer manufacturers treated DPI as equal to PPI and listed their printers as 300 DPI, regardless of how many dots of ink were actually required for them to print one pixel of image information. Nowadays, with photo printers using six or more colors of ink, man-ufacturers are trying to help you distinguish their printer's quality by listing its actual DPI, typically calculated by multiplying the number of inks by roughly 300. Regardless of how the DPI for your printer is calculated, the more dots of ink per inch, the higher the print quality will be because you can achieve gentle, sub-tle color variations. The weird thing, though, is that you probably won't be able to choose the DPI you want to use when you print a particular image because the DPI option is not usually listed in any print dialog box; instead, it's listed as Print Quality. So, to print a photograph with the highest DPI capability for your print-er, choose the highest photo quality it offers and, of course, use quality photo paper. So, let's just agree to ignore the acronym *DPI* for now and concentrate on the critical number, PPI, which describes an image's resolution.

▶ KEY TERM

DPI (dots per inch)—Used to describe printer output.

PPI (pixels per inch)— Used to describe an image's resolution or onscreen quality.

An image's resolution or PPI affects its onscreen size and actual print size as well as quality. First of all, the size of an onscreen image varies depending on the screen resolution of the monitor on which it is being viewed. In other words, if you're viewing an image with your monitor resolution set at 1280×1024, that same image will appear *bigger* (but with the same quality or level of detail) on a monitor set to a lower resolution, such as 1024×768. This little tidbit of informa-tion probably concerns you only if you're creating an image for the Web, where a viewer's monitor resolution affects the size in which that image appears.

The actual print size of an image also varies depending on its image resolution. Photoshop Elements calculates an image's default print size (called its *actual size*) by dividing its PPI by 220—the lowest image resolution you can use to produce a reasonable quality printout. For example, an image with a resolution of 2048×1536 pixels per inch (a 3MB image) has an actual print size of 9.3" $\times$ 6.9" ($2048/220 \times 1536/220$). If you ship the print to an online lab, you might be able to request a size larger than that because of the high-quality printers they use. Of course, you can always print an image smaller than its actual print size, which in this example is roughly 9" $\times$ 7". But if you try to print an image at home at a size larger than its actual print size, rendering it at less than 220 PPI image resolu-tion, you'll get a poor result. For example, if you try to print your 2048-x-1536 image in a large size, such as 10" $\times$ 8", you'll get poor results—fuzzy edges and lack of detail. Because of that, if you try to print any photo at a low resolution (again, less than 220 PPI), Photoshop Elements will warn you about the possible consequences.

You can, if needed, upsize an image without losing resolution by adding pixels to the image through a process called resampling. Of course, there are limits: Trying to double an image's size through resampling will indeed give you a larger image, maybe even with enough resolution (enough pixels per inch) to equal the print minimum of 220 PPI image resolution. But because the resampling process is not perfect, your larger image will most likely be fuzzy, be noisy (like a TV with poor reception), and have considerably less detail than the original. Thus, it's best to record digital images or scan printed photos at the highest resolution possible so you can print or display them in the size you want (actual print size or lower) without losing image quality. If you resize an image to make it smaller, you don't have to remove pixels, so you can skip the resampling part (which helps Photoshop Elements decide which pixels to keep). Keeping the pixels while reducing an image's size increases the image's resolution (the number of pixels per inch) and might produce a better-quality print.

Adding Text and Objects to an Image

When you decide to add text or drawn objects to a photo, you'll need to choose between *raster objects* and *vector objects*. The process of rendering raster (bitmap) objects onscreen is similar to using a Lite-Brite toy to draw a picture using small lights—the object is rendered as a series of dots. A *vector* is a mathematical formula that describes a line or curve. A vector object (such as a drawn rectangle or circle or some text) is therefore computed by the Editor *geometrically*, as a series of points connected by lines. Raster data can only be changed dot by dot, while vector data can be easily resized, moved, and recolored.

▶ KEY TERM

Raster object—Object comprised of individual pixels, each with its own hue, saturation, and brightness value.

Vector object—Object comprised of a series of mathematical formulas that plot the coordinates of points along the edges of the vector shape or text.

In the Editor, geometric elements such as shapes, curves, lines, and text are rendered on a vector *layer*. Image content (such as a digital photograph or a scanned image) and objects you paint with the **Brush** tool or draw with the **Pencil** tool are rendered on a raster layer. Normally, the edges of vector objects are smooth and clean because they are rendered mathematically, but because the Editor renders the contents of its vector layer on a grid with the same resolution as all the other raster layers in an image, curved or diagonal content might appear jagged or stair-stepped when viewed at a high magnification. This fact makes some vector data appear jagged when printed.

Not to worry though; the Editor can compensate for the jaggies through a process called *antialiasing*. Antialiasing smoothes curves by adding semitransparent pixels that soften the transition between the edge of the shape or text and the background. Your eye, as it turns out, will more readily forgive the watery borders caused by antialiasing than it will ignore the stair-step look of a non-antialiased curve.

▶ KEY TERM

Layer—A component of an image that contains its own data, which can be manipulated separately from other data in the image.

Antialiasing—The addition of semitransparent pixels along the curved edge of a shape or selection to help smooth curves.

▶ NOTE

When you resave a PSD file in any format other than TIFF (with the **Layers** option turned on), all vector data is converted to raster data.

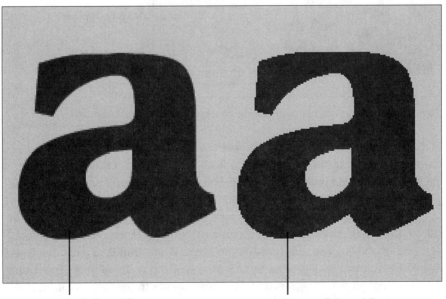

Antialiased Text   **Non-antialiased Text**

Antialiasing of this text blends otherwise jagged edges with their backgrounds by adding shades of the object color along its edges.

About Color Models and Optics

Digital images (such as photographs) are comprised of a series of pixels; each pixel has various characteristics that describe its color. For example, a pixel might be pale yellow-green. How the computer decides to make that pixel pale yellow-green depends on a specific color model. The Editor uses two color models: RGB (which describes the color of a pixel as a mix of red, green, and blue) and HSB (which describes a pixel with a given hue, saturation, and brightness). Color models become important whenever you're asked to make a color choice from the **Color Picker**. Neither color model is necessarily better than the other; you simply use the one you prefer to choose the exact color you want.

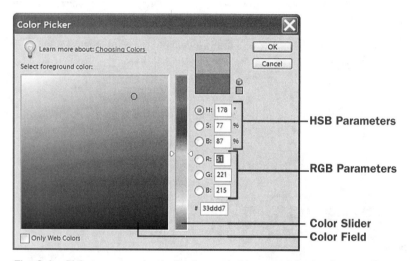

The Color Picker represents pixel colors using two models simultaneously.

With the RGB model, the relative amount of red, green, and blue contained in a color is displayed in the corresponding R, G, and B boxes in the **Color Picker**. The purest, brightest red is defined as an RGB value of {255, 0, 0}, or red with no green or blue. White is produced by mixing the three colors evenly at full strength: {255, 255, 255}. Black is produced on a monitor by adding no light at all: {0, 0, 0}. With the HSB model, the hue (H) value is represented by a color's location on the color wheel. There are 360° in a circle, and thus each hue is represented by its angle or degree on this circle, beginning with red at 0°. The saturation level (S) refers to how much of that hue appears in the final color, from 0 (white) to full color. Brightness (B) represents the blended color's degree of light. Here, a value of **0%** represents total darkness (black) and **100%** is a color with no black added at all. Using the HSB model, pure red is 0,100,100 (0 on the hue wheel, 100% saturation, and 100% brightness). Pure black is x,100,0 (any value for hue, 100% saturation, and no brightness), and pure white is x,0,100 (any value for hue, 0% saturation, and 100% brightness). You'll learn the specifics behind selecting a color using both the RGB and HSB color models in **71 Select a Color to Work with**.

▶ **NOTE**

Okay, there's a third way to specify color in the **Color Picker**: by entering a specific HTML color code in the # box. The code uses six hexadecimal (base-16) digits, where the first pair stands for the red value, the second pair for green, and the third pair for blue. Whereas we commonly use digits 0–9 with everyday numbers (base-10), hexadecimal proceeds from 0 to 9 and up to A–F (to represent 10–15). So, A0 represents 160 and FF represents 255.

Printing Great Photographs

You're probably used to printing mostly cards, letters, spreadsheets, and other everyday work documents, and you've come to expect that your printed results will match your onscreen view pretty closely. But when you print digital photographs, there may come a moment when you think, "That isn't how it looked onscreen." Not your fault really; no two devices ever worked so differently in reproducing color as your monitor and your printer. Your monitor produces colors with light, whereas your printer uses ink. Pretty obvious, really, but it's this difference that makes it difficult to get an image to print the way it looks onscreen.

Because the monitor and the printer use two different color models, one optical (RGB, for red, green, and blue) and the other ink-based (CMYK, for cyan, magenta, yellow and black) to reproduce color, it's up to your program (in this case, Photoshop Elements) to do the best job it can in translating between the two. Photoshop Elements uses ICC color profiles to help it translate color information from your monitor's RGB color model to your printer's CMYK color model. That way, what you see onscreen is very similar to what you'll get when you print a photograph. Windows typically installs a color profile for translating optical shades to printed shades so that what you see onscreen looks the same when printed. When you installed your printer, the software it uses might have overridden this default color profile with one that's better suited to your printer. But it might not have done so. In any case, this book will show you not only how to install the best color profiles for your system (see **63 Install a Color Profile**), but also how to make subtle color corrections to your images onscreen so that you'll get the best printed result.

Whether you plan to print a photograph locally or with a service, here are some tips for preparing the image properly for printing:

- **Start with enough pixels**—Typically, you'll want your final image resolution to be 220 *PPI* minimum, with 300 PPI a more realistic minimum. So, make sure that you capture digital images or scan print images at that resolution or higher. If you plan to resize and resample a scanned image to remove moiré patterns caused by the scanning process, scan at double that resolution or higher—400 to 600 PPI.

▶ TIP

Online services typically require images of only 150 PPI image resolution to achieve quality prints (because they use higher-quality printers, better inks, and Kodak paper). Because online services typically use better-quality papers and inks than what's available to the home user—and might even make minor corrections to your photos before printing them—you might want to use online services for the prints you want to keep. And better yet, sometimes the prints will cost less per copy than printing images at home! See **39** **Print Images Using an Online Service**.

- **Check the print size and resolution**—The actual print size and image resolution of a particular image can be viewed with the Editor's **Image, Resize, Image Size** command. Capturing photos at a high resolution (such as 5Mp or greater) means that their print sizes will be fairly large, but you can always reduce the print size of an image by resizing the image file in the Editor or resizing the image on-the-fly (without actually changing the image's size or resolution) using options in the **Print Preview** dialog box. However, you cannot increase an image's resolution or print size after it has already been shot, at least not with good results. For example, printing a 3Mp image at more than 5" × 7" produces a grainy, less-than-quality result.

- **Resize the image to fit the photo size you want**—If you are printing the image yourself, you can adjust its print size on-the-fly in the **Print Preview** or **Print Selected Photos** dialog box to approximate the proper photo size, although, as noted earlier, this might cause a loss of print quality if the resulting resolution becomes too low. This can also result in areas of the image being cropped (not printed) because Photoshop Elements adjusts an image size to fit the print size you select. It's better, therefore, to start your editing by cropping (if needed) and resizing the image to make it the size you want to print. This not only allows you to accurately judge its print quality onscreen, but also keeps you from losing portions of the image when printing. Resizing is especially important if you plan on sending your images to a photo lab for processing. Just follow the steps in **32** **Change Image Size or Resolution**.

▶ TIP

In the Editor, you can crop an image to an exact print size such as 4" × 6". See **65** **Crop a Portion of an Image**.

- **Work in Photoshop PSD or layered TIFF format; then resave the final result in format that preserves quality**—Non-layered TIFF format, a lossless format, is typically best to use to preserve your finished photographic images. TIFF files, however, are typically large. JPEG format allows for invisible, or semivisible, selective reductions in image quality to achieve smaller file sizes. If you plan to use an outside photo service that requires JPEG format, or you simply want as small a file as reasonably possible, edit your image first, working in Photoshop PSD or layered TIFF format. When you're completely done with the image, save a copy as JPEG, using as low an amount of compression as you can while still retaining visual quality. If the lab accepts TIFF format or if space is not a problem, use it instead because TIFF files provide higher-quality prints—just be sure to resave the working image in non-layered TIFF for the lab because they might not be able to read a layered TIFF image.

- **Merge layers before printing**—If you plan to print an image that has multiple layers from the Editor, merge the layers before printing to speed up the printing process. Save your working (***.psd**) image first, merge the layers, save the result in JPEG or TIFF format, and then print the JPEG/TIFF or send it out for printing. (See **28 About Saving Images** for details.)

▶ **TIP**

The **Layers** palette displays an eye icon in front of all currently visible layers. This icon also designates which layers will print. To print just some of the layers in an image, hide them temporarily by clicking the eye icon.

Using Photoshop Elements to Organize Photos

After beginning your foray into digital photography, it won't take long before you'll realize that your collection of images is getting almost too big to manage. This is where the Photoshop Elements Organizer comes in: Its purpose is to provide the tools you need to catalog images so you can locate them quickly, regardless of where they are stored—on the hard disk, a CD-R, a DVD, or a digital camera's memory card. Basically, you import images into the Organizer's catalog and then tag them with special markers that indicate what those images contain (for example, Fourth of July, Oklahoma City, or Granddad and Nana) or their purpose (for example, Family Reunion Invitation). Next, you'll use these markers to locate specific images for editing, printing, or using in *creations*. If you choose to edit an image, the Editor portion of Photoshop Elements appears, displaying its unique set of tools designed for making changes to images. To learn how to start the Editor and the Organizer, see **Using the Welcome Window**, later in this chapter. You'll learn how to use the Organizer and its tools in **❶ About the Organizer**.

▶ **TIP**

Creations—Greeting cards, calendars, web galleries, slideshows, and other things you can make with the images in the catalog.

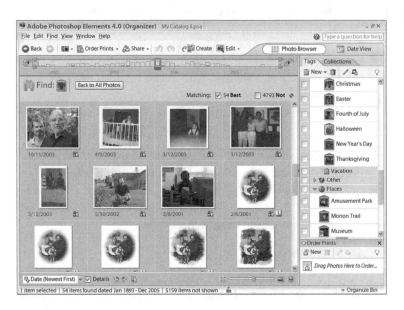

The Organizer enables you to quickly categorize your collection of digital images.

Using Photoshop Elements to Edit Photos

As you learned earlier, the portion of Photoshop Elements that enables you to edit and create graphic images is called the Editor. Although you can use the Editor to create buttons, banners, and other graphical gadgets for your web pages, its main purpose is to edit images. You can use the Editor's tools to retouch photographs, add text and other objects, and apply special effects. You'll learn how to start the Editor in **Using the Welcome Window**, later in this chapter, and to use the Editor's tools in **㉕ About the Editor**. Right now I want to show you how a graphics editor such as the Editor can make your images look better.

How to Use Layers

While editing or building an image, the Editor enables you to place data on multiple layers. The key purpose of layering is to give you a way to isolate individual parts of an image. For example, you might place your subject on a separate layer so you can lighten, recolor, resize, or position just it and not the entire photograph. In addition, data on upper layers obscures data on the layers below them, so you could copy a person onto a lower layer to place him behind other people or objects in a photograph. After using layers to manipulate elements of an image individually, you merge them together to create a flattened, single-layer image ready for printing or sharing.

▶ **NOTE**

After editing a PSD image, merge all the layers into a single background layer by selecting **Layer, Flatten Image**. If the results look good, save the image immediately in a shareable format such as JPEG or non-layered TIFF. (Retain the layer data in the PSD file by not saving over it.)

If you're still working in the PSD file, you can merge selected layers to reduce file size and make a complex image easier to work with. Of course, only merge layers when you're done with them. You can merge selected layers by selecting **Layer, Merge Layers**. Merge visible layers only by selecting **Layer, Merge Visible**. Merge the current layer with the layers below it by selecting **Layer, Merge Down**, or merge the current layer with layers linked to it by selecting **Layers, Merge Linked**. For the **Merge Down** and **Merge Linked** commands to work, the bottommost layer must be a raster layer. If it's a shape or text layer, simplify the layer first (which converts it to raster data) by selecting **Layer, Simplify Layer**.

You can build a complex image by isolating each element on its own layer.

▶ **NOTE**

When you select a region of an image to restrict editing to that region, you're also restricting your edits to that region on the currently selected layer—unless you specify otherwise when making the selection. See **52** **About Copying, Cutting, and Pasting Data Within a Selection**.

Layers are listed in the **Layers** palette. A digital photograph starts out with a single layer called the *background layer*. The background layer is locked and cannot be moved within the layer stack; if you try to erase pixels on a background layer, they are not made transparent, but instead are changed to the current background color. Also, the background layer's opacity (transparency) and blend mode (how its pixels blend with layers below) cannot be changed. If you want to make changes to the background layer, you must first convert it to a regular image layer by selecting the layer and selecting **Layer**, **New**, **Layer from Background**. The name of the current layer is highlighted in the **Layers** palette; with a few exceptions, any changes you make apply only to current layer. To select a layer for editing, click its name in the **Layers** palette. To select only the opaque pixels on a layer, press **Ctrl** and click the layer's thumbnail on the **Layers** palette.

▶ **KEY TERM**

Background layer—The lowest layer in an image; it cannot be moved in the layer stack until it is converted to a regular layer.

When needed, you can add layers to an image, including image layers (that contain a portion of an image), a fill layer (filled with color, gradient, or pattern), and vector layers (which are created automatically when you add text or shapes to an image). You can also add an adjustment layer to test an adjustment (such as a brightness change) without making that adjustment permanent to control the amount of an adjustment or to apply the same adjustment to several layers at once.

The **Layers** palette shows you which layers are on top of others and which are beneath, with upper layers obscuring the layers beneath them. Move layers up or down the layer stack by dragging them on the **Layers** palette; to hide a layer temporarily, click its **Visible** icon. You can control the capability of a layer to block the data in the layers below it by moving its **Opacity** slider at the top of the Layers palette. A layer that's 100% opaque is like new paint on a wall—it completely blocks the wall color beneath. Set the opacity to 50%, and the layer covers lower layers only partially—like a sheer veil. You can also control which areas of an image layer are seen by applying a clipping mask, which you'll learn how to do in **93** **Mask an Image Layer**. In a similar manner, a mask on a fill layer can block the fill from covering portions of the layers below. On an adjustment layer, a mask can act as a blanket, protecting selected parts of a layer from changes such as a color adjustment.

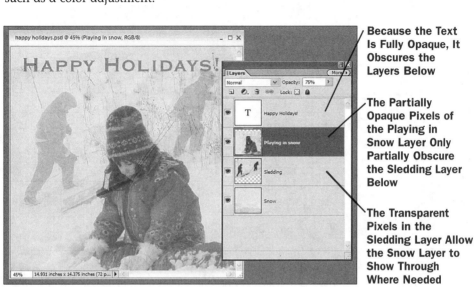

Because the Text Is Fully Opaque, It Obscures the Layers Below

The Partially Opaque Pixels of the Playing in Snow Layer Only Partially Obscure the Sledding Layer Below

The Transparent Pixels in the Sledding Layer Allow the Snow Layer to Show Through Where Needed

Upper layers can obscure lower layers, depending on their opacity.

▶ NOTE

To add a new layer, click the **New Layer** icon at the top of the **Layers** palette. The layer is added above the current layer in the **Layers** palette. To rename a layer, double-click its name on the **Layers** palette, type a new name, and press **Enter**. To delete the currently selected layer, click the **Delete Layer** button on the **Layers** palette.

To duplicate a layer and its contents, select the layer; select **Layer**, **Duplicate Layer**; type a name for the layer; and click **OK**. You can also use this command to copy a layer and place it in another image. You can quickly duplicate a layer by dragging it onto the **Create New Layer** button on the **Layers** palette. To copy a layer into another image quickly, drag the layer from the **Layers** palette and drop it in the other image window.

If a layer is locked so you can't make changes to it, the **Lock** icon displays to the right of the layer name. When the layer is locked, you cannot change its blend mode, opacity, or layer style. You also can't remove a locked layer from an image. Although the background layer is always locked, you can lock any layer by selecting the layer and then clicking the **Lock All** button at the top of the **Layers** palette. Click the icon again to unlock the layer. You can lock just the transparency of a layer if you want by clicking the **Lock Transparent Pixels** button at the top of the **Layers** palette. When a layer has locked transparency, you cannot edit the opacity of a pixel on that layer, but you can change the pixel's color, brightness, or saturation. The **Lock** icon appears on the layer, but you can tell that the layer is only partially locked by moving the mouse pointer over the **Lock** icon and reading the message that appears.

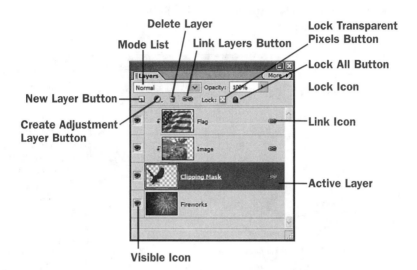

*The **Layers** palette uses various icons to show the properties of each layer.*

When you select a layer in the **Layers** palette, any layers linked to the active layer display the **Link** icon. When layers are linked, they work together as a group. You can move, copy, rotate, resize, skew, or distort the linked layers as if they were one. To link layers, select them by pressing **Ctrl** and clicking each layer; then click the **Link Layers** button at the top of the **Layers** palette. A link icon appears on the selected layers. Click the **Link Layers** button again to unlink the layers if you want to resize, rotate, skew, distort, copy, or move a single layer rather than the linked group.

Another way you can change how an upper layer's data affects the layers below it is through that layer's blend mode. By default, the blend mode for each new layer is set to **Normal**, which means that layer's pixels block data but do not blend with the data on layers below it. You can change a layer's blend mode by activating that layer in the **Layers** palette and selecting the blend mode you want to use from the **Mode** list at the top of the **Layers** palette. Refer to the Sams Publishing website for this book for a description of each blend mode and how it causes the pixels on the layer to blend with pixels on the layers below it.

About Selecting a Portion of a Photo

The Editor enables you to select a portion of a layer or layers to isolate that part of an image for editing. For example, if you select a portion of a layer and then begin painting, the paint affects only the selected area on that layer and none of the pixels outside it. Here, the selection acts as a kind of painter's tape, preventing the paint from spilling outside its borders and affecting the pixels you don't want to change. This same protection applies to any adjustment you might apply; for example, if you adjust the brightness after making a selection, only the pixels within the selected area are affected. You might also select an area when you want to delete, copy, rotate, resize, or move its pixels to another image or layer.

▶ **NOTE**

The Editor provides several tools for selecting the area you want to affect: the **Marquee** tools (which help you select a regularly shaped region such as a rectangle or circle), the **Selection Brush** tools (which enable you to paint or scribble over an area to select it), the **Lasso** tools (which enable you to select any region you can draw freehand or by tracing the edge of an object), and the **Magic Wand** (which selects pixels of a similar color with a single click). You'll learn how to use each of these tools later in this book.

The Editor gives you a variety of tools you can use to select the area you want to affect. You can combine tools, if you like, to select a complex area. Buttons on the **Options** bar (for all the selection tools but the **Selection Brush** tools) allow you to add, subtract, or intersect an existing selection. The selected area is marked with a *selection marquee* so you can easily see the area you selected and distinguish it from the rest of the image (the unselected area).

▶ **KEY TERM**

Selection marquee—Moving dashes that mark the boundary of a selection.

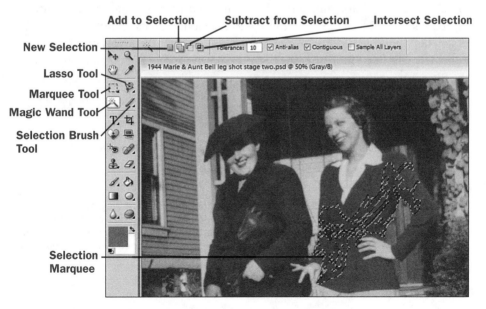

With a selection tool, you define where changes are to take place.

After you make a selection, the selection remains until you remove it. You can't make changes to the area outside a selection, so you'll need to remove the selection to affect other areas. To remove a selection, press **Esc** or choose **Select, Deselect**. To reselect the previous selection, choose **Select, Reselect**. To hide the marquee temporarily (but keep the selection in place), choose **View, Selection**.

You can modify a selection in many ways. You can move the selection marquee if needed to position the selected area precisely. Just click any of the selection tools, click inside the marquee, and drag the marquee into position. You can feather its edge to soften it, expand or contract it by a certain amount, smooth a selection's curved edges, or select just the area at the edges of a selection to create a border. To select everything *but* the current selection, invert the selection by choosing **Select, Inverse**.

Filters, Effects, and Layer Styles

Professional photographers often attach a filter to the front of the camera lens to bend the light coming into the camera and create visual effects. In the Editor, a *filter* can also be used to create a visual effect far beyond the capability of a mere lens attachment. For example, you can use a filter to change your image as though it were rendered by a watercolor brush, sketched with a charcoal pencil on coarse-bond art paper, or burned into a plate of steel with a blowtorch. You can also use filters for less artistic reasons, such as blurring the background around a subject, sharpening a photo, or removing scratches and small blemishes. You choose a filter from the **Filter** menu and configure its options using the dialog box that appears. You can also select a filter from the **Styles and Effects** palette by selecting **Filter** from the first drop-down list and then double-clicking the filter you want to apply. You'll learn how to apply various filters in upcoming tasks.

▶ KEY TERM

Filter—A series of computer instructions that modifies the pixels in an image.

▶ NOTE

Filters typically work on only RGB color images, although most work on grayscale images as well. See **38** **Change Color Mode** for help in changing color modes. In addition, you can't apply a filter to text unless you convert that text to raster data first. If you want to apply the filter to only a portion of an image, select that area first and then apply the filter.

Crystallize Filter

Solarize Filter

Stained Glass Filter

Colored Pencil Filter

Filters can apply many special effects to your images.

Effects are time-savers—typically, an effect is a collection of several filters and other image adjustments applied automatically in a particular sequence to create a special effect. Effects can be applied to an entire layer, to a selection, to text, or to a flattened image with no layers. You can't make adjustments to an effect as you can with a filter; effects are a take-it-or-leave-it kind of thing. To apply an effect, select **Effects** from the first drop-down list on the **Styles and Effects** palette. Then double-click the effect thumbnail to apply that effect. Most effects are applied to a copy of the current layer, but some effects are applied to the entire image, after first merging the layers. You can narrow the list of effects by selecting an effects group from the second drop-down list. If an effect's name includes the notation (**selection**), the Editor will flatten all layers first, insert a new layer above the flattened layer, and apply the effect on that new layer within the selection. If an effect's name includes the notation (**type**), that effect can be applied only to a text layer. If an effect's name includes the notation (**layer**), that effect will be applied to a new layer above the current one.

▶ KEY TERM

Effect—A combination of filters and other image manipulations applied together automatically.

A *layer style* is often applied to the edges of objects or text on a shape or text layer. These "edge styles" are listed in the first grouping in the **Layer Style** list box on the **Styles and Effects** palette. For example, you can add a bevel layer style to apply a chiseled look to your text. You can also apply a layer style to the object itself, filling that object with a special texture or pattern. For example, using the **Orange Glass** layer style, you can make an object or some text look as if it were made from orange glass. These filler styles are listed in a second grouping in the **Layer Style** list on the **Styles and Effects** palette.

▶ KEY TERM

Layer style—A design that's applied to layer data, meaning either all the objects on a layer, such as text or drawn objects, or to the layer as a whole. As new data is added to the layer, the style is applied to that data as well.

To apply a layer style, simply select an appropriate layer (a text layer, for example, for an edge style) and click the layer style you want to apply from those listed in the **Styles and Effects** palette. If you apply a layer style to a regular layer instead of a shape or text layer, the layer style may replace all the data on that layer, depending on what that data is. If the layer is filled with an image, for example, the filler styles typically replace the image and fill the layer. If the layer contains pixels you've painted or drawn with the **Brush** or **Pencil** tool, or if it contains objects you've simplified to bitmap data, the filler styles fill only the interior of those drawings and not the entire layer. If you later change the bitmap data (for example, paint with a brush on the layer), the layer style is applied to the new data as well. Layer styles are cumulative, so the order in which they are applied to a layer is often important because that order can produce different results. With filters, effects, and layer styles, it's typically best to apply the filter, effect, or style you're thinking about and then use the **Undo** button to remove it if it doesn't work out as you thought. To remove a layer style after it is applied, select **Layer**, **Layer Style**, **Clear Layer Style**.

▶ TIPS

You can adjust the scale of a layer style after applying it if you don't like the result. For example, if you apply the **Puzzle** layer style (it's grouped with the other **Image Effects** layer styles) and want the puzzle pieces to look smaller, select **Layer**, **Layer Style**, **Scale Effects**. Then select a percentage (less than 100% makes the pattern smaller; more than 100% makes it bigger).

When a layer style is added to a layer, a small, cursive *f* appears next to the layer's name on the **Layers** palette. Click this **f** to display the **Style Settings** dialog box , which enables you to make small changes to the layer style. Right-click the **f** and select **Clear Layer Style** to remove the layer style altogether.

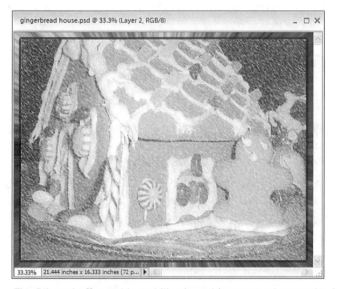

The Blizzard effect adds a chilly air to this scene, whereas the Angled Spectrum layer style applied to the border adds whimsy.

When to Use the Photoshop File Format

Your digital camera stores its photos in one of the universal image formats: perhaps JPEG, TIFF, or a version of RAW format customized by your specific camera manufacturer. Your digital scanner probably uses one of these formats as well. RAW format is uncompressed and can be considered a "digital negative" of your image, provided you have a program that can read the format. (Photoshop Elements can read most RAW formats, but you should check first before recording images you might want to edit later in RAW format.) But none of these formats is appropriate for saving work in progress—images with multiple layers, such as text, shape, and image layers.

True, TIFF format is capable of storing layer data. But a layered TIFF file might not be readable by some programs and will probably be considerably larger than Photoshop Element's default format—Photoshop (PSD) format. When you save an image in Photoshop format, all the image data is saved, such as layers, masks, saved selections, areas of transparency, and hidden data. When you complete your work on an image, you can merge all the layers and data into a single layer and then save the single-layer image in a smaller, universal format such as JPEG or non-layered TIFF. If you want the file to be useable on another computer and want the layers preserved, you can choose not to merge the layers and save them in a layered TIFF file that should be readable by most graphics editors. Even so, a lot of graphics editors these days can read PSD files easily, so converting your file to a layered TIFF might not be necessary.

Using the Welcome Window

Every time you start Photoshop Elements, you're greeted by the **Welcome** window. You can use its controls to start either the Editor or the Organizer, so you can quickly locate an image for editing, review a tutorial on an unfamiliar feature, watch the product overview, or start a new image or creation. To dismiss the **Welcome** window, click its **Close** button; to redisplay the **Welcome** window at any time, select **Window, Welcome** from the menu bar.

The buttons at the top of the **Welcome** window provide quick access to the most common tasks you'll want to perform at the start of a work session, such as importing images into the Organizer catalog, editing an image using **Quick Fix** or **Standard Edit** mode, beginning a new image, or starting a creation. You'll learn the specific steps for performing each of these actions in upcoming tasks.

To view the product overview, click the **Product Overview** button. To start a tutorial, click the **Tutorials** button at the top of the window. To open your web browser and display Adobe's home page, click the **Adobe** button at the bottom of the window.

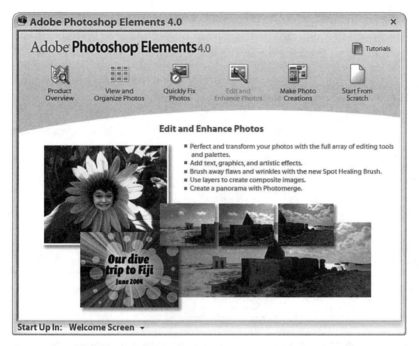

*The **Welcome** window provides a quick way to start your image editing session.*

Changing Preferences

Like most other programs, Photoshop Elements enables you to tweak its default settings to suit your needs. To change preferences in the Editor or the Organizer, select **Edit**, **Preferences** and then select the type of preferences you want to change from the submenu that appears. For example, in the Editor, select **Edit, Preferences, Saving Files** to change the way in which images are saved; in the Organizer, select **Edit, Preferences, Scanner** to change the default file type and resolution for images scanned into the Organizer catalog. The **Preferences** dialog box is then displayed with the appropriate page open.

▶ **TIP**

If you want to reset the currently displayed set of preferences back to default settings, in the Organizer, click **Restore Default Settings**. In the Editor, you can't reset to the defaults, but you can reset it to the way the dialog box looked like before you opened it by clicking **Reset**.

After making changes to a set of preferences, you can save those changes by clicking **OK**. To change from one set of preferences to another in the Editor **Preferences** dialog box, select the set of options you want to view from the drop-down list at the top of the dialog box or click the **Next** button to view the next set of preferences in the list. Return to a previous set of preferences by clicking **Prev** instead. To change to a different preference set in the Organizer **Preferences** dialog box, select that set from the list on the left.

Select Preference Set

Editor Preferences Dialog Box

Change Options as Desired

Organizer Preferences Dialog Box

*Use the **Preferences** dialog box to change the way in which the Editor or the Organizer performs basic tasks.*

How to Undo Mistakes

Like a lot of programs, both the Editor and the Organizer remember the changes you make to an image or the catalog and enable you to undo those changes as needed. When you click the **Undo** button on the **Shortcuts** bar or select **Edit**, **Undo** *XXX* from the menu (where *XXX* is the name of the action you want to undo), Photoshop Elements undoes the most recent change. To undo the next most previous change, click **Undo** or select **Edit**, **Undo** again. Whatever can be undone can also be redone. Just click **Edit**, **Redo** or click **Redo** to undo the most recent undo operation and return the image to the state it was in before you clicked **Undo**.

▶ **TIP**

If you save an image while you're working on it, you can undo changes you've made. After you close the image, you can't undo the changes. This is true in the Organizer as well: Changes to the catalog can be undone until you either close the catalog and open a different one or simply exit Organizer.

If you want to undo multiple changes in the Editor, use the **Undo History** palette. Select **Window**, **Undo History** to display the palette. Changes are listed in the order in which they occurred, with the most recent change appearing at the bottom. Drag the slider up from the bottom to undo changes, or simply select any change from the list. All the changes made up to that point are undone in one step (changes that have been undone appear faded to indicate that they no longer apply to the current image). You can still redo the changes by dragging the slider back down or clicking a change that's lower in the list than the last retained change. To clear the history list of all changes for the current image, click the **More** button and select **Clear Undo History** from the **More** menu.

▶ **NOTES**

To change the limit for the number of changes to an image the Editor can undo, select **Edit**, **Preferences**, **General**. Then adjust the **History States** value (the maximum value is 100) and click **OK**.

If you have several images open, the Editor remembers separate change histories for each image. When you display the **Undo History** palette, it lists only changes for the current image. Again, after an image is closed or you exit the Editor, you won't be able to undo your changes.

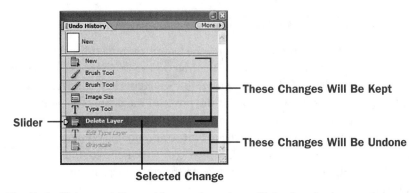

Slider

These Changes Will Be Kept

These Changes Will Be Undone

Selected Change

The **Undo History** palette enables you to undo multiple changes in one step.

2

Importing Items into the Organizer Catalog

IN THIS CHAPTER:

1. About the Organizer
2. Perform an Initial Scan for Media
3. Import Media from a Folder, CD-ROM, or DVD
4. Import Images from a Digital Camera
5. Import and Separate Multiple Scanned Images
6. Locate Moved Files
7. Back Up the Organizer Catalog
8. Copy Items onto CD-ROM or DVD

By now you have probably accumulated quite a collection of digital images and are more than ready to start organizing them using the Photoshop Elements's Organizer. With the Organizer, you can quickly categorize your images and easily locate them later. At the heart of the Organizer is its catalog—in the catalog, you can organize all your images, regardless of their location, into whatever categories you choose. For example, if you want to organize all the photos of your son into a single grouping, you can do so even if those photos are stored in various locations on the hard disk and on several CDs or DVDs. To keep the Organizer running smoothly, you must keep its catalog in order, so in this chapter you'll learn not only how to add images to the catalog, but also to remove them when needed, to update the catalog when an image's location has changed, and to back up the catalog periodically (a process that backs up the catalog information *and* the media files it references). Finally, you'll learn how to back up the images themselves onto CD-ROM or DVD—something you might do to easily share images or take them to a kiosk (such as a Kodak Picture Maker) for printing.

1 About the Organizer

→ **SEE ALSO**

3 Perform an Initial Scan for Media
7 Back Up the Organizer Catalog

The Organizer helps you categorize your digital images, video, and audio files by creating a list of those media files and their locations. In addition, the *catalog* keeps track of any creations you make using these media files. To create this initial listing of media files, you simply indicate the general location you want the Organizer to search. You'll learn the details of this procedure in **2** **Perform an Initial Scan for Media**. After compiling this initial listing (which is called the catalog), you'll want to repeat this process from time to time to add new media files, such as those located on a CD-ROM, DVD, digital camera, or scanner.

After your media files (images, video, and audio) are imported into the catalog (a process that does nothing to the original files but add their names, thumbnails, and file information to the catalog), you organize them by adding tags and collection markers. After adding these special markers, you can use them to quickly display a group of similar files, regardless of where they are stored—even if they are stored offline on a CD or DVD. For example, you might want to display all the photos of your dog so that you can pick out the best one to include in a family photo album. After displaying a set of similar images, you can browse through them full screen, or select a single image for editing within the Editor. You can perform other image tasks as well, including printing, sharing, and creating cards and calendars. *Captions* can be added to images, sound, video files, and creations to make them easier to locate and to enhance the creations (calendars, slideshows, and so on) you might make with them.

► KEY TERMS

Catalog—A organized collection of media files.

Captions—A text or audio description of a media file.

Because the catalog contains a list of each media file and its location, date, size, caption, markers, and other properties, it's important to create a backup copy of the catalog from time to time. The backup copy aids in data recovery, should something happen to the original catalog file. See ■ **Back Up the Organizer Catalog**. Backing up the catalog also copies your image, audio, and video files onto the backup disc, so performing a backup from time to time is critical. If you're ready to offload your images to a permanent location such as a CD-ROM or DVD, you can copy just those files to disc. See ■ **Copy Items onto CD-ROM or DVD**. As another protection against the loss of your original images, any changes you initiate from within the Organizer (whether you use the Editor or another graphics editor such as Photoshop to complete them) can be easily saved to a new image file.

► NOTE

The Organizer can recognize and import only particular image file types (PSD, JPEG/JPG, TIFF/TIF, BMP, PNG, and GIF to name a few), MP3 and WAV audio files, AVI, MPEG, and MOV video files, and PDF documents (Adobe portable document format files, which often contain images).

A Look at the Organizer Work Area

You can start the Organizer from the **Welcome** window (by clicking the **View and Organize Photos** button) or from within the Editor (by clicking the **Create, Photo Browser,** or **Date View** button on the **Shortcuts** bar). If this is your first time using the Organizer, you should perform an initial search for media files, as described in ■ **Perform an Initial Scan for Media**. After importing some media files into the catalog (well, actually, after importing just their thumbnails and information about the media files), you're ready to familiarize yourself with the Organizer work area. The work area can appear in one of two ways: as a browser or as a calendar. For now, I'll assume that you're using **Photo Browser** view because that's the default view. If you're using **Date View** (where images are displayed within a large calendar), see ■ **Find Items with the Same Date** for more information.

1

At the top of the Organizer work area is the menu bar; click a menu to open it, and then click the menu command you want. Below the menu bar are the **Shortcuts** bar, **Timeline**, **Organize Bin**, **Order Photos** palette, **Properties Pane**, **Find** bar, photo well, and **Options** bar. The **Find** bar looks like the one shown here only after you search for specific media files such as all the images of your daughter.

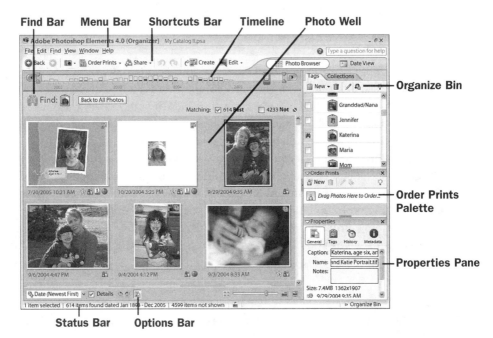

The Organizer work area.

▶ **NOTE**

The **Status** bar appears below the **Options** bar, and lists the total number of items currently being displayed. Occasionally, a **Notification** icon may appear in the middle of the **Status** bar; click it to display messages from Adobe, such as a new update or a sale on photo services

Shortcuts Bar

Below the menu bar, you'll find the **Shortcuts** bar—a toolbar of buttons for common commands such as importing media files into the catalog, sharing and printing images, and making creations. Some buttons on the **Shortcuts** bar require a bit more explanation than others. After you've searched for and displayed a group of similar media files, you can redisplay a previously selected group of items by clicking the **Back** button. To return to the most recent search results, click the **Forward** button. If you select an image in the photo well and click the **Edit** button, you'll see a menu of choices. Select either **Go to Quick Fix** or **Go to Standard Edit**, and the Editor automatically appears with the image displayed so that you can make changes to it. At the far right end of the **Shortcuts** bar, you'll see two buttons: click **Photo Browser** to display items in the photo well as shown here; click **Date View** to review items created on the same date, using a calendar format. See **23** **Find Items with the Same Date**.

▶ **TIP**

If you're unsure of the purpose of any button on the **Shortcuts** bar, simply move the mouse pointer over the button; a tooltip appears, displaying a description for that button.

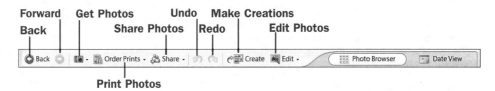

The Organizer Shortcuts bar.

Timeline

Under the **Shortcuts** bar, you'll find the **Timeline**. With it, you can quickly display items created on a particular date or within a range of dates. See **23** **Find Items With the Same Date**. Dates on which items were created are represented by a bar on the **Timeline** graph; the more items associated with a particular date, the taller the bar.

Find Bar

By dragging tags or collection markers onto the **Find** bar, you can display items that have the same content or purpose. You can also remove these restrictions quickly, redisplaying all media files in the catalog, by clicking the **Back to All Photos** button. The **Find** bar also displays how many items match or closely match your criteria, and how many do not. See **19** **Find Items with the Same Marker**.

Organize Bin

The **Organize Bin** displays the current list of tags and collection markers that you can attach to items in the catalog to identify their content or purpose. When you see a binocular icon in front of a particular tag or collection in the **Organize Bin**, it indicates that only items with that tag or collection marker are currently being displayed. To display all images again, click the **Back to All Photos** button on the **Find** bar. See **15** **Attach a Marker to an Item**. Below the **Organize Bin**, you'll find the **Order Prints** palette; use it to order prints online. See **39** **Print Images Using an Online Service**. You may also see the **Properties Pane**; it displays the properties of the selected item. See **30** **About Image Information**.

Photo Well

Images, video, audio files, and creations matching the current search criteria are displayed in the photo well, typically in date order with the more recent files displayed first. You can change the order of display, arranging files in reverse date order, by folder location, or by the batch in which they were imported into the catalog, and change the size of the image *thumbnails*.

▶ **NOTE**

Actually, audio files are not initially displayed in the photo well at all, even if they are added to the catalog. To control which file types are displayed, select **View**, **Media Types**, select the types to display (such as **Photos** or **Audio**), and click **OK**.

▶ **KEY TERM**

Thumbnail–A small version of an image generally appearing in a group of other small images, but just large enough so that you can easily distinguish it from the others.

Each item in the photo well is displayed with the date and time the file was originally created or scanned. If you edit an image, the date it was *modified* is saved, but the image's *creation* date is not changed. This enables you to always display images alongside other images taken that same day, whether or not you edit one of them. The date on which an item was imported into the catalog is also noted, so that you can group items by import batch. You can modify these dates if you find they don't reflect what you expect; see **11** **Change Image Date and Time**.

The thumbnails for selected files are surrounded by a blue outline. You might select several images, for example, to include them in a slideshow you want to create. To select one item, click it. To select multiple contiguous items, click the first item, press and hold the **Shift** key, and then click the last item in the group. To select items that are not contiguous, press and hold the **Ctrl** key as you click each item.

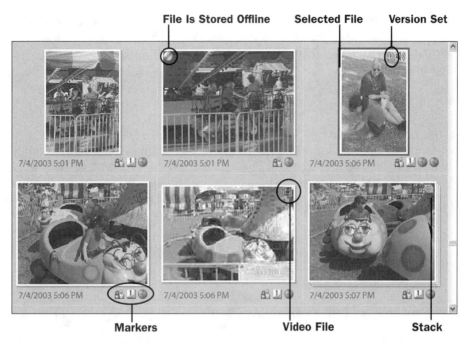

Icons in the photo well indicate various things.

Icons appear with each item as well, indicating various things:

- Whether the file is stored locally or offline (on a CD, for example)

- Whether the file is a video file

- Whether the file has been edited and stacked with the original in a version set

- Whether the image has been manually placed together with similar images in a stack

- Any associated tags or collection markers, such as a particular family member or event

Options Bar

The **Options** bar helps you control the sort order using the **Photo Browser Arrangement** list; you can sort items by date, folder, or import batch. If you sort by folder or import batch, similar items (such as the items in the same folder) are separated by a gray bar at the top of the group. Click this bar to quickly select all the items in that group. Change the size of the thumbnails using the **Thumbnail**

Size slider. Buttons representing the smallest and largest thumbnail sizes available appear on either side of the slider. Click either of these buttons to display images with very small thumbnails, or as single, large photos. You can also use the **Options** bar to quickly rotate an image, display the image in full screen view, display the **Properties** pane (with which you can change an item's properties, such as its text caption), and display each item's date, time, markers, and other properties.

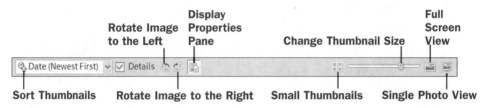

The Options bar.

2 Perform an Initial Scan for Media

→ **SEE ALSO**
_____

3 Import Media from a Folder, CD-ROM, or DVD
4 Import Images from a Digital Camera
5 Import and Separate Multiple Scanned Images

Before you can use Organizer, you must import some media files (images, music, and movies) into its catalog. When you start Organizer for the first time, it will ask if you want to import files. Click **Yes** and select the main folder containing your media. This method, although simple and straightforward, does not allow you to import media in several different folders at the same time or to place limits on the files that are imported. In this task, you'll learn how to scan your computer for media, and to import just the files you want.

After importing files into the catalog, organize them using tags and collection markers. See **15** **Attach a Marker to an Item**. If you copy new media files to your computer after this scan, you'll need to repeat these steps to add the new files to the catalog. If you have images on a digital camera, you can import them into the catalog and copy them to the hard disk in one step: see **4** **Import Images from a Digital Camera**.

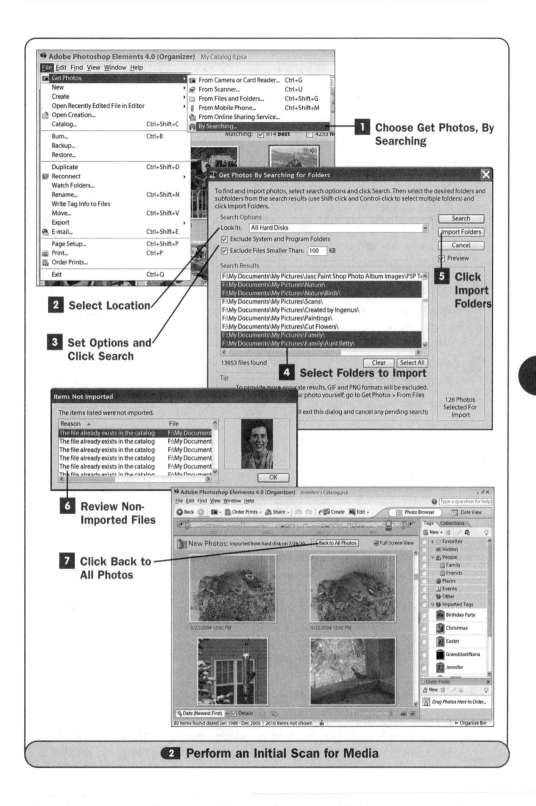

1 Choose Get Photos, By Searching

2 Select Location

3 Set Options and Click Search

4 Select Folders to Import

5 Click Import Folders

6 Review Non-Imported Files

7 Click Back to All Photos

2

▶ **TIP**

You can tell Organizer to scan particular locations for new media files periodically, and add any new files it finds to the catalog automatically. Choose **File, Watch Folders**. Click **Add**, select the folder to watch, and click **OK**. Choose whether you want to be notified when new media appears in that folder or if you want the media imported automatically. Click **OK**.

▶ **NOTE**

Importing does not really store the media files in the catalog; rather, the files are left where they are, and a thumbnail is created for viewing within the catalog. Information about the file (its file date, location, and so on) is also saved in the catalog. This means that, in order to protect your media files and the important information the catalog contains, you'll need to back up not just the catalog but the images, sound files, and video files themselves. See **7** **Back Up the Organizer Catalog**.

1 Choose Get Photos, By Searching

In the Organizer, choose **File, Get Photos, By Searching** from the menu bar. The **Get Photos by Searching for Folders** dialog box appears.

2 Select Location

From the **Look In** drop-down list, select the location you want to search. To search your entire computer, select **All Hard Disks**. To search only the main drive, select **Drive C**.

3 Set Options and Click Search

By default, the Organizer does not search the system or applications folders, but you can disable the **Exclude System and Program Folders** check box and search there anyway if you like, which can increase the scanning time considerably.

Also, by default, the Organizer does not look for files smaller than 100KB, under the assumption that smaller files are unlikely to be of high quality. You can disable the **Exclude Files Smaller Than 100k** check box, or modify the value to include smaller files in the search. You might want to do this, for example, if you take a lot of low-quality photos that you want to store in the catalog. Choose the options appropriate for the media you have on your computer and click **Search** to scan for media files.

4 Select Folders to Import

After the scan is complete, a list of folders that contain media files is displayed in the **Search Results** pane. Select the folders to import by either pressing the **Ctrl** key and clicking each folder or pressing **Shift** and clicking the first and last folder in a group. Selected folders are highlighted in blue. If you want to import from all the folders listed, click **Select All**.

▶ NOTES

The Organizer does not include GIF or PNG files in its **Search Results** list because you'll probably not want to import and organize Web graphics unless you've created them yourself. To import GIF and PNG files manually, see ■3 Import Media from a Folder, CD-ROM, or DVD.

To view what images are in a particular folder before you import it, click the folder in the results list, and its contents appears in the column to the right of the **Search Results** frame.

▅5 Click Import Folders

After selecting the folders you want to import, click the **Import Folders** button.

▶ NOTES

If the imported images contain metadata keywords (tags), the **Import Attached Tags** dialog box appears. You can add new tags to the **Organize Bin** to match the attached photo tags, or associate the attached tags with existing tags in the **Organize Bin**.

To remove an item from the catalog, select it and press **Delete**.

▅6 Review Non-Imported Files

The **Getting Photos** dialog box appears, displaying each photo as it's added to the catalog. You can click **Stop** if you want to interrupt the importing process for some reason; only photos already imported at that point will appear in the catalog.

After the import process is complete, the **Items Not Imported** dialog box may appear; it lists any files that were not imported because they were smaller than the limit specified, in an unsupported format, or already in the catalog. Review the list and click **OK**.

▅7 Click Back to All Photos

The Organizer might display a reminder that the only images being displayed right now are those you have just imported; click **OK** to dismiss this warning box. To redisplay all the images in the catalog, click the **Back to All Photos** button on the **Find** bar.

2

3   Import Media from a Folder, CD-ROM, or DVD

✔ **BEFORE YOU BEGIN**

2 Perform an Initial Scan for Media

→ **SEE ALSO**

4 Import Images from a Digital Camera

5 Import and Separate Multiple Scanned Images

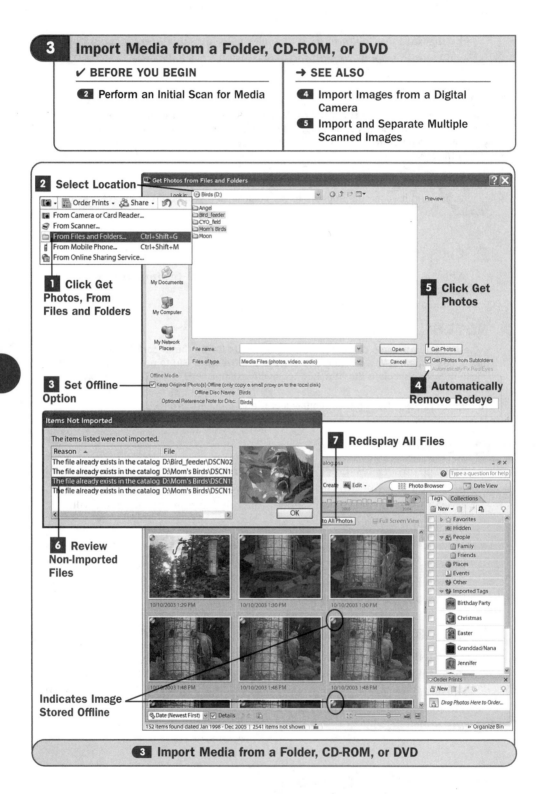

2 **Select Location**

1 **Click Get Photos, From Files and Folders**

3 **Set Offline Option**

5 **Click Get Photos**

4 **Automatically Remove Redeye**

6 **Review Non-Imported Files**

7 **Redisplay All Files**

Indicates Image Stored Offline

3 **Import Media from a Folder, CD-ROM, or DVD**

After you import an initial set of media files into the catalog by following the steps outlined in **2** **Perform an Initial Scan for Media**, you can import additional media files whenever you like. For example, you might have recently received some photos by email and saved those photos to the hard disk, or you might have gotten a CD or DVD or photos from a friend or a photo processing lab. Because Organizer can categorize your images, you don't have to organize them on the hard disk into particular folders. For example, you could have simply saved all the email images with your other photos in the **My Pictures** folder, or you could have created a special folder just for those photos. When importing images from a CD or DVD, you can choose to keep the photos *offline*, and not copy them to the hard disk. If you choose to do this, low-resolution thumbnails of the images are created and displayed in the catalog; if you attempt to edit an offline image, you'll be prompted to insert the CD or DVD on which it's stored.

▶ KEY TERM

Offline—Images in the Organizer catalog that are stored on a CD-ROM or DVD, and not copied to the hard disk.

▶ TIP

If you open a non-cataloged image in the Editor and make changes to it, you can add the image to the catalog when you save your changes. Just enable the **Include in the Organizer** option in the **Save As** dialog box.

1 Click Get Photos, From Files and Folders

In the Organizer, click the **Get Photos** button on the **Shortcuts** bar and then select **From Files and Folders** from the list that appears. You can also choose **File**, **Get Photos**, **From Files and Folders** from the menu bar.

If you've already inserted the CD or DVD, you can import the images by selecting **Organize and Edit pictures using Adobe Photoshop Elements** from the **What do you want to do?** list in the dialog box that Windows automatically displays.

2 Select Location

From the **Look in** drop-down list in the **Get Photos from Files and Folders** dialog box, select the drive that contains of the images you want to import. For example, if the files are located on the main drive, select **Local Disk (C)**. Select the folder that contains the images to import. Select multiple folders by pressing **Ctrl** and clicking each one. If you want to import the contents of any subfolders of selected folders, enable the **Get Photos from Subfolders** check box. If you're importing from a CD or DVD, and it doesn't contain any folders, skip this part.

3

3 Set Offline Option

If you're importing images from a CD or DVD and you want to keep the images offline (that is, you want to keep only low-resolution images in the catalog and leave the larger original images on the CD or DVD), enable the **Keep Original Photo(s) Offline** check box and type a name for the disc in the **Optional Reference Note for Disc** text box. If you do not enable the **Keep Original Photo(s) Offline** check box, the Organizer copies the files from the CD or DVD to the hard disk.

4 Automatically Remove Redeye

If the files you're importing are already on the hard disk, or if they're being copied there from a CD or DVD, you can have the Editor automatically remove red eye from the eyes of any people in the photos, before importing them into the catalog. Select the **Automatically Fix Red Eyes** option.

▶ **TIP**

The **Automatically Fix Red Eyes** option is perfectly safe; Photoshop Elements has an excellent red-eye fixer, and it saves its result in a new version of the image file in a version set. If you don't like the results for some reason, you can always delete the extra version of the image and go back to the original version. See **28** **About Saving Images** for more on version sets.

5 Click Get Photos

Click **Get Photos** to begin the importing process. The **Getting Photos** dialog box appears, displaying each photo as it's added to the catalog. You can click **Stop** if you want to interrupt the importing process for some reason; only photos already imported at that point will appear in the catalog.

6 Review Non-Imported Files

After the import process is complete, the **Items Not Imported** dialog box might appear; it lists any files that were not imported because they were in an unsupported format or already in the catalog. Review the list and click **OK**.

7 Redisplay All Files

The Organizer might display a reminder telling you that the only images being displayed right now are those you have just imported; click **OK** to dismiss this warning box.

If you kept the images offline, a small CD icon appears in the upper-left corner of each small thumbnail. To redisplay all files in the catalog, click the **Back to All Photos** button on the **Find** bar.

▶ **NOTE**

Before importing images into the catalog, you can use the Editor to rename, resize, retouch, and reformat them at the same time. For example, you could copy images from your camera onto the hard disk and then rename them. See **33** **Rename, Resize, Reformat, and Retouch a Group of Images**. After processing the images and saving the results to the hard disk, import the images into the catalog by completing the steps in this task.

If the imported images contain metadata keywords (tags), the **Import Attached Tags** dialog box appears. You can add new tags to the **Organize Bin** to match the attached photo tags, or associate the attached tags with existing tags in the **Organize Bin**.

4	**Import Images from a Digital Camera**	
✔ **BEFORE YOU BEGIN**		→ **SEE ALSO**
2 Perform an Initial Scan for Media		**3** Import Media from a Folder, CD-ROM, or DVD
		4 Import and Separate Multiple Scanned Images

You can import images directly from a digital camera and add them to the Organizer catalog. The method you use to do that, however, varies as much as digital cameras vary from one another. For a great many cameras, when you connect them to your computer using a USB, SCSI, or FireWire cable, Windows automatically detects the camera, reads its memory card, and displays the contents in a new drive window (a virtual drive) within **My Computer**. For example, your computer might have only one hard disk—drive C—but when you connect your digital camera, Windows presents you with a window that displays all the files on drive D, which is really the memory card inside your camera. At the same time, Photoshop Elements detects the virtual drive and launches its **Photo Downloader** to help you import the images into the catalog.

This same process occurs if you use a memory card reader. When you take the memory card out of the camera, insert it into the reader, Windows treats the contents of the memory card as a virtual (pretend) drive D or other drive letter. Once again, Photoshop Elements detects the virtual drive and launches the **Photo Downloader**.

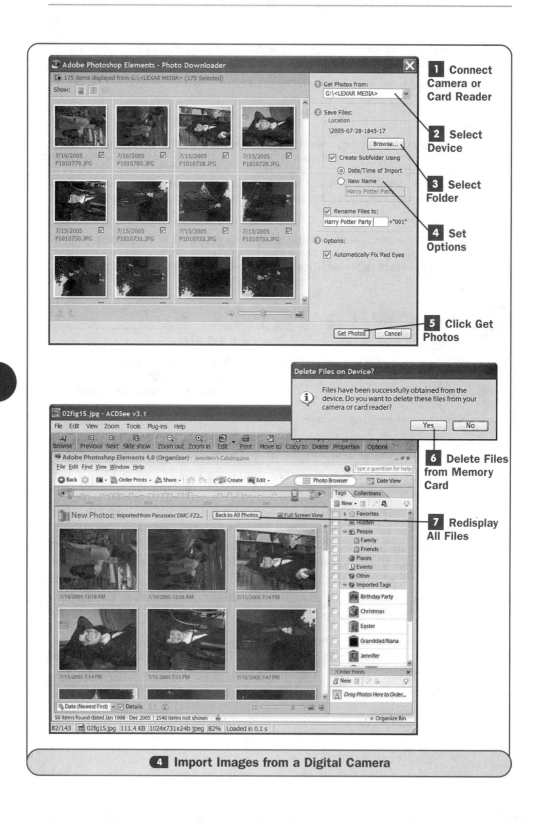

4

1 Connect Camera or Card Reader

2 Select Device

3 Select Folder

4 Set Options

5 Click Get Photos

6 Delete Files from Memory Card

7 Redisplay All Files

4 Import Images from a Digital Camera

■ Connect Camera or Card Reader

Connect the camera or the card reader to the computer, if it's not already connected. Adobe's **Photo Downloader** should automatically start and display the **Adobe Photo Downloader** dialog box. If Windows pops up a box asking if you want to use Adobe Photoshop Elements to organize and edit your files, click **Yes**, and the Downloader will start.

If the **Photo Downloader** does not start automatically, you can start it manually. In the Organizer, click the **Get Photos** button on the **Shortcuts** bar and select **From Camera or Card Reader** from the list that appears. You can also choose **File**, **Get Photos From Camera or Card Reader** from the menu bar. The **Get Photos from Camera or Card Reader** dialog box (which looks similar to the **Adobe Photo Downloader** dialog box shown here) appears.

▶ NOTE

If you can't get the Downloader to appear, use the driver that came with the camera to read its memory card. After copying the images to the hard disk using the camera's software, follow the steps in ■ **Import Media from a Folder, CD-ROM, or DVD** to import those images into the catalog.

■ Select Device

The card reader or camera should already be listed in the **Get Photos from** drop-down list. If not, open the list and select your camera or card reader (or its virtual drive letter) from the devices listed. After the memory card has been read, its images appear on the left side of the dialog box.

▶ TIP

You can change the camera preferences, such as the default folder in which images are stored, using the **Preferences** dialog box. Select **Edit, Preferences** from the Organizer main menu and then click **Camera or Card Reader.**

■ Select Folder

Your digital images will be copied to the **My Documents\My Pictures\ Adobe\Digital Camera Photos** folder. To change to a different folder, click the **Browse** button, select the folder into which you want to copy the new image files, and click **OK**.

■ Set Options

You can place the images you are importing into a subfolder of the folder you selected in step 3: First, enable the **Create Subfolder Using** check box. Then select either the **Date/Time of Import** option (if you want the subfolder to use the current date and time as its name) or **New Name** (if you want to name the subfolder yourself). If you chose the **New Name** option, type a name for the subfolder in the text box provided.

Because digital camera image files are typically given nondescript names such as **DSC00035.jpg**, you might want to tell the Organizer to rename the files as it imports them into the catalog. Just enable the **Rename Files to** check box and type a descriptive name in the text box. Organizer automatically adds a three-digit number to this description to create the filename. For example, if you type **Aunt Jane's Bday 2007** as the filename (notice the space I added at the end to separate the name from the number Organizer adds), files will be named **Aunt Jane's Bday 2007 001**, **Aunt Jane's Bday 2007 002**, and so on.

To automatically fix red eyes in any of your subjects, before importing the photos, select the **Automatically Fix Red Eyes** option.

▶ TIP

If you choose the **Automatically Fix Red Eyes** option, Photoshop Elements removes red-eye from each image and saves the result in an image file in a version set with the original image. If you don't like the results for some reason, you can always delete the extra version of the image and go back to the original version. See **28** About Saving Images for more on version sets.

5 Click Get Photos

Click the **Get Photos** button to begin the importing process. The files are copied to the hard disk; if Organizer is not already started, it is started for you automatically. The **Getting Photos** dialog box appears, displaying each photo as it's added to the catalog. Click **Stop** if you want to interrupt the importing process for some reason; only photos already imported at that point will appear in the catalog.

▶ NOTE

If the imported images contain metadata keywords (tags), the **Import Attached Tags** dialog box appears. You can add new tags to the **Organize Bin** to match the attached photo tags, or associate the attached tags with existing tags in the **Organize Bin**.

6 Delete Files from Memory Card

After the files are imported into the Organizer, You might see a dialog box listing images that were not imported; typically, this is because the images are already in the catalog. If so, make a note of the images that were not imported and click **OK** to continue. Next, you'll see a dialog box asking whether you want to remove the images from the camera's memory card. Click **Yes** or **No** as desired.

7 Redisplay All Files

The Organizer might display a reminder telling you that the only images being displayed right now are those you have just imported; click **OK** to dismiss this warning box. To redisplay all files in the catalog, click the **Back to All Photos** button on the **Find** bar.

---

5 Import and Separate Multiple Scanned Images

✔ BEFORE YOU BEGIN	→ SEE ALSO
28 About Saving Images	**89** Restore Quality to a Scanned Photograph

---

Although you can scan a photograph directly into the Organizer, using the **Get Photos, From Scanner** command, you might not want to. For example, if you think you'll need to edit the scan to remove spots and other imperfections or to improve the scan's color and contrast, why not import the scan directly into the Editor? After making changes, you can add the image to the Organizer when you save your edits.

Another reason why you might want to scan directly into the Editor is to exploit its capability to deal with multiple-image scans. If you've got multiple photographs to scan, you can lay them all on the scanner bed and perform a single scan. The Editor can then break up these images for you, creating the separate image files you need.

1 Choose File, Import

Lay the photograph(s) you want to scan on the scanner bed, leaving a small amount of space between them. This space enables the Editor to separate the images later on.

Choose **File, Import** from the menu bar and select your scanner from the list that appears. The program for your scanner automatically appears. My scanner happens to appear twice in the list—because it is *WIA* compliant, I'll choose that option.

5

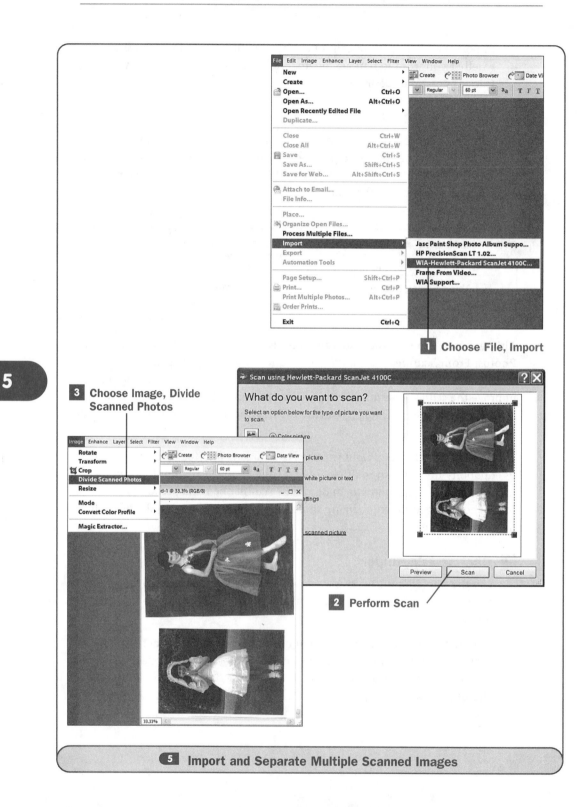

1 Choose File, Import

3 Choose Image, Divide Scanned Photos

2 Perform Scan

5 Import and Separate Multiple Scanned Images

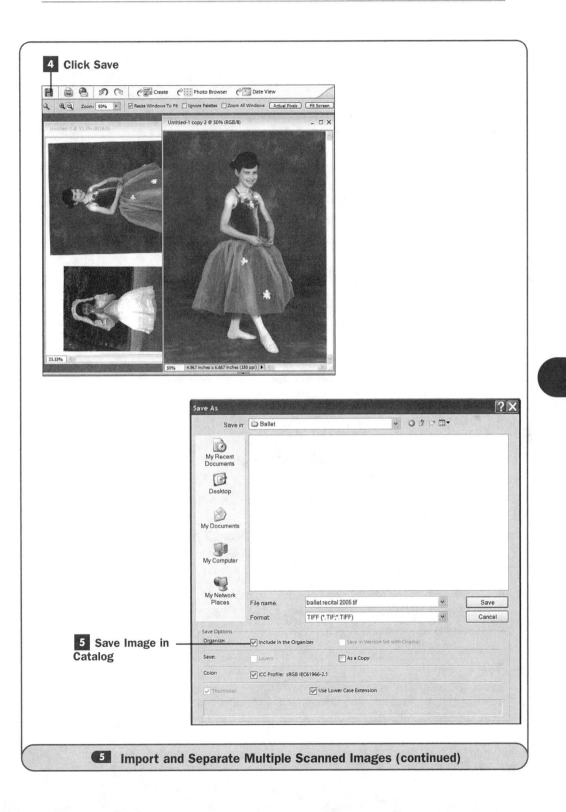

4 Click Save

5 Save Image in Catalog

5 Import and Separate Multiple Scanned Images (continued)

► **KEY TERM**

WIA and TWAIN— Technologies that allow graphical software programs to communicate directly with digital cameras and scanners. TWAIN was replaced by WIA in Windows Me and Windows XP.

► **TIP**

If your scanner is not listed, select **WIA Support** from the menu. This option enables you to access the WIA support built into Windows, which might be able to clear up the problem by scanning for WIA- and TWAIN-compliant devices.

2 Perform Scan

The dialog box that appears displays the options available to your particular scanner. Shown here are the generic Windows scanning options. Adjust the options as desired (in this dialog box you'd click **Adjust the quality of the scanned picture**) and click **Scan** to scan the image(s) into the Editor.

► **TIP**

I would choose as a minimum 70–100 PPI resolution for onscreen images, and 200–300 PPI for images you intend to print. Choosing higher resolutions for a scan can help you fix problems caused by scanning, such as moiré patterns.

3 Choose Image, Divide Scanned Photos

The image(s) appear in the Editor in a single, unsaved file. If you scanned multiple images, choose **Image, Divide Scanned Photos** from the menu. The Editor creates separate image files for you.

4 Click Save

None of the image file(s) are saved at this point. If you scanned multiple images, close the original scan window (the one with the multiple scanned images). Click **No** because you do not want to save this file.

Click each of the other image window(s), make changes as desired, and then click the **Save** button on the **Shortcuts** bar to save the image. The **Save As** dialog box appears.

► **TIP**

Scanned photographs often suffer from low brightness, poor contrast, low saturation, lack of sharpness, and may even contain moiré patterns. See **89** Restore Quality to a Scanned Photograph for help in improving your photographs after you scan them.

5 Save Image in Catalog

Select the folder in which you want to save the image from the **Save in** list, and type a name for the image in the **File name** box. Select an image type from the **Format** list. Select other options as desired (see **28** **About Saving Images**), but be sure to enable the **Include in the Organizer** option so that the image is placed in the Organizer catalog. Click **Save** to save the image.

6 Locate Moved Files

✔ BEFORE YOU BEGIN

2 Perform an Initial Scan for Media

As you are probably well aware by now, the Organizer catalog is not a collection of media files, but rather a listing of those files and their various locations on your hard disks, CDs, and DVDs. The Organizer is designed to keep track of any changes you initiate within its program (such as renaming, deleting, or editing images), but it is unaware of any file maintenance activities you perform on its media files outside of the program. If, for example, you use **My Computer** to move a file from one folder into another, the Organizer assumes that the file has simply disappeared. Similar problems arise if you rename or delete a file outside of the Organizer. Follow the steps in this task to remedy the problem, and reconnect the image thumbnail to its actual file on the hard disk.

To properly rename a file so that the Organizer keeps track of the modification, make the change within the Organizer using the **File**, **Rename** command. Move a file using the **File**, **Move** command. To delete a file from the Organizer catalog and from the hard disk (if you so choose), select it and press **Delete**.

▶ **TIP**

To tell Organizer to check for missing files periodically and to automatically reconnect them, choose **Edit, Preferences, Files** from the Organizer menu. Enable the **Automatically Search for and Reconnect Missing Files** option and click **OK**.

1 Select Moved Item

You may not know that a file's not connected to the catalog until you try to use it. Sometimes, a missing file icon will appear at the bottom of the image in the photo well. However you've identified a an image in the Organizer as being disconnected from its actual file, click the item in the Organizer to select it.

2 Choose File, Reconnect, Missing File

Choose **File, Reconnect, Missing File** from the menu bar. If you've moved a lot of files, you don't have to select any files in the catalog, but just choose **File, Reconnect, All Missing Files** instead. Typically, Organizer searches the hard disk so fast that it finds the missing file(s) right away, but if needed, click the **Browse** button in the searching box to display the **Reconnect Missing Files** dialog box.

3 Locate Actual File

In the **Reconnect Missing Files** dialog box, the original location and thumbnail of the missing image appear on the left. On the right side of the dialog box, the matching image and its new location appear. If Organizer didn't find the file (for example, you not only moved it, you also renamed it), from the drop-down list on the **Browse** tab, navigate to the folder in which the file is now located and select the file itself. You can select multiple files from the list on the left and choose the folder they are in on the right to reconnect a group of files.

4 Click Reconnect

Click the **Reconnect** button to update the file's location in the catalog. If you can't relocate the missing file and you no longer want the disconnected item in the catalog, click **Delete from Catalog** instead of **Reconnect**.

5 Click Close

You can reconnect files in other folders while the **Reconnect Missing Files** dialog box is open; just repeat steps 3 and 4. When you're through reconnecting files, click **Close**.

6 View the Result

After the file's new location is updated in the catalog, its thumbnail appears as normal in the photo well and the missing file icon is removed.

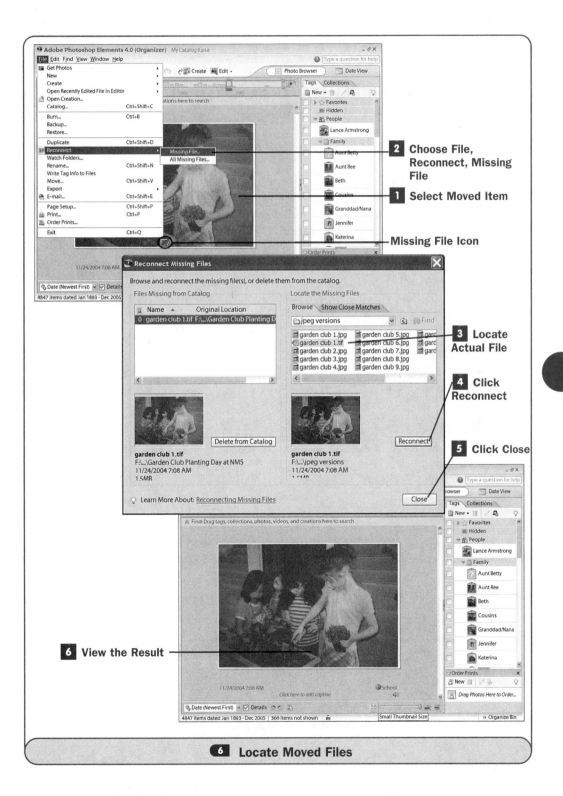

2 Choose File, Reconnect, Missing File

1 Select Moved Item

Missing File Icon

3 Locate Actual File

4 Click Reconnect

5 Click Close

6 View the Result

---

7 **Back Up the Organizer Catalog**

→ **SEE ALSO**

8 Copy Items onto CD-ROM or DVD

After you've imported lots of images into the Organizer catalog and have used its features to organize your images, you won't want to risk losing your hard work. True, the catalog does not contain the images themselves (only a listing of their locations and names), so if something were to happen to the catalog, you wouldn't lose any photographs. What you would lose, however, are the *properties* of each image, such as the various tags and collections to which an image is associated, plus any audio captions or text notes you've appended to the images. You would also lose your creations and organizational information, such as an item's location, file size, file type, and thumbnail. If something happened to the catalog (but your media files were still okay), you could always reimport all your media files and then retag, annotate, and caption them, but that would be a lot of work. Therefore, periodically, you should back up *both* the Organizer catalog *and* your media files onto CD, DVD, or another drive in case something happens to your media files or the catalog. Lucky for you, the Organizer provides an easy method for you to do both in one simple process.

▶ **KEY TERM**

Properties—Information associated with each media file, such as its creation date, modification date, tags, collections, audio or text captions, or notes.

1 Choose File, Backup

In the Organizer, choose **File**, **Backup** from the menu bar. The first page of the **Burn/Backup** wizard appears.

2 Choose Backup the Catalog

In Step 1 of the **Burn/Backup** wizard, select the **Backup the Catalog** option and click **Next** to continue. The **Missing Files Check Before Backup** dialog box might appear; if it does, use it to reconnect any moved files before continuing with the backup or simply click **Continue**. See **6** **Locate Moved Files.**

▶ **NOTE**

If something occurs to the catalog later on (such as a power surge that damages the file), you'll be prompted to recover the file—a process that fixes the damage. Simply choose **File**, **Catalog** from the menu, click the **Recover** button, and then click **OK**.

If the catalog file is so badly damaged that it can't be repaired using this method, create an empty catalog first by choosing **File**, **Catalog** and clicking **New**. Then choose **File**, **Restore** from the menu, locate the incremental backup file (if any, because it must be restored first), and click **Restore**. After the incremental backup file's restored, you'll be prompted to select the full backup file so that its data can be restored as well.

3 Select Backup Type

In Step 2 of the **Burn/Backup** wizard, select the type of backup you want to perform: To back up the entire catalog and all your media files, select **Full Backup**. To make an incremental backup that contains any new media files added to the catalog since the last backup, select **Incremental Backup**. Click **Next**.

4 Choose Backup Drive

In Step 3 of the **Burn/Backup** wizard, select the drive to which you want to copy the catalog and media files from the **Select Destination Drive** list. If you select a CD or DVD drive, you'll be prompted to insert the disc. Do so and click **OK** to return to the **Burn/Backup** wizard.

5 Set Options

If you are backing up the data onto a CD or DVD, type a **Name** for the disc. You can also adjust the write speed by selecting a different speed from the **Write Speed** list. You might do this if you have been having trouble with your CD-R drive and want to compensate for that by having the computer write the data more slowly.

If you are backing up to another hard drive and not a CD-ROM or DVD, you must select a folder into which you want the data copied. If you are performing an incremental backup, the folder you select must be different from the one you originally selected when you did the full backup. Click the **Browse** button next to the **Backup Path** text box, select a folder, and click **OK**.

If you're performing an incremental backup, you must tell the Organizer where the original backup file is located. Click the **Browse** button next to the **Previous Backup File** text box, select the file that contains the original backup, and click **OK**. If you backed up previously onto and a CD or DVD, you'll be prompted to insert that disc so that the Organizer can determine the backup set to which you want to add. You'll remove the disc later so that you can insert a new disc on which to copy the incremental backup.

7

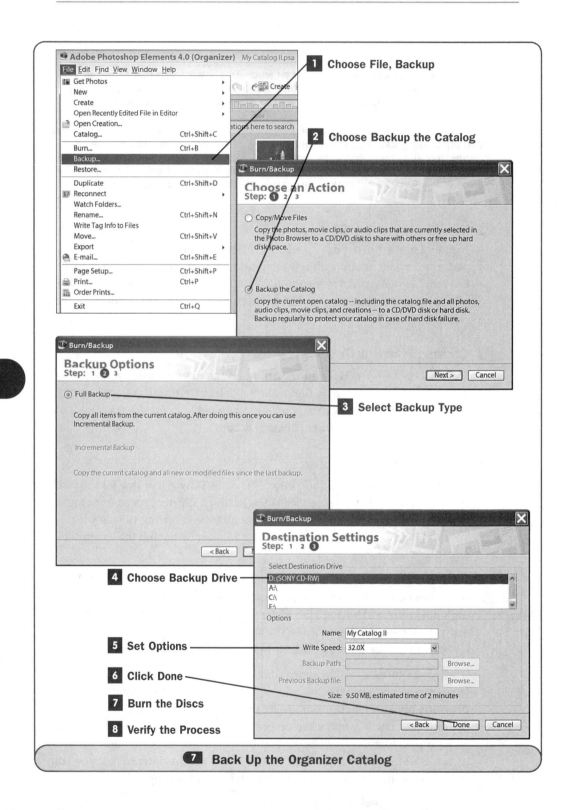

1 Choose File, Backup

2 Choose Backup the Catalog

3 Select Backup Type

4 Choose Backup Drive

5 Set Options

6 Click Done

7 Burn the Discs

8 Verify the Process

7 Back Up the Organizer Catalog

6 Click Done

Click **Done** to begin the backup process. If you are backing up the data onto a CD or DVD, you'll see a dialog box telling you how many discs you'll need to complete the backup. Click **Yes** to continue, and then follow the onscreen instructions.

If you are performing an incremental backup, the original backup disc is probably still in the drive (if you backed up to CD or DVD). If so, you'll be prompted at the proper time to remove the first disc and insert an additional disc on which to store the incremental backup. When the backup is complete, be sure to label any removable discs with the date and time of the backup.

7 Burn the Discs

The Organizer takes a moment to calculate how many discs you'll need and displays that information in the next dialog box. Click **Burn** to initiate the copy/move process. After a disc is completed, you'll see a reminder to label the disc properly.

8 Verify the Process

A message appears asking whether you want to verify the new disc. This process takes a while, but it also guarantees that the discs were created properly and can be read (which is time well spent if you later have to recover items from the discs). Click **Verify** to continue. At the end of the verification process, you'll be told whether everything is okay. If the verification detects any errors, repeat these steps to create a new series of discs. Otherwise, click **Don't Verify** to continue. window.

Click **OK** to continue. If an additional disc is needed to copy or move the files, you'll be prompted to insert additional discs until the procedure is complete.

---

8 **Copy Items onto CD-ROM or DVD**

→ SEE ALSO

7 Back Up the Organizer Catalog

In **7** **Back Up the Organizer Catalog**, you learned how to protect both your media files and the information in the catalog by backing it up onto disc. If you want to protect only some media, or share the files with friends or family, you do not have to back up the entire catalog to disc. Instead, you can copy just the items you want onto CD-ROM or DVD discs. During the process of creating the

CD or DVD, you can instruct the Organizer to change the status of the items to offline. If you choose this option, the Organizer copies the files from your hard disk to the CD or DVD, creates low-resolution copies of image files so that they can still be shown within the photo well, and then removes the files from the hard disk. Archiving files in this manner frees up hard disk space and yet still enables you to continue to view and work with those images, audio files, and movie files from the catalog. Offline images are marked with a small CD icon; if you attempt to edit one of these images or to use any offline media file in a creation, you'll be prompted to insert the disc onto which the original copies were transferred.

1 Select Items to Copy or Move

Select the items you want copied to CD/DVD. Select a contiguous group of items by pressing **Shift**, and clicking the first and last items in the group. Select noncontiguous items by pressing **Ctrl** and click each thumbnail. If the catalog is sorted by batch or folder, you can click the bar above a group to select all the items in that group (see **1 About the Organizer** for details about sorting).

Only the currently displayed items are archived, so you can use the **Find** bar to display the items you want to copy to CD/DVD instead of selecting them. See Chapter 4, "Finding Images, Movies, and Audio Files," for information about sorting and locating files.

▶ **NOTE**

Creations are not copied to the disc even if they are selected. To give someone a copy of most creations, convert the creation to PDF format and email it. To share an HTML photo gallery, post it on the Internet or simply copy it to CD.

2 Choose File, Burn

Choose **File**, **Burn** from the Organizer menu bar. The **Burn/Backup** wizard appears.

3 Choose Copy/Move Files

In Step 1 of the **Burn/Backup** wizard, choose the **Copy/Move Files** option and click **Next** to continue.

④ Set Offline Options

In Step 2 of the **Burn/Backup** wizard, set the offline options. For example, if you want to copy images to the CD or DVD and then erase them from the hard disk, enable the **Move Files** option. The images are then considered "offline," and to access them from the Organizer, you'll need to insert this disc when prompted.

If the selected images contain any stacks or version sets, you can copy or move all the images in the stack or version set (and not just the one used as a thumbnail), by enabling the **Copy/Move All Files in the Stack** and/or **Copy/Move All Files in the Version Set** options. See ⑩ **Stack Images** and ㉗ **About Editing Images**.

After selecting the offline options, insert a disc if you haven't already and click **Next** to continue.

⑤ Select Drive

In Step 3 of the **Burn/Backup** wizard, select the CD-ROM or DVD drive to which you want to copy the media files from the **Select Destination Drive** list.

▶ NOTE

You can copy items only to a CD-ROM or a DVD, and not to the hard disk.

⑥ Type Name and Click Done

In the **Name** text box, type a name (up to 70 characters) for the collection of items you want to copy. Use a name that will remind you later on which items are contained on the disc.

You can adjust the write speed by selecting a different speed from the **Write Speed** list. You might do this if you have an old CD drive and want to select a speed that matches it, or if you've been having trouble with your CD-R drive and want to compensate for that by having the computer write the data more slowly.

Click **Done**. If the selection includes any creations, you'll see a warning box telling you that they will not be copied to the disc. Click **OK** to continue.

7 Burn the Discs

The Organizer takes a moment to calculate how many discs you'll need and displays that information in the next dialog box. Click **Burn** to initiate the copy/move process. After a disc is completed, you'll see a reminder to label the disc properly.

8 Verify the Process

A message appears asking whether you want to verify the new disc. This process takes a while, but it also guarantees that the discs were created properly and can be read (which is time well spent if you later have to recover items from the discs). Click **Verify** to continue. At the end of the verification process, you'll be told whether everything is okay. If the verification detects any errors, repeat these steps to create a new series of discs. Otherwise, click **Don't Verify** to return to the Organizer window.

Click **OK** to continue. If an additional disc is needed to copy or move the files, you'll be prompted to insert additional discs until the procedure is complete.

8

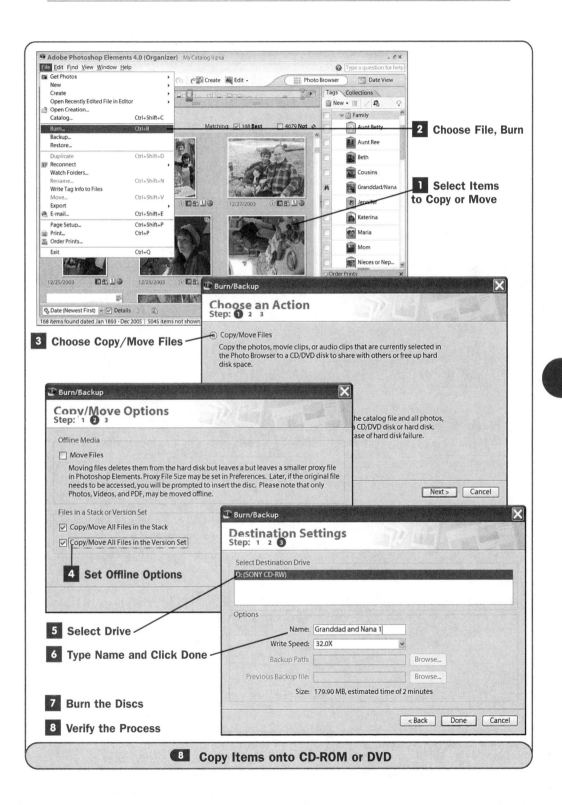

3

Organizing and Creating Items

IN THIS CHAPTER:

9   Review Images

10   Stack Images

11   Change Image Date and Time

12   About Organizing Items

13   Create a Tag

14   Create a Collection

15   Attach a Marker to an Item

16   Add a Text Caption or Note

17   Make a Creation

After importing images into a catalog, you can begin to work with them in the Organizer. In this chapter, you'll learn how to review images one at a time in an automated slide show, group different versions of the same image, and categorize images. You group similar media files together by adding the same tag or collection marker. For example, you might add a **John** tag to several audio files, movie files, and images that feature your son, John. Similarly, you might add a **Calendar** collection marker to the images you're gathering for a calendar you want to make. Finally, you'll learn how to annotate your images with a written caption or note.

▶ **NOTE**

The tasks in this chapter assume that you are using the Organizer in **Photo Browser** view. If you're currently displaying items in **Date View** (on a calendar), you can change to **Photo Browser** view by clicking the **Photo Browser** button at the right end of the **Shortcuts** bar.

---

9   **Review Images**

✔ BEFORE YOU BEGIN	→ SEE ALSO
16 Add a Text Caption or Note	**38** Print a Picture Package
18 About Finding Items in the Catalog	**39** Print Images Using an Online Service

9

You can automatically review each image in a group with a full-screen *photo review*. The ideal time to perform a photo review is just after importing a set of images into the catalog because you can stop the review when needed to edit, rotate, or delete an image; mark an image for printing; or add a tag or collection marker. You can also skip to a particular image when desired. In addition, you can split the screen and compare two images when needed. In this task, you'll learn the ins and outs of conducting your own private photo review.

▶ **KEY TERM**

Photo review—A controllable slide show in which each image is displayed onscreen, one at a time, in whatever order and at whatever speed you want.

1 **Select Photos to Review**

Photo review includes in its review only the images currently being displayed in the Organizer. So, if you've just imported some images you want to review, you can skip this step, because the newly imported images are the only ones currently showing. Otherwise, to limit the display, you can use the **Find** bar to show just the photos to review. (See **18** **About Finding Items in the Catalog**.) You can also select the images to review by pressing **Ctrl** as you click each one, or by pressing **Shift** as you click the first and last photo in a group.

▶ **TIP**

Even if they are shown, audio and creation files are excluded from the photo review. Video files, however, are played during the review in their entirety.

2 Click Full Screen View

Click on the **Options** bar at the bottom of the photo well. The **Full Screen View Options** dialog box appears.

3 Set Options

To play music while you're reviewing your photos, select a music file from the **Background Music** list or click **Browse** to locate the file. Select the number of seconds you want each image to appear onscreen from the **Page Duration** list. To fade in and out between images, select **Fade Between Photos**.

1 Select Photos to Review   **2** Click Full Screen View

9 Review Images

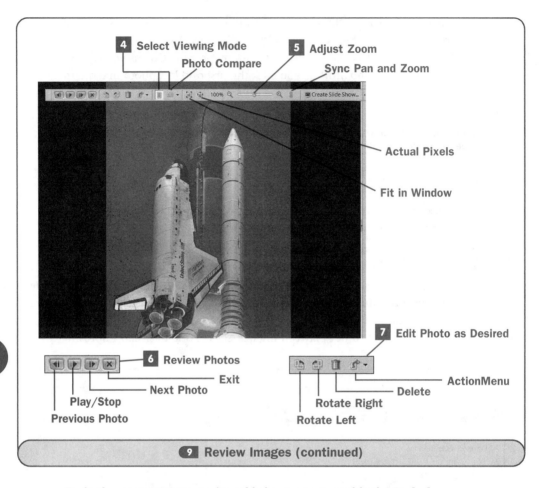

4 Select Viewing Mode

Photo Compare

5 Adjust Zoom

Sync Pan and Zoom

Actual Pixels

Fit in Window

7 Edit Photo as Desired

6 Review Photos

Exit

Next Photo

ActionMenu

Delete

Play/Stop

Rotate Right

Previous Photo

Rotate Left

9 Review Images (continued)

9

To display text captions you've added to images, enable the **Include Captions** option. To play audio captions you attached to any of these images, select **Play Audio Captions**. To allow photos to resize to fill the window, enable the **Allow Photos to Resize** option. To allow video files to resize to fill the window, enable the **Allow Videos to Resize** option. This option, however, can make low-resolution videos very grainy and hard to see.

To start the slide show automatically, select **Start Playing Automatically**. If you want the slide show to automatically repeat itself over and over until you stop it manually, enable the **Repeat Slide Show** option. To show the filmstrip (so you can view images in any order by selecting the one to view) select **Show Filmstrip**. Click **OK**.

4 Select Viewing Mode

If the slide show has started, you won't be able to set any options until you click **Stop**. Normally, each image is displayed one at a time during the show, but to display images side by side, click the **Photo Compare** button on the **Photo Review** toolbar (which you can display by moving the mouse at any time) and select either **Side by Side** or **Above and Below**.

5 Adjust Zoom

Adjust the zoom as desired: click the **Actual Pixels** button to display the photo in its original size (for a high-resolution photo, you'll have to scroll to see it all); click **Fit in Window** to shrink the photo so that all of it is displayed. You can also drag the **Zoom** slider to the left or right to adjust the zoom level. Click the **Sync Pan and Zoom** button to synchronize scrolling and zooming when displaying two images at a time.

6 Review Photos

Click **Play** to begin the slide show. Click **Stop** to pause the slide show temporarily to perform some action such as tagging an image, and then click **Play** to resume. If you do nothing but watch, each image is displayed and then you're returned to the photo well (unless you selected the **Repeat Slide Show** option in step 3, in which case the slide show will continue to repeat until you exit the photo review or stop it by clicking **Stop** on the review toolbar). If the filmstrip is displayed on the right, you can skip to an image at any time by clicking its thumbnail. You can also use the **Next Photo** and **Previous Photo** buttons to skip photos. The slide show will simply resume from that point.

If you're displaying two images at a time, you must switch from image to image manually. Click a pane to make that pane active (the active pane appears with a blue border), and then press ← or → on your keyboard, click **Next Photo** or **Previous Photo**, or click a thumbnail on the filmstrip to display that image in the active pane.

7 Edit Photo as Desired

If you're using **Photo Review** mode, click **Stop** to pause the slide show so that you can edit the displayed image. If you're using **Photo Compare** mode, click the pane that contains the image you want to edit.

Click the **Rotate Left** or **Rotate Right** button in the **Photo Review** toolbar to rotate the image sideways. Click **Delete** to remove the image from the catalog (and from the hard disk, if you want). Click the arrow on the **Action Menu** button to display a list of actions you can take, such as adding a tag or collection marker to the current image, or marking an image for printing later on. Click the **Create Slide Show** button on the right side of the toolbar to create a slide show using these images.

When you're through, click the **Exit** button to stop the review and return to the main Organizer window. If you used the **Action Menu** to mark photos for printing, a dialog box appears. Click **Print** to print those photos locally; click **Order Prints** to send the images to an online service for printing.

---

10 | **Stack Images**

✔ **BEFORE YOU BEGIN**

27 About Editing Images

If you're a picture-taking fool like I am, you probably record a lot of similar photos at an event, in the hopes that one of them will come out okay. The only problem with this approach to photography is that you can quickly end up with a lot of similar photos and a huge catalog as a result. If you find that you have a lot of copies of the same image—or lots of similar images taken at roughly the same time—you can still keep them all in the catalog without taking up too much room. Simply *stack* the images as explained in this task; the thumbnail of the latest image is all that shows up in the photo well. When needed, you can expand the stack and display all the related images in the stack.

▶ KEY TERM

Stack—A group of related images, typically displayed in the catalog with a single thumbnail.

▶ NOTE

If you use the Editor to edit an image and create a different version of it, you can save the image with the original in a version set. A version set is similar to the image stack discussed here, except that an image stack is created manually and can include any images you want to stack together. (See **28** About Saving Images to learn more about version sets.)

1 Select Images to Stack

In the Organizer, click the first image you want to stack, then press **Ctrl** and click additional images to stack. Selected images appear with a blue border. The images do not have to look alike for you to be able to stack them.

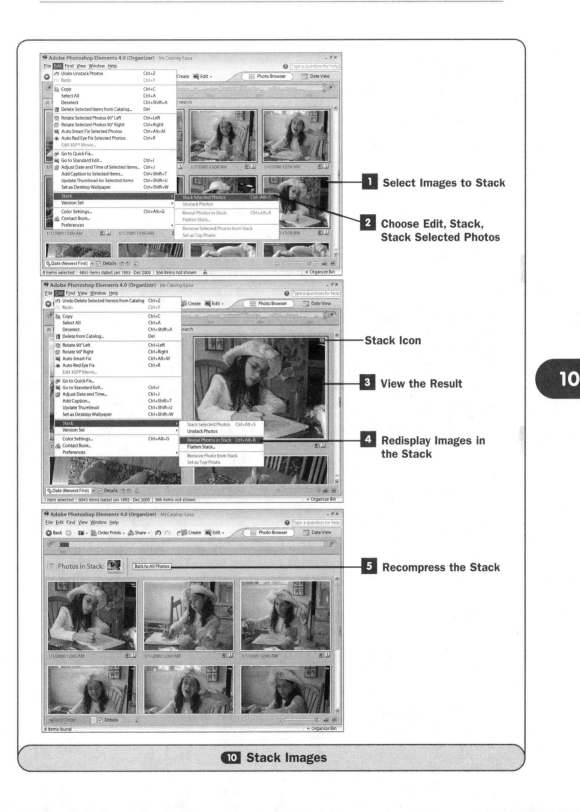

1 Select Images to Stack

2 Choose Edit, Stack, Stack Selected Photos

Stack Icon

3 View the Result

10

4 Redisplay Images in the Stack

5 Recompress the Stack

2 **Choose Edit, Stack, Stack Selected Photos**

Select **Edit**, **Stack**, **Stack Selected Photos** from the menu bar. The images you selected in step 1 are now stacked.

3 **View the Result**

A single thumbnail of the newest image (the one with the most recent modified date) now represents the stack of images. To remind you that the thumbnail represents a stack, the stack icon appears in the upper-right corner of the thumbnail.

4 **Redisplay Images in the Stack**

To redisplay the images in a stack later on, select the stack image (the one with the stack icon). Then choose **Edit**, **Stack**, **Reveal Photos in Stack**.

▶ **NOTES**

To unstack a stack of images so that each image is represented in the catalog by its own thumbnail once again, select the stack thumbnail and choose **Edit**, **Stack**, **Unstack Photos**.

If you don't want to keep the extra images in the stack, and you want to retain only the top photo in the catalog (the one displayed on the thumbnail), select the stack and click **Edit**, **Stack**, **Flatten Stack**. The extra images are removed from the catalog; you'll be asked whether you want to remove the extra photos from the hard disk as well.

5 **Recompress the Stack**

The stack is expanded and all its photos are displayed in a **Find** window. At this point, you can select a new photo to represent the stack by simply selecting an image and choosing **Edit**, **Stack**, **Set as Top Photo**. To remove a photo from the stack, select it and then click **Edit**, **Stack**, **Remove Photo from Stack** (this action does not remove the photo from the catalog or the hard disk). To hide the images in the stack again (to recompress the stack so that only one thumbnail represents the stack of images), simply click **Back to All Photos**.

11 **Change Image Date and Time**

➔ **SEE ALSO**

23 Find Items with the Same Date

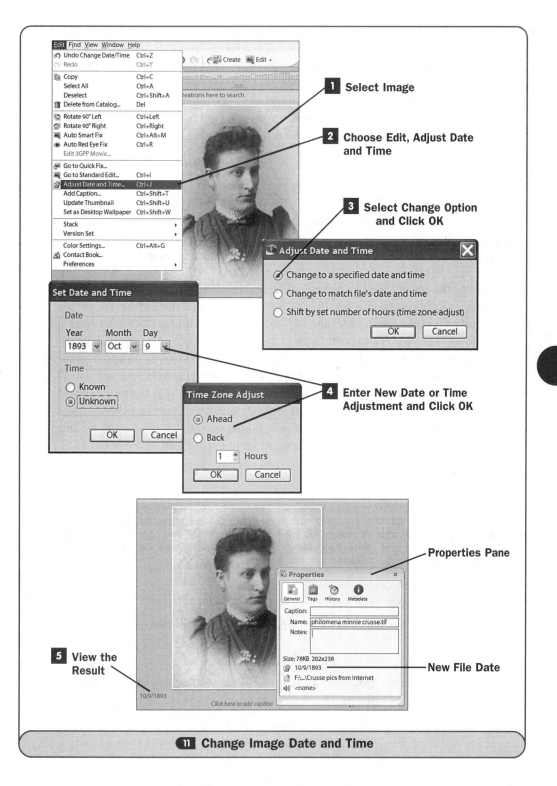

1 Select Image

2 Choose Edit, Adjust Date and Time

3 Select Change Option and Click OK

4 Enter New Date or Time Adjustment and Click OK

5 View the Result

Properties Pane

New File Date

Several dates are associated with each image: the *import date*, the *file date*, and the *modified date*. The modified date is changed when you edit an image, as long as you initiate the edit from within Organizer. The file date, reflecting the date on which an image was taken or created, is important because it's this date that appears in the photo well (assuming that the **Details** option on the **Options** bar is enabled). In addition, you might use the file date to locate an image in the catalog, so its accuracy is important.

▶ KEY TERMS

Import Date—The date on which an item was imported into the catalog.

File Date—The date on which an image was taken or scanned into the system.

Modified Date—The date on which an image was modified by either the Organizer or the Editor, or by launching another graphics editor from within the Organizer.

However, the file date might be wrong if you scanned in a photo, because the date is set to the day you scanned, and not when you took the picture. For example, unless you change the file date, the scan of Great-Grandma Kaster when she was 16 might appear in the catalog next to an image of your 6-year-old daughter taken years later. If you took a photo with a digital camera while on vacation in another time zone, the file date and time recorded were based on your home time, and not the local vacation time. Not that a difference of a few hours should matter much, but *it might matter to you*—especially if the difference between the two time zones (the vacation spot and your home) results in a different date, and thus, a different placement in the catalog when items are sorted.

▶ NOTE

The file date is also displayed on the **General** tab of the **Properties** pane. The import date and the modified date appear on the **History** tab of the **Properties** pane. The modified date is for your own purposes; you can't sort by that date. You can, however, search and sort using the import date. To display the **Properties** pane, click the **Show or Hide Properties** button on the **Options** bar.

1 Select Image

In the Organizer, click the image whose date or time you want to change.

2 Choose Edit, Adjust Date and Time

Select **Edit, Adjust Date and Time** from the menu. The **Adjust Date and Time** dialog box appears.

▶ **TIP**

You can change several images to the same date and time by selecting them all before continuing to step 2. If you select multiple images, you can adjust their file dates by shifting them. When you get to step 3, you'll see a fourth option, **Shift to new starting date and time**. Choose that, then enter the date and time for the earliest photo in the group. The file date and time for the selected images are shifted accordingly, using this earliest date/time as a starting point.

3 Select Change Option and Click OK

To change the file date and time to anything you like, select the **Change to a specified date and time** option. To change the file date so that it matches the current modified date, select the **Change to match file's date and time** option. To adjust the time portion only by a few hours or so, select the **Shift by set number of hours (time zone adjust)** option. Click **OK**.

4 Enter New Date or Time Adjustment and Click OK

If you selected the **Change to match file's date and time** option in step 3, the file date is changed immediately to match the modified date, and you're returned to the main Organizer window.

If you selected the **Change to a specified date and time** option in step 3, the **Set Date and Time** dialog box appears. Enter a **Year**, **Month**, and **Day**. If you don't know the actual date on which the photo was taken, and you'd rather list it as unknown, select **????** from the **Year** list. You can also select **??** from the **Month** or **Day** list if either is unknown. (Of course, this means that the image will not appear in **Date** view.) If you've entered a specific date, you can also specify the time the photo was taken. Click **Known** and enter the time, or select **Unknown**. Click **OK**.

If you selected the **Shift by set number of hours (time zone adjust)** option in step 3, the **Time Zone Adjust** dialog box appears. Select either **Ahead** or **Back** to indicate the direction in which you want the time adjusted and then enter the number of **Hours** to adjust the time of the photograph. Click **OK**.

5 View the Result

The Organizer immediately adjusts the file date and time based on your choices and displays that new date/time in the photo well, just below the image. Here, the file date for this photo of my great-grandmother on her wedding day originally displayed the date on which I scanned the photo into my computer. I changed the file date to October 9, 1893, her wedding date. I didn't know the exact time, so I chose **Unknown** for the time option in step 4.

11

▶ **NOTE**

Changing the file date of an image in the Photoshop Elements catalog does not affect the timestamp of the image's file as it appears in Windows Explorer. The file date is stored in the catalog and exists only there, which is why you can change it to anything you like by following the steps in this task. Again, the file date is the date shown below the image in the catalog. The image's modified date, which is changed when you actually edit an image, matches the date shown in Windows Explorer.

---

12 │ **About Organizing Items**

→ **SEE ALSO**

15 Attach a Marker to an Item
12 Find Items with the Same Marker

As you learned in **1** **About the Organizer**, you can display items grouped by import batch, file date or their location using the **Photo Browser Arrangement** list on the **Options** bar. Using the technique explained in **23** **Find Items with the Same Date**, you can also display a group of items created on the same date. To display photos shot over a *range* of days (with the same file date), drag the end markers on the **Timeline** to set the date range. To clear a date range you've set and redisplay all images, choose **Find, Clear Date Range**. Click a bar on the **Timeline** to quickly scroll to media files created within that month without limiting the display of items at all. For example, you might click a bar on the **Timeline** at **April 2005** to jump directly to the images taken on your birthday, plus any items you might have created that day. The advantage of these methods of organization is that you don't have to do anything to an item (other than import it) to locate that item when you need it. Still, these methods, though useful, have their limits. To locate images based on what they contain, the easiest method is to apply *tags* and *collection* markers.

▶ **KEY TERM**

Tag—A marker associated with a group of media files that contain similar content or subject matter.

Collection—A group of media files that share the same context or purpose, which have been manually arranged in a specific order by you.

With tags and collection markers, you can group similar items together quickly and easily. Tags are typically used to identify items with similar content—for instance, all images that contain Joan, taken during Christmas. Collections are used to group photos that might contain a variety of people or different types of subjects, but are important for their *collective purpose* (images, movies, and audio

**Click a Bar to Scroll to
That Month's Images**

**Limit Items Displayed with
These End Markers**

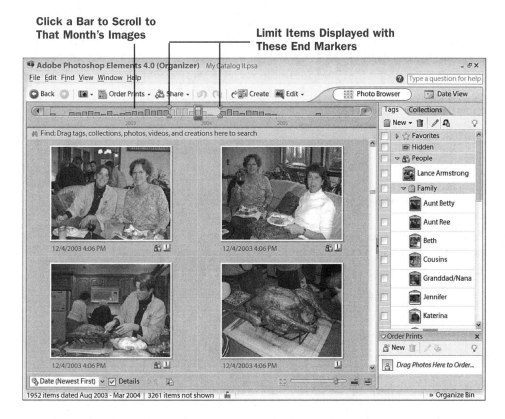

Use the Timeline to scroll within the catalog or to limit the display.

files you're gathering for a family history CD, a calendar, or slide show). The most useful aspect of a collection is that you can arrange the items in that collection so that they appear onscreen in whatever order you choose. Collections are useful for gathering images you intend to use for the same purpose, such as a calendar or photo album, and arranging them in the order in which you want them to appear in the creation you're planning to make.

The principal reason you would want to create a tag for images is because they contain some element that's important to you, and that you know you'll want to be able to search for later. Most often, that element is a person, such as yourself or a family member. It can also be a common place, such as a city you frequently visit, or a park, vacation home, festival, or sporting event. Think of a tag as identifying the *who, what,* or *where* of a photo, and a collection as identifying the *why,* as in "why am I keeping this photo?" or, "what do I intend to do with it?" Again, collections are perfect for gathering together various items for a project because you can arrange items in the collection in a specific order (unlike tags, which appear onscreen in whatever sort order you're using—typically file date order). Each item in a collection has a number that reflects its position within the collection. After displaying the items in a collection, just drag and drop them to rearrange their order. For example, you might rearrange images in the **Calendar** collection by months, making it easier for you to assemble the calendar in the **Creations Wizard** when you're done.

▶ **NOTE**

Markers do not appear on thumbnails in the photo well if you do not also display file dates. To display dates, turn on the Details option on the Options bar.

Tag and collection markers assigned to an item appear as small icons beneath an item's thumbnail in the catalog. To identify the tag or collection a particular image belongs to, hover the mouse pointer over that icon and a description appears. In **Single Photo** view, you'll see not only the marker icons, but the marker description as well. If you were to create a **Joan** tag and assign it to several images, you could quickly display just the images that contain Joan (maybe alone, maybe with other people); create a **Vacation** tag, and you could narrow your search to locate photos of Joan on vacation with you. See **19 Find Items with the Same Marker**. Being able to control the catalog display is one of the powerful results of using tags and collections to organize your catalog items.

Available tags are displayed on the **Tags** tab of the **Organize Bin**, located on the left side of the Organizer window. By default, tags consist of five main categories: **Favorites**, **People**, **Events**, **Places**, and **Other**. In addition, if you've imported images with tags already attached, those tags will appear in the **Imported Tags** category. (See **3 Import Media from a Folder, CD-ROM, or DVD**, for help importing images from various sources with their tags attached.) Under the **People** category, you'll find two subcategories—**Family** and **Friends**. You can use these existing categories and subcategories as tags, or you can create new ones. The **Favorites** category, for example, provides several tags you can use to rank your favorite images.

The Organizer does not provide any default collection markers for you, so you'll have to create your own. Also, collection markers do not use categories, but groups, to display similar collection markers together. Collection markers are displayed on the **Collections** tab of the **Organize Bin**. See **14 Create a Collection** and **13 Create a Tag**.

Number Icons Mark an Item's
Place Within a Collection

Category Markers

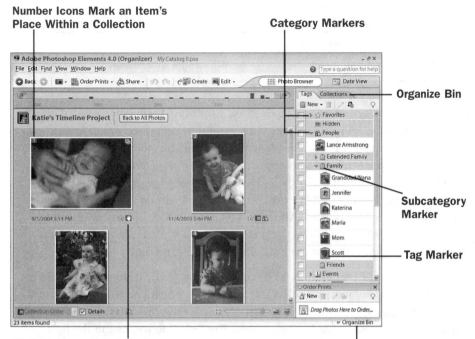

Organize Bin

Subcategory
Marker

Tag Marker

Markers Appear as Icons

Click to Hide/Display Organize Bin

Markers help you organize your images and display just those you want to work with.

12

▶ **NOTES**

The Organizer provides an additional tag category, called **Hidden**, that you can use to temporarily hide media files you don't use very often. Just assign this tag to any item you want to hide temporarily. To view the items again, redisplay all items with the **Hidden** tag.

You can hide the **Organize Bin** temporarily, and then later redisplay it by clicking the **Organize Bin** button at the right end of the **Status** bar.

▶ **TIP**

By default, the **Organize Bin** shows markers with a name and a small icon (this icon is actually a small photo, taken from the first image to which the marker is assigned). The **Organize Bin** sorts the tag and collection lists in alphabetical order. To change this arrangement, choose **Edit, Preferences, Tags and Collections.** Enable the **Manual** option if you want to drag and drop elements in the **Organize Bin** to arrange them yourself (tags normally appear in the order in which they are added). This way, the **Mom and Dad** marker can appear above little **Isabella** if you prefer elders to precede children in the list. In the **Tag Display** frame, you can set tags (but not collection markers) to appear without photos (as miniature folder icons) or as larger icons (big enough to see who's in them).

> **13   Create a Tag**
>
> | ✔ BEFORE YOU BEGIN | → SEE ALSO |
> |---|---|
> | **12** About Organizing Items | **14** Create a Collection |

To identify the content of images so that you can locate them when needed, you assign tags to those images. To make your various tags markers easier to use, you'll want to keep them organized by category. The **Tags** tab of the **Organize Bin** has several pre-existing tag categories for you to use: **Favorites**, **Hidden**, **People**, **Events**, **Other**, and **Places**. There are some subcategories in the **People** category as well: **Family** and **Friends**. To this list you can add as many categories and subcategories as you want. Although you can use the category and subcategory tags the Organizer provides to mark your images, you'll probably want to create at least a few tags that are more specific than just **Family** or **Events**.

When you create a new tag for your images, you assign it a unique name, add a descriptive note if desired, and select the category in which you want the tag to appear. New tags appear in the **Organize Bin** under the category you choose, at first with a generic icon that has no picture. The first time you assign the new icon to a photo, that photo is automatically applied as the icon for that tag. When you assign a group of photos to a new tag collectively, its icon is borrowed from the newest photo in that group. This task shows you how to create new tag categories and tag markers.

13

1 Click Tags Tab

To create a new tag category or subcategory, in the Organizer, click the **Tags** tab on the **Organize Bin**.

2 Click New Button

To create a new category or subcategory for tags, click the **New** button at the top of the **Organize Bin** and then select **New Category** or **New Sub-Category**. The **Create Category** or **Create Sub-Category** dialog box appears.

3 Enter Name

Type a name for the new tag category or subcategory in the text box provided.

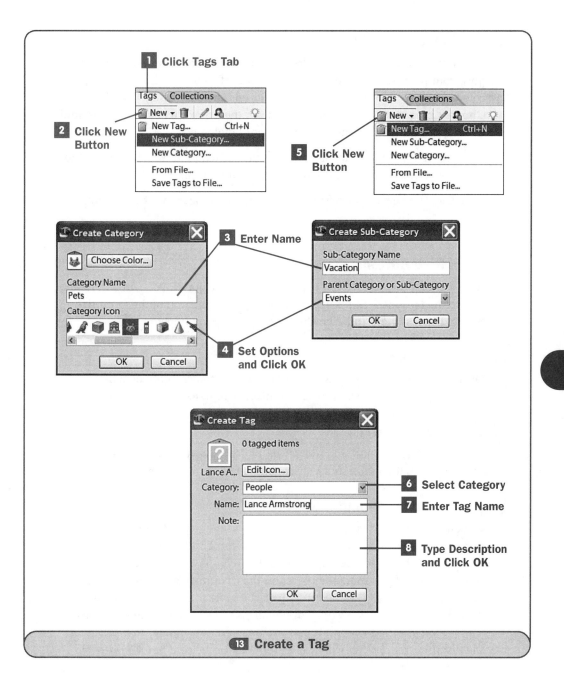

1 Click Tags Tab

2 Click New Button

3 Enter Name

4 Set Options and Click OK

5 Click New Button

6 Select Category

7 Enter Tag Name

8 Type Description and Click OK

13 Create a Tag

4 **Set Options and Click OK**

When creating a tag category, select the icon you want to represent the category from those shown in the **Category Icon** list. You can also change the color that appears at the top of the tags in this category by clicking the **Choose Color** button, selecting a color from the **Color Picker** that opens, and clicking **OK** to return to the **Create Category** dialog box.

If you're creating a tag subcategory, select the category to which you want to assign it from the **Parent Category or Sub-Category** list.

Click **OK**. The new category/subcategory marker appears on the **Organize Bin**.

5 **Click New Button**

After creating any needed tag categories or subcategories, you can add new tags to the **Organize Bin**. Click the **New** button at the top of the **Organize Bin** and choose **New Tag**. The **Create Tag** dialog box appears.

6 **Select Category**

Open the **Category** drop-down list and select the tag category or subcategory to which you want to assign this new marker.

7 **Enter Tag Name**

Type a name for the new tag marker in the **Name** text box. The name can include spaces if you like, but you are limited to 63 characters.

8 **Type Description and Click OK**

Click in the **Note** box and type a description of the tag if desired. This note appears only when you select a tag and click the **Edit** button (the pencil icon) at the top of the **Organize Bin**, so it's of limited use. Click **OK** to create the new tag marker. The marker appears on the **Organize Bin** underneath the category or group you selected in step 6. The marker is now ready to be assigned to any item you want—although you've probably noticed that its icon is blank at the moment. When you assign a new marker to a photo for the first time, the marker will grab that photo for its icon. See **15** **Attach a Marker to an Item**.

To remove a marker you no longer want, select it and click the **Delete** button (the trash icon) on the **Organize Bin**. The marker is automatically removed from any items to which it may have been assigned. To replace one marker with another, select both in the **Organize Bin**, right-click, and choose **Merge Tags**. Select the marker to keep and click **OK**. Items with the other marker are automatically tagged with the marker you kept, and the other marker is removed from the **Organize Bin**.

You can enlarge the size of the icon that appears next to a tag by choosing **Edit**, **Preferences**, **Tags and Collections**, and choosing the last option from the **Tag Display** frame. Notice that you can also forgo the photo icon altogether and display a small folder icon instead.

▶ **TIP**

You can drag existing tags on top of a category or subcategory on the **Organize Bin** to move that marker to that category/subcategory. To change any of the attributes associated with a category or subcategory, select it and click the **Edit** button (the pencil icon) at the top of the **Organize Bin**. To remove a category or subcategory and the tags within it, click the **Delete** button (the trash icon) instead.

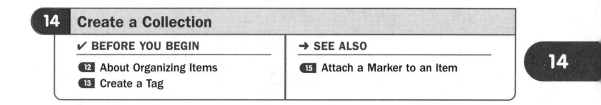

14 | **Create a Collection**

✔ **BEFORE YOU BEGIN**	→ **SEE ALSO**
12 About Organizing Items **13** Create a Tag	**15** Attach a Marker to an Item

14

Collection markers appear on the Organize Bin. You can organize collection markers into groups if you like, but by their very nature (gathering together a special group of images for a specific purpose such as an upcoming family reunion), collections are unique and you'll probably find that you don't need to group them much, although you'll learn how to do so in this task.

Creating a collection marker is similar to creating a tag (see **13** **Create a Tag**). It's after you create a collection marker and apply it that you'll discover the key differences between the two: Photos in a collection are organized *in sequence*, by number, unlike a set of photos that share the same tag (which are shown in the catalog using the chosen sort order). The sequence is important when you want to organize a group of photos, perhaps for a slideshow or other creation where sequence is critical. The Organizer provides no collection groups initially, although you can easily create the ones you need, and place into them any existing collections group.

1 **Click Collections Tab**

To create a new collection group (or subgroup, which is even more rare), click the **Collections** tab.

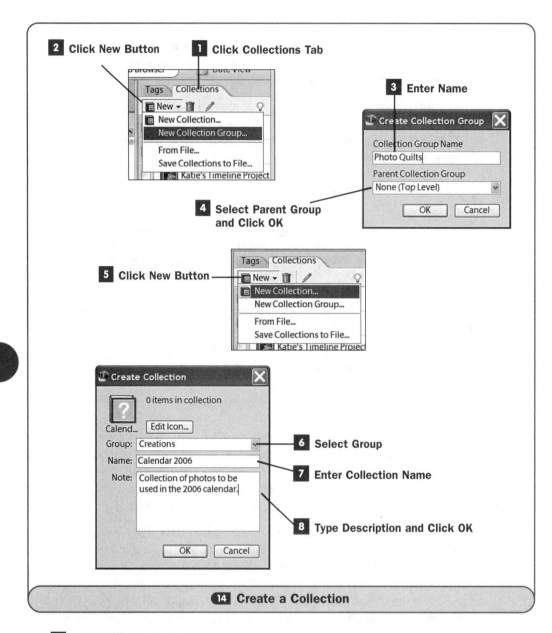

2 Click New Button

1 Click Collections Tab

3 Enter Name

4 Select Parent Group and Click OK

5 Click New Button

6 Select Group

7 Enter Collection Name

8 Type Description and Click OK

14 Create a Collection

2 Click New Button

To create a collection group or subgroup, click the **New** button on the **Organize Bin** and select **New Collection Group**. The **Create Collection Group** dialog box appears.

3 Enter Name

Type a name for the new collection group in the text box provided.

4 Select Parent Group and Click OK

To create a collection subgroup, select an existing group from the **Parent Collection Group** list. To create a collection group, leave this option set to **None**. Click **OK**. The new collection group/subgroup appears on the **Organize Bin**.

5 Click New Button

After creating any needed collection groups or subgroups, you can add new collection markers to the **Organize Bin**. Click the **New** button at the top of the **Organize Bin** and choose **New Collection**. The **Create Collection** dialog box appears.

6 Select Group

Open the **Group** drop-down list and select the collection group or subgroup to which you want to assign this new collection marker. If you don't want to group the new collection with other collections, choose **None (Top Level)** from this list.

7 Enter Collection Name

Type a name for the new collection marker in the **Name** text box. The name can include spaces if you like, but you are limited to 63 characters.

8 Type Description and Click OK

Click in the **Note** box and type a description of the collection if desired. This note appears only when you select a collection marker and click the **Edit** button (the pencil icon) at the top of the **Organize Bin**, so it's of limited use. Click **OK** to create the new collection marker. The marker appears on the **Organize Bin** underneath the group you selected in step 6 (if any). The marker is now ready to be assigned to any item you want—although you've probably noticed that its icon is blank at the moment. When you assign a new marker to a photo for the first time, the marker will grab that photo for its icon. See **Attach a Marker to an Item**.

▶ NOTE

To remove a collection marker you no longer want, select it and click the **Delete** button (the trash icon) on the **Organize Bin**. The marker is automatically removed from any items to which it may have been assigned. To replace one marker with another, select both in the **Organize Bin**, right-click, and choose **Merge Collections**. Select the marker to keep and click **OK**. Items with the other marker are automatically tagged with the marker you kept, and the other marker is removed from the **Organize Bin**.

14

▶ **NOTE**

You can drag existing collection markers on top of a group or subgroup on the **Organize Bin** to move that marker to that group/subgroup. To change any of the attributes associated with a group or subgroup, select it and click the **Edit** button (the pencil icon) at the top of the **Organize Bin**. To remove a group or subgroup and the collection markers within it, click the **Delete** button (the trash icon) instead.

15	**Attach a Marker to an Item**

✔ BEFORE YOU BEGIN

⓬ About Organizing Items
⓮ Create a Collection

To organize your media files into logical groups such as vacation photos, photos of the family dog, audio files of your daughter, movies of friends, and so on, assign tag and collection markers to them. After a marker has been associated with your media files, you can search for items with a particular marker and display just those files onscreen. For example, if you have a tag called **Hattie**, you could use it to instantly display photos of your pet Scottie dog.

14

▶ **TIP**

You can create new tags using the names of the folders in which images reside. Just display images by **Folder Location** by choosing that option from the **Photo Browser Arrangement** list at the left end of the **Options** bar, and click the **Instant Tag** button (located just after the folder name at the top of a folder group). A tag is created using the name of the folder, and all the images in that folder are automatically marked with the new tag.

1 Select Items

In the Organizer, select the item(s) you want to mark. To select multiple items, press **Shift** and click the first and last item in a contiguous group, or press **Ctrl** and click each item you want. If items are sorted by folder or import batch, you can click the gray bar above a group to select all items in that group.

2 Click Tags or Collections Tab

To assign a tag, click the **Tags** tab on the **Organize Bin**. To assign a collection marker, click the **Collections** tab instead.

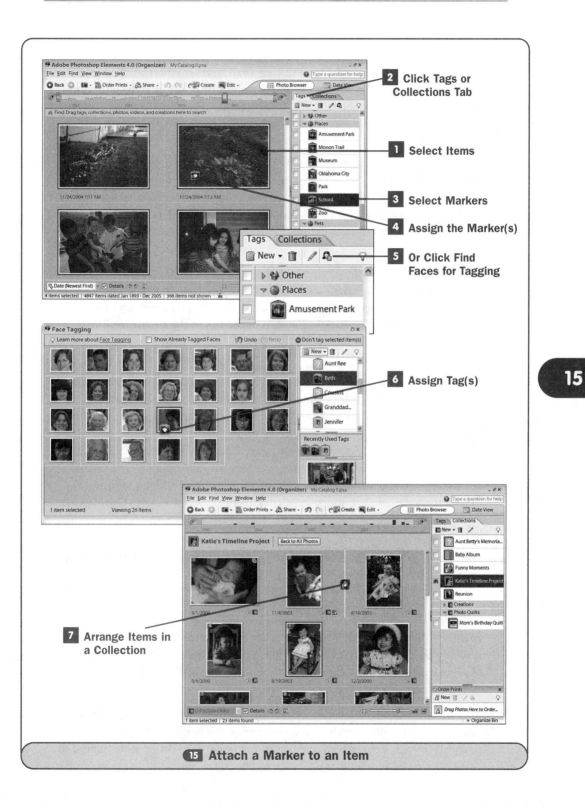

2 Click Tags or Collections Tab

1 Select Items

3 Select Markers

4 Assign the Marker(s)

5 Or Click Find Faces for Tagging

6 Assign Tag(s)

7 Arrange Items in a Collection

15

15 Attach a Marker to an Item

3 Select Markers

In the **Organize Bin**, press **Ctrl** and click each marker you want to assign to the selected items. (You can assign multiple tags or multiple collection markers in one step, but not both.)

4 Assign the Marker(s)

Drag the selected marker(s) onto any one of the selected items and drop the markers on the item. If you're assigning a new marker to an image for the first time, that image is used as the marker's photo icon. If you selected multiple images, the first image in the group is the one used. The markers you assigned appear as icons underneath the selected items.

5 Or Click Find Faces for Tagging

To use the faces in the selected photos you selected to help you assign tags (not collection markers), skip steps 2–4 and instead, after selecting images, click the **Find Faces for Tagging** button at the top of the **Organize Bin**.

6 Assign Tag(s)

Organizer searches the selected image(s) for faces and displays them in small thumbnails in the **Face Tagging** dialog box (if a face is turned partially away from the camera, it might not be picked up). Drag a tag from the list on the right and drop it on a thumbnail to assign the tag to that image. To view the image from which a face thumbnail was pulled, click the thumbnail. The thumbnail is removed from the **Face Tagging** dialog box, unless you've selected the **Show Already Tagged** Faces option. Continue until you've tagged all your images, then click **Done**.

▶ NOTE

You can review a group of photos and assign tags or collection markers to them during the review. See **9 Review Images.**

7 Arrange Items in a Collection

After assigning a collection marker to a group of items (images, sound files, and/or video files), you can display that group in **Collections Order** view by clicking the box in front of the collection name on the **Organize Bin**. (See **19 Find Items with the Same Marker.**)

Rearrange the items in a collection in any order you want by simply dragging them in the photo well. As you rearrange the items, the number assigned to each item (which appears in the upper-left corner of the item and denotes its position within the collection) changes.

16 | **Add a Text Caption or Note**

→ SEE ALSO

22 Find Items with the Same Caption or Note

With a text caption, you can provide a title for your "works of art" (your photographs). An image's caption appears in the photo well when you display the image using **Single Photo** view, and below each image in a photo review (see **9** **Review Images**). In addition, captions can be printed on a contact sheet and made to appear in various creations, such as a slide show, photo book, video CD, calendar, or HTML Photo Gallery. For longer descriptions or stories about an image, you can enter a note. Notes do not appear in the photo well, but only within the **Properties** pane.

▶ **TIP**

When searching for a particular image, you can search for text contained in its filename, caption, or note. See **22** **Find Items with the Same Caption or Note.**

1 **Select Image(s)**

In the Organizer, click the image to which you want to add a caption. If you want to add the same caption to multiple images, select them now.

2 **Click Show or Hide Properties Button**

If it's not already displayed, click the **Show or Hide Properties** button on the **Options** bar to display the **Properties** pane. You can also choose **Window**, **Properties** from the menu.

3 **Type Caption and/or Note**

If you selected one image, click the **General** button at the top of the **Properties** pane. Then type your **Caption**, such as **Alyce on Big Bear Mountain, July 2005** or **We watched the rain under the protection of a large maple tree**. Your caption can include up to 2000 characters, including spaces, but you'll want to keep it short so it displays fully onscreen and in creations. Longer descriptions can be typed in the **Notes** section if you like.

If you selected multiple images, click the **Change Caption** button. Type your **Caption**, select **Replace Existing Captions** (otherwise, if an image already has a caption, it won't be replaced), then click **OK**.

Close the **Properties** pane by clicking its **X** button or by clicking the **Show or Hide Properties** button on the **Options** bar.

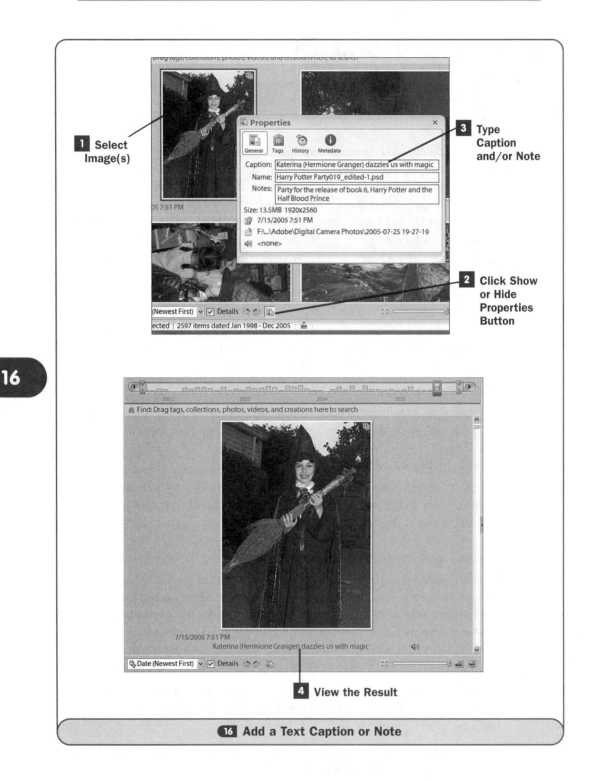

1 Select Image(s)

3 Type Caption and/or Note

2 Click Show or Hide Properties Button

16

4 View the Result

16 Add a Text Caption or Note

▶ **TIPS**

You can also enter text captions by double-clicking an image to display it in **Single Photo** view. Click where it says **Click here to add caption**, type a caption, and press **Enter**.

You can delete a text caption from either the **Caption** text box in the **Properties** pane, or from **Single Photo** view. Click the caption and then use the mouse to highlight the entire caption. Press **Delete** to remove the caption.

4 **View the Result**

Notes can only be seen in the **Properties** pane, and they are not used in creations. To view an image's caption, change to **Single Photo** view by double-clicking the image in the photo well or by clicking the **Single Photo View** button on the **Options** bar.

---

17 **Make a Creation**

✔ **BEFORE YOU BEGIN**

12 About Organizing Items

17

Organizing images is just one of the things Organizer helps you excel at; another is being creative. Using the images in the catalog, you can make a variety of creations, including slide shows, VCD (a collection of slide shows playable on your TV), calendars, photo books, greeting cards, and an HTML photo gallery (a browsable gallery of images). You can share creations you make in a variety of ways, such as emailing them to friends, burning slide shows or VCDs onto a CD, printing album pages, calendars, and cards at home, or uploading calendars and photo books to Adobe Printing Services for professional services.

You make creations using the **Creations Wizard**; the wizard steps you through the process of arranging your photos, selecting a template, choosing options, and saving, emailing, printing, or uploading the result. In this task, you'll learn the basic steps in making a calendar. Although each creation type has its own set of options, the process is similar for each type.

▶ **TIP**

To help you arrange multiple photos for a creation, create a collection first, and use the collection to arrange them in the order you want. See **15** Attach a Marker to an Item.

2 Click the Create Button

1 Select Image(s)

3 Select Creation Type

4 Set Options

17

17 Make a Creation

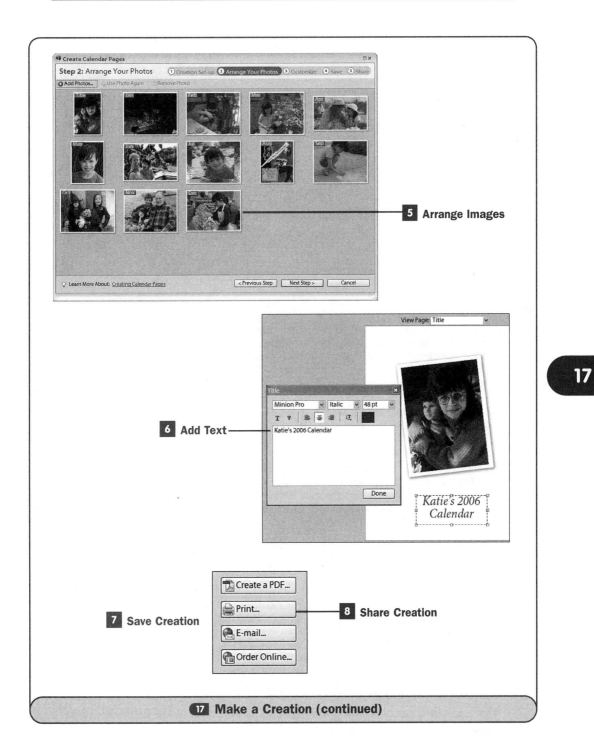

5 **Arrange Images**

6 **Add Text**

7 **Save Creation**

8 **Share Creation**

17 Make a Creation (continued)

1 Select Image(s)

In the Organizer, select the image(s) you want to use in the creation.

2 Click the Create Button

Click the **Create** button on the **Shortcuts** bar.

3 Select Creation Type

On the first page of the **Creations Wizard**, select the type of creation you want to make from those listed on the left. As you make a selection, a description of that choice appears on the right. Small icons appear above this description, indicating your choices (such as printing, burning to CD, ordering online, and so on) for this particular creation. Hover the mouse over an icon to see the choice it represents. Click **OK**.

▶ NOTES

VCDs, slide shows, and HTML photo galleries are not created using the **Creations Wizard**. If you choose **Slide Show** and click **OK** in step 3, a dialog box of options appears. Select the options you want for the slide show, and click **OK** to display the **Slide Show Editor**, which allows you to customize the transitions between each image, add music, text, and graphics.

If you choose **VCD with Menu** in step 3, the slide show(s) you selected appear; arrange the slide shows in the order in which you want them to appear on the VCD, select the VCD format, and click **Burn**.

If you choose **HTML Photo Gallery** in step 3, a dialog box appears in which you can choose the type of web page banner (heading) you want, adjust the size of the image thumbnails on the page(s), adjust the quality of the larger photos that appear when a thumbnail is clicked, and choose custom colors and fonts. Make your selections, choose a site folder in which to save the web pages that will be generated, and click **Save**.

4 Set Options

In Step 1 of the **Creations Wizard**, select a template from the list on the right. Set other options as desired. For example, in the calendar shown here, you can add a title page (you'll need an extra photo), image captions, and adjust the length of the calendar. Click **Next Step**.

5 Arrange Images

In Step 2 of the **Creations Wizard**, images appear in the order in which they were selected. Drag and drop images to rearrange them as desired. Click **Next Step**.

17

6 Add Text

In Step 3 of the **Creations Wizard**, you add text to the creation. Just double-click where indicated and type your text, set formatting by choosing the font, style, and size of the text, and click **Done**. Some creations have multiple pages; click the ➔ to flip through pages and add text as needed. You can also resize and move images on each page if you like. Click **Next Step**.

7 Save Creation

In Step 4 of the **Creations Wizard**, type a name for the creation in the box provided or select **Use Title for Name** to use the name from the **Title Page** as the creation's name. To display all the images you used in the creation in the photo well after the creation is saved, select **Show these photos in my Photo Browser when finished**. Click **Next Step**.

8 Share Creation

In Step 5 of the **Creations Wizard**, select how you want to share the creation. For example, to resave the creation in PDF format and attach it to an email message, click **Email**. Some creations are designed specifically to be printed professionally, although you can still print them at home if you want. To order a professionally printed copy of such a creation, click **Order Online**. (See **39 Print Images Using an Online Service** for more information on using an online service.) Options that are not applicable for this creation are grayed out. If you don't want to share the creation, click **Done**.

The creation appears with a special icon in its upper-right corner to help identify it as a creation. To redisplay all your creations, search by media type. See **18 About Finding Items in the Catalog**. You can also mark creations with tag or collection markers to help you locate them again. To edit a creation, double-click its thumbnail in the photo well. To display the items used in a collection in the photo well, right-click its thumbnail and choose **Show Creation Items in Photo Browser**.

17

4

Finding Images, Movies, and Audio Files

IN THIS CHAPTER:

18 About Finding Items in the Catalog

19 Find Items with the Same Marker

20 Find Items Using Metadata

21 Find Items with Similar Filenames

22 Find Items with the Same Caption or Note

23 Find Items with the Same Date

24 Find Items with the Same History

You'll know your digital photos, audio files, and movies are truly organized when you're able to quickly locate any item in the catalog without struggling to recall its exact filename or the folder you saved it in. As you learned in **15 Attach a Marker to an Item**, you can assign various collection or tag markers to an item, enabling you to locate it in multiple ways. For example, you could assign the **Christmas, Granddad, Uncle,** and **Kids** tags to the holiday snapshot, and locate it later on by searching for items with that unique combination of tags. Or you could assign a **Photo Album** collection marker to the images you used in a bound album, and recall them quickly for use in a new photo album creation. Because you're using the Organizer to categorize images and other media files, you can store all of them in the **My Pictures** folder if you like, without creating separate folders for various groups. You can even store media files offline, on CD-ROMs or DVDs. The Organizer doesn't care where files are located; it can organize them all easily.

By the way, tag and collection markers aren't the only things you can use to locate an image or other file, as you'll discover in this chapter. You can also search for media files based on file date, filename, caption, note, change history, file type, and other criteria.

18   About Finding Items in the Catalog

✔ **BEFORE YOU BEGIN**

12 About Organizing Items

Just because your catalog may have countless rows of thumbnails does not mean that it is less manageable, or that your media files are more difficult to find than when you had only a few dozen thumbnails to contend with. After each image file has been imported, the catalog automatically begins tracking that the item's filename, location, file date, and file type, and (in the case of images) the *Exchangeable Image File (EXIF)* data (also called *metadata*) that your camera/scanner stored in the file when the image was shot or scanned. This data typically includes the resolution, color gamut (color range), image size, compression, shutter speed, and f-stop of the image. An EXIF-aware application such as Photoshop Elements can use this data to adjust the image so that it appears, when displayed or printed, as closely to the way the image looked when shot as possible. In addition, through the **File Info** dialog box in the Editor, and the **Properties** pane in the Organizer, Photoshop Elements can amend the EXIF metadata to include tags, collection markers, title, description, and copyright information. Also, as you edit an image, its edit history is stored in the image's metadata. So, without doing any work other than importing a media file, you can locate an item immediately if you know any of its file data.

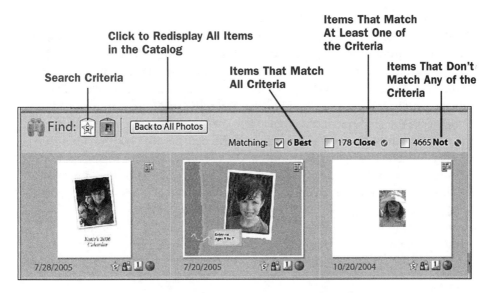

Search Criteria

Click to Redisplay All Items
in the Catalog

Items That Match
All Criteria

Items That Match
At Least One of
the Criteria

Items That Don't
Match Any of the
Criteria

The Find bar shows you the criteria for the currently displayed items.

▶ **KEY TERM**

EXIF (Exchangeable Image File)—Data attached to a photo file that contains the key settings the camera used when the photo was shot.

▶ **NOTE**

EXIF data such as image resolution will not be saved in a scanned image if you use Microsoft Office Document Imaging to perform the scan. It's best to use the software that came with the scanner. In addition, some scanners might not be capable of recording EXIF data—see the scanner documentation.

The true organizational magic begins, however, when you associate any number of markers to the items in the catalog. The markers enable you to keep track of what's important about a particular item—for instance, whether it's a holiday, party, or other special event, or whether the shot was taken indoors or outdoors. You can add notes and captions to your catalog items, making it even easier to locate a particular media file when needed. In upcoming tasks, you'll learn how to search for items in the catalog using the tags and collection markers you've assigned. You'll also learn how to search for items based on their file date, filename, caption, note, media type (such as creation, movie, audio file, and so on), and history (not just when an item was imported or edited, but also when it was sent via email, shared online, or printed).

When you perform a search of the catalog, the search criteria are displayed on the **Find** bar. For example, if you're searching for items with certain collection or tag markers, those markers appear in the **Find** bar. If you're looking for the photos you used in a particular slideshow, the **Find** bar reads **Used in** along with the name of that slideshow. If you're looking for only those items to which you've attached audio captions, the **Find** bar reads **Items with Audio Captions**. Underneath the **Find** bar, in the photo well, are the items that match your search. This means that, when you see something in the **Find** bar, all items in the catalog are not currently being shown; to display all items, click the **Back to All Photos** button on the **Find** bar. There is one exception here you should note: if you use the **Timeline** to limit the items displayed in the photo well (as described in **12 About Organizing Items**) nothing appears on the **Find** bar to notify you that all items are not currently being shown. To clear the **Timeline** limitations and redisplay all items, choose **Find, Clear Date Range**.

▶ **NOTES**

You can review the results of a previous search by clicking the **Back** button on the **Shortcuts** bar. You can return to the current search by clicking the **Forward** button.

18

If you always want to display both matching and closely matching items when you conduct a new search, choose **Edit, Preferences** and select the **General** tab. Select the **Show Closely Matching Sets for Searches** option and click **OK**.

When there's an active search in progress, the **Find** bar displays the number of matches and non-matches. After you perform a search, the matching items are displayed in the photo well and a check mark appears next to the *XX* **Best** box on the **Find** bar (where *XX* represents the number of exact matches to all your criteria). To display exact matches and items that match at least one of the criteria, enable both the *XX* **Best** and *XX* **Close** boxes. To show only those items that do not match any of the criteria, disable the *XX* **Best** and *XX* **Close** boxes, and enable the *XX* **Not** box instead. If you enable the *XX* **Not** box and the *XX* **Best** box, *all the items in the catalog* will appear, but the non-matches will show a red **Not** icon (a circle with a slash) similar to the one on the **Find** bar. Matches won't have this icon.

Normally, you cannot mix and match different types of search criteria. For example, if you're searching for items that contain one or more tags, and you begin a search for items you emailed to someone, the Organizer clears the current search by tags and processes your search by email as a new search. However, using an item's metadata (its filedate, shutter speed, aperture, tags, collection markers, edit history, and so on), you can create a unique search that combines the elements of these other, separate searches. For example, you can look for an item created on

July 12th, marked with a **Party** tag, and shot with a large f-stop of F4 or lower (which may indicate minimal available light, such as an indoor shot). See **20** **Find Items Using Metadata**.

There are so many ways to search for items in the catalog that we could not cover them all in the upcoming tasks. Because these search methods are really simple, I'll cover them briefly here. To locate items of a similar type (all creations or all videos), choose **Find**, **By Media Type**, then choose the type from the list that appears. For example, choose **Find**, **By Media Type**, **Videos**. To find images with similar content, select some sample images that show the content you want to find, and then choose **Find**, **Items by Visual Similarity with Selected Photo(s)**. Or just drag the similar images to the **Find** bar and drop them to create a search. With this type of search, it's best to select several items with similar content, because that makes it easier for Organizer to find more of the same. To find items with a date or time set to **Unknown**, select **Find**, **Items with Unknown Date or Time**. You might do this to locate and change items with unknown dates/times to something more specific.

To display images that have been edited and saved together with their originals in a version set, choose **Find**, **All Version Sets**. This command, however, does not display items you've grouped together manually in stacks. To display items that have not yet been tagged so that you can mark them, choose **Find**, **Untagged Items**. Items with collection markers and no tags will appear, along with items that have no markers at all. To find items that do not have a collection marker (but may or may not have a tag), choose **Find**, **Items Not in any Collection** instead.

19

---

19 **Find Items with the Same Marker**

✔ **BEFORE YOU BEGIN**

15 Attach a Marker to an Item
18 About Finding Items in the Catalog

The payoff of using tags or collection markers to help catalog your digital photos and other media files is that these markers can help you can find specific items quickly and easily. There are several different methods you can use to tell the Organizer which tag or collection markers are attached to the items you're looking for. After the Organizer knows the markers you're interested in, it searches the catalog for items that have those markers attached and displays them in the photo well.

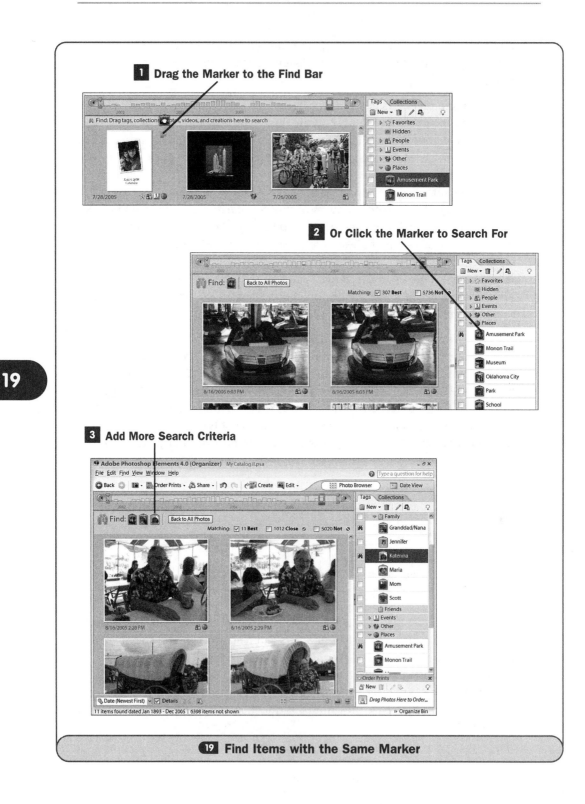

1 Drag the Marker to the Find Bar

2 Or Click the Marker to Search For

3 Add More Search Criteria

19 Find Items with the Same Marker

When selecting a marker to use in searching for a particular set of media files, keep in mind that if you select a category, subcategory, group, or subgroup marker, you automatically include all the tag or collection markers within that category/group or subcategory/subgroup as well. Although these extra markers won't appear on the **Find** bar, they are included by implication. For example, if you place the **Events** tag on the **Find** bar, items tagged with the **Events** category tag *plus* any items tagged with a specific **Events** tag such as **Family Reunion** or **Fourth of July** will also appear in the photo well.

▶ NOTES

Using the method explained here, you cannot combine tags and collection markers in a single search. In addition, you can specify only *one* collection marker to use in a search at a time. To specify both a tag and a collection marker for a search, use metadata. See **20** **Find Items Using Metadata**

You'll have to display the **Organize Bin** to complete this task. If it's not currently showing, select **Window, Organize Bin** from the menu or click the **Organize Bin** button on the **Status** bar to display it.

1 Drag the Marker to the Find Bar

In the Organizer, on the **Organize Bin**, click either the **Tags** or **Collections** tab. Drag the marker representing the items you want to search for and drop it on the **Find** bar. The marker appears on the **Find** bar, and matching items are displayed in the photo well.

2 Or Click the Marker to Search For

Another method for displaying marked items is to click on the **Organize Bin**, the small box to the left of the marker you want your items to match. A binoculars icon appears in the box, and the marker appears in the **Find** bar. Matching items are displayed in the photo well.

3 Add More Search Criteria

To search for items that have multiple tags, simply click the box in front of additional tags in the **Organize Bin** to add those tags to the search criteria, or drag more tags from the **Organize Bin** to the **Find** bar. Only items that match *all the tags* are shown in the photo well. To redisplay all items, click the **Back to All Photos** button on the **Find** bar.

▶ TIP

To exclude items with a particular a tag from an existing search, right-click that tag in the **Organize Bin** and select **Exclude photos with *XX* tag from search results** from the context menu.

19

20   **Find Items Using Metadata**

✔ **BEFORE YOU BEGIN**

18 About Finding Items in the Catalog

Images taken with a digital camera or scanned with a scanner typically include extra information, called EXIF metadata, that helps a monitor or printer display or print the image accurately. This metadata includes information such as the image resolution, f-stop, aperture, camera/scanner type, and so on. Audio and video files include metadata that tell a player what type of file it is so that it can be replayed accurately. To this metadata, Photoshop Elements adds other information such as an image's edit history, tags, collection markers, and so on. You can use this metadata to search for items in the catalog. An item's metadata appears on the **Metadata** tag of the **Properties** pane in the Organizer. It also appears in the **File Info** box in the Editor. You can use either of these two places to edit the metadata as well.

20

1 Choose Find, By Details (Metadata)

In the Organizer, choose **Find**, **By Details (Metadata)** from the menu. The **Find By Details (Metadata)** dialog box appears.

2 Enter Search Criteria

Old criteria from the last search appears; to remove any old criteria, click the – button to the right of the row.

To add criteria, from the first list, select the kind of metadata for which you want to search. For example, to search for images taken with an f-stop of f5.6 or less (a large aperture which you would use to take a photo in low light conditions), choose **F-Stop** from the list.

From the second list, select a criteria range such as **is less than**, **contains**, or **starts with**.

3 Add More Search Criteria

To add another criteria to further limit the search, click the + button to the right of the last criteria, then repeat step 2. Add as many criteria as you like. Here, in addition to the first criteria (which looks for low-light images taken with a large f-stop), I added criteria to narrow the search to include only low-light images with a **Katerina** tag and a file date (capture date) after July 9, 2005 (because I remember taking the photos I want to find sometime after that date).

1 **Choose Find, By Details (Metadata)**

Find	View	Window	Help	
Set Date Range...				Ctrl+Alt+F
Clear Date Range				Ctrl+Shift+F
By Caption or Note...				Ctrl+Shift+J
By Filename...				Ctrl+Shift+K
All Version Sets				Ctrl+Alt+V
By History				▸
By Media Type				▸
By Details (Metadata)...				
Items with Unknown Date or Time				Ctrl+Shift+X
By Visual Similarity with Selected Photo(s)				
Untagged Items				Ctrl+Shift+Q

Find by Details (Metadata)

Search for all photos that match the criteria entered below. Use the Add button to enter additional criteria, and the Minus button to remove criteria.

Criteria

F-Stop	Is less than	5.60	–
Tags	Include	Katerina	–
Capture Date	Is after	07/09/2005	– +

Choose from the list of F-Stop or aperture values

☐ Show Hidden Photos

2 **Enter Search Criteria**

3 **Add More Search Criteria**

4 **View the Result**

20

20 **Find Items Using Metadata**

To display hidden photos (images with the **Hidden** tag) that match the criteria you specify, select the **Show Hidden Photos** option. To begin the search, click **Search**.

4 **View the Result**

The criteria appear on the **Find** bar, and matching images are displayed in the photo well. If you need to tweak the criteria a bit, click the **Modify** button on the **Find** bar. To redisplay all items, click **Back to All Photos** on the **Find** bar.

21   Find Items with Similar Filenames

✔ BEFORE YOU BEGIN

18 About Finding Items in the Catalog

If you know something about the filename of the media file(s) you're looking for, but you're not quite sure of the actual filename, you might still be able to locate the file. For example, if you know that an image has the word *spring* in its filename, you can search for the text **spring** and get a list of items that contain that text, such as **Spring 2003-01**, **Jim's springer spaniel**, **Katie's spring recital**, and so on.

▶ NOTES

You can also search for letters in the filename extension. For example, to locate all images saved in TIFF format, enter the search text **.tif**, which will match images that use either the **.tiff** or **.tif** extension. Notice that, unlike searches you might conduct in other programs, you do not enter an asterisk before the filename extension here.

You can't search for a creation based on its filename because it doesn't have one—creations exist only within the catalog and not as separate files (at least, not until you save them manually as a PDF, if you do that). You can search for a creation using its title (caption). See 20 **Find Items Using Metadata**.

1 Choose Find, By Filename

In the Organizer, select **Find, By Filename** from the menu bar. The **Find by Filename** dialog box appears.

2 Enter Search Text and Click OK

Type the portion of the filename you know in the **Find items with filename containing** box. For example, type **jan** to search for files such as **January Snow**, **Jan's new car**, and **janyce 02**. The text you enter here is not case sensitive, nor does it have to be a complete word. If you typed **Erin**, for example, files whose names include **Katerina** are considered matches because the word *Katerina* contains the characters *erin*. Click **OK**.

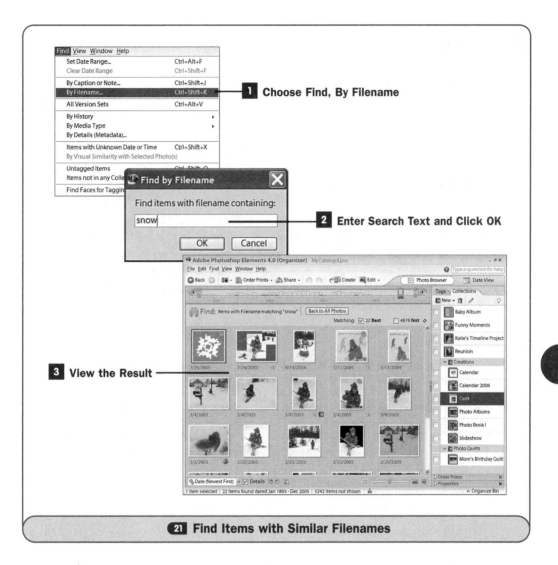

1 Choose Find, By Filename

2 Enter Search Text and Click OK

3 View the Result

21 Find Items with Similar Filenames

3 View the Result

Items whose filenames include the text you entered appear in the photo well. Here, I typed the word *snow* in the dialog box, and the Organizer displayed several photos, videos, and audio files whose names contained those letters. I got quite a variety of items as a result of my search, including a scan of a snowflake my daughter made, several photos from a Christmas card with a snowy scene, a squirrel in the snow, and an old photo of me building a snow fort. Notice that the **Find** bar displays the search criteria. To redisplay all items, click the **Back to All Photos** button on the **Find** bar.

22   Find Items with the Same Caption or Note

✔ **BEFORE YOU BEGIN**

16   Add a Text Caption or Note

18   About Finding Items in the Catalog

Ideally, the best way to ensure that items are easily located by category is to use tag or collection markers to group items, and then to search for items using those markers. However, markers might not tell the whole story about an image, audio file, movie, or creation. You can attach a brief description (a note) to any item in the catalog, and a title (a caption). If your catalog contains scans of printed photos bound in albums, for instance, you could use item notes to store the identity and location of the album to which each scanned photo belongs. Notes and captions for an item are displayed on the **General** tab of the **Properties** pane; captions also appear below an item when it's displayed in **Single Photo View**. In addition, captions can be made to appear below images in most creations.

22

▶ **NOTES**

The Organizer searches both captions and notes for matches to the text you supply. You cannot instruct the program to search through only one or the other.

Captions are written to an image's metadata (as the image's "description"), but notes are not; notes are stored in the catalog, however, as are captions. To protect the information you attach to items in the catalog from getting lost (such as markers, captions, and notes), you should back up your catalog often. See **7 Back Up the Organizer Catalog**.

1 **Choose Find, By Caption or Note**

In the Organizer, select **Find, By Caption or Note** from the menu bar. The **Find by Caption or Note** dialog box appears.

2 **Enter Text to Search For**

Type the known portion of the caption or note you want to search for in the **Find items with caption or note** box. The Organizer will search *both* captions and notes for this text. The search is not case sensitive, so don't worry about that when entering the search text.

3 **Choose How Matches Are Determined and Click OK**

Select the **Match only the beginning of words in Captions and Notes** option to make the Organizer search for the text you enter at the *beginning* of words only. For example, the search text **Erin** will not match the word *Katerina*. Selecting this option might speed up the search process.

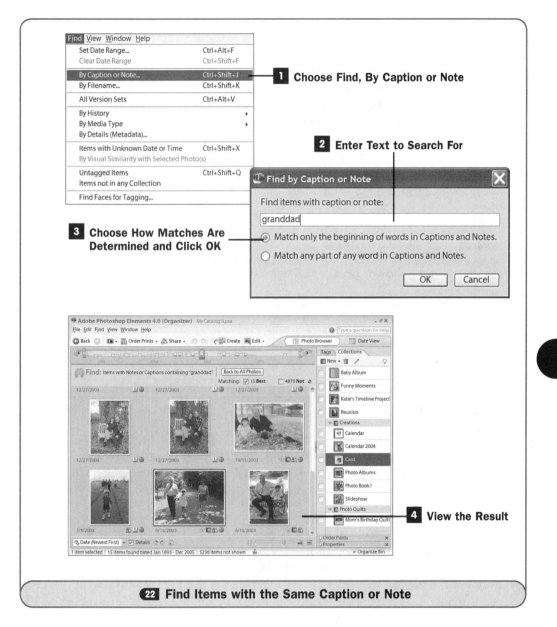

1 Choose Find, By Caption or Note

2 Enter Text to Search For

3 Choose How Matches Are Determined and Click OK

4 View the Result

22 Find Items with the Same Caption or Note

To search for matches throughout all characters (and not just those at the beginning of words), select the **Match any part of any word in Captions and Notes** option. With this option selected, the search text **Erin** does match the word *Katerina*. Click **OK** to begin the search process.

4 View the Result

The photo well displays only those items that match the search criteria. Click **Back to All Photos** to redisplay all items in the catalog. I needed to locate an image of my daughter skating at a park one day while we were visiting her granddad. The image had apparently been tagged only with her tag and not Granddad's, which I discovered after a search using both their tags and just his tag didn't locate the image, and a search using her tag alone resulted in too large a listing to browse through. So, I searched the notes and captions for any item that contained the word *granddad*, and came up with several matches, including the photo I was looking for.

▶ **NOTE**

Using the Organizer's new metadata search, I could also have found the images shown here by searching for items with the **Katerina** tag and with a caption/description that contains the text *granddad*. See ㉔ **Find Items Using Metadata**.

---

23 | Find Items with the Same Date

✔ BEFORE YOU BEGIN	→ SEE ALSO
⑱ About Finding Items in the Catalog	⑪ Change Image Date and Time
	⑫ About Organizing Items

To review a day's worth of photographs, movies, audio files, and creations, use **Date View**. There you can view each image, the first frame of each video, and the title page of each creation for the day you select from the calendar. If audio files are currently being displayed in the photo well, their thumbnails will appear as well.

While reviewing a particular day's items, you can add an event banner to the monthly calendar for that day, such as *Aunt Rheu's 90th Birthday* or *Baby Caitlyn Takes Her First Step*. These event banners, which display in bold teal text on a particular day in the monthly calendar, help you quickly identify that day, should you want to review it again. (Holidays are shown in purple.) You can also annotate the day's events with a **Daily Note**, which might also help you later identify the specific day you want to review.

▶ **NOTE**

Date View is best used when you want to review a group of media created on the same day. To quickly display a larger group of media created within a specific date range, use the **Timeline**, as explained in ⑫ About Organizing Items.

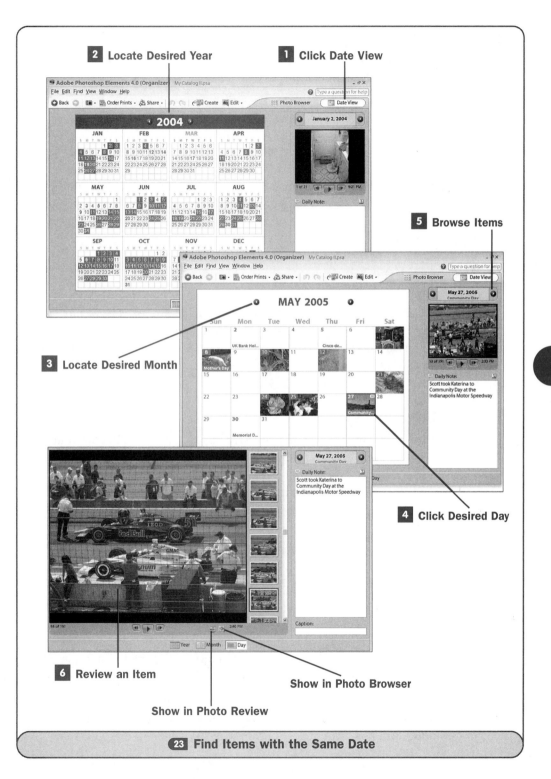

2 Locate Desired Year

1 Click Date View

5 Browse Items

3 Locate Desired Month

4 Click Desired Day

6 Review an Item

Show in Photo Browser

Show in Photo Review

1 Click Date View

In the Editor or the Organizer, click the **Date View** button at the right end of the **Shortcuts** bar. **Date View** appears, with items organized by month and year.

2 Locate Desired Year

If the year currently being displayed is the year containing the items you want to review, skip to step 3. Otherwise, change to a different year by clicking the **Year** button below the calendar. A yearly calendar appears; click the → or ← buttons at the top of the window to move to a different year. Dates with items associated with them appear with solid squares that are blue, or purple (if the date is an event or holiday).

3 Locate Desired Month

After you've changed to the year you want to review, click the **Month** button at the bottom of the yearly calendar. A monthly calendar reappears. To move to a different month, click the → or ← buttons at the top of the window. Dates with items associated with them are marked by an image thumbnail, and appear with blue squares around their dates (the squares are purple if the date is an event or holiday).

4 Click Desired Day

Click the day you want to review. The selected day is highlighted in blue, and the first item for the selected day appears in the preview window on the right. Below this preview are listed the total number of items for that day, and the number of the currently displayed item.

5 Browse Items

To scroll from item to item for the currently selected day, click the ← or → buttons below the preview window. To display items in sequence automatically until you stop it (as in an automated slideshow), click the **Start Automatic Sequencing** button. Click this same button to stop the playback.

6 Review an Item

After you've found the item you're interested in and have displayed it in the preview window, you can perform many tasks.

You can remove selected events that display on the calendar automatically, such as Lincoln's Birthday. Choose **Edit, Preferences, Calendar**. Then disable any **Holidays** you don't want to include on your calendar and click **OK**. You can also edit events you have added manually (as explained in the following bullet points), and elect to display Monday as the first day of the week:

- To add a note that describes the events that day, click in the **Daily Note** box under the preview window and type your note.

- To add a banner to the monthly calendar that describes the events of that day more succinctly, click the **Create Event** button. Type a brief description or event name such as **Family Reunion**, select the **Repeating event** option if this event happens on the same day every year, and then click **OK**. The event name appears on the monthly calendar, in teal (greenish-blue), on that day. Automatic events such as holidays, which are inserted into the calendar for you, appear in purple. The event name also appears below the date, but above the preview window, when that day is selected. In the example shown here, the event name, **Community Day**, was added to **May 27, 2005**.

- To display the current item (the item in the preview window) in the photo well, click the **Show in Photo Browser** button.

▶ NOTE

If an item's date was changed to **Unknown** (as explained in **11** Change Image Date and Time), it will not appear in **Date View**.

23

- To display the current item in a larger view, click the **Day** button below the monthly calendar. Other items for that day are displayed as thumbnails to the right of the large preview window. Click a thumbnail to display that item in the large preview window instead.

- To add a text caption to the current item, click the **Day** button if needed to display the item in a large preview. Then click in the **Caption** box on the right, and type your caption.

- To start a photo review of the items for the selected day, click the **Day** button if needed to display the item in a large preview. Then click the **Show in Photo Review** button.

To redisplay the photo well and exit **Date View**, click the **Photo Browser** button on the **Shortcuts** bar.

24   Find Items with the Same History

✔ BEFORE YOU BEGIN	→ SEE ALSO
18 About Finding Items in the Catalog	**39** Print Images Using an Online Service
	42 Share Images Using Email
	43 Share Images Using an Online Service

As soon as an item is imported into the catalog, a history is created. When you include an item in a creation, export it for use in some other application, share it via email or through an online service, or print it locally or through an online service, these events are noted and logged in that item's history. You can then use this history to recall a particular item for display. For example, suppose that you sent several images of a recent family outing to your brother in Colorado, and now you're ready to send some more but you can't recall which ones you've already sent! Luckily, you can simply ask the Organizer to display items you emailed to your brother, and then quickly review the recently sent ones.

24

▶ **NOTE**

Edits you make to an image are tracked by the Organizer—as long as you initiate those edits from within Organizer (whether or not you use the Editor or some other graphics editor). To locate an image you've edited on a certain date, see **23** Find Items with the Same Date.

1 Choose Find, By History

In the Organizer, choose **Find**, **By History** from the menu. A submenu of items tracked by history appears. Select an item from this list. For example, select **Find**, **By History**, **Imported On**.

2 Select Event(s)

A dialog box appears, listing the dates on which you performed the action you selected in step 1. For example, if you choose **Find**, **By History**, **Printed On** in step 1, a list of dates on which you printed some images appears. If you chose an event that involves a third party—for example, you selected **Find**, **By History**, **Shared Online**, you'll see a list of online services through which you've shared some images, and a list of dates on which you did that. Press **Ctrl** and click the events you're interested in, and then click **OK**.

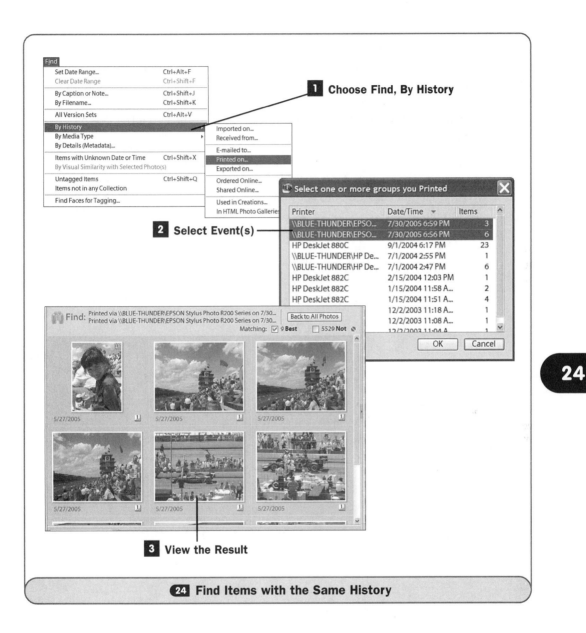

1 Choose Find, By History

2 Select Event(s)

3 View the Result

24 Find Items with the Same History

▶ **NOTE**

You can remove an event from history and reduce the size of the Organizer's catalog file by a little bit. Just select an event from the dialog box in step 2 and click **Delete**. Removing events you don't want to remember anymore will also reduce the size of the list displayed in the dialog box, making it easier for you to find the events you are interested in when needed.

3 View the Result

The items associated with the event you selected in step 2 appear in the photo well. Here, I had recently printed some photos from a day spent at the Indianapolis Motor Speedway. I wanted to print some more, but I just couldn't remember what I'd already printed. Luckily, the Organizer doesn't suffer from short-term memory loss.

After displaying the items associated with an event, you can make changes, print, share, organize, or use in a creation any of these items; when you're done, click the **Back to All Photos** button to redisplay all items in the photo well.

24

PART II

Working with Images

IN THIS PART:

CHAPTER 5	Creating, Opening, and Saving Images	117
CHAPTER 6	Printing and Emailing Images	169
CHAPTER 7	Selecting a Portion of an Image	203
CHAPTER 8	Using Multiple Layers to Edit Images	243

5

Creating, Opening, and Saving Images

IN THIS CHAPTER:

25 About the Editor

26 Create a New Image

27 About Editing Images

28 About Saving Images

29 Save an Image

30 About Image Information

31 Zoom In and Out

32 Change Image Size or Resolution

33 Rename, Resize, Reformat, and Retouch a Group of Images

34 Increase the Canvas Area Around an Image

35 Change Color Mode

The Editor comes with many tools for creating and manipulating graphics. With its help, you can restore old photographs, insert your missing brother into a family photo, or create a web page background. Before you can perform any of this graphics wizardry however, you must first open the image you want to work on or tell the Editor you want to start from scratch on a new image. In the tasks presented in this chapter, you will learn not only how to start something new, but also how to locate and open image files already saved to the hard disk. In addition, you'll learn how to save new or edited images in a variety of graphic formats and to perform simple image tasks such as resizing, renaming, and applying automatic image corrections.

▶ **NOTE**

Although you don't have to use the Editor to make changes to an image, if you use another program, you should initiate the edit from within the Organizer: First, select your preferred editor on the **Editing** page of the **Preferences** dialog box. Then select an image in the catalog and choose **Edit**, **Edit with XX**. If you don't initiate edits from within the Organizer, it won't know you've made changes to an image, and its thumbnail will not show correctly in the catalog. To manually update a thumbnail you've edited outside the Organizer without its knowledge, choose **Edit**, **Update Thumbnail**.

---

25 | **About the Editor**

→ **SEE ALSO**

27 About Editing Images

As you probably know by now, Photoshop Elements is made up of two components: the Editor and the Organizer. Although you can perform very basic image fixes in the Organizer, you'll use the Editor most often to fix photos. The Editor works in two modes: Standard Edit mode, shown here, and Quick Fix mode, which provides you with tools that automatically fix images but which limits your options. You'll learn how to use Quick Fix mode in **68** **Apply a Quick Fix**. Open images are displayed in the work area. You can have as many open images as you like; typically, each image is initially displayed within its own window that's sized so you can see all of the image. This image window contains its own **Minimize**, **Maximize**, and **Close** buttons, which (when the image window is maximized in the work area) appear at the right end of the menu bar, below the program window's buttons. When image windows are maximized, you're working in *Maximize mode*, and you can switch to it at any time (in other words, maximize all image windows) by clicking the **Maximize Mode** button. In this mode, you work on one image at a time, regardless of how many image files are open. Change from one open image to another by clicking its thumbnail in the **Photo Bin** at the bottom of the work area. If you have more images open than the **Photo Bin** has room to display, use the vertical scrollbar to scroll through the thumbnails.

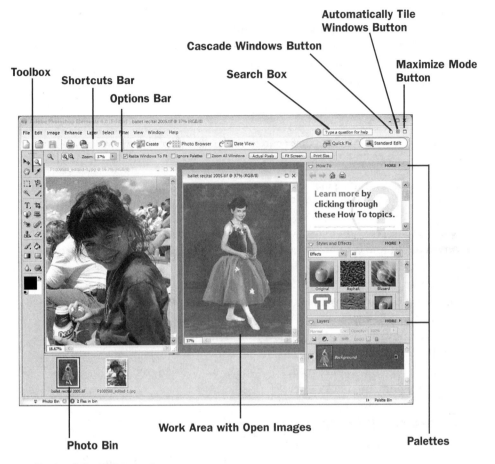

Parts of the Editor work area.

▶ **TIPS**

You can start the Editor in **Standard Edit** mode from the **Welcome Window** by clicking the **Edit and Enhance Photos** option. From the Organizer, you can start the Editor in **Standard Edit** mode by selecting an image, clicking the **Edit** button, and selecting **Go to Standard Edit**.

Display the **Photo Bin** if needed by choosing **Window**, **Photo Bin** or clicking the **Photo Bin** button at the left end of the **Status** bar.

To view multiple images at once, switch to *Multi-window mode*. Tile or cascade all open images by clicking the appropriate button: **Cascade Windows** or **Automatically Tile Windows**. To simply change from Maximize mode to viewing multiple windows in the same size and position they were in before you maximized them, click the **Multi-window Mode** button (which appears where the **Maximize Mode** button was). By the way, when the **Automatically Tile Windows** button is enabled, if you open a new image, it is automatically tiled with other open images.

▶ KEY TERMS

Multi-window mode—A setting that enables you to display more than one image in the work area at the same time.

Maximize mode—A setting that enables you to display only one image at a time, using as much of the work area as possible.

There are other ways to adjust your view of an image. For example, you can zoom in or out and display an image onscreen in the same size it will appear when printed. See **31** **Zoom In and Out** for help. You can zoom all images to the same level as the active image (regardless of whether you're in Multi-window mode or Maximize mode) by choosing **Window**, **Images**, **Match Zoom**. To have all images scroll to the area you're zoomed in on in the active image window, choose **Window**, **Images**, **Match Location**. These modes are helpful if you have several open photos that were taken at close to the same time—such as several portraits of the same family member—where you need to compare the same detail in each image side by side.

Use the Shortcuts Bar

Below the menu bar is the **Shortcuts** bar, which contains buttons for the most common commands such as opening, saving, and printing an image. Buttons with a sweeping right arrow on the left, such as the **Create**, **Photo Browser**, and **Date View** buttons, will launch the Organizer. At the right end of the **Shortcuts** bar, you'll find a pair of buttons that change the Editor from a full-featured graphics editor into a quick touch-up program, and back again. See **68** **Apply a Quick Fix** for more information.

*The **Shortcuts** bar provides fast access to common commands.*

Use the Toolbox and Options Bar

The **Toolbox**, located along the left side of the window, is the Editor's equivalent of a caddy on your desk where you keep all your brushes, pens, erasers, and scissors. To select a tool, click its button; the currently selected tool is highlighted. Some tools with similar purposes are located in the same slot on the **Toolbox**; you can identify these tool groups by the small black triangle in the button's lower-right corner. To access a hidden tool, hold the mouse down on a tool group button and select a tool from the menu that appears. After you select a tool, its available options appear on the **Options** bar, located just under the **Shortcuts** bar. You'll learn how to use the tools in the **Toolbox** and to set options in upcoming tasks.

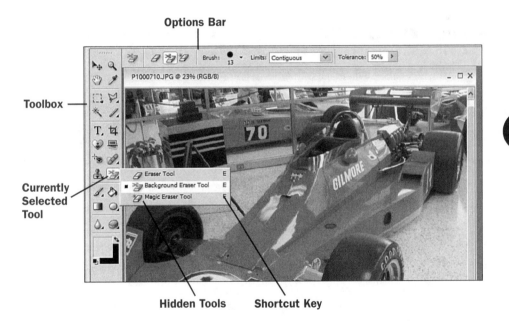

*The **Toolbox** contains tools you can use to edit images.*

▶ **NOTES**

To identify a specific tool, hover the mouse pointer over it. A tooltip appears with the name of the tool and its keyboard shortcut. You can press this shortcut key at any time to activate the tool currently displayed on the **Toolbox**. To choose a hidden tool, just keep pressing the same shortcut key. For example, to cycle through the erasers until you select the eraser tool you want, keep pressing E. Click the tooltip that shows the tool's name, and you'll get immediate help on that tool.

You can change to a different tool in a group   by clicking the icon on the **Options** bar for the hidden tool you want to use.

Use Palettes

On the right side of the Editor window, you'll see the *Palette Bin*, which contains a collection of *palettes*. By default, three palettes are displayed in the **Palette Bin**: the **How To** palette (which contains step-by-step instructions for completing common image modifications), the **Styles and Effects** palette (which displays thumbnails representing filters and effects you can apply to an image), and the **Layers** palette (which provides access to the multiple layers an image might contain). The **Palette Bin** helps you corral the palettes you currently want to use. You can add or remove palettes from the **Palette Bin** as desired, or you can display palettes in the work area. These palettes are called *floating palettes*. You can place several floating palettes together, forming a *group* (where only the tab of the active palette shows) or a *dock* (where palettes are stacked vertically).

▶ KEY TERMS

Palette Bin—A gathering place for the palettes you want to keep open.

Palette—A floating dialog box with tools or information that help you modify images.

25

- To display a palette, select it from the **Window** menu. If the palette is part of a group, the entire group appears; if the palette is docked with other palettes, they appear too. If the palette is docked in the **Palette Bin**, it's simply hidden or redisplayed when you choose its name from the **Window** menu.

- When a palette is displayed for the first time, it appears as a floating palette in the work area. You can move the palette around by dragging it by its title bar.

- To remove a floating palette from the screen, select its name again from the **Window** menu or click its **Close** button. Again, if the palette is docked or grouped with other palettes, this closes the related palettes too.

- To place any floating palette in the **Palette Bin**, click its **More** button and select **Place in Palette Bin** from the **More** menu, and then click its **Close** button. The palette closes—and reappears in the bin.

- To keep a palette in the **Palette Bin** but temporarily hide it, click the **down arrow** to the left of the palette's name on the title bar. To redisplay the hidden palette, click the **right arrow** that appears in its place, or choose the palette's name from the **Window** menu.

Docked Palettes   **Floating Palette**   **Hidden Palette**

More Button

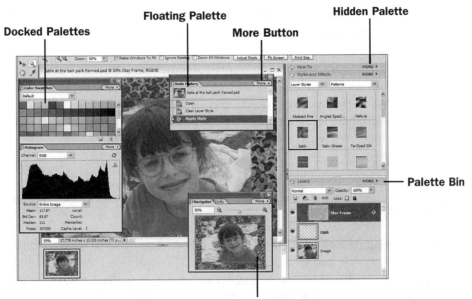

Palette Bin

Grouped Palettes

Palettes provide valuable information and tools for modifying images.

25

▶ NOTES

If you drag a palette out of the **Palette Bin** and into the work area, it becomes a float-ing palette. But if you close it, the palette returns to its home in the **Palette Bin**. To stop that from happening, click the palette's **More** button and uncheck the **Place in Palette Bin** option.

To place a palette in the **Palette Bin** temporarily, drag it by its tab and drop it on the bin. The temporary palette will hide and redisplay like a bin palette, but if you close the palette, it will be removed from the screen and not just hidden in the bin.

- To roll up a floating palette so that only its title bar shows, double-click its title bar. Double-click the title bar again to unroll it. To temporarily hide all floating palettes, press **Tab**. Press **Tab** again to redisplay them where they were. (The **Toolbox** can be dragged into the work area, where it acts like a floating palette.)

- If a palette is located in the **Palette Bin** or docked with other palettes, you can change its size vertically by dragging its bottom border up or down. If a palette is floating, drag the **Size box** (located in the lower-right corner) to resize it. (The **Histogram** and **Info** palettes cannot be resized.)

- To relocate any palette within the **Palette Bin**, drag it by its title bar up or down to a new location, and let go.

- You can make the **Palette Bin** skinnier by dragging its left border. This makes the work area (and the **Photo Bin**, if it's displayed) wider.

The **More** button provides access to commands other than **Place in Palette Bin**. Click the **More** button on a palette and select **XXX Help** (where **XXX** is the name of the palette) to get help working with a particular palette. Choose **Help Contents** to display the **Help Contents** page instead. Other commands on the **More** menu enable you to set options related to that particular palette.

▶ **TIP**

To reset all palettes to their default positions, choose **Window**, **Reset Palette Locations** from the menu.

You can group palettes together in a sort of tabbed dialog box so that the palettes are easily accessible and yet take up little room. To group one palette within another, drag a palette by its tab (and not its title bar) and drop it on top of the target palette. The palettes are grouped, and a tab appears for each palette. Only one palette in the group is fully visible at any one time. To switch to a different palette, click its tab. To remove a palette from a group, drag it by its tab outside the group to return the palette to a free-floating state.

You can dock multiple palettes together, creating mini-Palette Bins. These docked palettes can be moved, hidden, redisplayed, and closed with a single click. To dock a palette with another, drag the palette by its tab to the bottom edge of another palette. A double line appears along this bottom edge; release the mouse button to dock the palette. Click the **Minimize** button to roll up this floating bin, or click the **Close** button to remove it from the screen.

You'll learn more about the individual palettes throughout this book. For now, here is a brief description of the remaining palettes: **Color Swatches** (displays various collections of colors, patterns, and textures you can use with the painting tools); **Histogram** (a graph depicting the distribution of the brightness in an image); **Info** (displays information about the pixel under the cursor, and about the size of any shape, selection, or cropping border you're currently drawing); **Navigator** (provides an alternative method for zooming and scrolling an image); and **Undo History** (displays a list of actions you can undo).

Use the Rulers and Grid

Occasionally, you might want to turn on several tools to guide you as you make precise adjustments to an image. For example, when drawing objects of a specific size, you might want to display the ruler (choose **View**, **Rulers**). A vertical ruler appears along the left edge of each image window, and a horizontal ruler appears along the top edge. Using the ruler, you can make more precise selections with any of the **Selection** tools, create objects of an exact size and position, and position type more exactly. As you move the mouse pointer over the image, hash marks appear on the rulers to indicate the pointer's exact position.

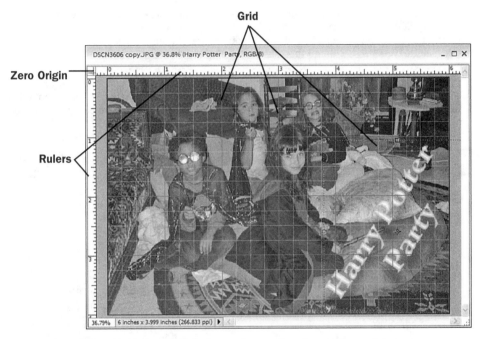

Use the rulers and the grid to help you make precise changes to an image.

If you want to measure from some point on an image, you can adjust the *zero origin*. Normally, zero is located in the upper-left corner of an image; to move the zero origin, click at the intersection of the two rulers (in the upper-left corner of the image window) and drag downward and to the right, to the point on the image from which you want to measure. Cross-hairs appear as you drag to help you precisely position the zero origin. Release the mouse button to set the zero origin. To reset the rulers so that the zero origin is once again in the upper-left corner, double-click the intersection of the two rulers.

Another useful tool for aligning objects perfectly is the grid, a set of vertical and horizontal lines that cross all over the image forming, well, a *grid*. You can automatically align objects to the gridlines by turning on the **View**, **Snap to Grid** option. You can see the gridlines by choosing **View**, **Grid**, although the grid does tend to obstruct your image; if you chose not to display the grid, you can still snap objects to the (invisible) gridlines by choosing only the **Snap to Grid** option.

When the gridlines are invisible, you still "feel" them (almost like they are magnetized) as you draw or move objects because the gridlines pull the edges of objects toward them.

▶ NOTES

Initially, the ruler uses inches as its unit of measurement, but you can change this by choosing **Edit**, **Preferences**, **Units & Rulers**, opening the **Rulers** list, and selecting a different unit of measurement. By the way, if you change the unit of measurement on the **Info** palette, you'll also change the rulers' unit of measurement.

To change the properties of the grid—for example, to make the gridlines further apart—choose **Edit**, **Preferences**, **Grid**. Here you can choose the distance between the horizontal/vertical gridlines, and the number of subdivisions between gridlines. You can also choose the color and pattern used for the gridlines.

---

26 | **Create a New Image**

→ **SEE ALSO**

28 About Saving Images
63 About Color Management

25

As with other programs, if you want to use Photoshop Elements to create new art, such as a decorative Windows wallpaper or a Web page button, you must start with a new, empty image file. You might also create a new image file when you want to combine portions of several photographs into a photo collage, scrapbook page, or panorama. After creating a new image file, you should save it in Photoshop format as described in **29** Save an Image.

When you create a new image file, you set several initial parameters, such as the image's width and height. You are not stuck with your initial choices; you can change your selections later on as you work. For example, it's easy to resize a photograph to make it bigger or smaller as needed. In addition to width and height, you determine how finely detailed the image will be (its resolution). Finally, you'll select the background color and the image *color mode*. As you make your selections, the resulting file size (taking into account only a single, basic background layer) is displayed at the bottom of the dialog box. If necessary, reduce the image size, resolution, or color mode to make the file size more manageable for your system.

▶ KEY TERM

Color mode—Determines the number of colors an image can contain.

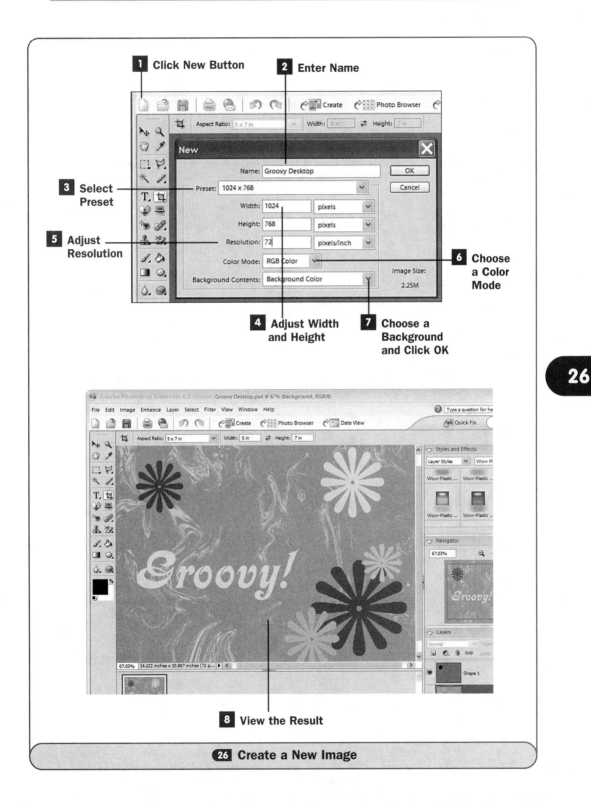

1 Click New Button   **2** Enter Name

3 Select Preset

5 Adjust Resolution

6 Choose a Color Mode

4 Adjust Width and Height

7 Choose a Background and Click OK

8 View the Result

26

26 Create a New Image

▶ **NOTE**

Before beginning any editing within the Editor for the first time, you should calibrate your monitor so that the colors you see onscreen will match what you get when you print a completed image. See **63** **About Color Management**.

1 Click New Button

In the Editor, change to **Standard Edit** mode and click the **New** button on the **Shortcuts** bar, or choose **File, New, Blank File** from the menu. The **New** dialog box appears.

2 Enter Name

Type a name for the new image in the **Name** box. The name you type will serve as the file's temporary name until you actually save the file as described in **28** **About Saving Images**. Because this is only a temporary name, you can skip this step if you like, and enter the permanent name for the file when you save it later on.

3 Select Preset

Open the **Preset** drop-down list and select one of the many common image types, such as a 5-by-7-inch photo or an 800-by-600-pixel Web background. You can modify the **Width**, **Height**, and **Resolution** settings that appear by following steps 4 and 5; otherwise, skip to step 6.

▶ **TIPS**

To create a new image that uses the same dimensions as a currently open image, select the image's name from the bottom of the **Preset** list.

If you want to create a new image using data currently on the Clipboard, see **58** **Create a New Image or Layer from a Selection** for help.

4 Adjust Width and Height

If your chosen preset doesn't match the image size you want exactly, select new **Width** and/or **Height** values.

5 Adjust Resolution

Depending on how detailed you want the image to appear, adjust the **Resolution** value. If the image will only be viewed onscreen or on the Web, an image resolution of 72 pixels per inch is sufficient; for images you intend to print, consider at least 300 PPI.

6 Choose a Color Mode

Open the **Color Mode** drop-down list and select the color mode you want to work with: **RGB Color** (for color images), **Grayscale** (for images in black, white, and grays), or **Bitmap** (for images in black and white only).

7 Choose a Background and Click OK

Open the **Background Contents** drop-down list and select the color you want to fill the bottom layer of your image—the background layer. You can choose **White**, **Background Color** (which makes the background the same color as the current background color as shown on the **Toolbox**), or **Transparent**. (The **Transparent** option is not available in **Bitmap** color mode.) After selecting a background, click **OK** to create the blank canvas for the new image onscreen.

8 View the Result

An image window opens with the dimensions and colors you choose. Use the Editor's tools to fill the image with color or data copied from another image. Apply filters, effects, or layer styles. After you've worked a little in your image, you'll want to save it so you don't lose your work. The best format for works in progress is Photoshop (***.psd**), as explained in **29 Save an Image**. After you work on the image, save the result in PNG, JPEG, or non-layered TIFF format as explained in **28 About Saving Images**, leaving your PSD image with its layers (if any) intact so that you can return at a later time and make different adjustments if you want.

Here, I created a quick image for use as a Windows background. I filled it with a purple background color, painted it with green and yellow droplets, and applied the **Glass**, **Wave**, and **Liquify** filters. Then I added some flowers using the **Custom Shape** tool, and some text.

26

27   About Editing Images

✔ BEFORE YOU BEGIN

25 About the Editor

The Organizer provides a few tools you can use to improve the photographs in its catalog. After selecting an image, you can rotate it by choosing **Edit, Rotate 90° Left** or **Rotate 90° Right**. You can apply a series of automatic corrections to color balance and image contrast by choosing **Edit, Auto Smart Fix**. Finally, if you didn't apply the automatic red eye fix when importing images, you can apply it now by choosing **Edit, Auto Red Eye Fix**. But for more control over the changes you make to an image, use the Editor. The Editor has two editing modes:

- **Quick Fix** mode allows you to make simple adjustments to an image's contrast, saturation, and sharpness, using slider controls that enable you to control the amount of adjustment that occurs. See **68** **Apply a Quick Fix** for help.

- **Standard Edit** mode provides complete control over any adjustments you apply. Here you can use any of the tools in the **Toolbox**, apply variable image adjustments, add layers, or apply filters and effects to correct or enhance an image.

To initiate an edit on an image in the catalog, select it and in the Organizer, click the **Edit** button on the **Shortcuts** bar and choose either **Go to Quick Fix** or **Go to Standard Edit**. If you're in the Editor, you can switch between editing modes by clicking the **Quick Fix** or **Standard Edit** buttons, located at the right end of the **Shortcuts** bar. When you edit an image in the catalog, the Organizer flags it with a marker that reads, *Edit in Progress*. The flag prevents you from attempting to share, print, or include the image in a creation while it's still being changed. The flag is automatically removed from the image thumbnail when you're done editing.

27

Quick Fix Window

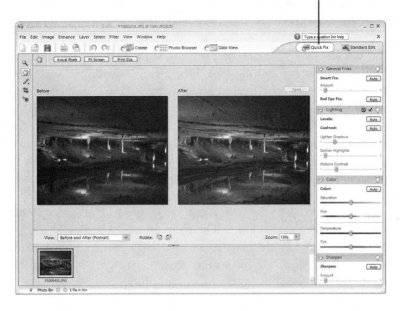

Standard Edit Window

*You can edit an image using either the Editor's **Quick Fix** or **Standard Edit** window.*

You should keep a few things in mind when you decide to edit an image. First, you will probably not want to make changes to an original file. If you make changes to a *copy* instead, you can always delete the copy and go back to the original if you feel that your edits took you in the wrong direction. When you edit an image and you save your changes, you can either make a copy of the file, or make a copy and link the new file with the original file within the catalog, in a *version set*. If you create a copy of an image when saving your changes to it, both the original and the copy will appear as thumbnails in the catalog. This can quickly lead to a fat catalog full of similar images. However, if you save the edited copy in a version set, the Organizer stacks the edited image with the original, leaving a single thumbnail in the catalog to represent both versions. The edited image is assigned the same file date as the original image, so the version set thumbnail appears where it belongs, amongst other images taken that same day. A version set thumbnail, by the way, is marked with a special icon, a larger version of which is shown in the figure. If you edit an image and make a copy instead of a version set, today's date is assigned to the resulting file, making the copy appear in a different location within the catalog than the original image.

27

▶ **KEY TERM**

Version set—Different edited versions of the same image, displayed as a single thumbnail in the catalog.

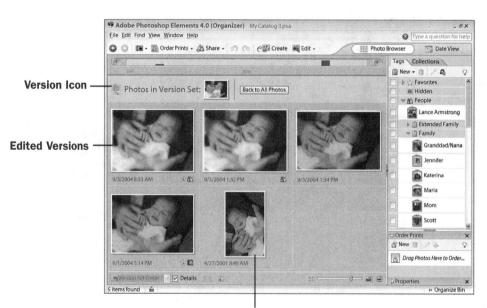

You can display the images in a version set.

Version sets are similar in functionality to stacks, which are images that have been manually grouped together in the catalog, as explained in **10** **Stack Images**. Like stacks, you can expand a version set when needed, to view the original image with its edited copies by choosing **Edit, Version Set, Reveal Items in Version Set**.

When the images in a version set are revealed, you can select a different image for use as the set thumbnail by clicking it and choosing **Edit, Version Set, Set as Top Photo**. The image you select to act as the new version set thumbnail (the top photo) will display first when you expand the stack, rather than the most recently edited version. You can remove all edited versions of an image (from the hard disk and from the catalog) and return to using the original image by selecting the original and choosing **Edit, Version Set, Revert to Original**. To close the version set and return to the catalog, click the **Back to All Photos** button on the **Find** bar. You can then remove the original image from the set (and from the hard disk if you want) by clicking the version set thumbnail and choosing **Edit, Version Set, Flatten Set**.

▶ NOTES

Only the topmost thumbnail appears in the catalog for a version set, so it's important to remember that this thumbnail is the only one you can work with when the version set is collapsed. If you add or remove a tag or collection marker for example, the Organizer removes the marker from only the top thumbnail in the set. If you select the thumbnail for a creation or to share using email, only the top image is selected, and not all the ones in the set. But if you want to do something to all the images in a set, you have to expand it first, and then work with the images as individual thumbnails. This caution applies to working with stacks as well.

If you expand a version set that contains multiple image edits, select the original thumbnail, and delete it, the remaining images are still kept together. However, the version set is converted to a stack, because the original image is no longer a part of the set.

---

28 **About Saving Images**

→ SEE ALSO

29 Save an Image

When working on an image in the Editor, you should save it in Photoshop (PSD) format. This format retains all your work—layers, vector-text and shapes, and so on—so that you can return at a later time and make more changes as needed. When you're through with an image, save the PSD file again, then resave it in a format that can be more easily printed or shared with your friends using email or over the Internet (such as non-layered TIFF or JPEG format). When you resave your working PSD file in non-layered TIFF or JPEG format, the vector data such as text and shapes are converted into raster data, and then the multiple layers are flattened into a single layer, making the file not only smaller but readable by a wide variety of programs.

▶ **NOTE**

If you open an image, make changes, and then save them, certain data might be lost forever when you close that file. For example, if you add a message to an image, it's stored on its own layer. Unless you save the image using the Photoshop or layered TIFF format, when you open the image later on, you'll find that the text has been flattened with the image data. You won't be able to edit, move, resize, or recolor the text, nor will you be able to erase the text and see the image data that used to be below the text. That's why you should always save an image in PSD format when beginning to edit it— so that you can retain your work should you need to make further changes.

The format you choose for the final version of an image depends on the purposes you have in mind for it. For example, if you want to use an image on a web page, you'll have to save it in a web-compatible format: GIF, JPEG, or PNG. If you're not planning on using the image on a web page, you might want to simply make it smaller, using JPEG, PNG, TIFF, or GIF format, which compresses the image by various amounts, making it smaller. Compressed images benefit web users who have lower bandwidth and, thus, longer download times. Compressed images are also great for emailing because they are smaller and easier to send.

You can resave a working Photoshop PSD file in a different format by choosing **File**, **Save As** from the menu. In the case of Web formats (GIF, PNG, and JPEG), you can also use the **File**, **Save for Web** command, which displays a special dialog box that allows you to preview how your selections affect the final result, and even preview the image in a web browser of your choice. Here's a description of each of the more popular formats, along with the options you can use while saving in that format:

**Image As It Will Look with
Current Settings Applied**

Set Options

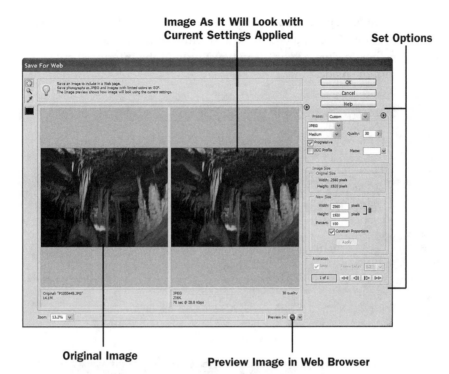

Original Image

Preview Image in Web Browser

*Save in a web-compatible format using the **Save for Web** dialog box.*

Because a **GIF** file can contain only 256 colors at most, GIF is great for use with line art such as cartoons, illustrations, and artwork with large areas of similar color, rather than photographic images. GIF format supports animation— basically multiple copies of almost-the-same image stored in one file. GIFs can also include fully transparent pixels. When a transparent GIF is placed on a web page, its rectangular edges disappear, and the image appears to sit right on top of the page as shown here.

When saving in GIF format, you can choose from various options. First, you can choose **Layers as Frames** in the **Save As** dialog box, to save each layer as a frame in a GIF animation. In the **Indexed Color** dialog box which appears next, you choose how to display similar colors not in the GIF's limited color palette, through a process called *dithering*. See **35 Change Color Mode** for more info. If you chose the **Layers as Frames** option in the **Save As** dialog box, the **Save For Web** dialog box appears instead of the **Indexed Color** dialog box so that you can set palette options and animation options such as a speed for the animation (**Frame Delay**) and whether to repeat the animation over and over automatically (**Loop**). In the **GIF Options** dialog box that appears next, choose how you want the GIF image to appear on a user's system when it's downloaded from the Web.

To have the image appear one line at a time from the top down, choose **Normal**; to have its details filled in gradually, choose **Interlaced**. If you use the **Save for Web** dialog box to choose your GIF options, turn off the **Interlaced** option to choose "normal" mode.

A transparent GIF blends into the web page background.

▶ KEY TERM

Dithering—A technique for simulating a color whose value does not appear in an image's palette by mixing pixels of the two closest available shades.

JPEG images are perfect for use with photographs or other images with lots of color. JPEG uses a lossy compression technique in which color values in similarly shaded regions are blended with one another in a barely noticeable way, resulting in a smaller color palette and image file. But because a JPEG file discards image data during compression, if you save a JPEG file over and over again, it will develop *artifacts*. So, you should save an image in JPEG format only when you are finished editing it. Artifacts might also appear in a JPEG file if it is compressed too much. If that happens to you, simply go back to your Photoshop PSD file and create a new JPEG using a smaller amount of compression. Artifacts might also appear in a JPEG file if the image contains sharp edges, such as a

28

border, a line, or the edges of large text. If that happens, save your Photoshop file in some other format, such as TIFF or PNG.

▶ KEY TERM

Artifacts—Unwanted blocks of color typically introduced in a digital photo by too much compression.

▶ NOTE

If you own a digital camera, it probably saves the photos it takes in JPEG format. As long as you choose high quality, however, the JPEG compression should be minimal and you'll still get a good quality image. However, if your camera gives you a choice between JPEG, TIFF, or RAW format, choose TIFF or RAW.

When saving in JPEG format, you can set various options in the **JPEG Options** dialog box. You can adjust the level of compression (**Quality**), and how you want the JPEG image to appear on a user's system when it's downloaded from the Web. To have the image appear one line at a time from the top down, choose **Baseline** (**"Standard"**) or **Baseline Optimized** (the **Optimized** option uses a newer compression scheme that's not compatible with very old Web browsers); to have the image appear all at once with details filled in gradually, choose **Progressive**. Also, since JPEG format does not support transparency, if the image has any transparent or semi-transparent pixels, they'll be blended with the **Matte** color you choose to create fully opaque pixels. (If you don't choose a color, white is used.) **JPEG 2000** or **JP2** format is similar to JPEG, but because it uses a different compression scheme, JPEG 2000 can produce smaller files while retaining image quality and produce minimal artifacts even at high compression. JPEG 2000 handles anti-aliased text better than JPEG, so if you have an image such as a photograph with text, JPEG 2000 might be the format to use. A JPEG 2000 file contains image information in its header about the color space (gamut) used, which helps to ensure that the file is displayed and printed properly. JPEG 2000 supports lossless and lossy compression, *alpha transparency*, and 16-bit color. However, if you use lossy compression, then, like JPEG format, a JPEG 2000 image can develop artifacts if resaved several times or if overly compressed. JPEG 2000's major drawback right now is that no web browsers currently support it (at least, not without third-party plug-ins), so you might not want to use this file type on your web pages.

▶ KEY TERM

Alpha transparency—Variable transparency—from fully transparent to partially transparent, which enables you to gradually fade the pixels along the edge of an image against a web page background, for example.

When saving a JPEG 2000 image, you can opt to use **Lossless** or **Fast Save** compression (save the file quicker, but with less optimization). You can also choose normal compression by specifying a target **File Size**. If you select **Fast Save** or normal compression, you can set the level of compression (**Quality**). You can opt to **Include Metadata** (such as copyright and saved selections information), **Include Transparency**, and make the file **JP2 Compatible** (for the few browsers that support JP2 format, but not the newer JPEG 2000 extended-JPF format). Finally, you specify how the image should appear when viewed with a compatible web browser: **Growing Thumbnail**, **Progressive** (whole, with increasing detail), or **Color** (first as grayscale, then in color).

PNG is supported by all but older web browsers, although few browsers support PNG's partial transparency option (alpha transparency), whereas PNG's full transparency is supported by newer web browsers. PNG is useful for full color images (photographs) and it also offers a lossless compression method (similar to what GIF uses), so it has that advantage over other web-compatible formats. PNG files, when compared to GIF files, are typically smaller. They also offer other advantages, such as gamma correction for cross-platform control, and faster *interlacing*. When saving in PNG format, you need set only one option, how you want the image to appear when viewed with a web browser: **Normal** (one line at a time, from the top down) or **Interlaced** (whole, with details filled in gradually). Using the **File**, **Save As** command results in a PNG-24 (24-bit) file; you can use the **File**, **Save as Web** command to save the file in PNG-8 format instead (8-bit limited color palette). See **35 Change Color Mode** for more information on the options related to a smaller color palette.

▶ KEY TERM

Interlacing—Also known as *interleaving*. A method of displaying a web graphic on a user's screen in which the image is displayed without much detail, and gains detail as it's downloaded.

TIFF/TIF format is great to use when saving photographs. Unlike JPEG, which uses a lossy compression scheme (loss of data during compression), TIFF offers two lossless compression schemes (LZW or ZIP). TIFF can also save image layers, which makes it a good format for saving your work in progress, if you need to use the unfinished work file on a system that does not have Photoshop Elements or Photoshop. Otherwise, use the PSD format for working images and reserve TIFF for saving copies after you've completed your work.

When saving in TIFF format, in the **Save As** dialog box, you can opt to retain **Layers**. Again, save your layer info in the working Photoshop PSD file rather than in a TIFF file—unless you need that option to be able to work on the image on a system that does not have Photoshop or Photoshop Elements. By not saving the layers, you can reduce the TIFF file size considerably. Also, layered-TIFF files may not be readable by some graphics programs. In the **Tiff Options** dialog box that appears next, you can choose the **Image Compression** you want: **None**, **LZW**, **ZIP**, or **JPEG** (which will result in some data loss). **LZW** is the most common choice here, but **ZIP** typically gives you smaller files. However, the **ZIP** option is not widely supported outside of Adobe applications. If you choose JPEG compression, also set the compression level (**Quality**). Next, select a **Pixel Order**: **Interleaved** or **Per Channel**. **Per Channel** (RRGGBB) order is typically faster, and is especially compatible with the **ZIP** option, but it's not widely supported outside of Adobe. **Interleaved** (RGBRGB) is the more common choice. Set a **Byte Order**: **IBM PC** or **Macintosh**. You can usually leave this set to **IBM PC**, but if you know that this image is destined for use on a Macintosh, you should select **Macintosh** instead. To save multiple resolutions of your image in the TIFF file, enable the **Save Image Pyramid** option. Some programs might then be able to display your image in the resolution you select when it's opened; Photoshop Elements simply displays such an image at its highest resolution. If the image has transparent pixels in it and you want to preserve them, enable the **Save Transparency** option. TIFF transparency is not compatible with all programs, so you might not want to use it. The **Discard Layers and Save a Copy** option is normally enabled. However, if you opted to save layers in the TIFF file, you can choose how those layers are saved: select **RLE** to create a file that's quicker to save yet larger; select **ZIP** for a smaller file that takes a bit longer to save.

RAW is a format used by many of the newer digital cameras today. You can't save images in RAW format using Photoshop Elements, but you can import RAW format images for editing. You can think of an image in RAW format as a digital negative—uncompressed, unprocessed raw image data that's been saved in a file. The only problem with the RAW format is that there's no standard—each camera manufacturer has its own particular version of it. Thus, the file extension varies from manufacturer to manufacturer, but look for extensions such as **.dcr**, **.orf**, **.nef**, and **.crw**. Lucky for you, Photoshop Elements can read the RAW files of the most popular digital cameras, making it the perfect format for taking pictures.

28

▶ **NOTE**

Although there is an option to save your work in Photoshop RAW format, note that this format is not the same as camera RAW format, and you should probably not depend on it since most programs cannot read its data. Still, you might use this format to save a RAW camera file that contains vital camera data you'd lose if you tried to resave the file in any other format.

29   Save an Image

✔ BEFORE YOU BEGIN	→ SEE ALSO
28 About Saving Images	33 Rename, Resize, Reformat, and Retouch a Group of Images
	35 Change Color Mode

After copying files from a digital camera onto your computer or scanning images using a scanner, your first step should be to perform some type of backup. Typically, this involves burning copies of the image files onto a CD-R. See **4 Import Images from a Digital Camera** for how to bring images into the catalog from your camera, and **7 Back Up the Organizer Catalog** for help on making the backup copies of the catalog and its images.

After importing an image into the catalog, backing it up, and beginning work on any touchups, you will most likely want to open the image in the Editor and save it in the Photoshop image format (PSD) by following the basic steps in this task. Using Photoshop PSD format ensures that you have access to all of the Editor's features, such as layers, transparency, vector objects, and masking, while also preserving the integrity of your original image's data. As you work on an image, you might want to save the image at various stages to which you can return later on, but not save these intermediate images in the Organizer, in a version set with the original image. To do this, select the **As a Copy** option from the **Save As** dialog box, as explained here in step 3. To make sure that this intermediate copy is not stored in the Organizer under its own thumbnail, be sure to deselect the **Include in the Organizer** option as well. When you are done working on an image, resave the Photoshop PSD file in a smaller, shareable format such as TIFF, JPEG, GIF, or PNG, again using the steps shown here. For this final, flattened copy of your image, be sure to select the **Save in Version Set with Original** and **Include in the Organizer** options in step 3, which will place the final version with the original under a single thumbnail in the catalog, where you can easily find them.

▶ TIPS

Photoshop Elements fully supports EXIF and PIM (Epson's Print Image Managing System, which its printers use to match printed output to how to an image looks onscreen), which means that you will not lose important digital camera data when you save your original file in Photoshop format.

If you have several photos that are similar to one another—such as several shots taken at around the same time—you can have the Editor make the same corrections to all of them simultaneously, and automatically save the results in whatever format you choose. See **33 Rename, Resize, Reformat, and Retouch a Group of Images** for details.

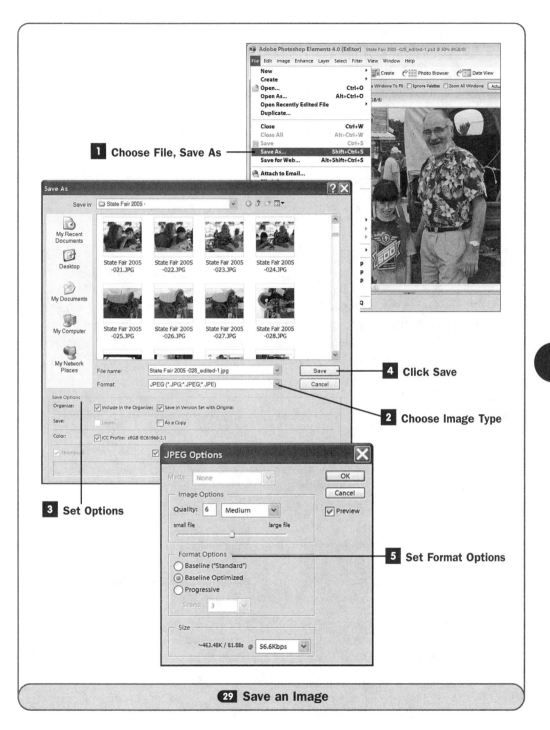

1 Choose File, Save As

4 Click Save

2 Choose Image Type

3 Set Options

5 Set Format Options

29 Save an Image

1 Choose File, Save As

To save changes and replace the current file, click the **Save** button on the **Shortcuts** bar, or choose **File, Save** from the menu. To save changes in a different file so you keep your original file intact (for example, to save your working PSD image in a flattened, sharable format such as JPEG as shown here), choose **File, Save As** instead. The **Save As** dialog box appears.

▶ NOTE

When you send an image from the catalog to the Editor for changes, you can click the **Save** button if you like, since it will automatically bring up the **Save As** dialog box, with options set so that you do not overwrite your original file with your edits.

2 Choose Image Type

From the **Format** drop-down list, choose the image type you want to use. If you're just beginning edits on an image, save the working file by choosing **Photoshop (*.PSD; *.PDD)**. If you're saving the final version of an image, select a type that matches your purpose, such as a web-compatible format (GIF, JPEG, or PNG), an email-friendly compressed format (JPEG or PNG), or high quality printer-friendly format (TIFF).

29

3 Set Options

Change to the folder in which you want to save the image. If this is the first time saving a new image file, type a filename in the **File name** text box. Normally, you do not have to edit the filename of an existing file when you save it because the options you select change the filename for you, as described below. Set options as desired:

- **As a Copy**—Select this option to save a copy of the image so that you don't overwrite the existing file. *The current image is kept open so that you can continue working*, but the image as it looks right now is saved in a new file with **copy** added to the original filename. Use this option to save copies of your working image at various stages in the editing process. Doing so allows you to go back to an earlier version if some of your edits don't work out.

- **Include in the Organizer**—Select this option to add the image to the Organizer catalog (if it isn't there already). By default, this option is already checked, but you can disable it if you like.

- **Layers**—Select this option when the format you've chosen supports layers (Photoshop PSD or TIFF format) *and* you want to make certain that the full content and identity of all layers are saved in your file. (This option is disabled if the format you select does not support layers.) With the **Layers** option disabled, the Editor merges all content in the file into a single layer before saving.

▶ NOTES

Typically, you'll enable the **Layers** option when saving a working Photoshop PSD image file; although you can enable this option when saving in TIFF, you probably won't want to since it makes the file larger than a regular TIFF and may also make it incompatible with some graphics programs. Layering is especially important when you're creating an image made up of parts of other images.

If you turn off the **Layers** option when saving a layered image, the **As a Copy** option is turned on for you. This prevents you from saving a merged (flattened) version of your image over top of the copy that contains the separate layers. So when you disable the **Layers** option, your layered, working image is kept open, and a merged, flattened copy is saved to the disk with a different filename.

- **Save in Version Set with Original**— Select this option to group the edited version of an image with its original version in the Organizer catalog, in a single version set. When this is done, both items share the same thumbnail in the catalog. In addition, when you chose this option, **edited-1** (or another number, if you've edited this image several times) is added to the original filename, creating a separate file so that you do not overwrite your original or other edited copies in the version set. (See **27** **About Editing Images**.)

- **ICC Profile**— Select this option to include the ICC color profile being used by your system, along with the other image data, in the image file. Knowing the name of this profile will help your printer or other computers render the image as you are seeing it now, rather than making color adjustments you don't want. See **63** **About Color Management**.

- **Thumbnail**—Select this option to save an image preview for applications that do not produce such previews for themselves. Admittedly, the number of applications that *can't* generate an image preview for themselves has grown quite few in recent years, but for these few, you might want to generate the preview for them. Normally, this option is on, but if you've changed your file-saving preferences so that image previews are not automatically created when you save, you'll be able to optionally save or not save a preview for particular images. Not saving a preview makes the image file smaller; however, having a preview enables you to view an image's content in the **Open** dialog box before you actually open the file. This option, by the way, has *nothing* to do with the Organizer's thumbnails, which it creates automatically when an image is added to the catalog.

29

▶ **NOTES**

To change your preferences for saving files (such as whether image previews are created), choose **Edit**, **Preferences**, **Saving Files** from the menu.

Not all image formats support the inclusion of thumbnails. For those formats, the **Thumbnail** option is not available.

- **Use Lower Case Extension**— Select this option to use lowercase letters in the filename extension—something that might be important if you intend to use the image on the Web or on a Linux computer, or if you're burning the image to a CD so that it can be read on a computer with a different operating system (such as a Mac). By default, this option is enabled, and it's typically best to leave it like that.

▣ Click Save

Click the **Save** button. If you see a note reminding you that you're saving this image as part of a version set, click **OK** to continue.

▣ Set Format Options

If you selected a particular file format from the **Format** list in step 2 (such as TIFF, JPEG, GIF, or PNG), an **Options** dialog box appears, allowing you to set options relating to that file format. See ㉘ **About Saving Images** for help selecting options,then click **OK**.

㉚ About Image Information

→ **SEE ALSO**

㉜ Change Image Size or Resolution
㉖ About Color Management

When needed, the Editor can display information about the basic characteristics of an image—its file type, resolution, size, and data specific to the conditions under which it was taken. To display this EXIF metadata for any image open in the Editor, select **File**, **File Info** from the menu bar. A dialog box opens, loaded with information about the current image.

Click a Category to Display Its Page

You Can Enter Some Metadata Manually

*The **File Info** dialog box contains lots of information about your image.*

On the left side of the **File Info** dialog box, you'll find a list of categories of information stored within the image file. Click a category to display its page of information. For example, click the **Camera Data 1** category to find out what the flash setting was when you took this photograph. You can enter some metadata yourself, simply by clicking inside any of the white boxes. For example, you might enter your name under **Author** or type in a **Copyright Notice**. Metadata you can view but not change is shown in gray. This kind of metadata is typically EXIF data that your camera recorded when the image was taken, such as shutter speed and f-stop.

▶ NOTES

You can also view an image's metadata on the **Properties** pane in the Organizer. Choose **Window**, **Properties** from the Organizer menu, then click the **Metadata** button at the top of the **Properties** pane.

Some metadata, such as an image's size and resolution, is added or changed by Photoshop Elements when you edit an image and save changes. So even if you have an image that started out as a scan of a printed photo, there might be information for you to view in the **File Info** dialog box.

You can change some of this metadata through the Organizer. For example, if you click the **Description** category on the left, you'll see the text caption you entered in the Organizer and any tags or collection markers you attached to the image (shown here as **Keywords**). Metadata you enter through this dialog box is permanently saved *only* if you store the image in PSD, TIFF, PNG, GIF, or JPEG format. At the bottom of the **Description** page, you'll find basic information about the image, such as the file date, modified date, and file type.

You can add a copyright notice on the **Description** page by changing the **Copyright Status** drop-down list to **Copyrighted**, and typing your copyright text in the **Copyright Notice** text box. You can add your web page address in the **Copyright Info URL** box. Note, however, that copyright data such as this is of limited use because anyone with a program capable of reading image metadata can change or remove it. Better to protect your images with a copyright that can't be removed—see **79** **Add a Text Caption or Label** for help in adding copyright text to an image.

As I mentioned earlier, metadata your digital camera recorded when the shot was taken—such as the camera type, date the photo was taken, and shot conditions such as f-stop, shutter speed, and focal length—can be found on the **Camera Data 1** and **Camera Data 2** pages in the **File Info** dialog box. Some of this data can be used by an EXIF-compatible printer to print your photo more accurately, with better color and brightness matching. To make sure that you don't lose this valuable EXIF data, save your digital camera file using an EXIF-compatible program (Photoshop Elements just happens to be one), in an EXIF-compatible format (Photoshop PSD, JPEG, or TIFF). See **64** **Install a Color Profile** for more information. Also on the **Camera Data 2** page, you'll find the image's current size in pixels, resolution, and ICC color profile (listed here as **Color Source**).

In the Organizer, the **Properties** pane can provide you with further information about the currently selected image. To display the **Properties** pane, click the **Show or Hide Properties** button on the **Options** bar, or choose **Window, Properties**. Although the **Properties** pane also displays EXIF data, it includes other information that you won't find in the **File Info** dialog box. In the **Properties** pane, you'll find information about where the image is stored, its file date, text caption, audio caption, and any notes you attached on the **General** tab. Markers you might have attached to an image are listed on the **Tags** tab. The file date, modified date, import date, and related information can be found on the **History** tab, and EXIF and other metadata is located on the **Metadata** tab. To display a condensed version of the metadata, select the **Brief** option; to display all the metadata, select the **Complete** option instead.

30

*The **Properties** pane enables you to access image information from the Organizer.*

31

31 Zoom In and Out

✔ **BEFORE YOU BEGIN**

25 About the Editor

Whether you're making changes to a photograph or some artwork you've created yourself, you must be able to view the image clearly to make precise changes. Typically, this means zooming in on some area that doesn't look right so that you can discern the problem, and later zooming back out again to see whether the change you made looks right when the image is viewed at its regular size. To zoom in on an image and back out again, use the **Zoom** tool. If you don't want to switch tools, you can also zoom in and out using the **Navigator** palette.

1 Click with the Zoom Tool

Open an image in the Editor and then click the **Zoom** tool in the **Toolbox**. Press **Alt** while clicking with the **Zoom** tool to zoom out. Click the **Zoom In** or **Zoom Out** button on the **Options** bar to determine the direction of the zoom, then click the point you want to zoom in on (or away from) within the image window. Drag an area with the **Zoom In** tool to zoom in on that area.

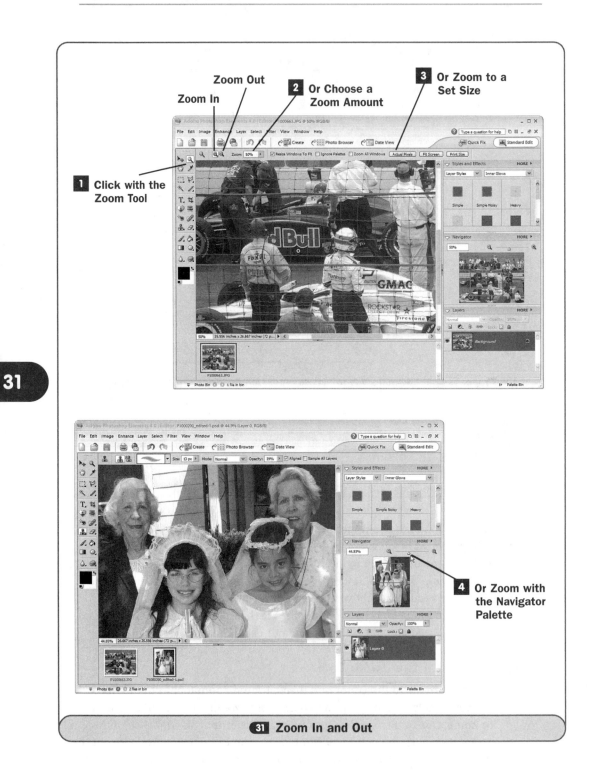

Zoom In

Zoom Out

2 Or Choose a Zoom Amount

3 Or Zoom to a Set Size

1 Click with the Zoom Tool

4 Or Zoom with the Navigator Palette

31

31 Zoom In and Out

▶ TIPS

To resize the image window as you zoom, enable the **Resize Windows to Fit** option on the **Options** bar. To allow the image window to expand below free-floating palettes, enable the **Ignore Palettes** option. To zoom all open image windows by the same amount, enable the **Zoom All Windows** option. (This option works only if you zoom using the **Zoom In** or **Zoom Out** buttons, and not the **Zoom** slider.)

To zoom in and out without actually selecting the **Zoom** tool first, press and hold **Ctrl+spacebar** and click the image to zoom in. Press and hold **Alt+spacebar** and click the image to zoom out.

2 Or Choose a Zoom Amount

You can also zoom by dragging the **Zoom** slider on the **Options** bar, or typing a percentage in the box and pressing **Enter**.

3 Or Zoom to a Set Size

To view the image at 100% (based on roughly 72 PPI, or optimum screen resolution), click the **Actual Pixels** button on the **Options** bar. To zoom the image as large as possible to fill the workspace, click the **Fit On Screen** button. To zoom the image to the approximate magnification it will be when you print it (based on the current image resolution), click the **Print Size** button.

31

4 Or Zoom with the Navigator Palette

Rather than switch from the tool you're using to the **Zoom** tool to zoom, use the **Navigator** palette: choose **Window, Navigator** if needed to display the palette. Select or type a zoom percentage in the box on the left side of the palette. You can also drag the slider on the **Navigator** palette to zoom. To zoom by a predetermined amount, click either of the **Zoom** buttons on the **Navigator** palette.

▶ TIPS

If you've zoomed in on an image, you can scroll to view hidden areas using the scroll bars, dragging the image with the **Hand** tool, or dragging the red rectangle on the **Navigator** palette. Hold down the **spacebar** to turn your pointer into the **Hand** tool for as long as you hold the **spacebar**.

When working with multiple images, you may want to use the **Navigator** palette to zoom, since the **Zoom** tool unarranges the windows.

32 | **Change Image Size or Resolution**

→ **SEE ALSO**

5 Import and Separate Multiple Scanned Images
34 Increase the Canvas Area Around an Image

As you learned in Chapter 1, "Start Here," an image's size is tied directly to the number of pixels in the image as well as the relative size of those pixels. When you create images with a digital camera or scan printed images with a scanner, you choose the resolution you want to use—for instance, 72 pixels per inch (ppi). The resolution you choose also determines the resulting print size. For example, an image that's 2048 pixels wide by 1536 pixels tall (the typical dimensions of an image taken with a 3-megapixel camera), whose resolution is 300 pixels per inch, will print at 6.827" by 5.120".

So what do you do if you want to print your image at a different size—larger or smaller—while maintaining or even increasing its resolution? Answer: You use *resampling*. When you resample to increase an image's print size and/or its resolution, new pixels are inserted between existing ones. The Editor determines the colors of the new pixels by sampling the color value of each surrounding pixel, calculating a value within the sample range, and assigning that value to that new pixel. Conversely, when you reduce an image's print size, resampling removes pixels from the image and then adjusts the colors of the pixels remaining in the image by approximating the blended color values of the pixels that were removed.

▶ **KEY TERM**

Resampling—The mathematical process applied during image resizing that evaluates the content of the pixels in the image to calculate the value of new pixels (when enlarging) or neighboring pixels (when reducing), and which re-interprets the result to minimize loss of detail.

Because resampling is based on best-guess estimation, using it to change an image's size or resolution by more than 20% often produces poor results. You can resize or change an image's resolution without resampling by telling the Editor that you want to turn resampling off, and therefore maintain the relationship between the size and the resolution. In this manner, you can double an image's print resolution by cutting its print size in half (the image contains as many pixels as it did before, but the pixels are smaller, and there are more of them per inch). Onscreen, you won't see any apparent change at all.

32

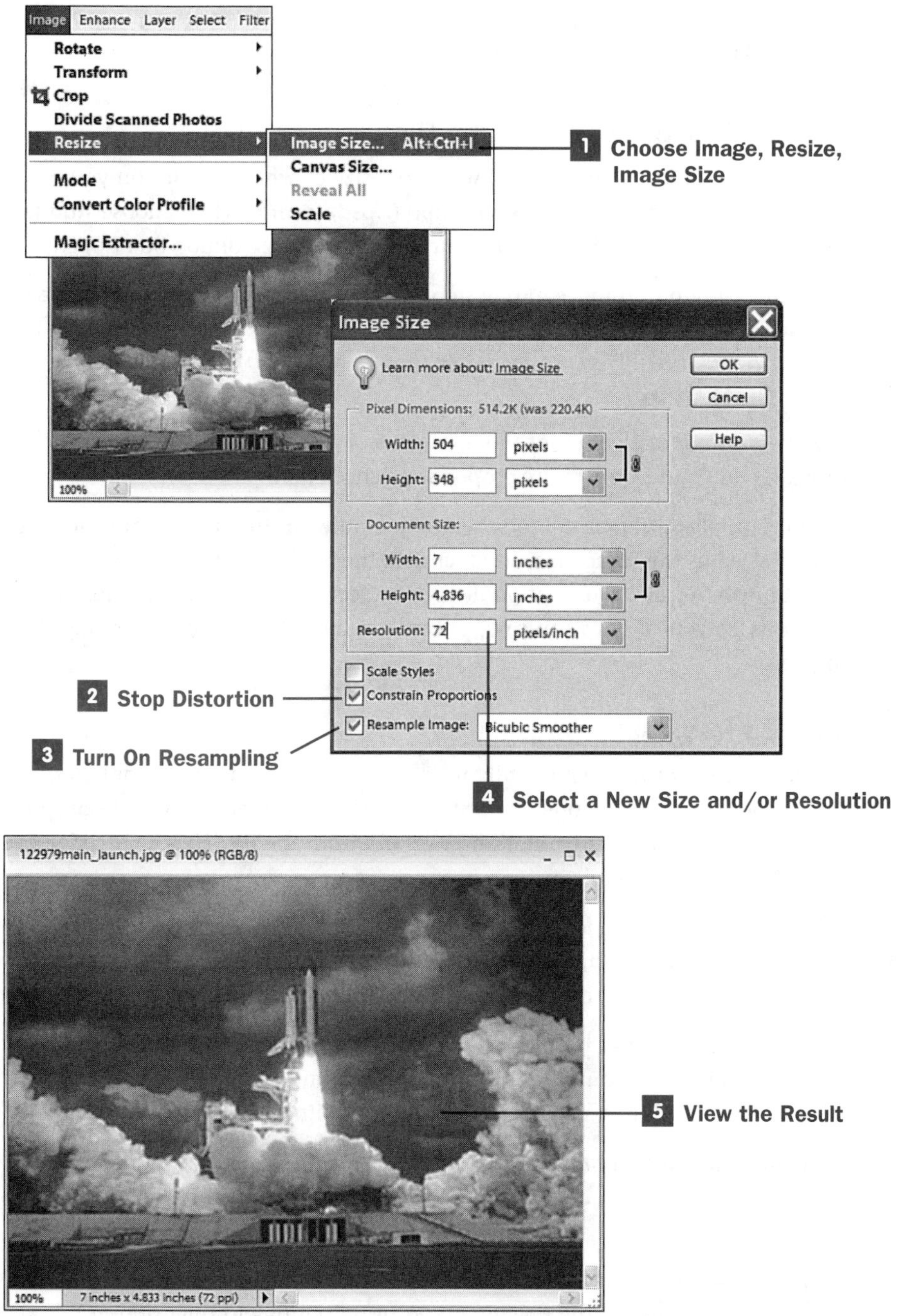

Image Enhance Layer Select Filter

- Rotate
- Transform
- Crop
- Divide Scanned Photos
- Resize
  - Image Size... Alt+Ctrl+I
  - Canvas Size...
  - Reveal All
  - Scale
- Mode
- Convert Color Profile
- Magic Extractor...

1 Choose Image, Resize, Image Size

Image Size

Learn more about: Image Size

Pixel Dimensions: 514.2K (was 220.4K)

Width: 504 pixels
Height: 348 pixels

Document Size:

Width: 7 inches
Height: 4.836 inches
Resolution: 72 pixels/inch

Scale Styles
Constrain Proportions
Resample Image: Bicubic Smoother

OK
Cancel
Help

2 Stop Distortion

3 Turn On Resampling

4 Select a New Size and/or Resolution

122979main_launch.jpg @ 100% (RGB/8)

100% 7 inches x 4.833 inches (72 ppi)

5 View the Result

32

32 Change Image Size or Resolution

▶ **NOTE**

To display an image in its print size, click the **Zoom** tool on the **Toolbox** and then click the **Print Size** button on the **Options** bar.

1 **Choose Image, Resize, Image Size**

In the Editor, open the image you want to resize or whose resolution you want to change and save it in Photoshop (*.**psd**) format. Then choose **Image, Resize, Image Size** from the menu bar. The **Image Size** dialog box appears.

To resize a group of images in one step, see **33** **Rename, Resize, Reformat, and Retouch a Group of Images**.

2 **Stop Distortion**

If you want to make sure that the image is not distorted during the resizing process, enable the **Constrain Proportions** check box.

If you've applied a layer style to the image and want the pattern of that style to be resized as the image is resized, enable the **Scale Styles** option as well. Note that the **Scale Styles** option does not affect the size of patterns formed by effects, so you might want to apply such embellishments after resizing the image.

3 **Turn On Resampling**

To have the Editor mathematically re-evaluate and re-render the content of the image when you change its print size or resolution, enable the **Resample Image** option and select a sampling formula from the list. Here's a brief description of the formulas:

- **Bicubic**—Estimates each new pixel's color value based on the values of the 16 pixels nearest to the new pixel's location relative to the original image, in a 4 × 4 array. This method is best used when enlarging an image.

- **Bicubic Smoother**—Similar to the **Bicubic** formula, except that the tendency of Bicubic resampling to create halos around highly contrasting edges is reduced. Best used when enlarging an image.

- **Bicubic Sharper**—Similar to the **Bicubic** formula, except the edges are sharper with even higher contrast. Best used when reducing the size of an image.

- **Bilinear**—Estimates each new pixel's color value based on the values of the four pixels nearest to the new pixel's location relative to the original image. This method is best used when reducing an image.

- **Nearest Neighbor**—Estimates each new pixel's color value based on the values of all the pixels that fall within a fixed proximity of the new pixel's location relative to the original image. Here, the pixel residing in the same proportionate location in the original image as that of the new pixel in the resized image is given the extra "weight" when estimating the new color value. This method is best used when reducing the size of an image, but only for those images with edges that have not been anti-aliased.

▶ NOTES

When you make your image larger or smaller, the rescaling process can introduce artifacts or patterns that resampling can eliminate. However, in smoothing out any possible artifacts or unwanted patterns, resampling after you resize can result in loss of detail, especially in the background or in small areas. So limit the number of times you resample an image to *once*; if you have detail in the background you don't want to risk losing, do not resample.

To avoid resampling an image, disable the **Resample Image** option and change either the **Height/Width** or **Resolution** values in the **Document Size** area. Just keep in mind that if you increase the **Resolution** without resampling, the image will be resized smaller.

If you want to print an image in some size other than its normal print size, you can "rescale" the image on the fly when you print it. If you print an image in a larger size than normal, however, the resolution is decreased proportionately to compensate (pixels are not added). If the resulting resolution falls below acceptable levels of quality, you'll see a warning so that you can choose a different print size. Regardless, with this method, the original resolution and print size of the image are left unchanged. If you get the warning, it's best to choose a smaller print size (or abandon printing and then resize and resample the image to the print size you want) by following the steps in this task.

4 Select a New Size and/or Resolution

If you know what size you want the final image to be, type a value in the **Document Size Width** box; the **Height** value changes proportionately (or vice versa).

You can also change an image's size by adding or removing pixels. When you add pixels while maintaining the same resolution, you make the image bigger. For example, if you want the image to be twice as big, in the frame marked **Pixel Dimensions**, for either **Width** or **Height**, type **200** in the text box, and from the adjacent drop-down list, choose **Percent**. This increases the number of pixels without affecting the size of the pixels (assuming that **Resample Image** is on).

To change the resolution, type a value in the **Resolution** box. Altering resolution in this manner does not change the image's print size unless you entered new values for **Document Size** earlier. Click **OK**. The image's size/resolution is adjusted as selected.

5 **View the Result**

After you're satisfied with the result of the resizing process, make any other changes you want and then save the final image in JPEG, PNG, or non-layered TIFF format, leaving your PSD image with its layers (if any) intact so that you can return at a later time and make different adjustments if you want.

Even though I increased the size of this photo by quite a lot (from roughly 4" × 3" to 7" × 5"), the quality (resolution) was maintained because I selected **Bicubic Smoother** resampling.

▶ **TIP**

Because resampling often leaves an image a bit fuzzy, it's best to follow up by applying an **Unsharp Mask**. See **99** Sharpen an Image.

32

---

33 **Rename, Resize, Reformat, and Retouch a Group of Images**

✔ BEFORE YOU BEGIN	→ SEE ALSO
28 About Saving Images	**32** Change Image Size or Resolution
68 Apply a Quick Fix	

It's easier than you might think to collect hundreds, if not thousands, of digital photos before you realize it. Managing these photos can become a full-time job if you don't establish a routine for processing new images that includes copying the files to your computer, backing them up onto CD-R or similar media, and converting those files you want to work with to PSD format or some other lossless format, such as TIFF. You should follow a similar process for images you copy to the computer using your scanner.

Luckily, the Editor provides a method for easily converting a group of files from one format to another *all at once*. In addition, you can rename the files (which you might want to do if they use generic names such as **DSC01982.jpg**), resize them (and even increase their resolution), and automatically adjust their brightness, contrast, and saturation.

▶ **TIP**

If you are processing files that are already in the catalog, you will need to update their catalog information. After you've processed the files, in the Organizer, choose **File, Reconnect, All Missing Files**. See **6** Locate Moved Files.

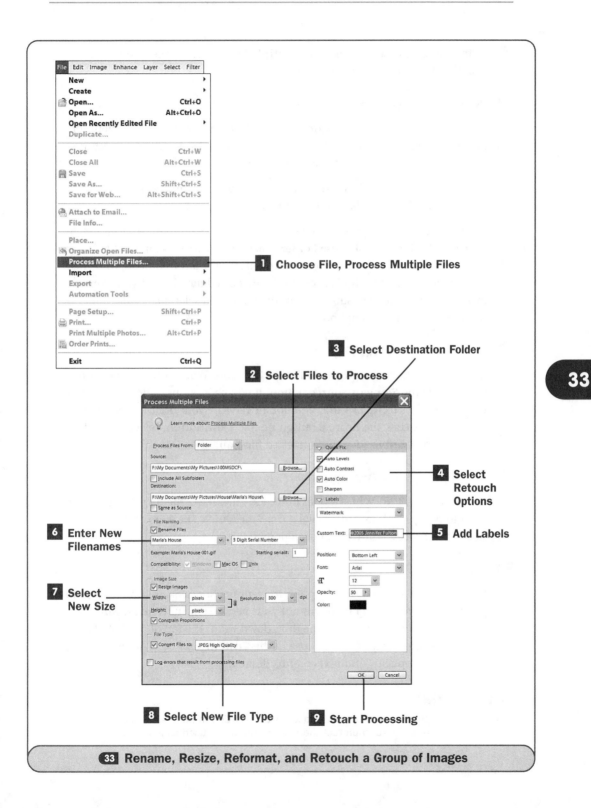

1 Choose File, Process Multiple Files

3 Select Destination Folder

2 Select Files to Process

33

4 Select Retouch Options

6 Enter New Filenames

5 Add Labels

7 Select New Size

8 Select New File Type

9 Start Processing

33 Rename, Resize, Reformat, and Retouch a Group of Images

1 In the editor, choose **File**, **Process Multiple Files** from the menu bar. The **Process Multiple Files** dialog box opens.

2 Select Files to Process

To import images from your scanner, digital camera, or a PDF document for processing, from the **Process Files From** list, choose **Import**. Then select the source you want to use from the **From** list.

To process all the files that are currently open in the Editor's workspace, from the **Process Files From** list, choose **Opened Files**.

To process all the images in a folder (and perhaps its subfolders), from the **Process Files From** list, choose **Folder**. Click the **Browse** button next to **Source**, select the folder that contains the files you want to process, and click **OK**. You're returned to the **Process Multiple Files** dialog box. If you want to include images stored in subfolders of the folder you selected, enable the **Include All Subfolders** option.

3 Select Destination Folder

If you want to save the processed files in the same folder in which they are now, enable the **Same as Source** option. If you choose this option, be sure to rename the files as well so that you don't overwrite your originals (see step 6). Otherwise, click the **Browse** button next to **Destination**, select the folder in which you want to save the converted files, and click **OK**.

4 Select Retouch Options

If you want to retouch the images automatically, select the adjustments you want to apply (such as **Auto Levels**) from the **Quick Fix** pane on the right side of the **Process Multiple Files** dialog box.

5 Add Labels

You can add a *watermark* or caption to identify your personal images and to protect them from being used without your permission. To create a watermark, select **Watermark** from the drop-down list at the top of the **Labels** pane. Enter the text you want to use in the **Custom Text** box. Adjust the font, size, position, opacity, and text color as desired.

▶ KEY TERM

Watermark—Slightly transparent text placed over a portion of an image, not only to identify its creator but also to protect the image from being used illegally.

33

To add a caption, select **Caption** from the drop-down list at the top of the **Labels** pane. Then select the text you want to include in the caption: **File Name**, **Description**, and/or **Date Modified**. You can choose as many of these text elements as you like—each appears on its own line in the image. The **Description**, by the way, is the same description you can enter on the **Description** page of the **File Info** dialog box or as an image caption in the Organizer. See **30** **About Image Information** and **16** **Add a Text Caption or Note**. Select a **Position** for the caption (such as **Bottom Right**), and adjust the font, size, opacity, and text color as desired.

▶ **TIP**

To enter the copyright symbol into the **Custom Text** box, press and hold **Alt** as you type **0169** on the numeric keypad.

6 **Enter New Filenames**

To rename the files, enable the **Rename Files** check box. By selecting items from one or both of the lists, you can use the existing properties of an image to create a unique filename. For example, you can use an image's date as part or all of its new name. You can also combine your own text such as **Jan's Birthday** with a sequence number, creating a unique filename for each image—**Jan's Birthday 01**, **Jan's Birthday 02**, and so on.

Start by choosing a property you want to use from the first list box in the **File Naming** area. To enter your own text, simply type it into the first list box. Choose a second property (such as **2 digit serial number**) from the second list box if desired. If you plan to use the converted files on a computer with a different operating system, select that system in the **Compatibility** area. As you make your selections, a sample filename appears in the **Example** area.

▶ **NOTES**

If you're using a serial number as part of the filename, you can change the starting number by changing the value in the **Starting serial#** text box.

The **Document Name** property simply refers to the image's current filename. Selecting that property will enable you to use the existing filename and add something to it by selecting an additional property from the second list. This way, for instance, you can change the filename **DCX0304987.jpg** to **Walt and Saundra's Wedding - DCX0304987.jpg** if the original filename is important to you. Also, if you select **document name** from the list and the file is currently named **BBQ Party.jpg**, the file will be renamed **bbq party.jpg**; if you select **DOCUMENT NAME**, the file will be renamed **BBQ PARTY.JPG**, and so on.

7 Select New Size

If you want to resize these images or change their resolution, enable the **Resize Images** option. Then enter new **Width** and **Height** values. Resampling will take place during resizing. To make sure that the images are not distorted as they are resized, enable the **Constrain Proportions** option. Enter a new **Resolution** if desired. See **32 Change Image Size or Resolution** for more information.

8 Select New File Type

If you want to convert these images to a different file type (such as from GIF to PSD), enable the **Convert Files to** option, and then open the drop-down list and select the file type to which you want to convert the selected files.

9 Start Processing

When you're satisfied with your choices, click **OK**. Each image appears briefly in the Editor window as it is being processed. To save any error messages that appear during processing in a text file that you can review later, enable the **Log errors that result from processing files** option before clicking **OK**. This log file is saved to the destination folder you identified in step 3.

33

---

34 Increase the Canvas Area Around an Image

✔ BEFORE YOU BEGIN	→ SEE ALSO
72 Select a Color to Work With	**32** Change Image Size or Resolution

---

Each image has a *canvas*—essentially the image's background layer—that can be stretched to increase the size of the area on which you can paint, draw objects, and insert text. For a newly imported digital photo, the image fills the canvas. You can expand the background layer (the canvas) of an image such as a photograph, for example, to make room for a frame, and fill the new area with color and apply a filter, style, or effect. Or you might simply want to expand the canvas to create more room in which to add a clip from another image, an object, or some text.

▶ KEY TERM

Canvas—The working area of an image, as defined by the image's outer dimensions.

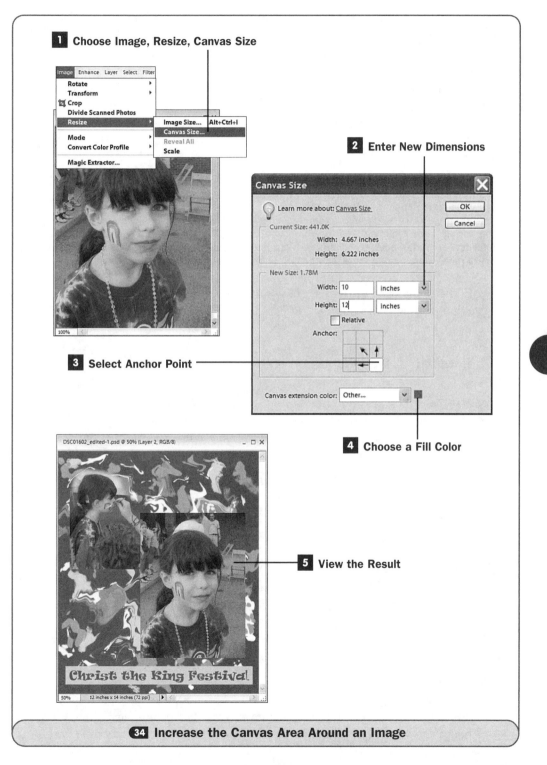

1 Choose Image, Resize, Canvas Size

2 Enter New Dimensions

3 Select Anchor Point

4 Choose a Fill Color

5 View the Result

34 Increase the Canvas Area Around an Image

When you expand the canvas of an image, you add new pixels around its edges in a color you select. If an image has no background layer—for example, if you created the image using the **File**, **New** command and made the bottom layer transparent, or you converted the original **Background** layer to a regular layer using the **Layer**, **New**, **Layer from Background** command—then the new pixels are made transparent. Every layer above the base layer—whether it's a background layer or a regular layer—is expanded by the same amount.

▶ **NOTE**

You can reduce the canvas size of an image. If you do, although all the layers are reduced in size, data is not removed from the upper layers—it's just placed off the canvas where it is not seen in the final image. You can then use the **Move** tool to move the data on these non-background layers to display exactly the portion you want. Data from the bottom layer is clipped and cannot be retrieved. But if you increase the canvas size later on (even after saving and closing the image), you'll see that the data on upper layers is now visible again. See **59 Move, Resize, Skew, or Distort a Layer or Selection**.

1 In the Editor, open the image whose canvas size you want to adjust and save it in Photoshop (***.psd**) format. Choose **Image**, **Resize**, **Canvas Size** from the menu bar. The **Canvas Size** dialog box is displayed.

34

2 Enter New Dimensions

The current dimensions of the image are displayed at the top of the **Canvas Size** dialog box. If you want to simply *add* a certain amount to the outer dimensions of the image, enable the **Relative** option. If the option is disabled, the dimensions you enter reflect the *total* width and height of the image.

In the **New Size** pane, select a unit of measure such as inches or pixels from one of the drop-down lists next to the **Width** and **Height** boxes (the other will change automatically). Then type values in the **Width** and **Height** boxes.

3 Select Anchor Point

Normally, the anchor point is in the center of the **Anchor** pad. This means that the added canvas is placed equally around the image. If you want to add canvas to just one side of the image, click the appropriate arrow on the **Anchor** pad.

4 Choose a Fill Color

If the bottom layer of the image is not a **Background** layer, the added canvas will be transparent. If the bottom layer is the **Background** layer, the added canvas will be set to the color you choose from the **Canvas extension** color list: **Background** (applies the current background color; **Other** displays the **Color Picker** with which you can choose a color. You can also click in the image to pick up that color with the dropper in the **Color Picker**. Click **OK**.

▶ **TIP**

To display the **Color Picker** without choosing **Other** from the **Canvas extension color** list, just click the box to the right of the list.

5 **View the Result**

After expanding the image canvas, make any other changes you want and then save the final image in JPEG, PNG, or non-layered TIFF format, leaving your PSD image with its layers (if any) intact so that you can return at a later time and make different adjustments if you want.

In the sample figure, the canvas was expanded above and to the left of the main image, text was added, and another image was pasted into the new space, creating a photo collage of a wonderful day spent at a local festival.

35	**Change Color Mode**	**35**

→ **SEE ALSO**

26 Create a New Image

One of the key factors affecting the size of an image file is the maximum number of colors it can include. If a file is theoretically capable of including a large number of colors—even though it may actually contain very few—the file's size will be large, just to ensure that capacity. If you're working on an image to be shared over the Internet, small file size is often a high priority. One way you can reduce a file's size is to change its color mode—the number of colors an image can contain, even if it doesn't actually contain that many. When you select certain file types that offer image compression, you'll be asked to make decisions on how to reduce the number of colors. You can also manually change to a different color mode, as explained in this task, and reduce the number of colors (and an image's file size) that way. Just keep in mind that reducing the number of colors in an image might lead to striation and patchiness in large areas of solid color.

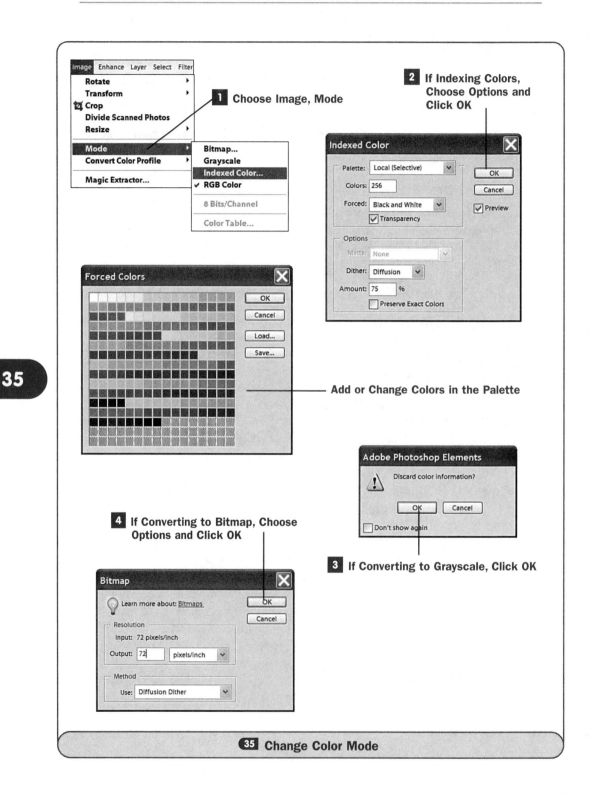

1 Choose Image, Mode

2 If Indexing Colors, Choose Options and Click OK

Add or Change Colors in the Palette

4 If Converting to Bitmap, Choose Options and Click OK

3 If Converting to Grayscale, Click OK

35 Change Color Mode

Photographs typically use **RGB color mode**, which gives them access to all 16 million-plus colors that standard video cards support. **Indexed color mode**, used in GIF images, provides a limited color palette of only 256 colors, although these colors are selected from all the 16,777,216 hues the standard video card produces. If your image is black and white, or black and white plus gray, there are other modes you can use to make your image file even smaller. How perceptible the difference is, when changing to a lower color mode, depends on the image you're working with. For this reason, the Editor makes it possible for you to sample different color reduction modes, enabling you to choose the least detrimental mode for your image.

▶ **NOTES**

Because some commands are available only for images that use RGB or grayscale mode, you might sometimes find yourself temporarily increasing an image's color mode (from grayscale to RGB, for example). This won't, however, improve the resolution or quality of a low-resolution image—increasing an image's color palette simply makes more colors available for use; it does not tell the Editor where to use them in an image to boost detail and clarity.

The color mode of an image appears after its name, in the image window title bar.

35

1 **Choose Image, Mode**

In the Editor, open the image you want to convert, and save it in Photoshop (***.psd**) format. Choose **Image, Mode** from the menu bar. Select the color mode you want to convert to from the submenu that appears:

- **Bitmap**—1-bit color in black and white; suitable for images in black and white only, with no gray tones.

- **Grayscale**—8-bit color in 256 shades of gray.

- **Indexed Color**—8 bits per pixel, in 256 colors, selected from the entire color gamut. Perfect for use with GIF images.

- **RGB**—24-bit color, with 8 bits per color channel, with more than 16 million colors available.

If you're increasing color depth, the image itself is not changed, but more colors become available for your use. If you're reducing color depth, a dialog box appears from which you must choose options. Continue to step 2, 3, or 4.

▶ **NOTE**

Technically speaking, the number of bits (binary digits) required for an image to encode the color value for one pixel is the base-2 logarithm of the maximum number of colors. In other words, 2 raised to that power equals the maximum number. It takes 8 bits to encode up to 256 values, and 24 bits to encode up to 16,777,216 values—thus the arithmetic behind the phrase *24-bit color.*

2 If Indexing Colors, Choose Options and Click OK

If you're reducing colors in an image with **Indexed Color** mode, select how you want the Editor to choose the colors for the palette by choosing from various options in the dialog box that appears. Before you begin making selections, enable the **Preview** option so that you can see how your selections affect the actual image. From the **Palette** list, choose one of the following options:

▶ **NOTE**

If the image already uses 256 colors or less, the **Palette** option is automatically set to **Exact**, which means that all colors in the image are added to the palette. You do not have to make a selection.

35

- **System (Mac OS)** uses the 256-color palette developed for the first color Macintosh computers. Select this palette to generate small files best displayed on Macs.

- **System (Windows)** uses the 256-color palette developed for Windows 3.0, which has been used as the backup palette for 8-bit color mode ever since.

- **Web** uses a 216-color palette (the last 40 index values are reserved), recommended for use in generating images for web pages because these are the 216 values that Mac and Windows machines have in common. Choosing this option ensures that the image will appear the same on both a Windows and a Mac computer.

- **Uniform** calculates 216 colors from equidistant positions in the RGB color gamut by rotating color index values from all-white to all-black. This setting ensures that your image uses colors sampled from throughout the image's color spectrum.

- The three **Local** options direct the Editor to create a palette based solely on the colors found in the currently open image.

- The three **Master** options instruct the Editor to create a palette based on the colors found in all the images currently open in the Editor.

Among the **Local** and **Master** options, **Adaptive** instructs the Editor to select 256 colors that are mathematically most similar to the colors in the original image.

Perceptual takes the 256 colors generated by the **Adaptive** algorithm and alters the selections slightly to favor colors that the human eye would tend to notice if they were changed—typically throwing away more colors in areas with the least amount of contrast, while favoring colors in areas with high contrast because the eye would notice that more.

Selective takes the 256 colors refined by the **Perceptual** algorithm and then weights the values to more closely resemble the Web spectrum, while also favoring broad areas of color within the image.

- Select **Custom** to make changes to any colors in the palette that the Editor is currently preparing to adopt. When the **Color Table** dialog box appears (which looks similar to the **Forced Colors** dialog box shown here), double-click the color in the palette you want to change. Select a new color from the **Color Picker** dialog box and click **OK**. To add a color to the palette, click an empty spot and then select a color to add. Repeat for any other palette colors you want to change or add, and click **OK** when finished. You're returned to the **Indexed Color** dialog box.

- Choose **Previous** to load the previously used custom color palette. Use **Previous** to convert a series of images to indexed color mode, using the same color palette.

▶ **TIP**

To reduce your file size even further, set **Colors** to a value less than 256 (to reduce file size *significantly*, select a value less than 128).

The options in the **Forced** list instruct the Editor to override some or all of its palette color choices and to include specific color values, some of which you can choose yourself from the **Forced Color** dialog box that appears. These "forced" choices may or may not be represented in the actual image, but they are included in the image's palette:

- **Black & White** forces the Editor to include pure black and pure white as two of the colors in the palette.

- **Primaries** forces the Editor to include the first eight colors of the old IBM Extended Graphics palette: red, green, blue, cyan, magenta, yellow, black and white. This allows a large measure of downward compatibility (if you really need it) with some of the first images ever produced for display on PCs.

35

- **Web** forces the Editor to include the entire 216-color Web palette (essentially the same as choosing **Web** from the **Palette** list).

- Choose **Custom** to enable you to change or add colors to the palette. Double-click a palette color. Select a new color from the **Color Picker** dialog box and click **OK**. To add a color, click an empty spot, select a color, and click **OK**. Repeat for any other palette colors you want to add or change and click **OK** when finished.

If the image has transparency but you don't want to retain it, disable the **Transparency** option. Then select from the **Matte** drop-down list a color to change the transparent pixels to. Semi-transparent pixels are blended with the color you choose to make them fully opaque. You can choose **Foreground Color**, **Background Color**, **White**, **Black**, **50% Gray**, or **Netscape Gray** (a lighter gray) from the list, or select your own color by choosing **Custom** from the **Matte** drop-down list and using the **Color Picker** that appears to select a color to use. To choose a color from the image, just click in the image with the **Eyedropper** tool.

If the image contains transparent pixels and you want to retain them, enable the **Transparency** option. If the image contains semi-transparent pixels, open the **Matte** list and choose a color to blend with them to make them fully opaque.

35

▶ NOTES

If you choose **None** from the **Matte** drop-down list, semi-transparent pixels are simply changed to fully opaque ones and are not blended with anything. Transparent pixels are made white.

Because it uses a mathematical formula, error diffusion (when used in images with a very limited color palette or large blocks of color, such as comics art) can sometimes generate artifacts in a color blended area, more so than if you use an ordered dither method such as **Pattern**.

To reduce the side effects caused by using a smaller number of colors than the original image contained, select the dither pattern you prefer from the **Dither** list:

- **Diffusion** instructs the Editor to apply an *error diffusion* algorithm to blend dissimilar colors by dividing the differences between them mathematically and spreading that difference to neighboring pixels, hiding the transition. When you make this choice, enter the relative percentage of error diffusion in the **Amount** text box. Enable the **Preserve Exact Colors** option to instruct the Editor not to dither any colors it encounters in the original image whose values exactly match any of those in the current reduction palette.

▶ KEY TERM

Error diffusion—Any of several mathematical techniques that attempt to compensate for large differences (errors) between the color of an original pixel and its replacement in a resampled image by dividing this difference into parts and distributing it to neighboring pixels, thus masking the obvious inaccuracy.

- **Pattern** applies a geometric dithering pattern, which might be noticeable in photographic images but is permissible in more patterned images such as original drawings.

- **Noise** scatters dithered pixels randomly.

- **None** turns off diffusion and causes the Editor to substitute the closest color in the palette for any color not in the palette.

To finalize your choices, click **OK**.

3 If Converting to Grayscale, Click OK

When you're converting a color image to various hues of gray (grayscale), click **OK**; if the image has multiple layers, you'll be asked whether you want to flatten all layers before proceeding. Click **Merge**.

▶ NOTE

If the color layers currently in the image use blend modes other than **Normal** to create its current appearance—especially if that appearance depends on how the color of one layer interacts with the colors of the layers beneath it—then these effects will probably be completely lost if the image is flattened while converting it to grayscale. To preserve the layers and their blend modes, click **Don't Merge** in step 3.

4 If Converting to Bitmap, Choose Options and Click OK

When converting an image to pure black-and-white (**Bitmap** mode), the Editor could simply make relatively dark pixels black and the relatively light ones white. However, the result might not be desirable, so you might want to apply dithering.

First, let the Editor convert your image to grayscale by clicking **OK**. It's easier for the Editor to convert grays to black-and-white than to convert colors directly to black and white. If there are multiple layers, the Editor warns you to flatten them first; click **OK** to have it do that and continue. In the **Bitmap** dialog box that appears, in the **Resolution** area, make sure that your image is set for the resolution of your output device. At first, this is set to the image's current resolution. To ensure best appearance, you might have to adjust

35

resolution—and thus, its size—accordingly. For on-screen use, choose 72 PPI as a minimum; for printing, choose 200–300 ppi as a minimum. Altering this setting resizes the image, both in print and on-screen.

In the **Method** area, choose how you want the Editor to apply dithering. The **50% Threshold** option applies no dithering whatsoever—light pixels are made white, and dark ones are made black. The **Pattern Dither** option applies a geometric dithering pattern, which might be adequate if your original image is a simple drawing—such as a corporate logo—rather than a photograph. **Diffusion Dither** applies an error diffusion pattern, distributing vast differences in brightness value over wider areas—which is generally more appropriate for photographs.

To finalize your choices, click **OK**.

After changing the color mode of your image, make any other changes you want and then save the final image in JPEG, PNG, or non-layered TIFF format (or GIF, if you've converted to **Indexed color** mode), leaving your PSD image with its layers (if any) intact so that you can return at a later time and make different adjustments if you want.

35

6

Printing and Emailing Images

IN THIS CHAPTER:

36 Print an Image

37 Print a Contact Sheet

38 Print a Picture Package

39 Print Images Using an Online Service

40 About Emailing

41 Manage Contacts

42 Share Images Using Email

43 Share Images Using an Online Service

In Photoshop Elements, printing is the final step you take in rendering a picture, a group of pictures, or a printed creation. As a first step before you do any editing of an image, you should calibrate your monitor (see **64** **Install a Color Profile** for instructions), so that what you see onscreen in Photoshop Elements is similar to what you should expect when you print. If you haven't calibrated your monitor, do that now. Then preview the images you want to print, using the newly calibrated monitor, and make any further adjustments to the images as needed before printing. You might also want to review the tips on printing great photographs discussed in Chapter 1, "Start Here," before printing any images.

▶ **TIP**

If you use more than one printer, select that printer before you edit, so that what you see onscreen is coordinated with the printer you intend to use. To select a printer for editing, choose **File**, **Page Setup** from the Editor or the Organizer. Select a paper **Size** and **Source** from the first **Page Setup** dialog box and click **OK**. In the second **Page Setup** dialog box that appears next, choose your printer from the **Name** list and click **OK**.

You can print single images from the Editor or multiple images the Organizer. Just before printing, you can adjust the printer options to change the print quality to **Best** and the paper type to photo paper or heavy bond paper (if you're printing a card, for example). And then, if you're printing photos, there are the endless choices you can make about what to print: multiple copies of the same image, single prints from a group of images, a set of prints in standard photo sizes, photo labels, or small thumbnails of each image you can use as a reference. You can also reverse the image on-the-fly when printing onto iron-on transfer paper. As a final option, you might choose not to print your images at all, but to upload them to an Internet printing service instead. In this chapter, you'll learn how to complete all these tasks.

You'll also learn how to share your photos. Photoshop Elements is not an email program, but it can work in close partnership with the email software you *do* have, allowing you to easily send photos via email whenever you like. In addition to individual pictures, you can email creations such as slide shows, photo albums, postcards, and calendars. You also can include sound and video files, but not automatically. You must manually attach them to the email message. If your friends and relatives have a slow connection to the Internet, you can share images using an online service. Not only does this make it quicker and easier for Grandma to view the latest photos of your daughter's birthday party, she can select the ones she wants to have copies of and have the service print and mail them directly to her. Of course, Adobe's online service, Adobe Photoshop Services, comes with built-in security so that you don't have to worry about someone viewing your photos if you didn't invite them to.

36 Print an Image

✔ BEFORE YOU START	→ SEE ALSO
64 nstall a Color Profile	**38** Print a Picture Package
	39 Print Images Using an Online Service

▶ **NOTE**

You can print an existing creation from the Organizer by selecting it and clicking the **Print** button on the **Shortcuts** bar and then selecting a printer and clicking **Print** from the **Print** dialog box that appears. You can also print a creation just after creating or editing it by clicking the **Print** button on the **Step 5: Share** page of the **Creation** wizard. See **17** Make a Creation.

After you're through making changes, you can print an image from the Editor. (To print multiple copies of an image or multiple images, use the Organizer; see **38** **Print a Picture Package**.) Although you can scale the image to fit a particular size (such as 5" × 7") the process may result in portions of the image being cropped (not printed). In addition, scaling the size of an image within the **Print Preview** dialog box may also reduce image resolution (and thus, in turn, quality), so in most cases, you should resize the image using the steps in **32** **Change Image Size or Resolution**. For prints that are smaller than the paper you're using, you can adjust *where* the photo prints on the paper (which may help you trim the print). You'll be able to add a colored border around the image, print the image filename and text caption, and select the specific ICC printer profile you want to use. Before printing, you can preview your selections to see how your image will look.

▶ **NOTE**

Printing low-resolution images in a large size results in poor quality (grainy) photos. If you took the photos using a low-resolution setting on your digital camera (or scanned them using a low-resolution setting), choose a small print size for best print results.

1 **Click Print**

Open the image you want to print in the Editor and save it in Photoshop (***.psd**) format. Calibrate your monitor if needed (see **64** **Install a Color Profile**), make any changes you want, including resizing the image to fit the print size you need, then save the result in JPEG, PNG, or non-layered TIFF format, leaving your PSD image with its layers intact so that you can return at a later time and make different adjustments if you want.

36

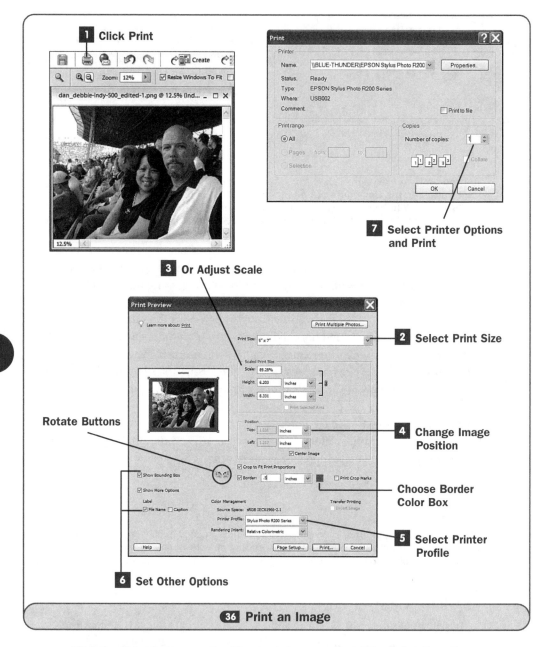

1 Click Print

7 Select Printer Options and Print

3 Or Adjust Scale

2 Select Print Size

Rotate Buttons

4 Change Image Position

Choose Border Color Box

5 Select Printer Profile

6 Set Other Options

36 Print an Image

36

Click the **Print** button on the **Shortcuts** bar, or select **File**, **Print** from the menu. The **Print Preview** dialog box appears.

2 Select Print Size

If you need to change the paper size, orientation, or paper type for this print job, click the **Page Setup** button to display the **Page Setup** dialog box. Select the paper **Size** and orientation; click the **Printer** button, select the printer to use, and then click **Properties** to display your printer's **Properties** dialog box where you can set the paper type.

The photo normally prints at its actual size (image size in pixels, divided by its image resolution or PPI). One way to scale the photo to print at a different size is to open the **Print Size** list and select the photo size, such as 5" × 7". The **Fit to Page** option from this list makes the photo as large as possible, while still fitting the paper size you chose. As noted earlier, scaling in this way could affect print quality. To resize correctly, see **32** **Change Image Size or Resolution**.

To adjust the photo to fit the print size you select (if not **Actual Size**), the Editor may crop portions of the image. To prevent cropping, disable the **Crop to Fit Print Proportions** option, and then the image will print at the largest size possible within the **Print Size** dimensions you've chosen.

After you select a photo size from the **Print Size** list, the Editor adjusts the photo as best it can to fit that size. Still, you can fine-tune the **Height** and **Width** values as desired.

▶ NOTES

For best results, change the **Print Size** only when the size you select is smaller than the actual print size. To print in a size larger than the image's actual print size, resize the image as described in **32** **Change Image Size or Resolution**.

You can print a photo in a custom size by selecting the **Custom Size** option from the **Print Size** drop-down list and entering the **Height** and **Width** dimensions. Alternatively, if the **Show Bounding Box** option is enabled, you can resize the image by dragging the corners of the bounding box that surrounds the image in the preview window.

3 Or Adjust Scale

You can also set the print size on an image as a percentage of the actual print size by entering a value in the **Scale** box. It's best to choose percentages that make for less awkward fractions. For example, 50% (1/2) or 75% (3/4) scale produces less degradation in the image than 95% (19/20) or 98% (49/50).

▶ NOTE

If you make a rectangular selection (with no feathering) before printing an image, you can enable the **Print Selected Area** option in the **Scaled Print Size** frame to print just the selected area. See **45** **Select a Rectangular or Circular Area**.

36

4 Change Image Position

Typically, the photo prints in the center of the page. To position the photo along the side (so that you can easily cut it) or anywhere else on the paper, disable the **Center Image** option and enter values in the **Position** frame that place the image relative to the **Top** and upper **Left** corner of the paper. A 1-inch **Top** value, for example, places the image 1" from the top of the page; –.5 places the image 1/2" above the top of the page, essentially cropping off the top of the image and not printing it.

▶ **TIP**

You can also reposition the image on the page by disabling the **Center Image** option and then dragging the image inside the preview area.

5 Select Printer Profile

Assuming that you've calibrated your monitor (see **64** Install a Color Profile), you've done half of what you need to do to ensure that the image you see onscreen is what you get when you print. To print properly, Photoshop Elements needs to know which printer profile you want to use, so it can match up the colors in your monitor profile with those in the printer profile you select from the **Printer Profile** list. To see this list, make sure that the **Show More Options** check box is enabled.

For best results, choose your printer's specific ICC color profile, or a profile designed for the photo paper you're using, *and* disable printer color management through the printer driver, whose icon is located in the Windows **Control Panel**.

In the absence of a printer color profile, your next best bet is choosing **Printer Color Management**, which assumes that your printer driver has its own color management routine (most photo printers do) and that *it's turned on*. If you don't like these results, try choosing **Adobe RGB**, with the printer driver's color management *turned off*. When you can't specify a specific printer profile to use, you can determine the methodology suited for approximating colors that don't exist in the printer's color space by choosing that methodology from the **Rendering Intent** list.

▶ **NOTE**

Whatever you do, *do not* choose your monitor's color profile (the one you created using Adobe Gamma in **64** Install a Color Profile) from the **Printer Profile** list because you are trying to select the color spectrum intended for your *printer* and not for your monitor.

6 Set Other Options

Enable the **Show More Options** check box to display all options related to printing, then select from among these additional options:

- Add a border around your image by enabling the **Border** option, setting the size, and then clicking the **Choose border color** box to select a color using the **Color Picker**.

▶ NOTE

When you change the width of the **Border** option to any value above **0**, the Editor scales the print size *down* to compensate. This can result in loss of print quality. You can adjust **Scale** back to 100%, but if you're working with a large image or with small paper, you could conceivably push the border off the edge of the page. Be sure to check the preview in the **Print Preview** dialog box to make sure that your image size is what you intend and that your bounding box falls completely within the page edges.

- To print crop marks (tiny **X**s at the corners) that can help you trim the image after it's printed, enable the **Print Crop Marks** check box.

- Print the image **File Name** or text **Caption** just below the photo by selecting the corresponding options. See **16** **Add a Text Caption or Note**.

- To flip the image so that you can print it backward onto iron-on transfer paper, enable the **Invert Image** option in the **Transfer Printing** frame. This way, when you iron the image onto your t-shirt, sweatshirt, or other material, the image will look correct.

- To rotate the image on the paper, click the **Rotate 90° Left** or **Rotate 90° Right** button below the preview window. When you do this, even though the upper-left corner of the image might be shifted to a different corner, the **Position** of the image remains relative to the upper-left corner of the area being printed.

7 Select Printer Options and Print

Click the **Print** button to display the **Print** dialog box. Because you selected your printer, paper type and page size in step 2, click **OK** to print the image.

---

37 **Print a Contact Sheet**

✔ BEFORE YOU START	→ SEE ALSO
64 Install a Color Profile	**36** Print an Image
	38 Print a Picture Package

37

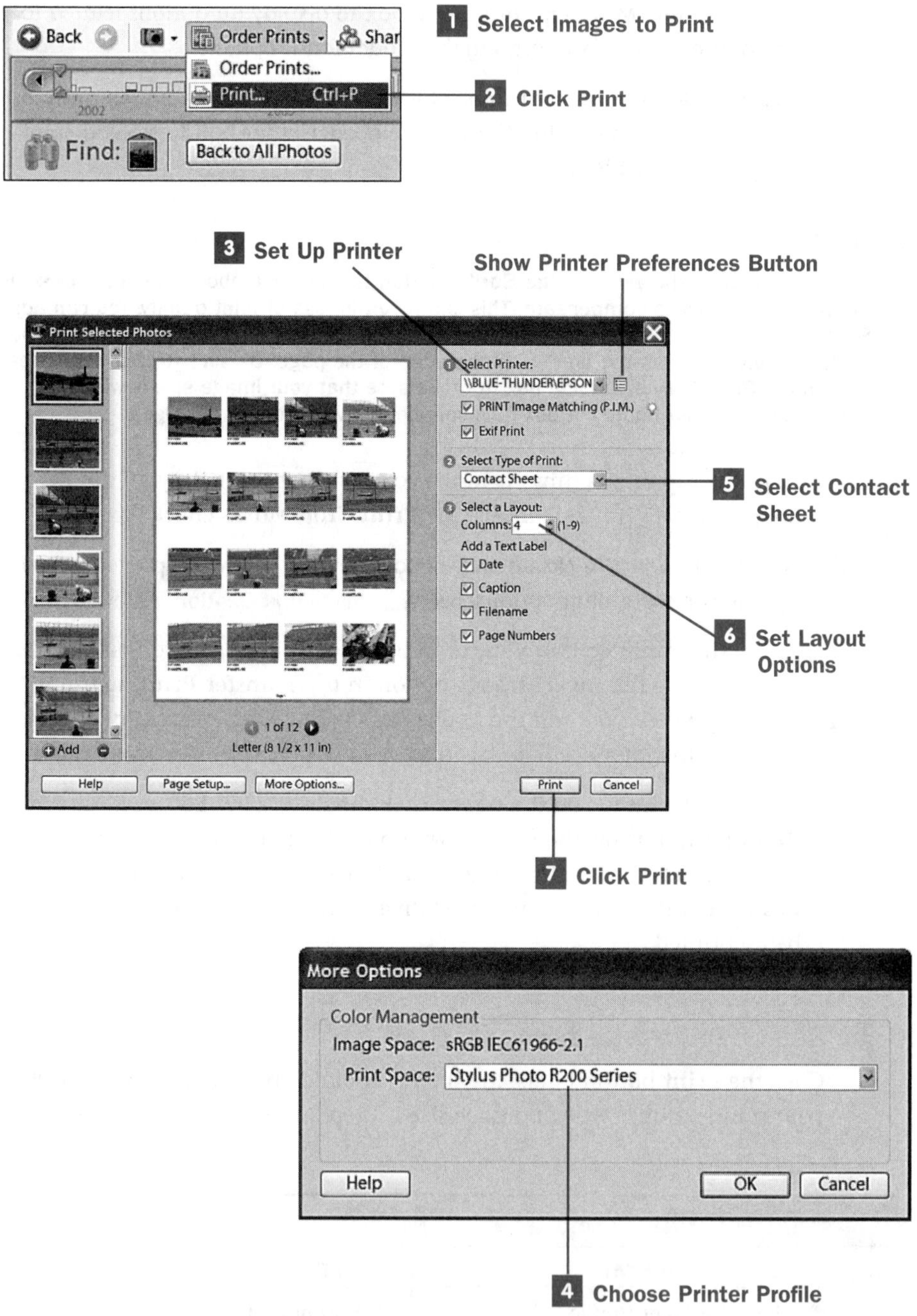
1 Select Images to Print
2 Click Print
3 Set Up Printer
Show Printer Preferences Button
5 Select Contact Sheet
6 Set Layout Options
7 Click Print
4 Choose Printer Profile
Back
Order Prints
Order Prints...
Print... Ctrl+P
Find:
Back to All Photos
Print Selected Photos
Select Printer:
\\BLUE-THUNDER\EPSON
PRINT Image Matching (P.I.M.)
Exif Print
Select Type of Print:
Contact Sheet
Select a Layout:
Columns: 4 (1-9)
Add a Text Label
Date
Caption
Filename
Page Numbers
1 of 12
Letter (8 1/2 x 11 in)
Add
Help
Page Setup...
More Options...
Print
Cancel
More Options
Color Management
Image Space: sRGB IEC61966-2.1
Print Space: Stylus Photo R200 Series
Help
OK
Cancel

37 Print a Contact Sheet

37

After importing a new batch of images into the Organizer, you may want to print a contact sheet so that you can decide which images are worth saving, which ones need work, and which ones are ready to print. A *contact sheet* is a printout of miniature photos or thumbnails, similar to the index sheet you get when you have photos commercially printed. Under each image, you can print its filename, text caption, and file date. Such a reference can make it easy, for example, to verify that the captions, filenames, and dates for your images make sense. You can use a contact sheet to quickly mark any information that seems wrong or incomplete so that you can later change it in the catalog. See **16** **Add a Text Caption or Note** and **11** **Change Image Date and Time** for help.

▶ KEY TERM

Contact sheet—A printout of a group of images, in miniature thumbnails, along with identifying labels.

1 Select Images to Print

In the Organizer, press **Shift** and click the first image in the group you want to print, and then click the last image in the contiguous group. Alternatively, click the first image then press **Ctrl** and click each additional image you want to print. If you don't make a selection, all the currently displayed images in the photo well are prepared for printing, along with any videos (the first frame of which will be printed).

▶ TIPS

If the catalog is sorted by batch or folder, you can click the gray bar above a group to select all the items in that group. To display a group of related images, such as all the images of your son or daughter, use the **Find** bar. (See **18** **About Finding Items in the Catalog.**)

You can send open images from the Editor to the Organizer to print on a contact sheet by choosing **File**, **Print Multiple Photos**.

2 Click Print

Click the **Order Prints** button on the **Shortcuts** bar and click **Print** from the menu that appears. You can also select **File**, **Print** from the menu. You may see a warning telling you that your selection contains creations and audio files that will not be printed; click **OK**. You may also see a warning box listing images or video thumbnails of low resolution, and therefore, low print quality. Click **OK** to dismiss the warning and continue. The **Print Selected Photos** dialog box appears.

37

3 Set Up Printer

If you have more than one printer, select your photo printer from the **Select Printer** list. Then click the **Show Printer Preferences** button to display the **Properties** dialog box for your printer. From this dialog box, you can select the type of photo paper you're using and the print quality you desire. Click **OK** to return to the **Print Photos** dialog box.

If you use a PIM-enabled printer, and if the image you want to print contains PIM data (presumably because you captured the image using a PIM-enabled digital camera), enable the **PRINT Image Matching (P.I.M.)** option and/or the **Exif Print** option (see your printer manual for more information on which options to choose). See **63** **About Color Management**.

4 Choose Printer Profile

Assuming that you've calibrated your monitor (see **64** **Install a Color Profile**), you've done half of what you need to do to ensure that the image you see onscreen is what you get when you print. To print properly, Photoshop Elements needs to know which printer profile you want to use, so it can match up the colors in your monitor profile with those in the printer profile you select. Click the **More Options** button and select the profile to use from the **Print Space** dialog box and click **OK**.

For best results, choose your printer's specific ICC color profile, or a profile designed for the photo paper you're using, *and* disable printer color management through the printer driver, whose icon is located in the Windows **Control Panel**.

In the absence of a printer color profile, your next best bet is choosing **Printer Color Management**, which assumes that your printer driver has its own color management routine (most photo printers do) and that *it's turned on*. If you don't like these results, try choosing **Adobe RGB**, with the printer driver's color management *turned off*.

▶ **NOTE**

Whatever you do, *do not* choose your monitor's color profile (the one you created using Adobe Gamma in **64** **Install a Color Profile**) from the **Printer Profile** list because you are trying to select the color spectrum intended for your *printer* and not for your monitor.

5 Select Contact Sheet

Open the **Select Type of Print** drop-down list and select **Contact Sheet**. The selected images are arranged as small thumbnails on as many pages as needed to meet the other options you select. To review the images on other pages, use the left and right arrows below the preview window.

37

▶ NOTES

To exclude a low-resolution image, select it from the pane on the far left side of the **Print Photos** dialog box and press the **Delete** key or click the **Remove Selected Items** button (the minus sign). This action does not remove the image from the catalog, just from the contact sheet you are setting up to print.

To add an image, click the **Add** button, select the images to add from the **Add Photos** dialog box, and click **OK**.

6 Set Layout Options

Control the size of each image by changing the number of thumbnails you want to appear in each row of the contact sheet by changing the **Columns** value.

Choose whether you want to display the **Date**, **Caption**, and **Filename** below each image by enabling the appropriate check boxes. You can also print the **Page Numbers** on each page of a multipage printout.

7 Click Print

To print the contact sheet using the options you have selected, click **Print**.

38

38	Print a Picture Package
✔ **BEFORE YOU START**	→ **SEE ALSO**
64 Install a Color Profile	**36** Print an Image

When you order prints from a professional photo lab, you're generally offered package deals where you can choose from multiple sizes of prints. To make the deal more economical, the lab lays out the different photo sizes on as few sheets of photo paper as possible, minimizing waste. The Organizer gives you similar options—the difference here being that you're doing the printing yourself. A *picture package* enables you to make maximum use of store-bought premium photo paper (generally 8 1/2" × 11") so that you can print various-sized photos of the same image or of multiple images, all at the same time. Some sizes may be rotated 90 degrees on the printed page to make room for other sizes. The program leaves enough margin between photos for you to cut between them with scissors.

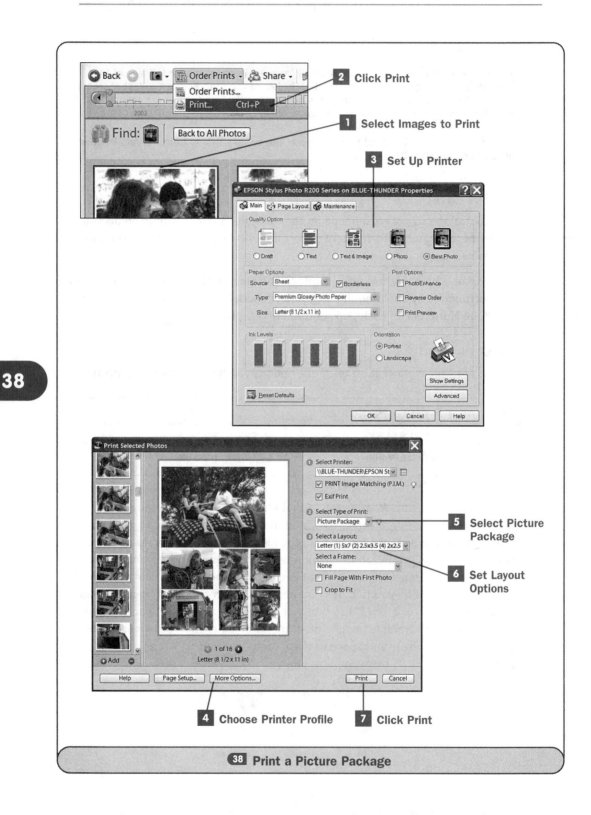

38 Print a Picture Package

▶ KEY TERM

Picture package—Multiple copies of one or more photographs, printed on a single sheet of paper, using standard print sizes such as 8.5" × 11", 5" × 7", and wallet.

1 Select Images to Print

In the Organizer, press **Shift** and click the first image in the group you want to print, and then click the last image in the contiguous group. Alternatively, click the first thumbnail, then press **Ctrl** and click each additional image you want to print. If you don't make a selection, all the currently displayed images in the photo well are prepared for printing, along with any videos (the first frame of which will be printed).

▶ TIPS

If the catalog is sorted by batch or folder, you can click the gray bar above a group to select all the items in that group. To display a group of related images, such as all the images of your son or daughter, use the **Find** bar. (See **18** About Finding Items in the Catalog.)

You can send open images from the Editor to the Organizer to print in a picture package, as well as a contact sheet, by choosing **File, Print Multiple Photos**.

38

2 Click Print

Click the **Order Prints** button on the **Shortcuts** bar and click **Print** from the menu that appears. You can also select **File, Print** from the menu. You might see a warning telling you that your selection contains creations and audio files that will not be printed; click **OK**. The **Print Selected Photos** dialog box appears.

3 Set Up Printer

If you have more than one printer, select your photo printer from the **Select Printer** list. You might also see a warning box listing images or video thumbnails of low resolution, and therefore, low print quality. Click **OK** to dismiss the warning and continue. Then click the **Show Printer Preferences** button to display the **Properties** dialog box for your printer. From this dialog box, you can select the type of photo paper you're using and the print quality you desire. Click **OK** to return to the **Print Photos** dialog box.

If you use a PIM-enabled printer, and if the image you want to print contains PIM data (presumably because you captured the image using a PIM-enabled digital camera), enable the **PRINT Image Matching (P.I.M.)** option and/or the **Exif Print** option (see your printer manual for more information on which options to choose). See **63** About Color Management.

4 Choose Printer Profile

Assuming that you've calibrated your monitor (see 64 **Install a Color Profile**), you've done half of what you need to do to ensure that the image you see onscreen is what you get when you print. To print properly, Photoshop Elements needs to know which printer profile you want to use, so it can match up the colors in your monitor profile with those in the printer profile you select. Click the **More Options** button, select the profile to use from the **Print Space** dialog box, and click **OK**.

For best results, choose your printer's specific ICC color profile, or a profile designed for the photo paper you're using, *and* disable printer color management through the printer driver, whose icon is located in the Windows **Control Panel**.

In the absence of a printer color profile, your next best bet is choosing **Printer Color Management**, which assumes that your printer driver has its own color management routine (most photo printers do) and that it's turned on. If you don't like these results, try choosing **Adobe RGB**, with the printer driver's color management turned off.

38

▶ **NOTE**

Whatever you do, *do not* choose your monitor's color profile (the one you created using Adobe Gamma in 64 **Install a Color Profile**) from the **Printer Profile** list because you are trying to select the color spectrum intended for your *printer* and not for your monitor.

5 Select Picture Package

Open the **Select Type of Print** drop-down list and select **Picture Package**. The selected images are arranged in the standard package: one 3" × 5" print of each image on as many pages as needed to print all the images you've selected. To review the images on other pages, use the left and right arrows below the preview window.

▶ **TIPS**

You can drag and drop images from the strip on the left side of the dialog box to fill any vacancies in the picture package layout. If a picture was placed on the layout in a size you don't want it to be, just drag a different photo onto that location in the preview window.

To exclude a low-resolution image, select it from the pane on the far left side of the **Print Photos** dialog box and press the **Delete** key or click the **Remove Selected Items** button (the minus sign). This action does not remove the image from the catalog, just from the picture package you are setting up to print.

To add an image, click the **Add** button, select the images to add from the **Add Photos** dialog box, and click **OK**.

6 Set Layout Options

To select a different picture package, open the **Select a Layout** list and choose the picture package layout you want to use. This list features all the layout possibilities for your current printer paper size. Each entry in the list shows the quantity and size of the images that will be printed per page. For example, if your paper size is listed as 4" × 6", you might see entries such as 2.1" × 2.8" or 4" × 6".

You can add a picture frame border around each image by choosing one from the **Select a Frame** list.

To print each photo multiple times using the picture package layout you've chosen, check the **Fill Page with First Photo** option.

To crop photos so that they exactly fit the photo sizes you've selected, check the **Crop to Fit** option. (This option is not available with all layouts.)

▶ NOTES

The Organizer crops equal amounts of content from opposite sides of an image where necessary for certain sizes to make that image fit the proportions of that size. For certain packages, you might notice that some sizes are cropped more than others.

You can print photo labels by choosing **Labels** from the **Select Type of Print** list in step 5, instead of **Contact Sheet**. Select the type of label to use from the **Select a Layout** list. If you've selected multiple images, you can arrange them on the label pages however you like. Adjust the alignment of the photos to the label page using the **Offset Print Area** settings.

7 Click Print

To print the photos using the package options you've selected, click **Print**.

39

39 Print Images Using an Online Service

→ SEE ALSO

42 Share Images Using Email
43 Share Images Using an Online Service

If you don't have a photo printer or a printer capable of printing on photo paper, or you're looking for professional results, you can link directly from the Organizer or the Editor to Adobe Photoshop Services (an online service), upload your images, have the service print the images (perhaps with professional corrections), and ship you the results—in some cases, by next-day air!

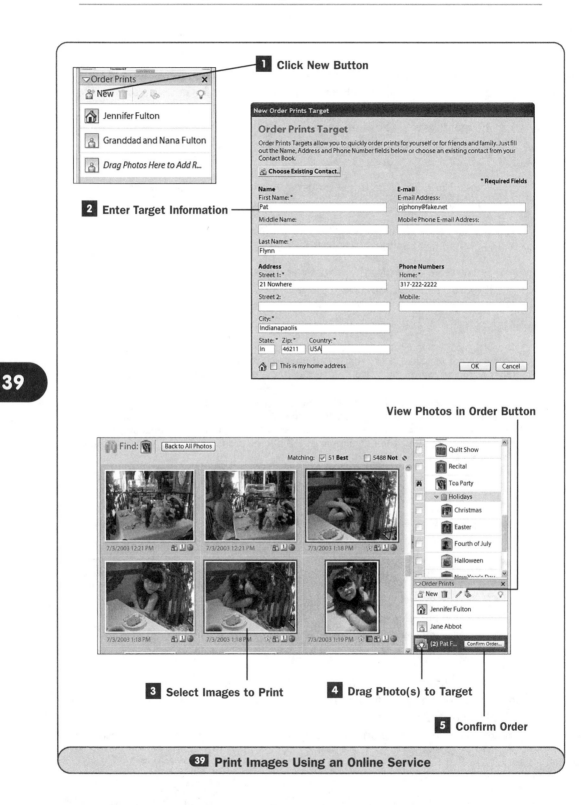

1 Click New Button

2 Enter Target Information

View Photos in Order Button

3 Select Images to Print

4 Drag Photo(s) to Target

5 Confirm Order

39 Print Images Using an Online Service

Before printing, however, you should prepare your images properly: Select each image in the Organizer, send it to the Editor, save the file in PSD format, and make any necessary improvements to the image's color, contrast, saturation, and sharpness. Resize the image as needed to ensure that its print size matches the size you want to use when printing, and that it has a high-enough resolution to produce a good quality print. See **32 Change Image Size or Resolution** for help. Finally, save a copy of your image in a shareable format you can upload to an online service, such as TIFF or JPEG.

The simplest way to order prints from an online service is to use the **Order Prints** palette. There, you set up various *targets* (people to whom you want to ship the finished prints), and then simply drag and drop photos from the Organizer catalog onto a target—so that most of the order information is already completed for you!

■ Click New Button

If you have not set up a target for the person to whom you want the photos sent, do that now. On the **Order Prints** palette, click the **New** button. (To display the palette, choose **Window, Order Prints**.) The **New Order Prints Target** dialog box appears.

■ Enter Target Information

Enter information for the chosen target, completing at least all the required fields (those marked with an asterisk). If you enter other information such as an email address or mobile phone email, this data is added to the **Contact Book** so that you can use it to email photos at a later time.

If this person is already in your **Contact Book**, click **Choose Existing Contact**, select a contact, and click **OK** to copy the contact's information into the dialog box. See **41 Manage Contacts**. Click **OK** to save the target. The target appears alphabetically with those listed in the **Order Prints** palette.

▶ TIPS

If you're setting up yourself as a target, enable the **This is my home address** option, which causes your name to appear with a special house icon at the top of the **Order Prints** palette instead of alphabetically by last name. If you enable this option for more than one target, the targets will appear at the top of the palette, listed alphabetically by last name.

To change a target's information, select the target in the **Order Prints** palette and click the **Edit** button (the pencil icon).

3 **Select Images to Print**

After you've prepared each image for printing, in the Organizer, press **Shift** and click the first image in the group you want to upload for printing, and then click the last image in the contiguous group. Alternatively, click the first image, press **Ctrl**, and click each additional image you want to upload for printing.

4 **Drag Photo(s) to Target**

Drag the selected photo(s) to the **Order Prints** palette, and drop them on the icon for the target to which you want them shipped. You can select other photos, and then drag and drop them to the target as needed.

5 **Confirm Order**

When you're ready to send the selected photos to the online service, click the **Confirm Order** button next to the target on the **Order Prints** palette. You'll be asked to register for the service, providing your email address and password to use. After you register, you can log on to the online service, then select the print sizes you want for each photo, enter your billing and shipping information, and place the order.

After the images are uploaded, a confirmation screen appears, displaying your order number and an order summary. You'll also receive an email message confirming your order and providing a delivery date. Now simply wait for your selected delivery service to deliver your prints!

▶ **TIPS**

To preview the photos you've collected before you confirm your order, select the target in the **Order Prints** palette and click the **View Photos in Order** button.

You can also order prints by selecting images in the Organizer (or opening images in the Editor) and choosing **File**, **Order Prints** or (in the Organizer) clicking the **Order Prints** button on the **Shortcuts** bar.

You can print an existing creation using an online service by clicking the **Order Prints** button. Send a new creation to Adobe Photoshop Services by clicking the **Order Online** button on the **Step 5: Share** page of the **Creation Wizard**. Certain creation types (such as a slide show) cannot be uploaded to an online service for printing.

39

---

40 | **About Emailing**

→ **SEE ALSO**

41 Manage Contacts

42 Share Images Using Email

Photoshop Elements can use Microsoft Outlook, Outlook Express, or Adobe's own *email client* to send photos to anyone you like. After initiating the email sharing process from within the Editor or the Organizer, the Organizer prepares the photos for sending, identifies them as email attachments, and even packages them in an email message with a fancy background if you like. It then hands off the process of emailing to your email client. If you use an independent program such as Eudora or AOL Mail, you can still use Photoshop Elements to prepare your images for sending and then manually attach them to an email.

▶ **KEY TERM**

Email client—A program that sends and receives email. Popular email clients/programs include Outlook and Outlook Express.

You have several options when sending email. Using Organizer's **Photo Mail** option, you can embed the photos (with or without captions) within a fancy background of your choice, such as picture frames or birthday balloons. If you don't want to embed the photos, you can attach them as files to the email message instead. When you chose this option, you can opt to convert the images to JPEG and compress them. In addition, you can set the compression level (quality) of the image files. If you increase the quality, you lower the compression, making the files larger and a bit more difficult to send and receive. It's best to choose a happy median—slightly smaller files with acceptable quality. If you don't want to compress the images, you can choose to send them as is. As a final option, instead of embedding the images or attaching the image files, you can choose to bundle the images in a PDF slideshow and attach that to the message. Again, you can choose the quality (compression level) of the slide show images or incorporate them into the slide show as is.

▶ **NOTE**

Some email programs transmit only text. If so, Photoshop Elements might not be able to embed pictures in email messages using its fancy collection of layouts and formats. It will, however, create email attachments and prompt you to attach the files manually to a text message.

You can send also send a creation, but just one at a time. Note that you cannot send photos at the same time you're sending a creation. You can, however, send

40

photos, video files, and audio files in one message if you like. The Organizer can help you keep track of recipient's email addresses using its **Contact Book**, or you can skip the process of selecting recipients when you send photos and use your email client's address book after the email message is packaged by the Organizer. See **41** **Manage Contacts**.

Before you begin emailing with Photoshop Elements, you need to designate the email client you want to use. In the Organizer, choose **Edit**, **Preferences**, **Sharing**. Choose the email client to use from the **E-Mail Client** list: Microsoft Outlook, Outlook Express, or Adobe E-Mail Service. By enabling the **Write E-mail captions to catalog** option, you can also tell Organizer to write the captions you type under particular images while creating a Photo Mail message to the catalog with the appropriate image.

Use this dialog box to make Photoshop Elements ready for emailing.

41	**Manage Contacts**
✔ **BEFORE YOU BEGIN**	→ **SEE ALSO**
40 About Emailing	**42** Share Images Using Email

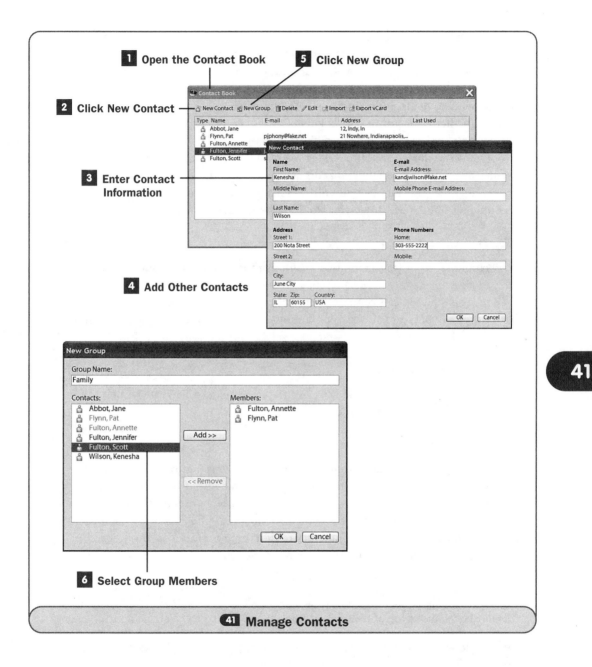

1 Open the Contact Book

5 Click New Group

2 Click New Contact

3 Enter Contact Information

4 Add Other Contacts

6 Select Group Members

41 Manage Contacts

If you regularly send photos to certain individuals or groups, you can keep track of their email addresses in the Organizer **Contact Book**. The **Contact Book** is an address book similar to those you might have in your email client or in other applications that use name and address information, such as Microsoft Word. When sending items using email, sharing them through an online service, uploading items for printing (and later sharing), or sending photos to a cell phone or other device, you can use the addresses already entered in your **Contact Book** to designate who should receive the photos or be notified that you want to share them online. Although you can always enter addresses through your email client after the associated email notifications have been created, it's a lot easier to set up at least the few people you regularly send items to in the **Contact Book**.

1 Open the Contact Book

From the Organizer menu, select **Edit**, **Contact Book**. The **Contact Book** dialog box opens. If you have already added contacts to the book, the names and email addresses of those people are listed in the dialog box in alphabetical order. The icons in the **Type** column tell you whether the contact is an individual or a group.

41

2 Click New Contact

To add a new individual to your **Contact Book**, click the **New Contact** button. The **New Contact** dialog box opens.

3 Enter Contact Information

Enter the person's **First Name** and **Last Name**, and **E-Mail Address**. If you think you might want photos you've had printed online sent directly to this person, enter the contact's street address and phone numbers to save you from having to enter it later. If you'd like to email photos to this person's mobile phone, enter the contact's **Mobile Phone E-mail Address**. Click **OK**. The name and contact information are added to the **Contact Book**.

▶ TIPS

To import addresses you have already entered in your Outlook mail client, click the **Import** button at the top of the **Contact Book**.

Be sure to add yourself to the **Contact Book** so that you can easily upload images to Adobe PhotoShop Services for printing and sharing.

To change a contact's email address, open the **Contact Book**, select the contact from the list, and click **Edit**. (If the contact is set up as a print target on the **Order Prints** palette, you'll need to edit it there, and not in the **Contact Book**. See **39** Print Images Using an Online Service.) To delete a contact, select it and click **Delete**. Click **OK**.

4 Add Other Contacts

Repeat steps 2 and 3 to add other names to the **Contact Book**.

5 Click New Group

To create a group of related email addresses, such as the addresses of your parents and siblings, click the **New Group** button. The **New Group** dialog box opens.

6 Select Group Members

In the **Group Name** box, type a name for the group such as **Family**. All the names currently in your **Contact Book** appear in the **Contacts** list on the left side of the **New Group** dialog box. Select any or all of these names (press **Ctrl** or **Shift** to make multiple selections). Click the **Add** button. The names are added to the **Members** column on the right side of the dialog box. When you're finished adding contact names to the group, click **OK**.

The group is added to the **Contact Book**. When sending a message, you can select a group name to send the message to every member in that group. Click **OK** to close the **Contact Book**.

42

---

42 | Share Images Using Email

✔ BEFORE YOU BEGIN	→ SEE ALSO
40 About Emailing **41** Manage Contacts	**18** About Finding Items in the Catalog **43** Share Images Using an Online Service

---

If you have selected your preferred email client in the **Preferences** dialog box, you can send anything you create in Photoshop Elements to anyone who has an email address. Just select what you want to send from the Organizer catalog or open an image in the Editor, decide who to send it to, add a message, and give the order to **Send**. And you can do all this without shutting down or minimizing the Editor or the Organizer window and switching to your email program. You do all the work in Photoshop Elements, and the application then hands off the message to your email client to process and send.

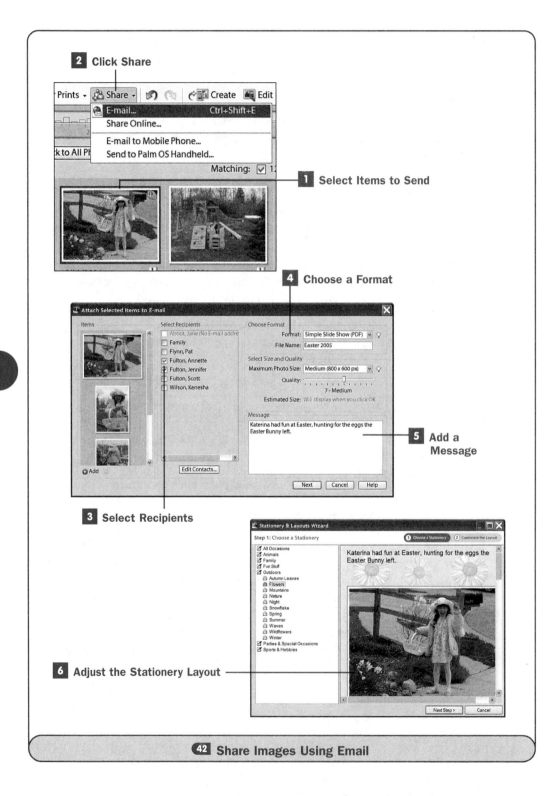

42 Share Images Using Email

6 Adjust the Stationery Layout

7 Send the Email

When you send images, tags are sent as well (with the exception of **Hidden** and **Favorites** tags), so if the recipient uses Photoshop Elements, the images will already be tagged when they import them into their catalogs. In addition to individual pictures, you can send creations such as slide shows, photo albums, postcards, and calendars. You also can include sound and video files with your photos, but not in the same email message as you send creations: Only one creation can be included in an email message, and you can't send it with any other item type.

1 Select Items to Send

In the Organizer catalog, select one or more items to send. To select contiguous items, click the first item, press and hold the **Shift** key, and click the last item in the group. To select noncontiguous items, click the first item, hold the **Ctrl** key, and click each additional item.

▶ TIPS

If no items are selected, all displayed items are included in the email. To send a group of related images, such as the photos of a recent family outing, use the **Find** feature to display them in the catalog (see **18** About Finding Items in the Catalog). If the catalog is sorted by batch or folder, click the gray bar above a group to select every item in a group.

You can send an image from within the Editor by saving it first and then choosing **File**, **Attach to Email**. The **Attach to E-mail** dialog box appears.

2 Click Share

Click the **Share** button on the **Shortcuts** bar. From the menu that opens, select **Email** or **Email to Mobile Phone**. The **Attach Selected Items to E-mail** or **Send to Mobile Phone** dialog box opens. The items you selected to send are displayed on the left.

To email open images from the Editor, choose **File**, **Attach to E-Mail** or click the **Attach to E-Mail** button on the **Shortcuts** bar. If this is your first time emailing photos, you'll be asked to confirm your choice of email client. Do so and click OK.

▶ TIP

To send a creation immediately after making it, click the **Email** button in the last step of the **Creations Wizard**.

3 **Select Recipients**

In the **Select Recipients** section of the dialog box, check one or more of the names in your **Contact Book** to identify those you want to receive the message.

If a recipient's name doesn't appear on this list, click the **Edit Contacts** button to add the name to your **Contact Book**. See **41** **Manage Contacts** for details of how to add a contact.

▶ **TIPS**

You do not have to designate recipients at this stage. If you are using Outlook or Outlook Express, you can add recipients using the address book of your email client in step 7.

If you forgot an item you wanted to send, click the **Add** button at the bottom left. Select the items to add and click **OK**.

If you've set up Photoshop Elements *not* to use an email client (such as Outlook) but to instead save email attachments directly to the hard disk (choose **Edit**, **Preferences**, **Sharing**, **E-mail Settings** to access these options), then skip step 3. One reason you'd do this is because you want to use your web mail client (such as YahooMail or GMail) or AOL, and not Adobe, Outlook, or Outlook Express. In step 4, you can choose a slide show or file attachments, and set the quality (photo size) you want. The images or PDF file is then prepared and placed in the folder you designated in your preferences.

42

4 **Choose a Format**

If you are sending a creation, it will be converted to PDF format before sending. Enter a **File Name** for the resulting file and select a **Size and Quality** option.

If you're emailing to a mobile phone, the images are converted to JPEG and attached as individual files in the **Maximum Photo Size** you set. You can choose a similar option when sending to a regular email address by selecting **Individual Attachments** from the **Format** list. Enable the **Convert Photos to JPEGs** option to have the Organizer compress the attachments using JPEG compression and the **Maximum Photo Size** and **Quality** you choose. If you don't convert the images, they are attached to the email as is. Because some email systems place limits on the file sizes they will handle, try to send small files whenever possible so that you do not exceed that limit.

If you're sending images, audio files, or video files to a regular email address (no creations), you can embed them in a fancy background. Open the **Format** list and choose **Photo Mail (HTML)**. To include captions from the catalog, select **Include Captions**.

▶ **NOTE**

Aware that viruses are often planted with embedded graphics, some email systems strip the illustrations from HTML mail and send them as attachments instead.

If you're sending just images to a regular email address, you can combine that can be played on the recipient's computer using Adobe Reader. Select **Simple Slideshow (PDF)**. Type a **File Name** for the file. Adjust the quality of the resulting slide show by selecting a **Maximum Photo Size** and **Quality**.

5 **Add a Message**

If you want to include a message to the people who are receiving the selected items, type it in the **Message** text box. Click **Next**.

6 **Adjust the Stationery Layout**

If you are using the **Photo Mail** format, the message appears in the **Stationery & Layouts Wizard**. Select the stationery to use from those listed on the left. Click **Next Step**, and set options to customize the stationery (such as text font, background color, borders, and layout). For images that don't have a caption, click **Enter caption here** under the image and type a description. These captions are saved to the catalog if you set that option in the **Preferences** dialog box, as explained in **40** **About Emailing**. Click **Next**.

7 **Send the Email**

Organizer prepares the images, creates the message, and hands the result to your email client. At this point, you can do anything the email program allows, including adding or subtracting recipients and editing the message text. Click **Send** to send the email.

▶ **NOTES**

Photoshop. You might want to take this opportunity to replace it with something more personal.

If any items you selected were not embedded in the email message or attached for you, you can attach them yourself. Follow the steps for adding attachments using your particular email client. For example, both of the Outlook programs have an **Attach** button. Click it to select the files to attach.

42

43 Share Images Using an Online Service

→ **SEE ALSO**

39 Print an Image Using an Online Service

42 Send Images Using Email

As you learned in **42** **Share Images Using Email**, you can use email to quickly send photos to friends and family members, as long as the photos are small enough to travel through the Internet mail system without being rejected by an email server. Small files, particularly if they're compressed for transmission, often leave much to be desired in terms of quality. An additional problem with email is that not everyone has an email connection at home, and many people rely on the service they have available at work. Receiving your pictures on office email systems does not always go over well with employers.

An alternative is to post your pictures on the World Wide Web using Adobe Photoshop Services with Kodak EasyShare Gallery. There, you can display pictures in larger sizes and at higher resolution. Your recipients can check out your images at times convenient to them; using a web browser to view images is much easier for most people than dealing with an email client. Your photos are secure because you decide with whom to share them. If they want, visitors can select images for printing by Kodak.

43

▶ **NOTES**

Rather than upload your images to Kodak's EasyShare Gallery to share them, you can create an **HTML Photo Gallery**. Most web service providers will let you have a bit of free space for storing files to share. An **HTML Photo Gallery** creation will take your images and build a series of interlinked web pages for you, featuring thumbnails of your images, with links to larger versions. If you don't want to post the pages on the Web or you're not sure how, you can always copy the web pages and supporting folders to a CD instead. The pages will make it easy for even a novice to browse through the images on the CD, using his web browser. See **17** **Make a Creation**.

Another way to share images is with a slideshow, which can also be copied to a CD for sharing. If you create a series of slideshows, you can organize them all on a VCD, which is playable on a DVD player.

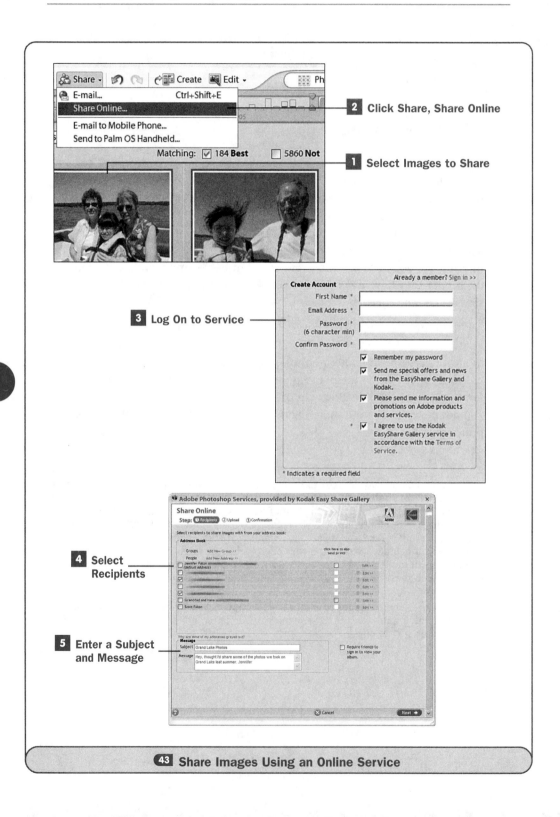

43

2 Click Share, Share Online

1 Select Images to Share

3 Log On to Service

4 Select Recipients

5 Enter a Subject and Message

43 Share Images Using an Online Service

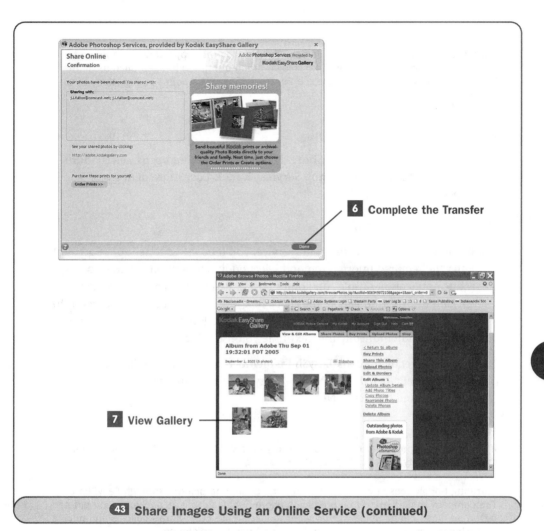

6 Complete the Transfer

7 View Gallery

43

43 Share Images Using an Online Service (continued)

1 Select Images to Share

In the Organizer, review the images you want to share and edit them as needed so that they look their best. You might also want to give each image a text caption to help identify and explain it when people visit your online gallery (see **16** Add a Text Caption or Note).

When you're ready, select the images you want to share. To select a single image, click it. To select multiple images, click the first one, press and hold the **Ctrl** key, and click each additional thumbnail. To select a range of contiguous images, click the first image, press and hold the **Shift** key, and then click the last image of the group.

▶ **TIP**

If the catalog is sorted by batch or folder, you can click the gray bar above a group to select all the items in that group. To display a group of related images, such as all the images of your son or daughter, use the **Find** bar. (See ⑱ **About Finding Items in the Catalog.**)

② Click Share, Share Online

On the **Shortcuts** bar, click **Share**. From the menu that opens, select **Share Online**. The **Adobe Photoshop Services Kodak EasyShare** dialog box appears.

③ Log On to Service

If this is your first time using the service, you'll be asked to set up an account. Enter the required information and select additional options (such as automatic notification of sales and other offers). Read the **Terms of Service** by clicking its link, and enable the check box to indicate that you agree with the terms. Enable the **Remember my password** check box to have the Organizer log you in automatically the next time you use this service.

If you're already a Kodak EasyShare member and you asked that your password be remembered, click **Next**. Otherwise, enter your email address and password, and then click **Next**.

▶ **NOTES**

If you want your password remembered and you forgot to indicate that initially, select the **Remember my password** option when you log in.

Currently, Kodak doesn't charge its customers for sharing pictures through EasyShare. The company makes money on producing photo prints, as well as packages and gift sets based on those prints. Still, you may want to investigate EasyShare's policies and pricing through its website (http://www.easyshare.com) before registering.

④ Select Recipients

On the **Step 1 Recipients** screen, a list of people in your **Contact Book** appears on the left. Enable the check boxes in front of the persons with whom you want to share these photos. You can also order prints of the shared photos for each person you selected (assuming that you've also entered street addresses for those contacts)—just click the **click here to also send prints** check box to the right of their names. If you chose this option, a few extra pages in the wizard appear so that you can select the number of prints and their sizes.

▶ TIPS

If you simply have the email notification sent to you, you can use the addresses already in your email client's address book to forward the message onto your friends and relations.

If you want to see your own online photos, add your own email address to the address list and select your name as one of the recipients in step 4.

To add a new address to the **Contact Book**, click the **Add New Address** link, enter the address data, and click **Next** to return to this screen. If a person's name is grayed out, you must complete her information by clicking **Edit** to the right of her name, entering the rest of the email and address data, and clicking **Next** to return.

5 Enter a Subject and Message

Type a **Subject** and **Message** in the email notification form near the bottom of the dialog box. Click **Next**.

6 Complete the Transfer

To make each invitee join Kodak EasyShare and sign in to view the images, enable the **Require friends to sign in to view your album** option. Without this option, anyone who knows the link to the album web page can view your photos. Click **Next** to upload the images.

After the images are uploaded, the **Confirmation** screen appears, displaying the list of names with whom you shared the photos, and a link to the website.

If you ordered prints, the **Confirmation** screen will include an order summary. Click the **Print this Confirmation** button to print a copy of this page.

Click **Done**. The wizard closes, and you return to the catalog. Recipients will receive email invitations to look at your images.

7 View Gallery

You should receive an email confirming the location of the gallery. Open the email and click the **View Photos** link. Your web browser opens; you're taken to the EasyShare Gallery website. Log in to your account using your email address and password and view a slideshow of the image you just uploaded. You can mark images for printing while reviewing the show if you like.

43

When you're through, click the **View & Edit Albums** tab to review other galleries you've shared. Albums appear as icons; click one to view its images. From there, you can rearrange photos, delete photos, and perform other maintenance tasks including, deleting the album totally.

43

7

Selecting a Portion of an Image

IN THIS CHAPTER:

44 Make Areas of an Image Easier to Select

45 Select a Rectangular or Circular Area

46 Draw a Selection Freehand or by Tracing Its Edge

47 Select Areas of Similar Color

48 Paint a Selection

49 Expand, Shrink, or Add Similar Areas to a Selection

50 Smooth and Soften a Selection

51 Save and Reload a Selection

52 About Copying, Cutting, and Pasting Data Within a Selection

53 Create a New Image or Layer from a Selection

Many of the modifications you make to an image in Photoshop Elements are applied to only a portion of the image. For example, you might want to delete an item from the background or change the color of part of the image. To make modifications to any portion of an image, you must first select the area to change. Selecting an area enables you to make modifications to only that portion of the image without affecting the rest of the image.

In this chapter, you will learn how to make selections using the different selection tools available in Photoshop Elements. You will see that the tool you choose to make selections is based on the type of selection you want to make. You will learn to select geometric portions of the image (such as a rectangle or an oval) or to select specific objects by tracing the object's borders (such as selecting only the light post in front of a house). You will also learn how to select specific portions of the image based on their color, such as selecting only the red balloons in a balloon bouquet. You'll learn how to save selections and then reuse those selections to edit the image. You'll see how selections can be used to create a new image or layer. We'll also show you how data can be pasted directly into a selection.

Regardless of how you select a portion of the image, after you've done that, all the editing commands you then make affect only that portion. So, you can change the color of only the red balloons to blue or use the **Dodge** tool on just the light post without affecting the house. For more information about some of the image-editing commands available to you after making a selection, see **52** **About Copying, Cutting, and Pasting Data Within a Selection.**

---

44   **Make Areas of an Image Easier to Select**

✔ BEFORE YOU BEGIN	→ SEE ALSO
Just jump right in!	**46** Select an Object Freehand or by Tracing Its Edge
	47 Select Areas of Similar Color

Photoshop Elements has tools that can help you select objects in a photo—to pluck them right out of a scene. But those tools only work effectively when they can distinguish the boundaries and periphery of the objects you're trying to isolate. For example, if the lighting was not good when you took the photo, the subject may not be sufficiently distinguished from its background. In such a situation, it would be more difficult for you to use the **Magnetic Lasso** to trace the subject's edge. If you're trying to select an area based on color, and that area doesn't contrast well enough with the surroundings, that can make using the **Magic Wand** tool difficult if not impossible to use. If this is the case, you can use filters to make adjustments that change the area you want to select and make the selection easier.

1 Duplicate the Layer

2 Choose a Filter

3 Adjust Settings

4 Make a Selection

5 Create Editing Layer

6 Make Desired Edits

7 View the Result

In the technique you're about to see, you create a duplicate layer in your image, and apply the **Threshold** filter to convert the new layer's contents to pure black and white. Although that might seem counter-intuitive at first, realize that the borders between pure black and pure white are very easy to ascertain; and once those borders have been found on the duplicate layer, those same boundaries can be applied to the original, full-color layer. With this technique, everything in the duplicate layer whose brightness level falls below a specified level is converted to black; the rest become white. With a similar technique that involves the **Posterize** filter, you specify the number of varying brightness levels you want for the duplicate layer (with the **Threshold** filter, you only have two).

1 Duplicate the Layer

Open an image in the Editor in **Standard Edit** mode and save it in Photoshop (***.psd**) format. In the **Layers** palette, select the layer that contains the data you want to select. If you're working with a single-layer image, this layer is called, by default, the Background layer.

Select **Layer**, **Duplicate Layer** from the menu. Accept the default layer name of **Background copy** and click **OK**. The new layer is added to the **Layers** palette, just above the **Background** layer. See **54** **Create a New Image Layer**.

2 Choose a Filter

In the **Layers** palette, choose the **Background copy** layer. Apply the adjustment that helps isolate the area you want to select: From the menu bar, select **Filter**, **Adjustments**, **Threshold** or **Filter**, **Adjustments**, **Posterize**.

3 Adjust Settings

If you chose the **Threshold** filter, the **Threshold** dialog box appears, displaying a histogram. Specify the threshold level by sliding the pointer below the histogram, or by typing a **Threshold Level** value. In the duplicate layer, all pixels whose brightness fall below this level are changed to black; the rest are made white. You want to make plainly obvious the outline of the object you intend to select. See **91** **About an Image's Histogram** for more information about how a histogram works.

If you chose the **Posterize** filter, type the number of brightness levels you need to thoroughly distinguish the object you want to select from its surroundings. Now, you won't be able to calculate this number in your head, so enable the **Preview** option, try a *low* number (such as **4**) and see what happens. Again, your goal is to make plainly obvious the outline of the object you intend to select.

44

When you're ready to apply your adjustments to the **Background Copy** layer, click **OK**.

4 Make a Selection

With the **Background Copy** layer still active, use any selection tool, or any number of them collectively, to select the region you want. For example, you can select a band of neighboring pixels that are now all the same color or are black or white, using the **Magic Wand** (see **47** Select Areas of Similar Color). Here, I quickly painted a border along the left side of Katie's head, and then clicked twice with the **Magic Wand** to select her head, chest, and right leg which are too dark and need brightening. I feathered the selection so that the adjusted area will blend with the rest of the image.

5 Create Editing Layer

Now that you've selected the region you want to change, in the **Layers** palette, click the eye icon beside **Background Copy** to hide it temporarily, then click the **Background** layer. I make it a habit never to make major edits to the **Background** layer directly, to avoid any chance of losing the information on that layer; for this next step, I'll create another copy of the background layer to which I'll apply my edits. Select **Layer**, **Duplicate Layer**, keep the name **Background Copy 2**, and click **OK**.

6 Make Desired Edits

Here's where you make good use of all your hard work. In the **Layers** palette, choose **Background Copy 2**. Make any change you want to the selected area. Here, I used the **Brightness/Contrast** command to brighten the girl's face, chest, and leg, restoring detail there.

▶ NOTE

If you have no other use for the **Background Copy** layer (the one to which you applied the **Posterize** or **Threshold** filter) at this point, you can delete it. Select the layer and choose **Layer**, **Delete Layer**. However, you can also keep the layer around. As long as its visibility remains turned off, when you save your image in a standard format (*not* Photoshop format) with the **Layers** option disabled, the copy and any other invisible layers won't be merged into the saved copy.

7 View the Result

After you're satisfied with the result, make any other changes you want and save the PSD file. Resave the result in JPEG, PNG, or non-layered TIFF format, leaving your PSD image with its layers (if any) intact so that you can return at a later time and make adjustments if you want.

In this example, I wanted to brighten my daughter's face and body a bit, since she's the subject of this photo. I used the **Threshold** command to quickly isolate the dark areas of her face, chest, and right leg. I feathered the selection and then applied the **Brightness/Contrast** command to lighten the selected areas. The result is subtle, which is what I wanted—I did not want her to shine out like a light bulb. Nonetheless, her concentration and posture as she almost sinks the putt is now much easier to see.

---

45   **Select a Rectangular or Circular Area**

✔ BEFORE YOU BEGIN	→ SEE ALSO
69 About the Toolbox	**46** Draw a Selection Freehand or By Tracing Its Edge

---

You can use the **Marquee Selection** tools to select any rectangular or elliptical area in an image. These are the most common selection tools in this or any other image editing program. But you might be wondering, now that you know you can select *just* the subject of your image or *just* some element you want to remove, why would you *want* to select something that's rectangular or elliptical? Rectangles are the most common shapes for *frames*, ovals the second most common. For example, to apply many of the frame effects on the **Styles and Effects** palette, you must make a selection first.

44

1 Select the Marquee Tool

Open an image in the Editor in **Standard Edit** mode and save it in Photoshop (***.psd**) format. In the **Layers** palette, click the layer that contains the data you want to select. Select the **Rectangular Marquee** or **Elliptical Marquee** tool on the **Toolbox**.

2 Set Options

On the **Options** bar, click the **New Selection** button. Set other options as desired. For example, to soften the edge of your selection, adjust the **Feather** value and turn on the **Anti-aliased** option.

The default **Mode** setting is **Normal**, which means that you control the size of the selection yourself. If you want to specify the proportions of your selection, choose **Fixed Aspect Ratio**. To specify an exact size, choose **Fixed Size** instead. For the **Fixed Aspect Ratio** or **Fixed Size** option, enter the proportions or exact measurements you want (in pixels) in the **Width** and **Height** boxes.

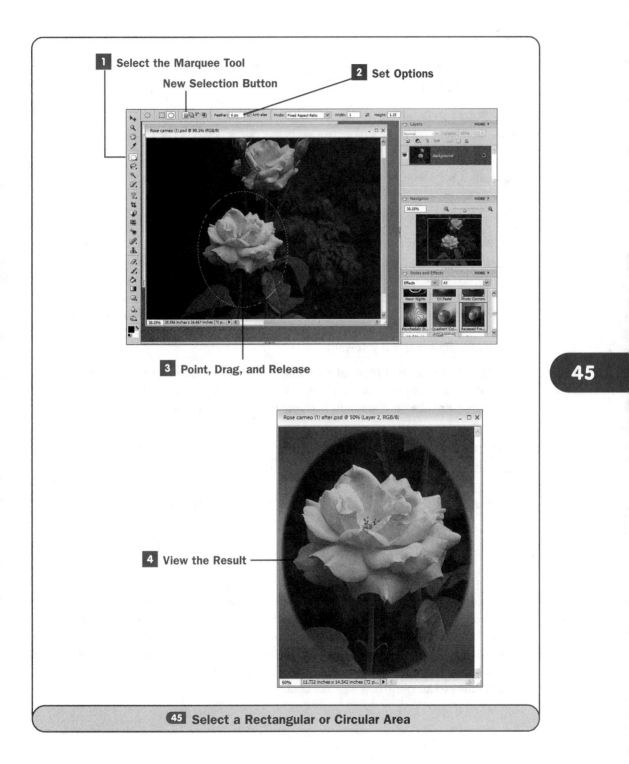

1 Select the Marquee Tool

New Selection Button

2 Set Options

3 Point, Drag, and Release

4 View the Result

45

3 Point, Drag, and Release

Drag to create the selection. If the **Mode** setting is **Fixed Size**, just click without dragging.

▶ TIPS

If you want to create a perfectly square or circular selection instead of a rectangular or elliptical selection, press and hold the Shift key as you drag to create the selection.

To create a circle from the center out, press Alt+Shift as you drag.

4 View the Result

Add to or subtract from the selection using the same **Marquee** tool or a different selection tool. Make changes to the area within the selection, copy or cut it to another image or layer, or delete the data. After you're satisfied with the result, make any other changes you want and then save the PSD file. Resave the result in JPEG, PNG, or non-layered TIFF format, leaving your PSD image with its layers (if any) intact so that you can return at a later time and make adjustments if you want.

Here, I've used the **Elliptical Marquee** tool with feathering set to **6**, to cut a rose out of one photo and paste it into this new, blank layer. I then added a layer painted with a gradient to create a frame for the rose.

---

46   **Draw a Selection Freehand or By Tracing Its Edge**

✔ BEFORE YOU BEGIN	→ SEE ALSO
Just jump right in!	**45** Select a Rectangular or Circular Area
	48 Paint a Selection

The principal reason you'd want to use one of the Editor's lasso tools is so you can select a region in your photograph whose shape does not fit within a rectangle, square, or circle, and also so that you don't select anything else in the photo except for that region. For example, you can use a lasso tool to designate the head of a person or an animal lying on the ground, or a naval destroyer, or even a respectable approximation of the edge of a dandelion puff-ball, while at the same time *excluding* the object's surroundings.

CHAPTER 1
How to Use Layers

You can build a complex image by isolating each element on its own layer.

CHAPTER 1
How to Use Layers

Upper layers can obscure lower layers, depending on their opacity.

CHAPTER 1
Filters, Effects, and Layer Styles

The **Crystallize** filter makes your image look like wavy glass.

CHAPTER 1
Filters, Effects, and Layer Styles

The **Solarize** filter makes your image look like it has been burned into the film.

CHAPTER 1
Filters, Effects, and Layer Styles

The **Stained Glass** filter creates a tiled look for an image.

CHAPTER 1
Filters, Effects, and Layer Styles

With the **Colored Pencil** filter, you can make an image look as if it were hand drawn.

CHAPTER 4
23 Find Items with the Same Date

*Using the Organizer's **Calendar** view, you can quickly locate photos taken on the same day.*

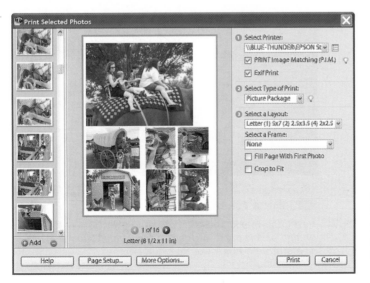

CHAPTER 6
38 Print a Picture Package

The Organizer can help you print multiple photos in multiple sizes, on a single page.

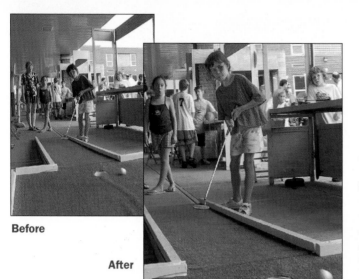

Before

After

CHAPTER 7
44 Make Areas of an Image Easier to Select

*The **Threshold** filter was used to quickly isolate areas of my daughter's face, chest, and right leg so that I could apply a **Brightness/Contrast** adjustment.*

Before

After

CHAPTER 7
46 Draw a Selection Freehand or By Tracing Its Edge

*I used the **Magnetic Lasso** to trace the edges of these Chicago skyscrapers and select the original drab, almost-white sky, replacing it with this more dramatic background.*

CHAPTER 7
48 Paint a Selection

*I used the **Magic Selection Brush** to select the background of this photo with just a few strokes, enabling me to blur it a bit and lower its saturation.*

CHAPTER 8
54 Create a New Image Layer

To this photo of my great-nephew, I added a new layer with the **Clouds** filter and painted a yellow halo and a blue pillow on two other new layers.

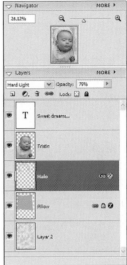

CHAPTER 8
60 Rotate the Data in a Layer or Selection

Using the **Move** tool, I rotated the layer with the flag and then changed the layer's blend mode to **Soft Light** so that it would blend with the red, white, and blue background.

CHAPTER 8
61 Mask an Adjustment or Fill Layer

After applying a **Levels** adjustment to this entire image to brighten it, I masked the adjustment so that it affects only the subject, leaving the background darker and less distracting.

Before

After

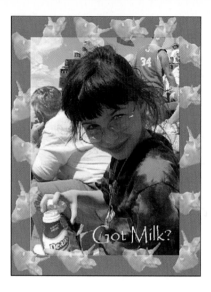

CHAPTER 10
70 Create Your Own Brush Tips

I created a new brush tip from a photo of a calf and used that new tip to create a unique frame for this photo of my daughter enjoying some milk.

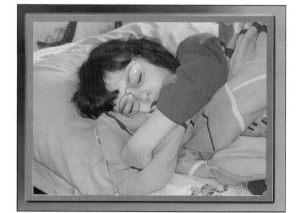

CHAPTER 10
76 Fill an Area with a Gradient

After making a rectangular selection and inverting it, I filled the frame-shaped selection with a gradient comprised of colors that matched the photo.

CHAPTER 10
79 Add a Backscreen Behind Text

Placing a backscreen behind this text made it easier to read against the texture of the sidewalk.

CHAPTER 10
80 Create Metallic Text

*Using the **Brushed Metal** effect and a slight **Hue/Saturation** adjustment, I was able to create golden text for this little princess.*

CHAPTER 10
82 Fill Text with an Image

*Using a photo of fall leaves, I filled a text selection created with the **Horizontal Type Mask** and caught the spirit of this very happy Thanksgiving.*

Before

After

CHAPTER 11
86 Restore Color and Tone to an Old Photograph

*I used the **Levels** command to remove the color cast and improve the contrast in this old photo. I then increased the saturation lost by time, and the result is a lovingly restored old photograph.*

Before

CHAPTER 12
97 Sharpen an Image

*I used the **Unsharp Mask** to sharpen the subject in this photo, where the camera had focused perfectly on the background. I then blurred the background to create an illusion of depth.*

After

CHAPTER 12
98 Blur an Image to Remove Noise

*Because of the long zoom needed to take this image, this photo was filled with noise. To remove it, I tested two different filters: **Smart Blur** and **Reduce Noise**.*

Before

Smart Blur

Reduce Noise

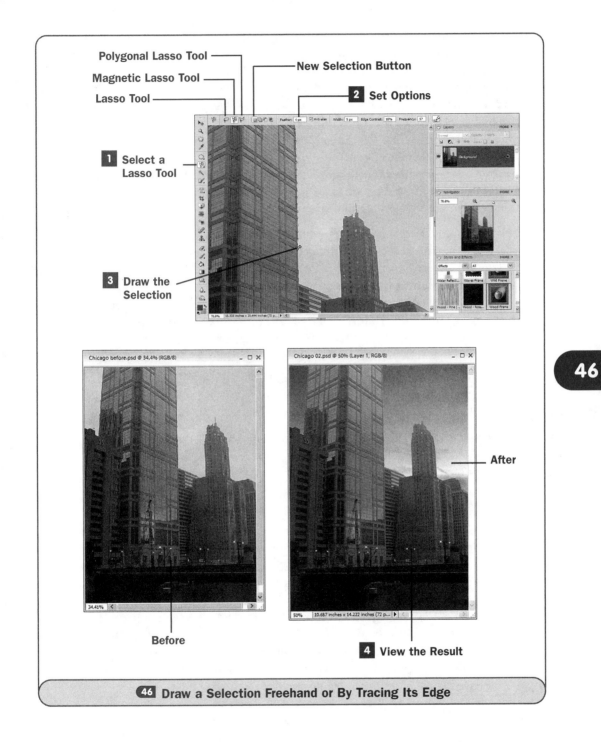

Polygonal Lasso Tool

Magnetic Lasso Tool

Lasso Tool

New Selection Button

2 Set Options

1 Select a Lasso Tool

3 Draw the Selection

After

Before

4 View the Result

46

To use the standard **Lasso** tool, you drag it around the area you want to select as though you're drawing a chalk boundary around it. With patience, you can trace intricate shapes with the **Lasso** tool. However, in the case of objects whose color and shade are clearly distinguished from its surroundings—for example, a grey skyscraper against a clear blue sky—you can use the **Magnetic Lasso** tool. With this tool, the boundary you draw automatically snaps to the edges of objects you drag near. When you use the **Magnetic Lasso** tool, you must specify settings that help Photoshop Elements locate the edges of your object. For example, you can indicate a pixel **Width** value to define the width of the area near where you drag; Photoshop Elements looks in this area to locate the object edge. Photoshop Elements places the selection line along the edge it finds in that search area.

The **Polygonal Lasso** tool becomes most helpful in best-guess scenarios, such as selecting a fuzzball or a cloud or a stream of water, where exact edges won't be ascertained anyway, and it might not matter too much whether you end up selecting indetectably small swatches of sky or background. With the **Polygonal Lasso**, you mark points along the edge of the image that you want to select, and the Editor automatically connects those points with straight lines.

46

1 Select a Lasso Tool

Open an image in the Editor in **Standard Edit** mode and save it in Photoshop (***.psd**) format. In the **Layers** palette, click the layer that contains the data you want to select.

Select the desired lasso tool from the **Toolbox: Lasso**, **Magnetic Lasso**, or **Polygonal Lasso**. The icon for the last lasso tool you used is the one displayed in the **Toolbox**.

2 Set Options

Click the **New Selection** button. Set the desired options for the tool on the **Options** bar, such as **Feather** and **Anti-alias**. If you choose the **Magnetic Lasso** tool, adjust the **Width** (1 to 256 pixels) to the area you want the Editor to look within, in order to identify the edge of the object (pixels whose brightness contrast with their neighbors). The **Edge Contrast** option indicates the amount of contrast to look for, between **1%** and **100%**. If your object has low-contrast edges, use a higher value. The **Frequency** option indicates the rate at which you want the lasso to set the anchor points along the object's edge as you drag. Enter a frequency value between **0** and **100**. Use a higher value to have the Editor set border points more often.

▶ **TIP**

If you are using a pen and drawing tablet, select the **Pen Pressure** option. When this option is enabled, if you increase the pen pressure, the **Width** value increases for the selection.

3 Draw the Selection

The hotspot for each of the lasso tools is the tip of the little loop in the lower-left corner. For the **Lasso** tool, just drag to draw a freehand selection. Make sure that you draw your selection so that it ends at the same point you started. When you release the mouse button, the Editor completes the selection by connecting the start and end of your selection.

For the **Magnetic Lasso** tool, click the location on the image where you want to start your selection. Continue holding down the left mouse button and drag the mouse pointer along the edge of the object to select. The Editor drops selection points along this edge, identifying the edge by looking for high contrast within the **Width** area surrounding where you drag. You can drop a selection point yourself by just clicking. Double-click to connect a selection's starting and ending points.

For the **Polygonal Lasso** tool, click the location on the image where you want to start your selection, move the mouse pointer to where you want to create a corner in the selection, and click again. As you reposition the mouse pointer, a springy line extends between the last anchor point and the mouse pointer so that you can see how the selection line will lay against the area you are selecting. Continue to click to set corner points; double-click to close the selection.

▶ **TIP**

With the **Magic Lasso** or **Polygonal Lasso** tool, you can remove selection points as you drag by simply pressing the **Backspace** key as many times as necessary. Points are removed in reverse order. Removing points allows you to correct a bad selection; for example, if the Editor selected something far from the edge of the object.

4 View the Result

Add to or subtract from the selection using the same **Lasso** tool or a different selection tool. Make changes to the area within the selection, copy or cut it to another image or layer, or delete the data. When you are satisfied with the result, congratulate yourself, then make any other changes you want and save the PSD file. Resave the result in JPEG, PNG, or non-layered TIFF format, leaving your PSD image with its layers (if any) intact so that you can return at a later time and make adjustments if you want.

46

In this example, I used the **Magnetic Lasso** tool to draw the boundaries between these Chicago skyscrapers and the sky. I could have used the **Polygonal Lasso** tool, but I would have missed the faint ridges that make up the texture of the center building; the **Magnetic Lasso** tool found them automatically. Selecting this rather cloudy and, frankly, uninteresting sky enabled me to remove it and replace it with a more striking background.

47   Select Areas of Similar Color

✔ BEFORE YOU BEGIN	→ SEE ALSO
69 About the Toolbox	**46** Draw a Selection Freehand or by Tracing Its Edge
	48 Paint a Selection

Despite its name, don't expect the **Magic Wand** tool to select exactly the region you want in an image with just one touch. The reason is because most things in a digital photograph are not often composed of a single color (although they may seem to be), but rather, several shades of a single color or closely matching colors. Although you might see a landscape composed of leaves, branches, sky, clouds, and water, how Photoshop Elements' Editor sees it is a cluster of pixels of various colors.

46

When you click a pixel in your image with the **Magic Wand** tool, the Editor evaluates neighboring pixels (or all the pixels in the image, if the **Contiguous** option is disabled) for color similarity, the degree of which is based on the **Tolerance** setting you specify in the **Options** bar. For example, if the **Tolerance** value is low, only pixels adjacent to the one you click, whose color values are very similar, are selected. Specify a higher **Tolerance** setting to widen the range of colors that are selected, such as the shadows in the petals of a red rose or variations in the green of the picnic grass. Sometimes you'll need to make these adjustments intermittently while you touch the image with the **Magic Wand** a handful of times, each time building onto the existing selection—or perhaps removing a small portion from it—until its final selection becomes something you can work with.

1   Select Magic Wand Tool

Open an image in the Editor in **Standard Edit** mode and save it in Photoshop (***.psd**) format. In the **Layers** palette, select the layer that contains the data you want to select. Select the **Magic Wand** tool on the **Toolbox**.

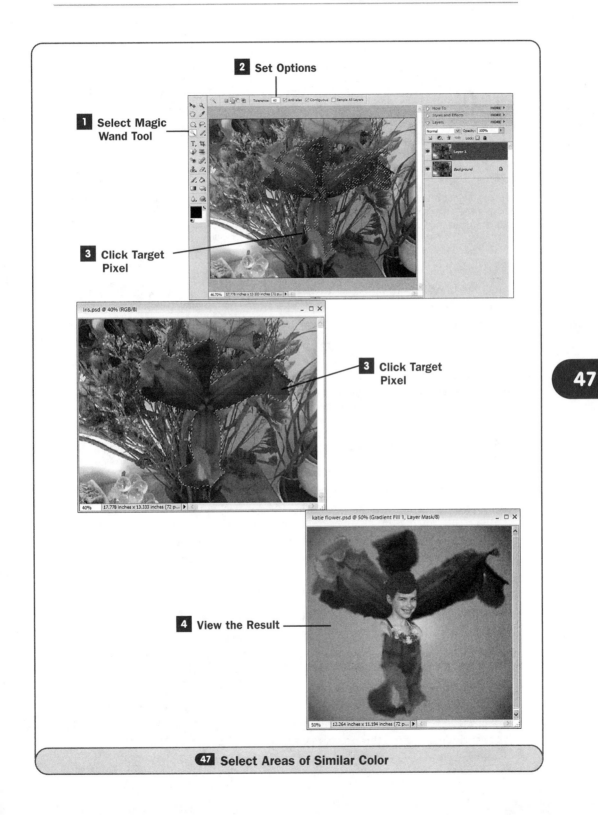

2 Set Options

1 Select Magic Wand Tool

3 Click Target Pixel

3 Click Target Pixel

47

4 View the Result

47 Select Areas of Similar Color

2 Set Options

On the **Options** bar, click the **New Selection** button. Adjust the **Tolerance** value to fit the similarity of the pixels you want to select; with very similar pixels, you can set a low **Tolerance** and still select the area you want with just a few clicks. Set the other options, such as **Anti-aliased, Contiguous,** and **Sample All Layers.** See 69 **About the Toolbox.**

▶ TIP

You can select all pixels in a layer with an opacity of 50% or higher by pressing **Ctrl** and clicking the layer's thumbnail in the **Layers** palette. To select all pixels, regardless of their transparency, choose **Select, All** from the menu bar.

3 Click Target Pixel

In the image window, locate the point that best exemplifies the pixels you want to select, and click that point. The Editor selects similar pixels in accordance with your option settings.

▶ TIP

You cannot use the **Magic Wand** tool with an image that uses **Bitmap** or **Indexed Color** mode. If you want to use this tool, you must first choose **Image, Mode, Grayscale** or **RGB Color** from the menu bar to convert the image.

4 View the Result

Add to or subtract from the selection using the **Magic Wand** tool or a different selection tool. Make changes to the area within the selection, copy or cut it to another image or layer, or delete the data. When you're satisfied with the result, make any other changes you want and save the PSD file. Resave the result in JPEG, PNG, or non-layered TIFF format, leaving your PSD image with its layers (if any) intact so that you can return at a later time and make adjustments if you want.

In this example, I wanted to isolate the iris from the rest of the bouquet so that I could use it to frame a photo of my daughter. There are several regions of differing hues in this iris, obviously including the deep blues, but also incorporating the light lavenders (which contain a small hint of red tint, optically) and the bright yellows of the stamen. So even with a relatively loose **Tolerance** setting of 40, I still had to select about eight different contiguous regions, and then trim the result using the **Lasso** tool in **Subtract from Selection** mode, especially for the purple daisies along the side that I wanted to exclude. But even this process was faster and less tedious than trying to draw around the perimeter of the iris with the **Magnetic Lasso** tool.

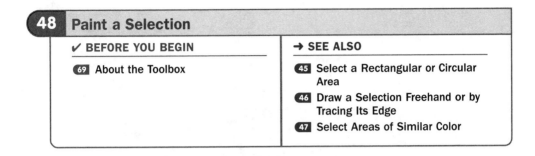

48 Paint a Selection

✔ BEFORE YOU BEGIN

69 About the Toolbox

→ SEE ALSO

45 Select a Rectangular or Circular Area

46 Draw a Selection Freehand or by Tracing Its Edge

47 Select Areas of Similar Color

The Editor's selection brushes work in either of two ways: With the conventional **Selection Brush** tool, whatever your paintbrush touches becomes selected. With the new **Magic Selection Brush** tool, after you've applied your "paint" stroke, the selected region takes on the characteristics of the **Magic Wand** tool (explained in 47 **Select Areas of Similar Color**). All the pixels throughout the image whose color and brightness characteristics are similar to those you brushed are also selected. You could use this tool to select an oddly shaped object, such as a leaf set against the sky, by painting inside of it and then letting the Editor expand the painted region to encompass the entire leaf, right to the edges.

The **Selection Brush** tool can be rigged to work the opposite way, using what the Editor calls **Mask** mode. Here, you paint a mask, represented by a red overlay, over the areas of the image you *do not* want to select. You can switch between **Mask** and **Selection** modes by changing the **Mode** option on the **Options** bar. When the Editor is in **Mask** mode, the mask covers the unselected areas, and the "windows" left open by the red mask overlay reveal the parts of the image ready to be changed with a filter or other adjustment.

▶ **NOTE**

Although the process is similar, the **Mask** mode of the **Selection Brush** tool is not the same kind of mask you paint to protect lower layers from the effects of a fill or adjustment layer. The painted mask is also different from a clipping mask, which you can use to block parts of an upper layer from covering lower layers.

1 Choose the Selection Brush Tool

Open an image in the Editor in **Standard Edit** mode and save it in Photoshop (***.psd**) format. In the **Layers** palette, click the layer that contains the data you want to select. On the **Toolbox**, choose the **Selection Brush**.

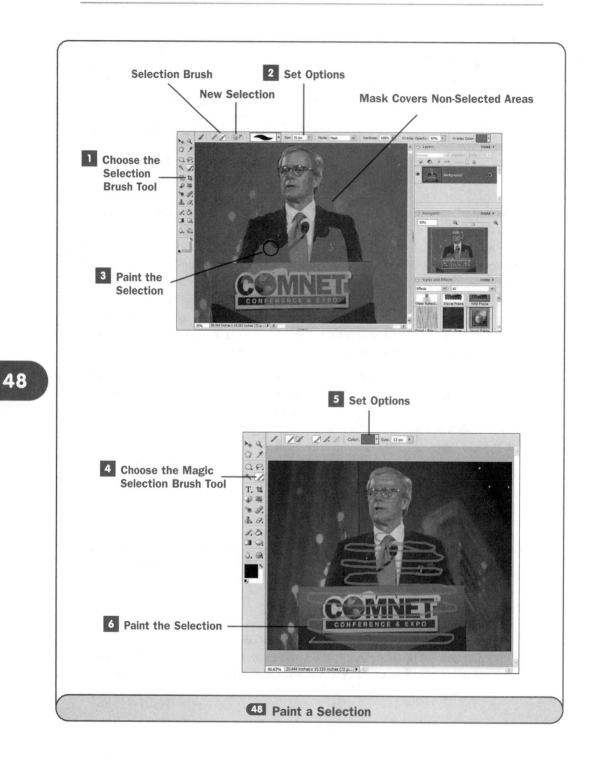

48

48 Paint a Selection

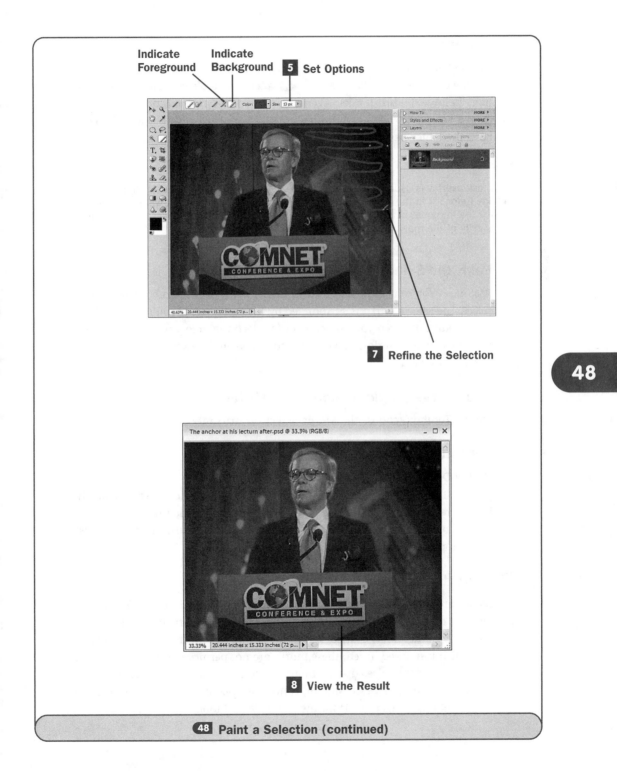

Indicate Foreground

Indicate Background

5 Set Options

7 Refine the Selection

The anchor at his lecturn after.psd @ 33.3% (RGB/8)

8 View the Result

48 Paint a Selection (continued)

48

2 Set Options

On the **Options** bar, choose a brush tip, **Size**, and **Hardness**. A soft round brush works well in most cases. See 🔘 **About the Toolbox** for more information. To have the brush select everything you paint, in the **Mode** list, if you choose **Selection** then everything you paint with the brush is selected; to have the Editor deselect everything the brush paints, choose **Mask**.

▶ TIP

The mask overlay is usually red, but you can select a different mask color from the **Overlay Color** list in the **Options** bar. Typically, you select a color that will stand out against the image so that you can easily identify the masked area. You can also adjust the opacity of the mask with the **Overlay Opacity** value.

3 Paint the Selection

Assuming you're using the **Selection** mode, paint over the area you want to select. The selected area is surrounded by the marquee. If you're using **Mask** mode, paint the area you do *not* want to select; the area you paint is marked by the red mask overlay. You can change between the two modes as needed to select the area you want.

48

4 Choose the Magic Selection Brush Tool

On the **Toolbox**, choose the **Magic Selection Brush** tool.

5 Set Options

On the **Options** bar, you only need to select a brush **Size** because the only purpose the brush serves when you use this tool is to indicate *very roughly* the item or region you want selected. The only purpose for the **Color** setting (which, by default, is red) is to let you see what you're brushing; the color is never applied to the image or layer you're painting on.

6 Paint the Selection

Make sure that the **New Selection** is enabled on the **Options** bar. Then brush over the area you want to select, making sure that you brush over a good sampling of the pixels that comprise the region you want to select. The area you brush is marked in red; these marks are not permanent and do not affect the image. After you release the mouse button, the Editor analyzes the pixels you've marked, and selects similar, contiguous pixels. (Note there is no tolerance option here, as there is for the **Magic Wand** tool.)

7 Refine the Selection

To add to the pixels being sampled so that the Editor can make a broader approximation of the region you want selected, click the **Indicate Foreground** button on the **Options** bar (it is automatically selected after the first brush stroke), then brush another area of the image as you did before. You can remove regions from the current selection by clicking **Indicate Background**, and then brushing the area (this mark shows up in blue, by default) that represents the general color and variety of pixels you want *removed* from the current selection.

8 View the Result

Add to or subtract from the selection using the **Selection Brush** or a different selection tool. Make changes to the area within the selection, copy or cut it to another image or layer, or delete the data. When you're satisfied with the result, make any other changes you want and save the PSD file. Resave the result in JPEG, PNG, or non-layered TIFF format, leaving your PSD image with its layers (if any) intact so that you can return at a later time and make adjustments if you want.

In this example, I was never particularly pleased with this photo of a keynote speaker at a networking conference. If you're thinking, "Hey, that looks like Tom Brokaw," well, *it is*, but that's not the problem: The photo is a little fuzzy up front, and the background is too blue and distracting. After selecting Tom, I sharpened him. I then inverted the selection, blurred the background, and lowered the saturation, making the resulting background area much more tolerable.

49

---

49 | **Expand, Shrink, or Add Similar Areas to a Selection**

✔ **BEFORE YOU BEGIN**	→ **SEE ALSO**
Just jump right in!	**50** Smooth and Soften a Selection

After you've made a selection with a lasso tool or the **Magic Wand** tool, adjusting that selection so that it encompasses a larger or smaller region is a simple matter. You can inflate or deflate a selection just like controlling the air in a balloon, using the **Select, Modify, Expand** and **Select, Modify, Contract** commands, respectively. For example, you might select a subject, expand the selection and fill it with color, then place the layer with the filled selection below the subject, creating a frame that perfectly traces the object's outline.

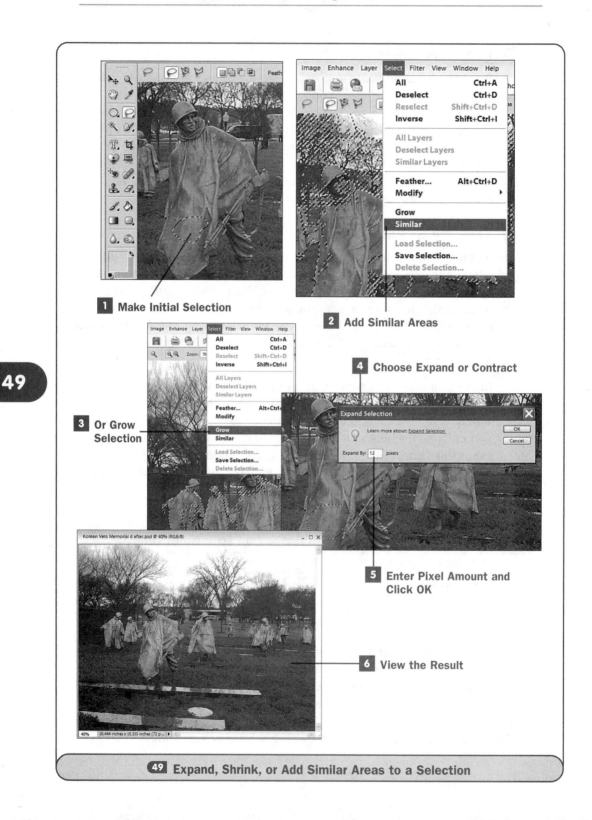

1 Make Initial Selection

2 Add Similar Areas

4 Choose Expand or Contract

3 Or Grow Selection

5 Enter Pixel Amount and Click OK

6 View the Result

49 Expand, Shrink, or Add Similar Areas to a Selection

Another technique that will come in handy when perfecting a selection is the ability for the Editor to select all the pixels in the image whose color values are close to those in the current selection. For this equally simple technique, you use the **Select**, **Similar** command. Suppose, for instance, that you have a photo of a troupe of costumed dancers, and you've selected just a portion of a single blue costume. The **Select**, **Similar** command selects not only the rest of the original blue costume, but all similarly colored blue costumes in the image. If you want to select only similarly shaded pixels adjacent to the current selection—for example, only the remainder of the single blue costume—choose the **Select**, **Grow** command instead.

1 Make Initial Selection

Open the image you want to select in the Editor in **Standard Edit** mode and save it in Photoshop (***.psd**) format. In the **Layers** palette, choose the layer that contains the data you want to select, and then use any selection tool to make the initial selection. The colors and tone in this selection will be used to find matching pixels in the image. In this example, I made a small selection in the front statue in this photo of the Korean War Memorial in Washington, D.C.

2 Add Similar Areas

Choose **Select**, **Similar** to select all areas in the image that are similar in color and tone to the area you selected in step 1. In my image, this command causes all of the medium-gray pixels to be selected, including the other statues, parts of the sky, and the marble "rice paddies."

▶ **TIP**

With both the **Grow** and **Similar** commands, you can control how closely pixels must match your original selection before being included in the expanded selection by simply adjusting the **Tolerance** value on the **Options** bar when the **Magic Wand** is selected. Seems strange, but true. So, select the **Magic Wand** tool, adjust the **Tolerance** to suit your needs, then apply the **Grow** or **Similar** command as explained here.

3 Or Grow Selection

Alternatively, choose **Select**, **Grow** to expand the current selection to include only neighboring pixels of similar color and tone. In my image, the command causes the selection to expand to include the rest of the soldier's cape I originally selected only partially, plus the capes of two neighboring soldiers whose pixels are contiguous to (happen to be touching) the original soldier.

49

4 **Choose Expand or Contract**

Choose **Selection**, **Modify**, **Expand** to expand the selection at all points by the same amount, or **Selection**, **Modify**, **Contract** to shrink it uniformly along all points. The **Expand Selection** or **Contract Selection** dialog box appears; both are remarkably similar.

5 **Enter Pixel Amount and Click OK**

In the **Expand Selection** or **Contract Selection** dialog box, enter the number of pixels you want to expand or contract by, and then click **OK**. The selection is immediately modified. With my original, small selection, I expanded it by 12 pixels; this adjustment simply made the small oval a little bigger.

▶ **TIPS**

You can refine a selection by adding to or subtracting from it, or by creating a new selection from the intersection of two selections, using the buttons on the **Options** bar for most of the selection tools (**Selection Brush** excluded): **Add to Selection**, **Subtract from Selection**, and **Intersect with Selection**. To build a selection, you can switch from selection tool to selection tool freely, using each tool to your advantage when trying to snag a particular area.

49

To select the outline of a selection, choose **Select, Modify, Border**. Enter the number of pixels on either side of the outline to include, then click **OK**. You might use this command to create a narrow frame around a selection. You can also use the **Stroke** command to create a frame: Create the selection first, then choose **Edit, Stroke (Outline) Selection**. Enter the **Width** for the frame and choose a **Color**. Select whether you want the frame created on the **Inside**, **Center**, or **Outside** of the selection border. Choose a blend mode and **Opacity**. To preserve the transparency within a selection and not stroke those pixels, choose **Preserve Transparency**. Click **OK**.

6 **View the Result**

Add to or subtract from your original selection using a combination of tools and commands. When you're satisfied with the selection, make changes to the area within the selection, copy or cut its data to another image or layer, or delete the data within the selection. Save the PSD file and then resave the file in JPEG, PNG, or non-layered TIFF format, leaving your PSD image with its layers (if any) intact so that you can return at a later time and make adjustments if you want.

Using the **Grow** command, I was able to expand my small selection to include almost all the closest soldiers. I saved this selection and then started over, growing a similar selection until I had selected all the soldiers on the right. Then I combined the two selections using the **Select, Save Selection** command. When I had all the soldiers selected, it was easy to lighten them a bit and adjust their color to restore their original greenish overcast.

50 Smooth and Soften a Selection

✔ **BEFORE YOU BEGIN**	→ **SEE ALSO**
Just jump right in!	**49** Expand, Shrink, or Add Similar Areas to a Selection

After you've used the **Magic Wand** tool to select a region from an image, there's a good chance the selection will have a number of pits and bumps. Photoshop Elements's **Smooth** command analyzes the color values of selected pixels and uses that information to decide how to adjust a selection border to smooth it visually. In this way, the **Smooth** command does not select pixels outside a selection that are obviously different in color. The goal of the **Smooth** command is to make a selection border less jagged. It's quite possible that, after smoothing, some portion you might have meant to exclude could end up being included, and other portions you meant to include could end up excluded. That's because the **Smooth** command actually changes the selection marquee here and there, smoothing out jagged ins and outs. The purpose of this kind of smoothing is not to create precise selection areas but more general ones—areas that appear more naturally cut out, especially when pasted into another image. The **Smooth** command can also be used to include previously non-included pixels within a selection that obviously should be included—for example, lighter green pixels in a leaf that were not included when you clicked with the **Magic Wand**.

Another common modification you might find yourself making to a selection is *feather* it, either when making the selection, or after the fact, with the **Feather** command. When you feather a selection, semitransparent pixels are added to the edge of the selection to soften it. Feathering a selection is often preferable when you intend to copy the selection and place it on a different background, or to fade the edge of a selection gradually to white or black, creating an old-fashioned photographic vignette. Feathering is also preferred when you intend to change the color or tone of the data within the selection, or apply a filter or effect, and you want the resulting data to blend into surrounding pixels. By feathering the edges of the selection, the edges seem softer and appear to fade into whatever background on which you place the object.

▶ **KEY TERM**

Feathering—The addition of partly selected pixels along the edge of a selection, often to help blend a relocated selection into its new surroundings.

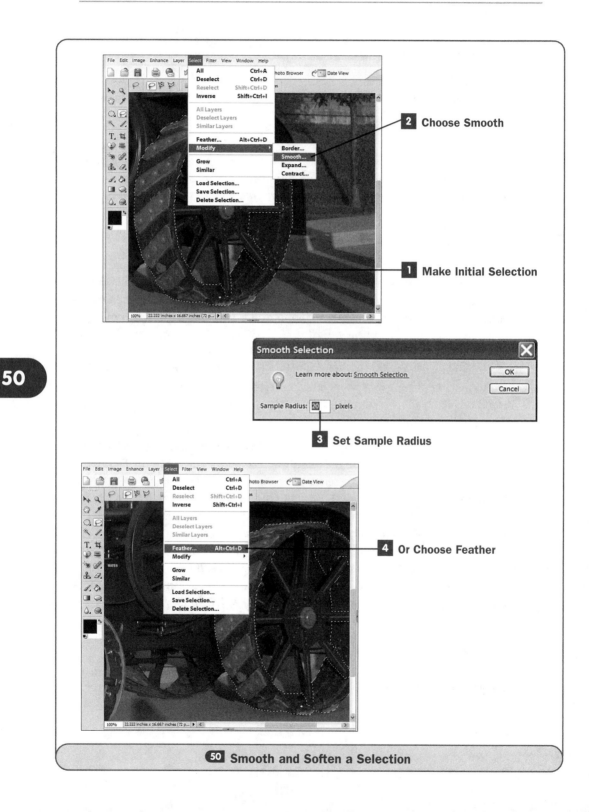

50

2 Choose Smooth

1 Make Initial Selection

3 Set Sample Radius

4 Or Choose Feather

50 Smooth and Soften a Selection

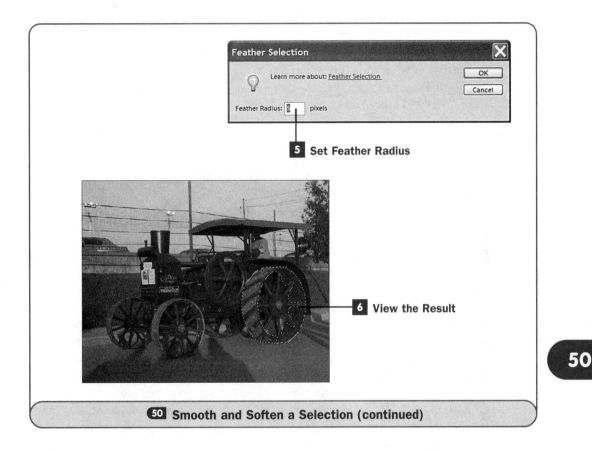

5 Set Feather Radius

6 View the Result

50 Smooth and Soften a Selection (continued)

50

▶ NOTES

Feathering occurs on both sides of the original selection marquee. When you feather the selection within your image, however, you will not see the feathering in the selection itself. For example, if you feather the edge of a selection by 10 pixels, the marquee will shrink by that amount to surround only the area of 50% or more selected pixels. If you copy or cut the data and then paste the selection into another image or onto another layer however, you'll notice that the copied data includes the partially selected pixels outside the marquee where the feathering occurred.

Although feathering, anti-aliasing, and smoothing might appear to be synonymous, each actually refers to a different concept. Feathering a selection's border enables pixels along the very rim to be partly selected, for a fuzzy border. This causes a regular change in opacity to the pixels along the entire border of a selection. Anti-aliasing adjusts the opacity of certain pixels only to help a selection look less jagged along the edges. Smoothing, like anti-aliasing, also makes a selection look less jagged by changing the border of a selection and not by partially selecting pixels.

▮1 Make Initial Selection

Open the image you want to work with in the Editor in **Standard Edit** mode and save it in Photoshop (***.psd**) format. In the **Layers** palette, choose the layer that contains the data you want to select and then use any selection tool to make the initial selection in the image.

▮2 Choose Smooth

To include the stray pixels around the current selection, choose **Select**, **Modify**, **Smooth** from the menu bar. The **Smooth Selection** dialog box displays.

▮3 Set Sample Radius

In the **Sample Radius** field, specify a number between **1** and **100** that indicates the maximum number of pixels that the Editor will add to or subtract from either side of the existing selection border to smooth out any jagged ins and outs it finds. This number represents how much change you'll allow to the existing selection perimeter. With a high value, your selected region could conceivably become much smaller. On the other hand, pockets of unselected pixels in the original region could become selected when smoothed because the **Smooth** command doesn't look just outside a selection for similar pixels, but inside as well. Also, because higher resolution images have pixels that are closer together (more dense), you might have to set the **Sample Radius** value higher than you would in a lower-resolution image to get the same result. Click **OK** to proceed.

▮4 Or Choose Feather

Choose **Select**, **Feather** from the menu bar to display the **Feather Selection** dialog box.

▮5 Set Feather Radius

In the **Feather Radius** field, type a value larger than **0** to indicate the number of pixels inside the marquee that will be used to create a fuzzy border around the selection. Click the **OK** button to close the **Feather Selection** dialog box.

50

▶ NOTES

Setting the **Feather** value in the **Options** bar when you make the initial selection with the **Lasso** or **Marquee** tools does the same thing as opening the **Feather Selection** dialog box after the selection has already been made. However, using the **Feather** command after the fact allows you the freedom to undo the feathering and adjust its value until you get the effect you want.

The **Magic Wand** and **Selection Brush** tools do not allow you to specify feathering on the **Options** bar, although the **Selection Brush** does enable you to lower the **Hardness** of its tip, which creates the same effect as feathering. For the **Magic Wand**, however, you must add feathering after the fact (if desired) by following the steps in this task.

6 View the Result

When you're satisfied with the selection, make changes to the area within the selection, copy or cut its data to another image or layer, or delete the data within the selection. Save the PSD image and then resave the file in JPEG, PNG, or non-layered TIFF format, leaving your PSD image with its layers (if any) intact so that you can return at a later time and make adjustments if you want.

In this example, I used the **Magnetic Lasso** to select the back wheel of a 1929 Rumely Oil-Pull farm tractor I photographed at a State Fair parade. The reason I did this was to adjust the lighting on this rubber-treaded steel wheel, which unfortunately caught too much shadow from the early evening sun. The **Magnetic Lasso** did a pretty good job, but the curves on the tractor wheels' edges looked like they'd been through a muddy pit. A quick smoothing, using the **Select**, **Modify**, **Smooth** command with **Sample Radius** set to 20, rounded out those curves easily.

51

---

51 Save and Reload a Selection

✔ BEFORE YOU BEGIN	→ SEE ALSO
45 Select a Rectangular or Circular Area	**52** About Copying, Cutting, and Pasting Data Within a Selection
46 Draw a Selection Freehand or By Tracing Its Edge	

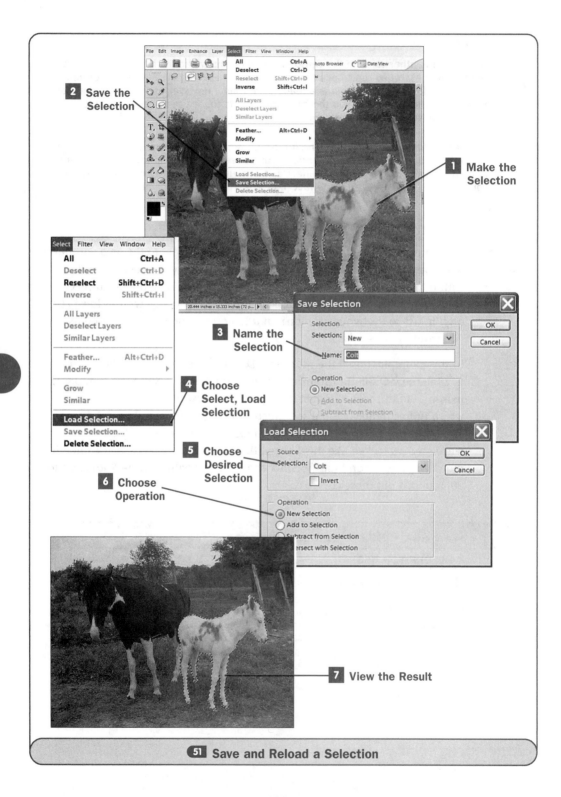

51

2 Save the Selection

1 Make the Selection

3 Name the Selection

4 Choose Select, Load Selection

5 Choose Desired Selection

6 Choose Operation

7 View the Result

51 Save and Reload a Selection

Sometimes, image attaining the perfectly selected region is a hard-won victory. It's difficult to cast aside the fruits of that victory to work on some other region. For this reason, Photoshop Elements makes it easy for you to save the *pattern* of a selection. Note that you don't save the *contents* of the selected region, just the shape, in case you need to use that shape to select the same region—or a different region with the same shape—later. When you save a selection, the Editor records the exact position and shape of the selection marquee, and whether it had any feathering, anti-aliasing, or smoothing at its edges. That recording becomes part of the image's Photoshop .PSD file. Saved selections are also useful for creating masks, frames, or for making the same-shaped selection in several images.

After you save a selection pattern, you can reload it at any time from within the image where you saved it. You can reload the saved selection to the same layer or to another layer. You can even add or subtract the saved selection from a current selection, creating a complex selection such as an oval frame. You build complex selections like these by making the outer selection, saving it, shrinking the selection, and subtracting this modified selection (the "hole") from the first selection ("the outer border"), leaving a selection "rim." When you reload a selection, pixels within its border are instantly selected, even if those pixels are different from the ones you originally selected when you saved the selection border.

1 Make the Selection

Open an in the Editor in **Standard Edit** mode and save it in Photoshop (***.psd**) format. Use any of the selection tools in any combination to create your selection.

2 Save the Selection

Choose **Select**, **Save Selection** to display the **Save Selection** dialog box.

▶ **NOTE**

Selections can be saved only in PSD, JP2 (JPEG 2000), and TIFF files. So if you saved a selection in a file with one of these formats, and then resaved that image in a different format (such as JPEG), the selection is no longer contained in the JPEG file and you won't be able to reload it. The selection should still be in the original PSD, JP2, or TIFF file—assuming that you saved that file again after saving the selection.

3 Name the Selection

In the **Save Selection** dialog box, choose **New** from the **Selection** drop-down list. In the **Name** field, type the name you want to assign to the selection. You can use any combination of characters to name the selection, but the selection name cannot be longer than 32 characters. Click **OK** to save the selection to the image.

After you've saved the selection, you can keep on working as usual. For example, you could make changes to the area within the selection, copy or cut its data to another image or layer, or delete the data within the selection. You can make other changes and even make another selection without fear of losing the original saved selection, which can be recalled when needed. When you're satisfied with all your changes, save the PSD image. Resave the result in JPEG or TIFF format, leaving your PSD image with its layers (if any) and selections intact so that you can return at a later time and make adjustments if you want.

▶ NOTE

You can modify an existing saved selection by making a selection and redisplaying the **Save Selection** dialog box. Select the name of the previously saved selection from the **Selection** drop-down list and then select the desired type of modification from the **Operation** area and click **OK**. For example, if you choose the **Add to Selection** operation, the current selection is added to the saved selection you chose from the **Selection** list.

51

4 Choose Select, Load Selection

At a later point in time, you might want to recall this selection. For example, you might want to perform further adjustments to the object you originally selected. Perhaps you want to adjust everything *but* that object; if so, you can invert the selection as you load it.

When you're ready to reuse the stored selection, select the layer that contains the pixels you want selected, then choose **Select, Load Selection** from the menu bar. The **Load Selection** dialog box is displayed.

5 Choose Desired Selection

From the **Selection** drop-down list, choose the name of the previously saved selection you want to load. If the **Load Selection** command is grayed out on the **Select** menu, the current image does not contain any saved selections. If you want to load a pattern that includes everything *except* the saved selection, enable the **Invert** check box.

6 Choose Operation

If you made a selection in your image before step 4, then under **Operation**, choose one of the following:

- **New Selection**—Replaces any existing selection in the image with the pattern you choose.

- **Add to Selection**—Produces a selection in the image that joins the existing pattern with the one you choose.

- **Subtract from Selection**—Removes the pixels included in the selection you choose, from the pattern currently in the image.

- **Intersect with Selection**—Produces a selection that includes only the pixels that the existing pattern and the pattern you choose have in common.

To finalize your choice, click **OK**.

▶ TIPS

For a neat effect, create a text selection (using the **Horizontal** or **Vertical Type Mask** tool), save it, and then make a new selection to act as the text background, such as a rectangle or a freely drawn shape. When the background for the text is just as you like, reload the text selection with the **Subtract from Selection** option so that it cuts out of the second selection an area in the shape of the text. Fill this new selection with a color or pattern, and the result looks impressive and unusual.

To use your saved selection in another image, just reload the selection in the original image as explained here. Then open the other image in which you want to use the selection, choose any selection tool other than the **Selection Brushes**, enable the **New Selection** button, position it over the selection, and then drag the selection into the image and drop it.

7 View the Result

After loading the selection, make changes to the area within the selection, copy or cut its data to another image or layer, or delete the data within the selection. When you're satisfied with the result, make any other changes you want and save the PSD file. Resave the result in JPEG, PNG, or non-layered TIFF format, leaving your PSD image with its layers (if any) and selections intact so that you can return at a later time and make adjustments if you want.

This example has as many as five components: the two horses, the ground, the part of the image that's above the ground, and the tree in the upper-right corner. To make the most of this image, I selected and stored each of these parts separately. The benefit of storing patterns for the horses first is that it's easy to select the ground (everything from the horizon line down) and then subtract the already stored horses from that area to attain just the region that needs to be edited. Here you can see the **Colt** selection in its entirety.

51

52   **About Copying, Cutting, and Pasting Data Within a Selection**

✔ **BEFORE YOU BEGIN**

45 Select a Rectangular or Circular Area

46 Draw a Selection Freehand or By Tracing Its Edge

→ **SEE ALSO**

53 Create a New Image or Layer from a Selection

Most Windows applications have some permutation of the **Edit**, **Cut** or **Edit**, **Copy** command, for placing a selection on the Clipboard, and the **Edit**, **Paste** command for pasting the contents of the Clipboard onto a designated location. In a word processor or a spreadsheet application, the blinking cursor indicates where the pasted data is going to go. Normally, image data pasted into Photoshop Elements's Editor is pasted onto a new layer above the current layer, so your choice of layers on the **Layers** palette usually answers the "Where?" question.

But just as you can select a region for limiting the extent of a flood fill or a drawing operation, you can select a region to have the Editor paste its Clipboard data into that area only, using the **Edit**, **Paste into Selection** command. For example, in an image of a tree trunk, you can make a heart-shaped selection in the trunk and then paste a snapshot of you and your boyfriend (that you've copied from another image) into that heart, using the **Edit**, **Paste Into Selection** command.

You can also use the **Paste** command to paste data from one layer to another in the same image, although there's an easier way: If you're working with a single image, you can bypass the Clipboard and copy or cut data in one step. Just make a selection and choose either **Layer**, **New**, **Layer via Copy** or **Layer**, **New**, **Layer via Cut**.

52

▶ NOTES

Pasted data is always placed on a new layer *above the current layer*, regardless of whether you use the **Paste** or the **Layer**, **New** command. If, however, you paste data into a selection, or onto a new, completely empty layer, the data is placed *on* the current layer and a new layer is not created.

Data is always pasted at its original resolution, even data that's pasted into a selection. Thus, if you want to copy data from one image to another, you should adjust the source image so that its resolution matches the resolution of the destination image. See **32** Change Image Size or Resolution.

When you copy the data within a selection in the Editor, you can either copy the data on the current layer only (using the **Edit**, **Copy** command), or on all visible layers of the image (by selecting **Edit**, **Copy Merged**). When you use the **Copy Merged** command, the Editor actually creates a merged copy of the data in all the layers visible in the image. Because the data in the visible layers is merged when you **Paste** the copied selection, the selection is pasted to a single layer (instead of the multiple layers the data was in when you copied it).

Suppose that you have an image with multiple layers that include both image layers and text, such as the *Happy Birthday* image shown in this figure. If you choose **Edit, Copy** with the **Ivy** layer active, only the contents of that layer are copied, even if you have selected data on multiple layers using various selection tools. If you paste what you've copied, you'll only get data from the **Ivy** layer. If you choose **Edit, Copy Merged** instead, it doesn't matter what layer is current or if you've selected data on only the current layer; everything within the selection (data on all visible layers) is copied. When you paste what you have copied, the contents of all layers—in this example, the **Ivy** layer, the text layer, and the layer being used as a text background—are all merged into one layer that is pasted onto the new layer or selection.

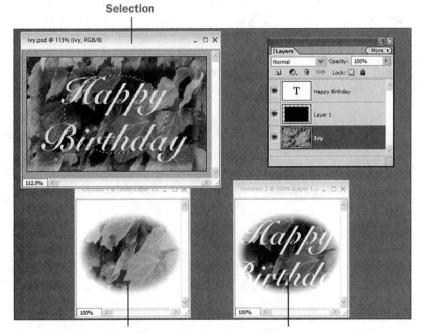

Selection

Pasted from Copy Command   **Pasted from Copy Merged Command**

*The **Copy** command copies data on the current layer only; the **Copy Merged** command copies all visible pixels within the selection.*

▶ NOTES

In this example, the text is simplified (converted to bitmap) before it is pasted, whether you use the **Copy** or **Copy Merged** command. This means the text will not be editable when it's pasted in its new home. You can, however, copy a text layer into another image and keep it editable by dragging it from the **Layers** palette and dropping it in the other image window.

The **Copy Merged** command selects data on all visible layers; to exclude data on a particular layer, hide that layer temporarily by clicking the layer's eye icon on the **Layers** palette.

You can quickly select all the data on a layer by pressing **Ctrl** and clicking the layer's thumbnail on the **Layers** palette.

Photoshop Elements has its own clipboard, separate from the Windows Clipboard. This means that data you cut or copy within the Editor is available to be pasted only within Photoshop Elements. Fortunately, Photoshop Elements does provide the ability to paste data into other programs, but you must enable the **Export Clipboard** option on the **Preferences** dialog box if the option is not already on (which it typically is). To display the **Preferences** dialog box so that you can check, from the Editor, choose **Edit, Preferences, General**. Enable the **Export Clipboard** option and click **OK** to save your changes.

52

Export Clipboard Option ————

Enable the **Export Clipboard** option in the **Preferences** dialog box if you want to use data you copy in the Editor in other Windows programs.

The Photoshop Elements clipboard can hold only one selection at a time. Therefore, when you copy or cut a selection, that selection replaces any previous contents in the clipboard. The contents remain in the Photoshop Elements clipboard until you close Photoshop Elements, which clears the clipboard. The next time you open Photoshop Elements, the clipboard will be empty. If you have enabled the **Export Clipboard** option in the **Preferences** dialog box, the situation changes slightly. When you choose **Edit**, **Cut** or **Edit**, **Copy** for a selection in the Editor, the selection is automatically copied to *both* the Photoshop Elements clipboard and the Windows Clipboard. If you close Photoshop Elements, the selection remains in the Windows Clipboard until you copy something else into that Clipboard from another Windows program. With the data safely stored on the Windows Clipboard, you can continue to paste a selection from an Editor image into other applications, even if you close Photoshop Elements.

▶ **TIP**

The **File**, **Place** command helps you bring an image from a PDF document, Adobe Illustrator, or EPS (Encapsulated PostScript) file into an Editor image. Using **File**, **Place** rather than **Edit**, **Copy** and **Edit**, **Paste** causes the Editor to automatically convert the incoming data's resolution and size to fit the image into which you copy the data.

When you make a selection, instead of cutting and pasting the data in it, you can move the data around on the layer using the **Move** tool on the **Toolbox**. Just click inside the bounding box with the tool and drag to move the data around on the layer. You can copy instead of moving by pressing **Alt** as you drag. You can move or copy data into another image by dragging the selection into the other image window. If you move data on the Background layer (and not a regular layer) or a layer that does not support transparency (the option is turned off), the location where the selection was originally positioned on the layer becomes the background color. For example, if the background color for the current image is set to white, the location where the selection was originally located is also white. On regular layers, the vacancy left by the moved data becomes transparent.

▶ **NOTE**

Using the **Move** tool, you can copy or move data on the active layer only. If you make a selection that includes the contents of other layers, anything in those layers is ignored.

Normally, only selected data on the current layer is moved with the **Move** tool. If you enable the **Auto Select Layer** option on the **Options** bar, data on the topmost layer on the **Layers** palette—which is also located under the **Move** tool when you begin dragging—is the data that's moved, even if that data is not located on the current layer. There are two different types of moving you can perform using the **Move** tool. To move the selection marquee to adjust its position (without moving the data in the marquee), choose a selection tool (except for one of the **Selection Brushes**), click the **New Selection** button in the **Options** bar, and drag the marquee.

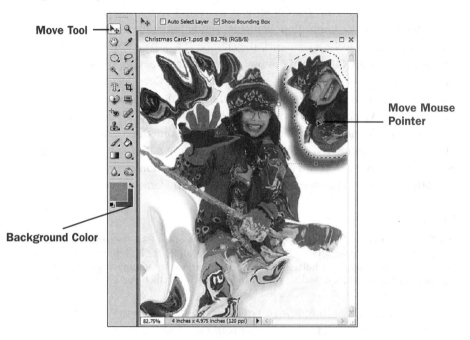

Move Tool

Move Mouse Pointer

Background Color

*Use the **Move** tool to move data in the current selection to a new location on the layer or into another image file.*

If you want to remove a specific portion of an image, you can select that area and then delete the selection by either pressing the **Delete** key on the keyboard or selecting **Edit**, **Delete**. You will also notice with this option that the location of the selection is replaced with the current background color if you remove data from the background layer or a layer that does not support transparency. Otherwise, the vacancy is filled with transparent pixels. Like the **Move** command, the **Delete** command removes data on only the current layer, even if the selection includes data on other layers, too.

53 | Create a New Image or Layer from a Selection

✔ BEFORE YOU BEGIN

52 About Copying, Cutting, and Pasting Data Within a Selection

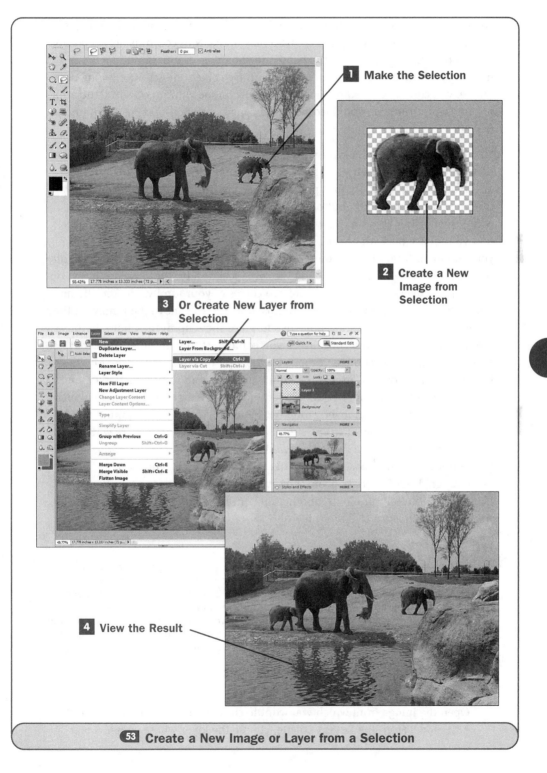

1 Make the Selection

2 Create a New Image from Selection

3 Or Create New Layer from Selection

4 View the Result

53

53 Create a New Image or Layer from a Selection

You can create new images in the Editor by using selections from other images. For example, you might want to create a new image that contains only a portion of the original image, such as the head and shoulders of a person taken from a full-length photo of that person. When you have copied the selection to the new image, you can make modifications to the new image without affecting the original image. In this task, you'll learn how to copy a selection and create an image from it.

You can also create a new layer with data you've copied from a selection instead of an entire image. When you use layers, you can isolate portions of an image and make changes to only that portion. If you create a selection of your family from a larger image taken in front of your house, you can create a new layer with just your family on it. Now you have two layers: your family on one layer and your house plus your family on another. The composite image still shows your family in front of your house because the copy of your family, when initially pasted to the new layer, is in exactly the same location on that layer as it was on the original layer—in effect, there are two copies of your family, one directly on top of the other. You can do a lot of things now. You can move the family on the top layer over to one side, and have two families show up in the photo. Because the family is isolated on its own layer, you can adjust the brightness and contrast of just the family; select a blend mode on the top layer that causes the families to blend in such a way that makes the family appear more saturated, darker, or artfully colored; blur the entire bottom layer and make the duplicate family (which remains sharp on its own layer) stand out better against the background; resize the top family and move it to one side so they appear as a miniature with themselves; or you can replace the layer containing your house with an image of the White House. Just that easily, you've taken your family on "vacation" to Washington, D.C. The tricks begin, however, by first selecting the family and transferring that selection onto another layer in the same image, which is one of the things you'll learn to do in this task.

▶ **NOTE**

When you're copying data from one image to another, you're using the Photoshop Elements clipboard. If you have enabled the **Export to Clipboard** option in the **Preferences** dialog box, data on this clipboard is also copied to the Windows Clipboard for use in other programs—the purpose of that option is to help you get data *out of Photoshop Elements*; thus, that option does not have to be on for this task to work, even if you want to create a new image from data copied from another program (the option has nothing to do with data coming *into* Photoshop Elements).

1 **Make the Selection**

Open the image from which you want to copy data in the Editor in **Standard Edit** mode. From the **Layers** palette, choose the layer whose contents you want to copy—in whole or part—into a new image. Make your selection using the tools of your choice.

2 Create a New Image from Selection

To create a new image from the selected data, select **Edit**, **Copy** from the menu bar to copy the selection to the Photoshop Elements clipboard. To copy all visible pixels within the selection, regardless of what layer they are on, choose **Edit**, **Copy Merged** instead. See **52** **About Copying, Cutting, and Pasting Data Within a Selection** for help.

Now that the data's on the clipboard, select **File**, **New**, **Image from Clipboard** to create a new image from the contents of the clipboard. The new image is sized to match the actual size of the data within the clipboard. In other words, if the selection was 400 × 400 pixels in size, that will be the size of the new image.

When you create a new image file, the existing image file from which you copied the selection remains open. (You can see the open files in the **Photo Bin** at the bottom of the screen.) The Editor indicates the selected image file by outlining it in blue.

53

▶ TIP

To create an image using data you capture from your computer screen, arrange the monitor display to show the programs or elements you want to capture and press the **Print Screen** key. Return to the Editor and select **File**, **New**, **Image from Clipboard** to create a file containing whatever data was displayed on your computer monitor.

3 Or Create New Layer from Selection

To create a new layer in the current image using the data you've selected, you do not have to copy it first. Instead, select **Layer**, **New**, **Layer via Copy** to copy the current selection to a new layer. This new layer appears above the current layer in the **Layers** palette. The selection appears in the same location on the new layer as it occupied in the original layer, but you can move it with the **Move** tool.

You can also select **Layer**, **New**, **Layer via Cut** to cut the current selection from its existing layer and paste it in a new layer. If used in this example, the selected baby elephant would be cut from the **Background** layer and pasted on the new layer. A hole would be left in the **Background** layer where the baby elephant was originally located, and that hole would be filled with the background color, or transparent pixels (if the background layer had been converted to a regular layer, such as **Layer 0**).

▶ **NOTE**

If your purpose is to copy data from one image to another, just select it and choose **Edit**, **Copy** or **Copy Merged**; then change to the other image and choose **Edit**, **Paste**. The data is pasted onto a new layer automatically, just above the current layer.

4 **View the Result**

Save the new image in Photoshop (***.psd**) format. Make any changes you want and save the PSD file again. Resave the final result in JPEG, PNG, or non-layered TIFF format, leaving your PSD image with its layers (if any) intact so that you can return at a later time and make adjustments if you want.

In this example, I used the **Magnetic Lasso** tool to select the walking baby elephant. I then used the **Layer via Copy** command to move just the baby elephant onto a new layer all to himself. I wanted to make the photo a bit more interesting by adding another elephant, but to disguise that fact, I resized him slightly and moved him closer to his mother. See **59** **Move, Resize, Skew, or Distort a Layer or Selection**. I had to clone in the missing trunk and leg that was hidden behind the rock on the original elephant. See **86** **Repair Minor Tears**. I still have some more work to do, adding a shadow and a reflection in the water, but even now the effect is pretty convincing.

53

8

Using Multiple Layers to Edit Images

IN THIS CHAPTER:

54 Create a New Image Layer

55 Create a Layer Filled with a Color, Gradient, or Pattern

56 Create an Adjustment Layer

57 Erase Part of a Layer

58 Replace a Background with Something Else

59 Move, Resize, Skew, or Distort a Layer or Selection

60 Rotate the Data in a Layer or Selection

61 Mask an Adjustment or Fill Layer

62 Mask an Image Layer

The use of layers to edit an image is the most powerful feature in Photoshop Elements. Using multiple layers, you can isolate each element of the image, in the same way a cartoonist isolates each element of a scene by placing them on sheets of clear acetate. You could put the sky and a roadway on the bottom layer, a sports car on the next layer, and your son on the top layer. Separating your image into layers gives you the ability to make adjustments to any one of the objects within the image—such as the location of the sports car or the sharpness, brightness, and tone of your son—without affecting the background or other objects on different layers. When elements in an image are separated, you can apply effects, filters, and layer styles to specific objects without applying them to the entire image.

In Chapter 1, "Start Here," you learned about the different layer types available: image layers, fill layers, and adjustment layers. In this chapter, you'll learn how to create them. You'll learn how to erase part of a layer to let the background show through, and how to erase the background layer so that you can place the graphic seamlessly on a Web page or your desktop. You'll learn how to move, resize, rotate, skew, and distort the data on a layer or in a selection so that it looks exactly how you want. You'll also learn how to mask a portion of a layer to create special effects such as picture frames or to insert fake backgrounds behind a subject.

54 Create a New Image Layer

✔ BEFORE YOU BEGIN	→ SEE ALSO
Just jump right in!	55 Create a Layer Filled with a Color, Gradient, or Pattern
	56 Create an Adjustment Layer

You can add a new image *layer* to just about any image you have open in the Editor. Because an image layer can hold any type of raster data, you might insert an image layer so that you can paint or draw on it, make a selection on the new layer and copy data into that selection, create a clipping mask to partially block data on another layer, or fill the layer using a filter or effect, such as a rendering of clouds. However, you don't have to create an image layer if your plan is to copy data from some other layer or image into this image; the Editor will paste the data on a new layer automatically.

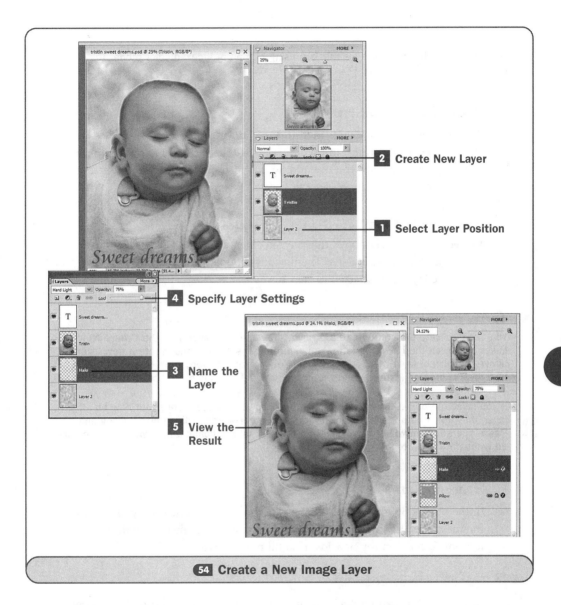

54 Create a New Image Layer

When you add the new layer, you must first determine the location for the layer within the layer stack. To specify the layer location, select the layer *below* where you want the new layer (in other words, the new layer is added above the current layer). For example, to insert a new layer at the top of the layer stack, you select the top layer in the **Layers** palette. If the only layer is the **Background** layer, the new layer is always placed on top of the **Background** layer because you cannot place any layers below the **Background** layer—unless you first convert the **Background** layer to a regular layer by choosing **Layer**, **New**, **Layer from Background**.

▶ **NOTE**

You cannot add layers to images that are using bitmap or indexed color mode. To change color modes, see **35** Change Color Mode.

1 **Select Layer Position**

Open an image in the Editor in **Standard Edit** mode and save it in Photoshop (***.psd**) format. In the **Layers** palette, select the layer you want to be below the new layer you are adding. Photoshop Elements will insert the new image layer directly above the selected layer.

2 **Create New Layer**

To create a new layer above the selected layer, click the **Create New Layer** button on the **Layers** palette. The new layer appears on the **Layers** palette above the layer you selected in step 1.

▶ **TIPS**

You can duplicate the contents of a layer by dragging that layer onto the **Create New Layer** button on the **Layers** palette. You can make a selection and create a new layer above the current layer by choosing **Layer**, **New**, **Layer Via Copy** from the menu bar. A new layer is created instantly, and the data in the selection is placed on that layer.

If you select an object from another layer and copy and paste it onto your new blank layer, the copied data is placed on that layer. In other words, unlike normal **Copy** and **Paste** operations in which new layers are created automatically, *a new layer is not created when data is pasted onto an empty layer*.

3 **Name the Layer**

In the **Layers** palette, double-click the default layer name and type a **Name** that describes the layer's content or purpose. Press **Enter**. I know that I want to create a halo on my new layer, so I'll name it **Halo**.

4 **Specify Layer Settings**

After you have created the layer, it is ready for you to add data to it. A new image layer is filled with transparent pixels so that, at least initially, it does not block any layers below it. However, as you add opaque pixels, they will block the data below (or blend with them, if you select a blend mode other than **Normal** as explained here). Paint or draw on the new layer, or copy data there.

Next, play with the blend mode and opacity of the layer to get the effect you want. Typically, I play with these settings as I work, making frequent

54

changes. The *blend mode* of a layer specifies how the pixels on that layer mix with pixels in the layer(s) below. The blend mode for a new layer is set to **Normal** by default. To select a different blend mode, open the **Blend Mode** list at the top of the **Layers** palette and select the one you want to use. See the website for this book (start at www.samspublishing.com) for more information on blend modes.

The opacity of a new layer is set to 100% by default. To reduce the overall opacity of the new layer, adjust the **Opacity** value at the top of the **Layers** palette. The lower the **Opacity** setting, the more transparent that layer's pixels appear. If you add semi-transparent pixels to this new layer, the **Opacity** setting reduces their overall transparency even more.

5 View the Result

When you're satisfied with the image, save the PSD file. Then merge the layers together and resave the result in JPEG, PNG, or non-layered TIFF format, leaving your PSD image unflattened so that you can return at a later time and make adjustments if you want.

I started with a photo of my great-nephew sleeping peacefully. I added some text, and then inserted a new layer and used the **Clouds** filter to create a puffy cloud background. I moved this clouds layer (**Layer 2**) to the bottom of the layer stack so that it would be behind the baby and not on top of him. Next I inserted the **Halo** layer, on which I painted a yellow halo. I set the blend mode to **Hard Light** and set the **Opacity** to 75% so the halo would be semi-transparent. I added an **Outer Glow** *layer style* to complete the halo effect. I inserted a **Pillow** layer just above the **Cloud** layer and used the **Brush** tool to paint a pillow for the baby's head. I locked the transparency on this layer so that I could brush soft texture along the edges of the pillow, giving it some dimension.

55

---

55 | **Create a Layer Filled with a Color, Gradient, or Pattern**

✔ **BEFORE YOU BEGIN**	→ **SEE ALSO**
Just jump right in!	**54** Create a New Image Layer
	56 Create an Adjustment Layer
	61 Mask an Adjustment or Fill Layer

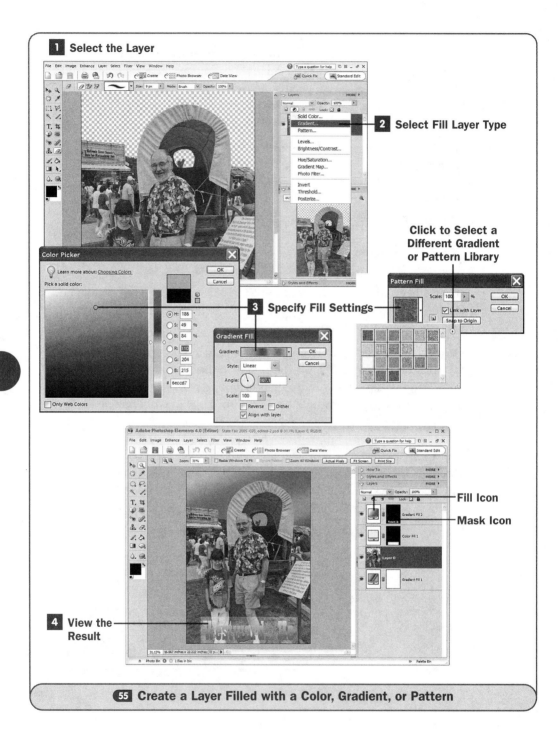

1 Select the Layer

2 Select Fill Layer Type

Click to Select a
Different Gradient
or Pattern Library

3 Specify Fill Settings

Fill Icon

Mask Icon

4 View the
Result

55 Create a Layer Filled with a Color, Gradient, or Pattern

If you want to insert a layer completely filled with a color, pattern, or gradient, create a fill layer. True, you could insert an image layer and fill it with a color or pattern (using the **Paint Bucket** tool) or a gradient (using the **Gradient** tool), but you can accomplish things with a fill layer that you can't easily duplicate with an image layer. For example, you could erase the background around a subject, allowing a more interesting background created by a gradient or pattern fill layer to show through. See **88** **Remove Unwanted Object from an Image**. You could mask out the center of a fill layer so the fill layer only shows through along the edges, creating a "frame" around the layer(s) below it. See **61** **Mask an Adjustment or Fill Layer**. And because you used a fill layer, you can change the fill type (from a pattern to a gradient, for example) until you find the right look for your frame.

You might place a pattern fill layer over another layer, lower its opacity, and use the pattern to give that layer a "texture." Or you could make a selection and instantly fill the selection with a color, gradient, or pattern. The selection in this case is not *actually* filled, but its shape is used on the fill layer's mask to block the layer's fill from appearing anywhere else but within the confines of your selection. Although you could use this technique to fill any selection shape with the contents of a fill layer, you can also fill text you created using the **Horizontal** or **Vertical Type Mask** tool with a pattern or a gradient—something you can't do using the ordinary text tools.

55

1 Select the Layer

Open an image in the Editor in **Standard Edit** mode and save it in Photoshop (***.psd**) format.

In the **Layers** palette, select the layer *below* where you want the new fill layer to be. The Editor will insert the fill layer directly above the selected layer. To create a fill layer that automatically fills only the area within a selection, select that portion of the layer now.

2 Select Fill Layer Type

Click the **Create Adjustment Layer** button on the **Layers** palette and select **Solid Color**, **Gradient**, or **Pattern** from the menu that appears.

3 Specify Fill Settings

A dialog box for the fill type you selected in step 2 appears. If you selected a **Solid Color** fill layer, choose a color from the color picker and click **OK**. See **72** **Select a Color to Work with**.

If you selected a **Gradient** fill layer, select a **Gradient** from the list box. Choose a gradient **Style** and adjust the **Angle**, which controls the direction in which the gradient transitions from one color to the next. By lowering the

Scale, you can have these transitions occur more often. Enable the **Reverse** option to reverse the colors in the gradient. Enable the **Dither** option to reduce jagged transitions, especially in lower-resolution images. Enable the **Align with Layer** option to use the layer's outer perimeter to calculate the gradient. Click **OK**. See 🔢 **Fill an Area with a Gradient** for help.

If you selected a **Pattern** fill layer, select a pattern and adjust its **Scale**. Click the **Snap to Origin** button to reposition the pattern so that it's aligned with the image borders. Enable the **Link with Layer** option so that you can click in the image and move the pattern on the layer until you get its position just right for your purposes. Click **OK**.

▶ **TIPS**

To display a different set of gradients or patterns, click the triangle button to open the pop-up menu, and select the library of gradients or patterns to use.

Several gradient patterns use the current *foreground color*. Before creating a gradient fill layer, select the desired foreground color to make finding the right gradient colors easier. See 🔢 **Select a Color to Work with** for more information on selecting the foreground color.

55

If you want to make modifications to a fill layer later on, double-click the fill thumbnail on the **Layers** palette. The corresponding dialog box reopens so that you can adjust the fill's settings.

4 **View the Result**

The new fill layer is created using the color, pattern, or gradient option you selected. If desired, you can change the layer's **Opacity** and **Blend Mode** using those options at the top of the **Layers** palette. Notice that in the **Layers** palette there are two icons for the layer: The first icon shows the type of fill that was added. For example, if you created a color fill, the icon contains the color that was used. The second icon shows the mask. It's white where the fill shows through to other layers and black where the fill is blocked. Unless you made a selection in step 1, you'll notice that the mask is initially white, meaning that the fill completely shows through at the moment, covering all data on the layer below. You'll learn how to edit the mask to block the effects of the fill in 🔢 **Mask an Adjustment or Fill Layer.**

When you're satisfied with the image, save the PSD file. Then merge the layers together and resave the result in JPEG, PNG, or unlayered TIFF format, leaving your PSD image unflattened so that you can return at a later time and make adjustments if you want.

In this example, I removed the background around my subjects and added a gradient fill layer behind them to act as a new "sky." To add a gradient to the text, I added another gradient fill layer and masked it (so that only part of the gradient fill shows through) the text caption.

---

56 **Create an Adjustment Layer**

✔ BEFORE YOU BEGIN	→ SEE ALSO
Just jump right in!	**55** Create a Layer Filled with a Color, Gradient, or Pattern
	61 Mask an Adjustment or Fill Layer

If you want to make adjustments to the color, contrast, brightness, or saturation of the *layers* in your image, you can add an *adjustment layer*. An adjustment layer changes the appearance of the layers below it in the layer stack without affecting the actual contents of those layers. Adjustment layers let you try out various adjustments without making any permanent changes to the image layer(s). If you don't like the result, you can open that adjustment dialog box again and make other changes, which is the same as if you had clicked **Undo** and had started over. However, in this case, you can change your mind at any time, even way down the editing process! You can also remove the adjustment layer and its effects completely.

56

▶ **KEY TERM**

Adjustment layer—A special layer that allows you to make a specific color or contrast adjustment to the layers underneath it.

There are several types of adjustment layers you can create:

- **Levels**—Allows you to adjust the highlight, midtone, and shadow values for a single color channel (the red, green, or blue channel) or the entire tonal range. You can also remove a color cast using **Levels**. See **93** **Improve a Dull, Flat Photo.**

- **Brightness/Contrast**—Allows you to decrease or increase the general amount of brightness and contrast for all pixels on the affected layers. See **92** **Improve Brightness and Contrast.**

- **Hue/Saturation**—Allows you to adjust the hue, saturation, and lightness of all pixels on the affected layers. See **97** **Adjust Hue and Saturation Manually.**

- **Gradient Map**—Applies the colors in the gradient you select to the pixels in the affected layers, based on their brightness value.

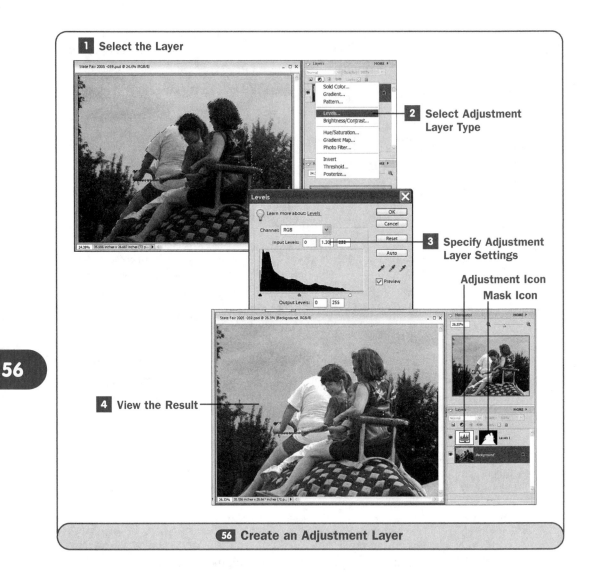

56 Create an Adjustment Layer

- **Photo Filter**—Allows you to apply an effect that simulates the use of a particular photo filter to the affected layers. For example, if you want your image to have a sepia appearance, apply the **Sepia** photo filter.

- **Invert**—Changes the pixels on the affected layers so they are reversed in color and tone.

- **Threshold**—Allows you to convert the pixels in the affected layers to either black or white. Light areas are converted to white and dark areas are converted to black, depending on the threshold you select. See **44** **Make Areas of a Photo Easier to Select**.

- **Posterize**—Allows you to control the number of tones in the affected layers by specifying the number of brightness levels you want. The brightness of each pixel is then adjusted to fit within one of these tonal levels. See **44** **Make Areas of a Photo Easier to Select.**

1 Select the Layer

Open an image in the Editor in **Standard Edit** mode and save it in Photoshop (*.psd) format. In the **Layers** palette, select a layer; all layers below the layer you choose will be affected by the adjustment layer. The adjustment layer will appear in the **Layers** palette above the layer you select and will affect all layers below. To create an adjustment layer that automatically adjusts only the area within a selection, select that portion of the image now.

2 Select Adjustment Layer Type

Click the **Create Adjustment Layer** button on the **Layers** palette and select the type of adjustment layer you want to create.

3 Specify Adjustment Layer Settings

Depending on the type of adjustment layer you create, a different dialog box displays. For example, if you select the **Levels** adjustment layer type, the **Levels** dialog box displays. Make your selections for the type of adjustment you want to make and click **OK** to apply the adjustment filter.

▶ TIPS

If you want to make modifications to an adjustment layer later, double-click the adjustment thumbnail on the **Layers** palette.

Because its effects are easy to change or remove, an adjustment layer is preferable to applying that same adjustment directly to a layer. In addition, by adding a mask, you can easily limit the adjustment to particular portions of the layers below, *and even change your mind on which portions* you want affected, any time you want. See **61** **Mask an Adjustment or Fill Layer.**

4 View the Result

The new adjustment layer is created using the adjustment settings you specified. If desired, you can change the layer's **Opacity** and **Blend Mode** using those options at the top of the **Layers** palette. Notice that in the **Layers** palette there are now two icons for the layer: The first icon shows the type of adjustment that was added. The second icon shows the mask. It's white where the adjustment is applied to other layers and black where the adjustment is blocked. Unless you made a selection in step 1, you'll notice that the mask is initially white, meaning that the adjustment is currently being applied to all layers below. You'll learn how to edit the mask to block the effects of the adjustment in **61 Mask an Adjustment or Fill Layer**.

When you're satisfied with the image, save the PSD file. Then merge the layers together and resave the result in JPEG, PNG, or non-layered TIFF format, leaving your PSD image unflattened so that you can return at a later time and make adjustments if you want. In this example, I selected my subjects and inserted a **Levels** adjustment layer. I then changed the settings to make that area brighter, without losing the details in the shadows. Because the adjustment affected only the subjects, the background remained dull, drawing more attention to the subjects.

56

57 Erase Part of a Layer

✔ BEFORE YOU BEGIN	→ SEE ALSO
Just jump right in!	**58** Replace a Background with Something Else
	62 Mask an Image Layer

One advantage of using layers is the ability to isolate changes to various elements in an image, such as applying a contrast adjustment to just the subject and not the entire image. Another advantage of using layers is that you can easily add and remove data from a layer without affecting the other layers in your image. In fact, when you erase data from a layer using one of the eraser tools, the pixels are changed to transparent ones, and the contents of the layers below become visible "through" the area you just deleted. If you attempt to "erase" data from a layer that has transparency locked (such as the **Background** layer), the pixels are not made transparent but are instead filled with the current background color. To erase the pixels on a background layer, convert it to a regular image layer by choosing **Layer**, **New**, **Layer from Background**.

1 Select Eraser Tool

2 Adjust Eraser Settings

Click to Select a
Different Brush Library

3 Erase Unwanted Pixels

6 Erase Unwanted Pixels

5 Adjust Eraser Settings

4 Select Magic
Eraser Tool

7 Select Background
Eraser Tool

8 Adjust Eraser
Settings

9 Erase Unwanted Pixels

10 View the Result

57

To erase part of a layer, you use the eraser tools: the regular *Eraser*, the *Background Eraser*, and the *Magic Eraser*. The **Eraser** works just as you might expect, making transparent the pixels the brush passes over. The **Background Eraser** works a little differently. As you drag the **Background Eraser** tool, pixels under the brush that match the pixel in the center of the brush tip crosshair are made transparent. How closely these pixels must match before being erased is controlled by the tool's **Tolerance** level, which is set on the **Options** bar. With the **Magic Eraser** tool, you erase matching pixels by clicking a sample pixel. Pixels that match the sample you clicked are erased from the layer. Again, the **Tolerance** option controls how closely this match must be before pixels are erased (made transparent). These tools work well if there is a lot of difference between the pixels you want to erase and the portion you want to remain. The Magic Eraser is best at removing large areas of similar color. To remove a background with lots of different colors, it's easier to use the **Background Eraser** because you can drag and you do not have to click each color to remove.

▶ KEY TERMS

Eraser—A tool that erases (makes transparent) the pixels under its brush.

Background Eraser—A tool that erases pixels (makes transparent) that match the pixel under its crosshair as you drag.

Magic Eraser—A tool that erases (makes transparent) pixels that matches any pixel you click.

▶ TIPS

You can also erase data by making a selection and pressing the **Delete** key.

Another way you can erase the background from around a subject is to use the **Magic Extractor**, a dialog box with tools that allow you to select areas to erase, preview your changes, and make adjustments *before* the pixels are actually erased from the image. See **58** Replace a Background with Something Else.

1 Select Eraser Tool

Open an image in the Editor in **Standard Edit** mode and save it in Photoshop (***.psd**) format. On the **Toolbox**, select the **Eraser** tool.

2 Adjust Eraser Settings

On the **Options** bar, select the **Mode** (**Brush**, **Pencil**, or **Block**), which determines the shape of the brush tip. For the **Brush** and **Pencil** options, you can further refine the tip by selecting an option from the **Presets** list. Set the **Size** and **Opacity** for the brush. If you lower the **Opacity**, for example, the eraser only partially erases (it makes the pixels partially transparent instead of fully transparent).

▶ TIPS

When selecting a brush tip from the **Presets** list for any of the eraser tools, you can display a different set of brush tips by clicking the triangle button to open the pop-up menu and choosing a different library of brush tips.

Before using any of the eraser tools, you can make a selection to limit the erasure to that area so that you don't accidentally erase something you don't want to. For example, to erase the sky around a girl's face who also happens to be wearing a blue hat, draw the selection boundary omitting the hat so that it isn't mistaken for the background and isn't erased as you work at removing the background from around her face.

3 Erase Unwanted Pixels

In the **Layers** palette, change to the layer you want to erase. If you want to erase pixels on the background layer using the **Eraser** tool, you'll need to convert it to a regular layer first by choosing **Layer**, **New**, **Layer from Background**. To preserve the data on the layer against possible mistakes you might make while erasing, consider duplicating the layer and erasing the new layer instead. To do that, choose **Layer**, **Duplicate Layer**.

In the image area, drag with the **Eraser** tool; pixels under the tip are erased (made transparent). I used the **Eraser** here to erase large areas of the background where I'm not afraid of accidentally erasing the subject—the flowers.

4 Select Magic Eraser Tool

Select the **Magic Eraser** on the **Toolbox** (if an eraser tool is already selected, just click the **Magic Eraser** icon in the **Options** bar).

5 Adjust Eraser Settings

Set the **Tolerance** to a value that tells the Editor how closely you want pixels to match the one you click before they are erased. A low **Tolerance** level indicates that only pixels that are very similar to the pixel you click will be erased. The higher the **Tolerance** value, the broader the range of pixels that will match.

Enable the **Anti-Aliased** check box to make sure that the edges are smooth around the area that is erased. Enable the **Contiguous** check box to erase only pixels that are adjacent to the pixel you click. If you clear the **Contiguous** check box, Photoshop Elements will find all the pixels in the layer or selection that match the pixel you click. Enable the **Sample All Layers** check box to remove pixels on the current layer, based on the blended color (from all layers) that you click. Adjust the **Opacity** value to only partially erase matching pixels.

57

6 Erase Unwanted Pixels

In the **Layers** palette, change to the layer you want to erase. If you choose the background layer, the **Magic Eraser** tool automatically converts the layer to a regular layer as soon as you begin erasing. To preserve the data on the layer against possible mistakes you might make while erasing, consider duplicating the layer and erasing the new layer instead. To do that, choose **Layer, Duplicate Layer**.

Click a pixel that matches the ones you want to erase. Pixels that match closely enough (based on the **Tolerance** setting) to the one you click are erased. Continue the process until you have removed the unwanted portion of the layer. Here I use the **Magic Eraser** to remove large sections of a background, especially where the background is mostly one color (as it is here) where it's a blend of colors from several layers (I can enable the **Sample All Layers** option).

7 Select Background Eraser Tool

Select the **Background Eraser** on the **Toolbox** (if an eraser tool is already selected, just click the **Background Eraser** icon in the **Options** bar).

8 Adjust Eraser Settings

On the **Options** bar, select the brush tip you want to use by clicking the arrow next to the brush tip and choosing a **Diameter** (size) and **Hardness**.

To control which pixels are similar enough to warrant erasure, adjust the tool's **Tolerance** and **Limits** options. When you set **Limits** to **Contiguous**, the **Background Eraser** tool samples the pixel under the *hotspot* (located at the center of the brush tip and marked by a crosshair) and erases similar pixels under the brush that touch the hotspot or another similarly colored pixel. When **Limits** is set to **Discontiguous**, the tool erases any and all similarly colored pixels under the brush tip, regardless of their position. By default, the **Limits** value is set to **Contiguous**, but this setting might make it difficult to erase the background if it peeks through your subject (as the sky does through tree branches). Use **Discontiguous** in such a case.

9 Erase Unwanted Pixels

In the **Layers** palette, change to the layer you want to erase. If you choose the background layer, the **Background Eraser** tool automatically converts it to a regular layer as soon as you begin erasing. To preserve the data on the layer against possible mistakes you might make while erasing, consider duplicating the layer and erasing the new layer instead. To do that, choose **Layer, Duplicate Layer**.

Click and drag with the **Background Eraser** tool. Pixels within the circular area of the brush tip, that are a relative match for the pixel under the hotspot, are erased.

10 View the Result

When you're satisfied with the image, save the PSD file. Then merge the layers together (if any) and resave the result in JPEG, PNG, or non-layered TIFF format, leaving your PSD image unflattened so that you can return at a later time and make adjustments if you want.

In this example, I erased the background behind the floral bouquet, expanded the canvas, added a colorful background and some text, and created a nice Mother's Day greeting.

---

58 | **Replace a Background with Something Else**

✔ BEFORE YOU BEGIN	→ SEE ALSO
Just jump right in!	**57** Erase Part of a Layer
	90 Remove Unwanted Objects from an Image

58

One of the simplest special-effects tricks you can pull off is to remove the background from around a subject and replace it with something else. For example, are you the only one who didn't make it to a recent family reunion? There's no reason you have to remember that fact forever—just use any of the eraser tools (see **57 Erase Part of a Layer**) or use the **Magic Extractor**, as explained in this task, to remove the background from a recent photo of yourself, and then replace the background with the reunion photo. After a few minutes' work, you'll be partying with your cousins. Of course, there are legitimate reasons for needing to replace an image background as well—for example, if you have a photo of a man in a black suit on a dark background, you won't be able to do much using the Editor's contrast controls to separate them visually. Better to select the man and place him on a lighter background that provides more contrast.

The **Magic Extractor** differs from the eraser tools in that it is used exclusively for removing the background from around a subject. The process is simple: You use the tools in the **Magic Extractor** dialog box to mark the area you want to keep and the area you want to get rid of. You can preview the results of your selections and make adjustments as needed. When you close the dialog box, the area you marked for removal is erased (made transparent).

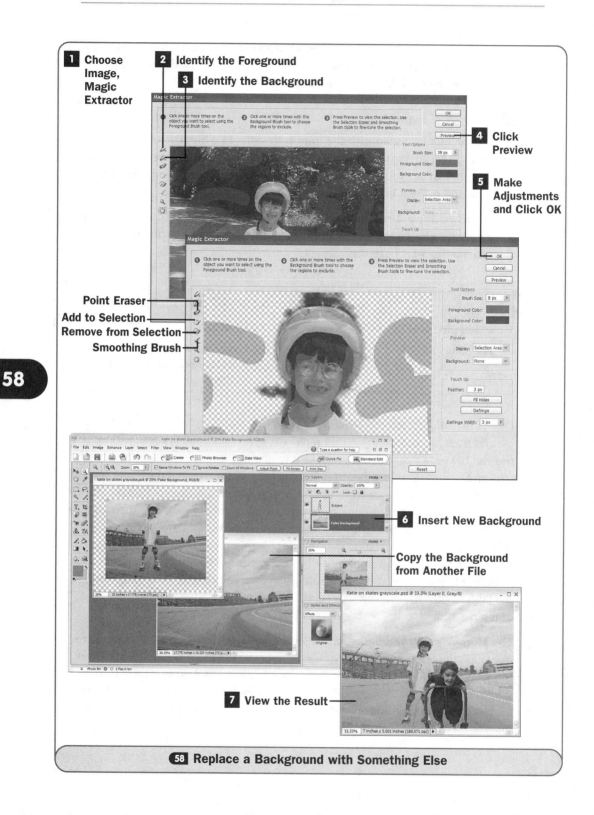

1 Choose Image, Magic Extractor

2 Identify the Foreground

3 Identify the Background

4 Click Preview

5 Make Adjustments and Click OK

Point Eraser

Add to Selection

Remove from Selection

Smoothing Brush

58

6 Insert New Background

Copy the Background from Another File

7 View the Result

58 Replace a Background with Something Else

1   Choose Image, Magic Extractor

Open an image in the Editor in **Standard Edit** mode and save it in Photoshop (***.psd**) format. Choose **Image, Magic Extractor**. The **Magic Extractor** dialog box appears.

2   Identify the Foreground

The **Foreground Brush** tool is automatically selected; in the image area within the dialog box, click or drag with it a few times to mark the area you want to keep. You can adjust the **Brush Size** if desired, and the **Foreground Color** used by the brush.

3   Identify the Background

Click the **Background Brush** tool, adjust the **Brush Size** and **Background Color** used by the brush if desired, then click or drag with it a few times in the image area of within the dialog box to mark the area you want to remove.

4   Click Preview

Click the **Preview** button. The background you identified in step 3 is removed (made transparent). The red and blue squiggles you made remain so that you can see where you might need to add more squiggles to properly identify the foreground (the area to keep) and the background (the area to remove).

The **Display** box shows **Selection Area**; to redisplay the original image and your squiggles, but not actually remove the indicated background area, choose **Original Photo** from the **Display** menu. To display white, black, or gray in the area marked for removal, make that selection from the **Background** menu. You can also display the result as a mask (in which the foreground area is displayed as white and the area to be removed appears normally. In addition, you can choose **rubylinth**, which displays a light red overlay on top of the area to remove, while displaying the image as-is in the foreground area.

5   Make Adjustments and Click OK

Make adjustments as needed until the background is fully removed. Click the **Foreground Brush** or **Background Brush** and click or drag some more in the foreground or background area. Remove marks you've made using the **Point Eraser** tool. To see these changes to your image, click **Preview** again.

To add or remove portions of the image without having to click **Preview** to see them, use the **Add To** or **Remove From Selection** tools. To add/or remove

58

a large area, drag a line with either tool to separate the foreground from the area to remove, and then click the **Fill Holes** button.

Smooth the edges around the area you want to keep by adjusting the amount of **Feather**. You can also drag over any areas you want to smooth using the **Smoothing Brush** tool. To remove random colors left between the foreground and background, set a **Defringe Width** and click the **Defringe** button.

Click **Reset** if you want to start all over; otherwise, when you've specified the right area to remove, click **OK**. The area you designated as the background is removed from the image. Name this layer **Subject** because what remains in the layer after you've removed the background is undoubtedly the subject of the image.

6 Insert New Background

After erasing the background from around a subject, you can replace the background with something else. Open the image you want to use as the background, and if necessary, select the layer you want to use from the **Layers** palette. Choose **Select**, **All** to select all the pixels in your background image that reside on that particular layer, and then choose **Edit**, **Copy** to copy them to the Clipboard.

Paste the new background into the image you're editing by activating its window again and then choosing **Edit**, **Paste**. This action creates a new layer with the contents from the Clipboard (the new background you want to use). Rename the layer **Fake Background**.

In the **Layers** palette, drag the **Fake Background** layer below the **Subject** layer so that the new background appears in the holes created by the **Magic Extractor**. Resize and reposition the **Fake Background** layer if needed. See **59** Move, Resize, Skew, or Distort a Layer or Selection.

▶ TIPS

As you're using the Magic **Extractor** to remove an image background, click the **Zoom** tool to zoom in. To zoom back out, press **Alt** and click. Scroll the image with the **Hand** tool.

If you want to place the original image on a web page background or your Windows desktop, skip step 6 and leave the background around the subject transparent. To retain the transparent pixels when you resave the completed PSD file, use **GIF**, **PNG**, or **JPEG 2000** format.

58

7 View the Result

When you're satisfied with the result, make any other changes you want and save the PSD file. Resave the result in JPEG, PNG, or non-layered TIFF format, leaving your PSD image with its layers intact so that you can return at a later time and make adjustments if you want. For example, you might want to try out some different backgrounds and have some fun!

After seeing this photo of my daughter trying out her new roller skates, I couldn't help but imagine her racing someplace sportier. I just happened to have a photograph of the Indianapolis 500 track (taken while my husband was driving around it in his sports car), so I merged the two to create a cute photo. I combined the result with a photo of my sister Pat pushing a walker around our driveway when she was little.

Because the walker image was in grayscale, I changed the image mode in my daughter's photograph to grayscale before copying the image of my sister into the master PSD file. I then resized and positioned my daughter just behind my sister with her walker.

---

59 **Move, Resize, Skew, or Distort a Layer or Selection**   **59**

✔ BEFORE YOU BEGIN	→ SEE ALSO
54 Create a New Image Layer	**60** Rotate the Data in a Layer or Selection

---

One advantage of layers is that you can move, resize, *skew,* or *distort* the contents of each individual layer without affecting the data on other layers. For example, you might decide to reduce the size of a layer so that its contents fit better with the proportions of the contents of the other layers. This is common procedure after pasting data onto a new layer taken from a different image. For example, if you paste your dog into a family photo, you'll probably need to move and resize him so that he doesn't look out of proportion with the rest of the family members. You can skew or distort data to tilt or stretch it—sometimes just for fun, and sometimes to correct for perspective. For example, if you take a photo of a tall object while looking up, the base looks wider than the top, even if the object (such as a building) is the same size all the way up. By distorting the image, you can pull the base of the building inward, eliminating the illusion of a wide base.

▶ KEY TERMS

Skew—To tilt (slant) a layer right, left, up or down.

Distort—To stretch a corner of a layer in any one direction.

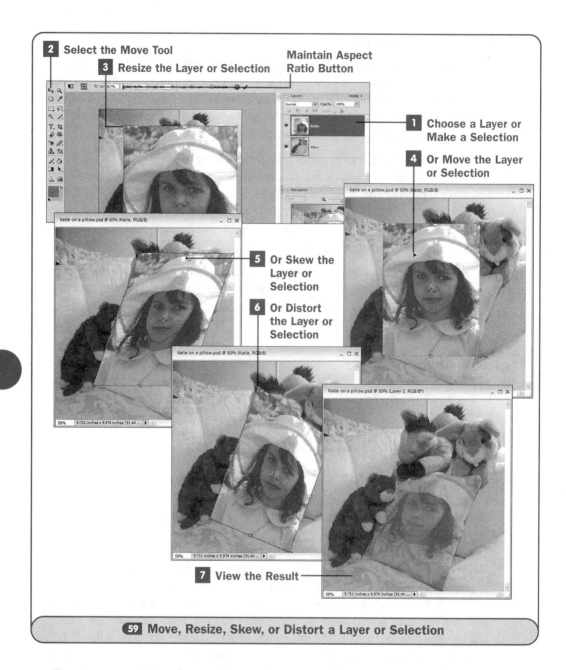

2 Select the Move Tool

3 Resize the Layer or Selection

Maintain Aspect Ratio Button

1 Choose a Layer or Make a Selection

4 Or Move the Layer or Selection

5 Or Skew the Layer or Selection

6 Or Distort the Layer or Selection

7 View the Result

59 Move, Resize, Skew, or Distort a Layer or Selection

You can move, resize, skew, or distort a layer using the **Move** tool. You can also perform these same functions on a shape or text object or on a selection. When you move, resize, skew, or distort the data in a selection, however, the hole that is left by the selection's former location is filled with transparent pixels (if the layer supports transparency). For the **Background** layer, which does not allow transparency, the hole left by the altered selection is filled with the current background color. If you alter a selection surrounded by colored pixels on any other layer, the hole is filled with transparent pixels. You can then fill the hole by cloning the surrounding data.

1 Choose a Layer or Make a Selection

Open an image in the Editor in **Standard Edit** mode and save it in Photoshop (***.psd**) format. In the **Layers** palette, select the layer you want to modify. To alter the entire **Background** layer, you must first convert it by choosing **Layer, New, Layer from Background**. If you want to alter a portion of the layer, make that selection now.

2 Select the Move Tool

On the **Toolbox**, select the **Move** tool. On the **Options** bar, enable the **Show Bounding Box** option. To automatically grab whatever object or layer under the mouse pointer is highest in the layer stack, enable the **Auto Select Layer** option as well. These two options disappear from the **Options** bar as soon as you start making adjustments, so be sure to set them before you continue.

The mouse pointer changes to a solid black arrow, and assuming that you have enabled the **Show Bounding Box** option, a bounding box appears around the edges of the selection or layer. If the layer is a shape or text layer, the bounding box appears around the edges of the shape or text object.

59

3 Resize the Layer or Selection

If you're altering an entire layer rather than a selection, maximize the image window and adjust the zoom so that the image is smaller than the window itself. This arrangement will give you the space you need to grab the layer handles properly.

To resize the contents of the layer or selection, position the mouse pointer over one of the handles on the edge of the bounding box until it changes to the **Resize** pointer (a straight line with arrows on each end). Drag to resize the layer or selection. Press **Shift** as you drag a corner handle to retain the proportions of the layer, selection, or object. If you begin resizing and then realize that the object is out of proportion, stop dragging and click the **Maintain Aspect Ratio** button that appears on the **Options** bar. The object's size is adjusted to fit its original proportions, and if you start dragging again, these proportions are maintained.

▶ **NOTE**

You can enter a percentage in the **W** and **H** boxes on the **Options** bar after beginning to drag. The selection, object, or layer is then instantly scaled by that amount, such as 50%.

4 Or Move the Layer or Selection

To move the layer or selection, click in the center of the bounding box and drag the layer or selection to the desired position. To move in one-pixel increments, press the arrow keys. To move in 10-pixel increments, hold down the **Shift** key while you press the arrow keys.

5 Or Skew the Layer or Selection

If you want to skew the layer or selection (tilt it horizontally or vertically in one direction), press **Ctrl+Shift** and then position the mouse pointer on a side (not a corner) handle. The mouse pointer changes to a gray arrow with a small double-headed arrow beneath it. Drag left or right to skew horizontally; drag up or down to skew vertically.

▶ TIPS

You can also skew by first clicking the **Skew** button on the **Options** bar (it might not be showing yet; it appears when you begin to resize, skew, or distort) or by selecting **Image**, **Transform**, **Skew** and then dragging any side handle in the direction you want to skew.

You can also distort by selecting **Image**, **Transform**, **Distort** and then dragging any handle in the direction you want to stretch.

59

6 Or Distort the Layer or Selection

If you want to distort the layer or selection (stretch one corner), hold down the **Ctrl** key and position the mouse pointer on a corner or side handle. The mouse pointer changes to a gray arrow. Drag the handle of the bounding box inward or outward.

7 View the Result

When you're satisfied with your changes, click the **Commit** button (the check mark) on the **Options** bar. To undo all changes made with the **Move** tool this session, click the **Cancel** button (the circle-with-a-slash icon) instead.

Make any other changes you want in the image and save the PSD file. Then merge the layers together (if any) and resave the result in JPEG, PNG, or non-layered TIFF format, leaving your PSD image unflattened so that you can return at a later time and make adjustments if you want.

In this example, I took a photo of a pillow surrounded by some much loved stuffed animals and combined it with a photo of my daughter, which I first resized and then skewed to the left. I then distorted the corners of the photo, positioning them exactly over the corners of the pillow. The result was a photo of my daughter that exactly matched the shape of the pillow below. It was then a simple matter to change the photo layer's blend mode to **Multiply** and set the **Opacity** to 62%, causing the photo of my daughter to blend into the pillow on the layer below, making it look as if her face was lightly painted on the pillow.

---

60 **Rotate the Data in a Layer or Selection**

✔ BEFORE YOU BEGIN	→ SEE ALSO
Just jump right in!	**59** Move, Resize, Skew, or Distort a Layer or Selection

---

It is not uncommon to have to rotate the data in a selection or layer. You might have just pasted your daughter's pretty face onto a layer and want to rotate it just a bit so that it faces your son, who is located on another layer. Or you might want to rotate a shape that's on the same layer as another shape, or to rotate some text. No matter what the goal, the rotation process is basically the same in all instances: Select the data or layer to rotate and use the **Move** tool to spin it around.

This task teaches you what is essentially free rotation—you can rotate a selection or layer by whatever amount you choose. If you want to rotate by 90° left or right, or by some exact amount you already know (such as 120°), or if you want to flip the data rather than rotate it, choose the appropriate command from the **Image**, **Rotate** menu. To rotate/flip the entire image, choose **90° Left/Right**, **Custom**, or **Flip Horizontal/Vertical**. To rotate or flip a layer by a set amount, choose **Layer 90° Left/Right**, **Layer 180°**, or **Layer Flip Horizontal/Vertical**. If your goal is not rotation, but resizing, moving, or somehow distorting the data in a selection, see **59** **Move, Resize, Skew, or Distort a Layer or Selection**.

▶ **NOTE**

If you rotate a selection on the **Background** layer, the hole it leaves is filled with the background color; on other layers, the selection is filled with transparent pixels. You can then fill the hole by cloning the surrounding data. If you don't want to leave a hole where the original selection was located, you should paste your selection into a new layer before rotating it. See **53** Create a New Image or Layer from a Selection.

1 **Choose a Layer or Make a Selection**

Open an image in the Editor in **Standard Edit** mode and save it in Photoshop (***.psd**) format. In the **Layers** palette, choose the layer to rotate. To rotate the entire **Background** layer, you must first convert it by choosing **Layer**, **New**, **Layer from Background**. If you want to rotate a portion of the layer, make that selection now.

60

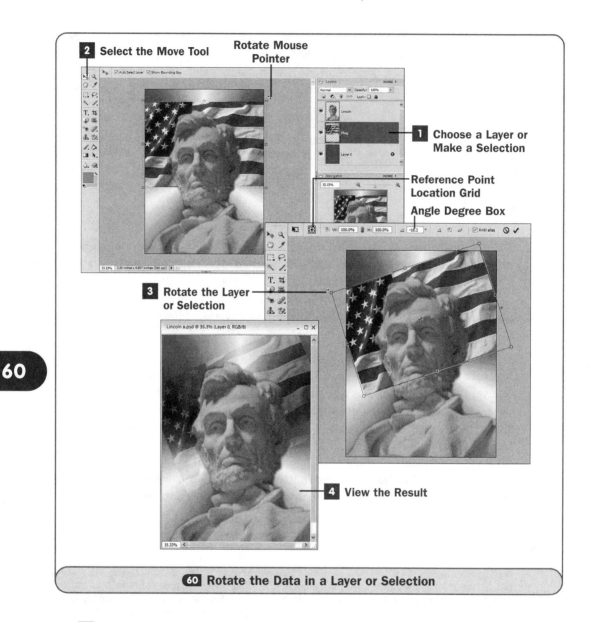

60 Rotate the Data in a Layer or Selection

60

2 Select the Move Tool

If you're rotating an entire layer rather than a selection, maximize the image window and adjust the zoom so that the image is smaller than the window itself. This arrangement will give you the space you need in step 3 to grab the layer and rotate it.

Select the **Move** tool on the **Toolbox**; the mouse pointer changes to a solid black arrow. Enable the **Show Bounding Box** option in the **Options** bar. To automatically grab whatever object or layer under the mouse pointer is highest in the layer stack, enable the **Auto Select Layer** option in the **Options** bar as well. These two options disappear from the **Options** bar as soon as you start rotating, so be sure to set them before you continue.

The mouse pointer changes to a solid black arrow, and assuming you enabled the **Show Bounding Box** option, a bounding box appears around the edges of the selection or layer. If the layer is a shape or text layer, the bounding box appears around the edges of the shape or text object.

▐3▌ Rotate the Layer or Selection

Position the mouse pointer over a corner handle on the bounding box; the pointer changes to a curved arrow like the one shown. Drag in the direction you want to rotate. You can also use any of the following techniques to rotate:

- To rotate a copy of a selection, press **Alt** as you drag. This technique cannot be used to rotate and copy a layer.

- To rotate by 15-degree increments, press **Shift** as you drag.

- To alter the reference point around which rotation takes place, click the reference point you want to use in the **Reference Point Location** grid on the **Options** bar.

- To rotate by a specific amount, type the number of degrees to rotate in the **Angle Degree** box on the **Options** bar.

When you're done rotating the selection or layer, click the **Commit** button (the check mark) on the **Options** bar. To cancel your adjustment, click **Cancel** (the circle-with-a-slash icon) instead.

▐4▌ View the Result

When you're satisfied with the results, make any other changes you want and save the PSD file. Resave the result in JPEG, PSD, or non-layered TIFF format, leaving your PSD image with its layers (if any) intact so that you can return at a later time and make adjustments if you want.

For this example, I wanted the flag to appear diagonally behind ol' Abe, so I rotated the layer containing just the flag image. To get the see-through effect, I changed the flag layer's blend mode to **Soft Light**.

60

---

61 **Mask an Adjustment or Fill Layer**

✔ BEFORE YOU BEGIN	→ SEE ALSO
55 Create a Layer Filled with a Color, Gradient, or Pattern	**62** Mask an Image Layer
56 Create an Adjustment Layer	**74** Paint an Area of a Photo with a Brush

Unless you made a selection when you created an adjustment or fill layer, the fill or adjustment layer initially "flows through" to the layers below, affecting all of them. That's because the *mask* for the layer (the thing that controls what portions of the layers below are affected) is *all white*. White on a mask shows you where the pixels on a fill or adjustment layer affect the layers below.

▶ KEY TERM

Mask—The part of an adjustment or fill layer that acts as a filter, blocking the adjustment or fill from affecting the other layers that lie beneath it in the layer stack.

You might decide after inserting an adjustment or fill layer that you do not want its effect to be applied to your entire image. For example, if you created an adjustment layer and selected the **Brightness and Contrast** adjustment, you might want to apply the adjustment to just your subject and not to the entire image layer below. To prevent adjustment and fill layers from affecting areas of an image, you must edit the mask for that layer—basically painting parts of the mask black, which causes the mask to block the effect in that area of the layers below. If you use gray to paint on the mask, the effects of the adjustment or fill layer are only partially blocked. You can use any painting tool to accomplish this, such as the **Brush**, **Pencil**, or **Paint Bucket**. You can also apply a black-to-white gradient, for example, to fade the effect of the fill or adjustment layer in one direction. You can also apply any filter or effect that works on grayscale images to a mask, or use the **Text** or **Shape** tools to draw the area you want to block.

1 Select Layer

Open an image in the Editor in **Standard Edit** mode and save it in Photoshop (***.psd**) format. In the **Layers** palette, select the adjustment or fill layer whose mask you want to edit.

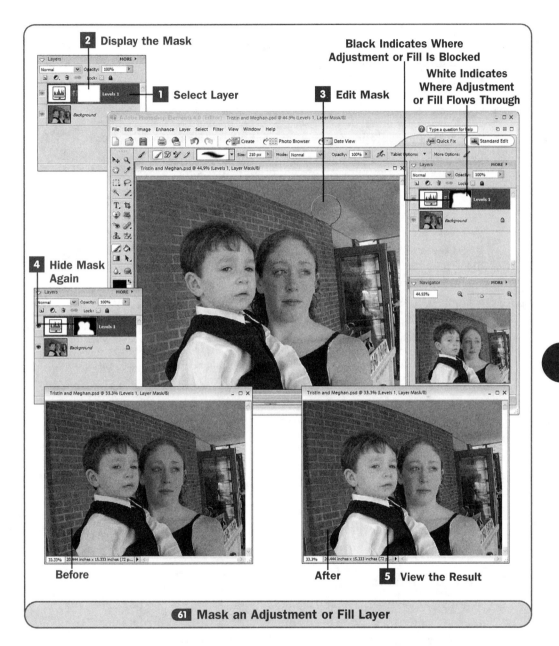

2 Display the Mask

Black Indicates Where
Adjustment or Fill Is Blocked

White Indicates
Where Adjustment
or Fill Flows Through

1 Select Layer

3 Edit Mask

4 Hide Mask Again

Before

After **5 View the Result**

61 Mask an Adjustment or Fill Layer

2 Display the Mask

Press **Alt+Shift**, and on the **Layers** palette, click the mask thumbnail (the thumbnail on the right) for the adjustment or fill layer you want to change. This displays the mask in the image window as a red overlay (so that you can see the image through the mask). To display the mask in black and white (so that the mask covers the image), press **Alt** as you click instead. If you haven't edited the mask, the entire mask layer will be white (indicating that the adjustment or fill layer is affecting all the pixels on the layers below it in the layer stack).

3 Edit Mask

Click one of the painting tools in the **Toolbox**, set the foreground color to black, and paint on the mask in the area where you want to block the adjustment layer's effect. Paint with gray to partially block the layer's effects. Paint with white again to let the layer's effects flow through.

You can use any tool, filter, effect, or command that works with grayscale images to edit the mask, such as the **Gradient** tool, **Text** tool, **Shape** tool, **Paint Bucket** tool, **Brightness/Contrast** or **Levels** command, or **Posterize** filter.

▶ TIPS

After the mask is displayed, you can copy data onto it and use that data as your mask. For example, you could select a portion of your image or another image, and paste that onto the mask. The data appears in grayscale; the black pixels (represented by the darkest parts of the image you pasted) block the fill or adjustment layer, and the lighter gray pixels only partially block it.

If you need to reposition the mask on the fill or adjustment layer, you must unlink it first by clicking the link icon (the chain), located between the layer thumbnail and the mask thumbnail. Use the **Move** tool to reposition the mask, and then click the link icon again to re-link the mask to the fill/adjustment layer.

4 Hide Mask Again

To view the image again and hide the mask, press **Alt** and click the mask thumbnail on the **Layers** palette. Notice that the mask thumbnail has been updated to reflect your changes to the mask.

5 View the Result

When you're satisfied with the image, save the PSD file. Then merge the layers together (if any) and resave the result in JPEG, PNG, or non-layered TIFF format, leaving your PSD image unflattened so that you can return at a later time and make adjustments if you want.

▶ TIP

You can temporarily turn off a mask (and let the fill or adjustment flow through freely) by pressing **Shift** and clicking the mask thumbnail for the adjustment/fill layer on the **Layers** palette.

In this example, I first applied a **Levels** adjustment to improve the contrast in my niece and great-nephew's face. But I didn't like what it did to the background (it made it too bright and distracting). So, I displayed the mask by following steps 1 and 2 and then painted the background black (to stop the **Levels** adjustment). The result is a subtle yet striking difference.

---

62 **Mask an Image Layer**

✔ BEFORE YOU BEGIN	→ SEE ALSO
Just jump right in!	**61** Mask an Adjustment or Fill Layer

A mask blocks data on a layer from covering up data on the layers below it. Masks are automatically created when you insert an adjustment or fill layer. For an adjustment layer, the mask blocks the adjustment from affecting certain areas of the layers below. For a fill layer, the mask simply blocks the fill from appearing in particular areas of the layers below.

But what do you do if you want to mask an image layer rather than an adjustment or fill layer? For example, suppose you want a flag to appear within the contours of an American eagle? You could use the **Cookie Cutter** tool to cut the flag into an eagle shape (if it had an eagle shape to use, which it doesn't). But even if the **Cookie Cutter** tool had the shape you wanted, you couldn't reposition the flag image within the eagle shape after committing the change. The simplest way to create what you want is to use a *clipping mask* in the shape of an eagle to control what portions of the flag appear in the final image. Unlike an adjustment or fill mask, in which black is used to block data and white is used to allow data on upper layers to show through, in a clipping mask, opaque pixels (regardless of their color) allow data to show through, and transparent or partially transparent pixels block data fully or partially.

▶ **KEY TERM**

Clipping mask—Controls what portions of any upper layers grouped with the mask appear in the final image.

1 **Add Clipping Mask Layer**

Open the image you want to mask in the Editor in **Standard Edit** mode and save it in Photoshop (***.psd**) format. Insert a new layer for the clipping mask by clicking the **Create new layer** button on the **Layers** palette. Name this new layer **Clipping Mask**.

62

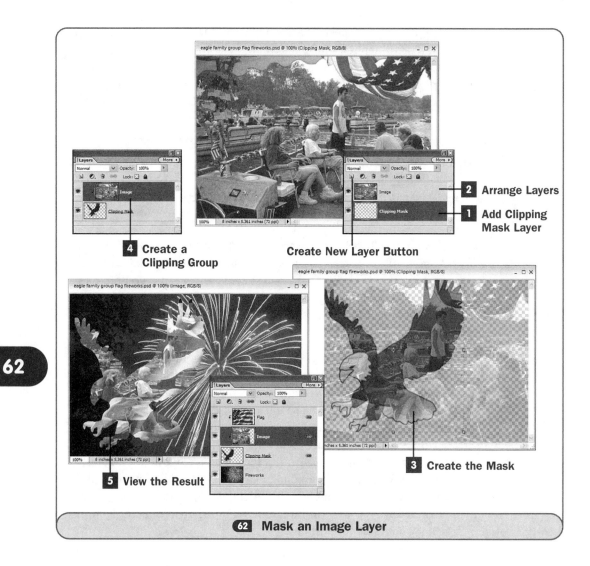

62 Mask an Image Layer

2 Arrange Layers

The **Clipping Mask** layer must go beneath the layer(s) you want to mask. So, if necessary, in the **Layers** palette, drag the **Clipping Mask** layer into position under the layer you want to mask.

▶ **NOTE**

To move the **Clipping Mask** layer below the background layer, you must first convert the background layer to a regular layer by choosing **Layer, New, Layer from Background**. In the **New Layer** dialog box that appears, you can name the converted layer **Image** if you like, so that you'll remember what it contains.

3 Create the Mask

On the **Layers** palette, select the **Clipping Mask** layer. Lower the **Opacity** of the **Image** layer so that you can see the data on the **Clipping Mask** layer more clearly as you work. To create a mask on this layer in the shape you want, you have the following choice of methods:

- Paint on the **Clipping Mask** layer with any color using the **Brush** tool, or draw with the **Pencil**. To create a feathered effect, select a soft brush to apply semi-transparent pixels to allow the upper layers to show partially through. Remember: Where you paint or draw, that portion of the image layer will show through in the final image. See **73** **Draw on a Photo with a Pencil** and **74** **Paint an Area of a Photo with a Brush**.

- Draw any shape you want onto the **Clipping Mask** layer, using any of the shape tools, such as the **Rectangle** tool or the **Custom Shape** tool. If you want more than one shape on the **Clipping Mask** layer, or if you want to create an object with a complex shape made up of several different shapes (such as a rectangle and two circles), draw your shapes with the **Add to Shape Area** button enabled on the **Options** bar. Again, the portion of the image layer that appears in the final image will be in the shape you draw. See **78** **Draw a Shape**.

- Fill the layer with a gradient, using the **Gradient** tool. The upper layers will be blocked only where the gradient is fully transparent, will show through partially where the gradient is partially opaque, and will show through fully where the gradient uses fully opaque pixels, so keep that in mind when selecting a gradient preset. See **77** **Fill an Area with a Gradient**. In a similar manner, you can fill the **Clipping Mask** layer with a *pattern*. See **76** **Fill an Area with a Color or Pattern**.

- Use the **Selection Brush** to create a selection in the shape you need, then fill the selection with any color using the **Paint Bucket** tool. The image layer will show through only in the area you fill. If you feather the edges of the selection, the upper layers will show through at the edges, but only partially. This might enable you to blend the masked area more smoothly into the layers below. See **48** **Paint a Selection**.

▶ TIP

You can create a clipping mask layer using any of the selection tools to select an object in another image that's in the shape you want to use and copying that object into your image, to a new layer below the image layer you want to clip. This process saves you from having to create a clipping mask layer manually because pasting data from a different image always results in a new layer. Skip step 1 here that creates a **Clipping Mask** layer, remove the **Clipping Mask** layer if you've already created one, or merge the layer you pasted into the image with the **Clipping Mask** layer so that there's just one layer.

62

- Type text, and then merge the text layer into the **Clipping Mask** layer by selecting the text layer in the **Layers** palette and choosing **Layer**, **Merge Down**. The upper masked layer(s) will then appear only within the outline of the text. See **79** **Add a Text Caption or Label**.

4 Create a Clipping Group

In the **Layers** palette, choose the **Image** layer. Group this layer with the **Clipping Mask** layer by choosing **Layer**, **Group with Previous**. On the **Layers** palette, the **Image** layer is indented, indicating that the upper layer is being clipped (masked) by the layer below. Data on the **Image** layer is now masked by the **Clipping Mask** layer and shows through only where the **Clipping Mask** layer is partially or entirely opaque.

You've just created a clipping group. Now, if you'd like to clip other layers as well, you can add those layer(s) just above the **Image** layer to the clipping group—there cannot be any other layers in between. In the **Layers** palette, select the layer above the **Image** layer and choose **Layers**, **Group with Previous** to group the layer with the clipping group. In this same manner, add as many other layers as you like to the clipping group.

5 View the Result

After you're satisfied with the result, make any other changes you want and then save the PSD file. Resave the result in JPEG, PNG, or non-layered TIFF format, leaving your PSD image with its layers intact so that you can return at a later time and make adjustments if you like.

To create this image, I used the shape of an eagle to mask two layers—one of my sister's family enjoying the Fourth of July on their pontoon boat, and another layer of an American flag. I blended these two layers together so that you can just see the ripple of the flag across the family photo, and the result was clipped by the eagle mask. On the bottom layer, I placed an image of the fireworks we enjoyed later that evening. By placing the fireworks layer on the bottom, its contents are obstructed by only the portion of the image layer that's clipped by the mask.

PART III

Editing Images

IN THIS PART:

CHAPTER 9   **Making Quick Corrections to a Photograph**   279

CHAPTER 10   **Retouching Photos with the Tools**   307

CHAPTER 11   **Repairing and Improving Photographs**   353

CHAPTER 12   **Correcting Brightness, Contrast, Color, and Sharpness**   375

9

Making Quick Corrections to a Photograph

IN THIS CHAPTER:

63 About Color Management

64 Install a Color Profile

65 Crop a Portion of an Image

66 Straighten an Image

67 Correct Red Eye

68 Apply a Quick Fix

Using the Editor, you can easily make adjustments to your photographs before printing them. For example, you might want to rotate or straighten an image, or crop it to remove distractions from around your subject. If the image is pretty good, you might want to give it only a quick fix (a series of simple, automated adjustments to an image's brightness, contrast, saturation, and sharpness), rather than a more complex, manual editing job. You'll learn how to perform all these simple, easy corrections in this chapter. For images that require a bit more work before you can print them, see upcoming chapters for help.

The Organizer provides a way for you to make automatic improvements to a selected image without invoking the Editor. The **Edit**, **Auto SmartFix** command makes automatic adjustments to color and tone *without any input from you*. However, you'll most likely prefer the results you get with the Editor's **Quick Fix** tool, which allows you to select not only the type but the amount of the automatic adjustment you want to apply. See **68 Apply a Quick Fix**. For full access to all adjustments and tools, choose **Standard Edit** mode in the Editor; see upcoming tasks for information on how to use the Editor's tools. Before editing on any image, however, you must adjust your monitor so that the colors you see onscreen will match the colors you get when you print an image. See **63 About Color Management**.

63   About Color Management

✔ BEFORE YOU BEGIN	→ SEE ALSO
Just jump right in!	**36** Print an Image
	64 Install a Color Profile

What you see onscreen when you view an image is often very different from what you get when you print an image on paper. Not only do your monitor, printer, and even your scanner use different methods to render color images, each device works with its own separate range of possible colors (also called a *gamut*). What this means is that, when representing an image onscreen, your monitor might display a grayish red for an area of an image, which is not reproducible by your printer as *an exact* match. The printer, in such a case, simply substitutes a *close* match to the grayish red from similar colors in its gamut. So, when the image is printed, you get something that's close to what it looked like onscreen, but not exactly. The best way you can deal with this messy situation is to create an environment that simulates onscreen (as nearly as possible) what an image will look like when it's finally printed. To do that, you use *color management*.

▶ KEY TERMS

Gamut—A palette comprised of all the individual colors that can be reproduced by a device. Your monitor, printer, scanner, and your digital camera each have separate gamuts, and sometimes colors within them might match closely but not precisely.

Color management—The process of coordinating the color gamut of your monitor with that of your scanner and printer so that the same colors are reproduced throughout your system.

Microsoft Windows has the unenviable task of translating colors from one device to another using specific ICM (Image Color Management) profiles for the devices involved. All devices that use color should have one of these profiles installed (specifically, your monitor, printer, scanner, and some digital cameras). Usually, the color profile for a device is located on the manufacturer's disc, and you install it at the time you install the device driver and other software for that device—monitor, printer, scanner, and digital camera. With a profile installed, Windows translates colors between devices, so that "rosy red" shows up as exactly that on your monitor, printer, and scanner. Sounds easy, but it isn't. For example, suppose you scan in an image. Windows translates the colors from the scanner's profile into a set of colors matching those in the monitor's profile. If there is no monitor profile installed, Windows translates the scanner colors into colors within its own standard color gamut. This result goes through a further translation by your video card, using its own methodology and driver. (For good reason, high-end video cards do not trust Windows's results, and so they typically tweak these colors before displaying them.) Photoshop Elements takes this one step further by making minor adjustments to these monitor colors with some help from a program called Adobe Gamma.

63

▶ NOTES

Adobe Gamma creates an ICC color profile of its own, using information provided by the video card through Windows. The resulting profile is what Photoshop Elements uses to represent colors onscreen. You'll learn how to create and install the profile Adobe Gamma creates in **64** Install a Color Profile.

Because paper plays a critical role in the quality of photos printed at home, manufacturers of paper for inkjet and photo printers are now releasing ICC color profiles for their various grades and bonds of paper. How you use one of these profiles depends on how your printer driver manages color. Newer printer drivers can incorporate separate paper profiles along with their existing printer profiles. Some printer manufacturers' brands of paper—for instance, HP and Epson—provide color profiles that override the existing profiles for their older models of printers (those that don't manage paper profiles separately), thus becoming combination "printer + paper" profiles.

Earlier, I mentioned that some digital cameras have color profiles you need to install. Most cameras, however embed their color profiles within recorded images and therefore, cameras of this type do not need to have a color profile "installed" on your system. The color gamut for an image is saved in the image's EXIF data, which you can view on the **Metadata** tab of the **Properties** pane in the

Organizer, and on the **Camera Data 2** page of the **File Info** dialog box in the Editor. (See 🔟 **About Image Information**.) For most digital cameras, the gamut saved in an image file is sRGB. If you turn color management on within the Editor, the gamut used by the digital camera (and included in an image's EXIF data) is used to translate the image to the screen. For images that don't have a gamut listed in their EXIF data (again assuming you turn on color management within Photoshop Elements), you can choose which gamut to use. Again, sRGB is the gamut typically used by most digital cameras, so it's a good choice for use in the Editor if you're prompted to make a choice when opening an image.

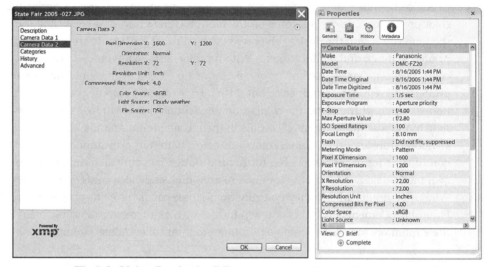

File Info Dialog Box in the Editor   **Properties Pane in the Organizer**

You can view the EXIF data attached to an image using the Editor or the Organizer.

▶ **NOTE**

Some cameras tag their images with the sRGB color space (gamut), even if that is not the actual gamut used by the camera. This causes a noticeable color cast in all images from that camera, when viewed in Photoshop Elements because the program assumes that sRGB was actually used, and uses that gamut to display the image onscreen. When your digital camera is pretending to use sRGB and it really isn't, you'll want to ignore the EXIF data when saving an image and have Adobe Gamma provide the color space data instead. Simply choose **Edit**, **Preferences**, **Saving Files** from the Editor menu, enable the **Ignore Camera Data (EXIF) Profiles** check box, and click **OK**.

Printing and Color Management

Now that you understand more clearly how an image is translated to the screen, let's take a closer look at the translation to the printer. When Photoshop Elements sends an image to the printer, Windows just passes it along, because when

Windows processes the image to display it on the screen, its Graphics Device Interface bases its color decisions partly on the current printer driver. If you have no printer installed, the GDI translates color information using Windows's generic printer driver. Which is why it's a really good idea to make sure that the printer you intend to use is selected in the **Printer** dialog box, before you go making a lot of changes to an image. (You can choose which printer to use from the **Page Setup** dialog box in the Editor; see **36** **Print an Image**.)

▶ **NOTE**

It's important to note that I'm talking about translation here—getting the image data from the file and onto the screen with some degree of accuracy, and then getting that data from the screen to the printer correctly. The data in an image file itself isn't changed at all during this translation process—neither by Windows nor by the printer. Image data can be changed by Photoshop Elements, of course, as you edit an image to make it ready for its final use. As you edit, however, it's important not to lose any image data that will help in printing the image, which is why you should be careful to protect the original EXIF information in your digital camera images.

After Windows passes the image data to the printer, most photo printers tweak it a bit using the EXIF data in the image file. The EXIF data helps the printer translate the image data into as accurate a reproduction of the onscreen image as possible. So it's important that you don't remove EXIF data from an image file, which will happen if you save the image in anything other than JPEG, TIFF, or PSD format. Some printers do not interpret EXIF data. Recently, Epson has engineered a system for its inkjet and photo printers that gives the printer the EXIF data for an image directly, by way of a bypass driver. Epson calls its system Print Image Management (PIM), and it enables its printers to see with a high degree of accuracy (albeit through two translators) what a PIM-enabled digital camera saw when it recorded an image, and to be able to print that image as accurately as possible. Essentially, PIM—and its successor, PIM II—ensure that both the Epson printer and the PIM-enabled digital camera interpret color and present EXIF data in the same way. If you plan to use the PIM feature of your printer as it was intended, you should purchase or use a digital camera that explicitly supports PIM as well—and thankfully, many do, but you *do* have to look. When PIM is involved, the color management scheme changes. Software called the *PIM plug-in* bypasses Windows color management and the ICC color profile, presenting EXIF data from an image directly to Photoshop Elements.

63

Setting Monitor Chromaticity

Assuming that you have a desktop monitor, or a newer notebook (post-2004, with 15" monitor or larger), you should calibrate your monitor, using a utility called Adobe Gamma. (Older or less expensive, newer notebooks cannot be easily calibrated because their colors change too much depending on the lighting and angle of viewing.) Keeping your monitor calibrated is the best way for you to ensure that the image you see onscreen is the same image you get when you print. Photoshop Elements includes a tool for calibrating your monitor called Adobe Gamma. Using Adobe Gamma, you should calibrate your monitor at least twice per year, plus every time you replace your video card or update your video drivers. Monitor calibration affects how data is displayed onscreen, not just in Photoshop Elements, but in all your Windows applications.

You'll learn how to use Adobe Gamma in **64 Install a Color Profile.** Before you jump to that task, however, there are some technical terms you must understand to complete the steps, and the first one is called *monitor chromaticity*. Basically, every monitor has its own idea of how to display pure red, green, and blue, and that information is stored in the monitor's *ICC color profile*. If you have already installed a monitor profile, or if you're using the default sRGB color space that Windows provides when no profile is present, you'll have no problems in Adobe Gamma, because it will read values currently in use. However, you might still need to make changes to these values to enable the colors you *see* to more closely approximate the colors that the current profile would have you see. The sRGB color space is often inadequate for many brands of monitors—it makes a best-guess estimate of what colors you should see, and might be off-target. If you haven't installed a profile (because you couldn't find one for your monitor), you'll need to make some guesses, and in the next task, we'll show you how.

63

▶ KEY TERM

Monitor chromaticity—A particular monitor's definition of pure red, green, and blue. A monitor's chromaticity is stored in its ICC color profile.

---

64 Install a Color Profile

✔ BEFORE YOU BEGIN	→ SEE ALSO
63 About Color Management	**36** Print an Image

To ensure that what you see onscreen when viewing an image is what you get after printing that image on paper, you must perform certain steps that involve installing color profiles and properly calibrating your monitor. When you use the Adobe Gamma program for monitor calibration, you rely on your own eyes as the best gauge for what looks right. First, your monitor should be warm and stabilized so that colors and contrast don't appear washed out. For best results, leave your monitor running and active (that is, not in standby mode) for at least 30 minutes before running Adobe Gamma. When you're ready to begin, turn down any lights near your computer so that you can make a good assessment of the settings you select.

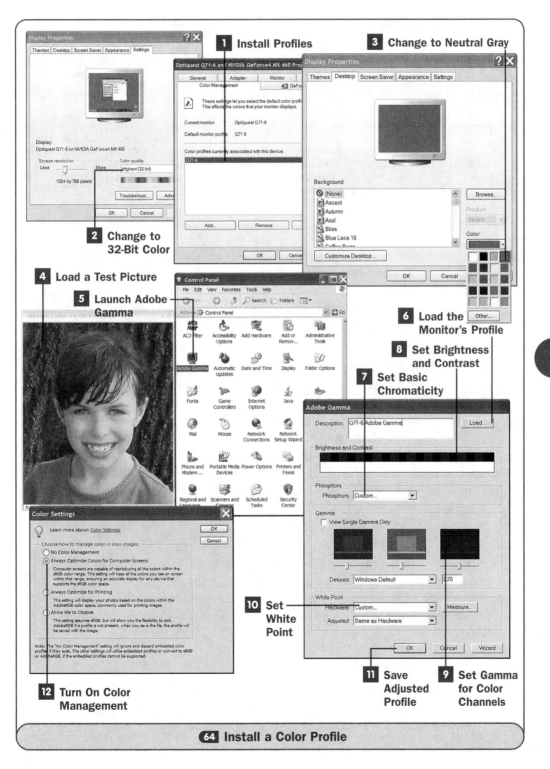

1 Install Profiles

3 Change to Neutral Gray

2 Change to 32-Bit Color

4 Load a Test Picture

5 Launch Adobe Gamma

6 Load the Monitor's Profile

7 Set Basic Chromaticity

8 Set Brightness and Contrast

9 Set Gamma for Color Channels

10 Set White Point

11 Save Adjusted Profile

12 Turn On Color Management

64 Install a Color Profile

Adobe Gamma has two operating modes. The **Wizard** mode leads you by the hand, step by step, with each option presented in its own individual panel. The **Control Panel** mode displays all options in a single window, without description. This task shows you how to use the **Control Panel** mode to make your selections and to save them in a new ICC color profile.

▶ **KEY TERM**

ICC color profile—Also known as an ICM profile. Each imaging device should have its own color profile installed; the file is used to translate image data from one device (such as a monitor) to another (such as a printer), so that the colors delivered by both devices match up as much as possible.

1 **Install Profiles**

Before beginning work with Adobe Gamma, copy the ICM color profiles for your monitor and printer to your system (if they are available). Save the files **Windows\System32\Color** folder. If you have profiles for your scanner and digital camera, copy them to these same folders as well. You might find profiles on the disc that came with the hardware or on the manufacturer's website.

After copying profiles to your computer, install them. To install the printer or scanner profile, open the **Control Panel**, and right-click the device's icon and choose **Properties**. The **Properties** dialog box appears. For the monitor, just double-click the **Display** icon in the **Control Panel** to open the **Properties** dialog box, then click the **Settings** tab and click **Advanced**. Then, for all devices, click the **Color Management** tab, and then click **Add**. Select the profile, and click **Add**. Click **OK** to close the **Properties** dialog box. With a printer, you have the additional step of selecting the profile to use and clicking the **Set As Default** button.

2 **Change to 32-Bit Color**

If needed, reopen the monitor's **Display Properties** dialog box and click the **Settings** tab. Open the **Color quality** drop-down list and choose **Highest (32 bit)**. If this option isn't available, it's because your system does not have enough video memory to support it; in that case, choose the highest setting you can.

3 **Change to Neutral Gray**

Click the **Desktop** tab in the **Display Properties** dialog box and choose **None** from the **Background** list. Set **Color** to a neutral gray by clicking the gray swatch on the right side of the color swatches drop-down list. Click **OK**.

64

▶ **NOTES**

Do not bother calibrating older laptops or newer, inexpensive laptops because the results will not be satisfactory; instead, install the appropriate monitor and printer profiles, turn on color management, and leave it at that.

If you've enabled any color correction features in your video card driver (for example, NVIDIA's **Digital Vibrance** option), be sure to disengage those features or reset them to their defaults before beginning monitor calibration with Adobe Gamma. You should make any video driver adjustments (if needed, and it's pretty rare that you might ever need to do so, typically only when you have a slightly malfunctioning monitor) *after* creating an Adobe Gamma profile.

4 Load a Test Picture

You won't be able to tell whether the settings you're about to make are "right" unless you have a test print to compare them to. In the Editor, open an image you've already printed out so that you can compare its onscreen version with its printed version as you work.

5 Launch Adobe Gamma

Open the **Control Panel** and double-click the **Adobe Gamma** icon to start the program. If prompted, select the **Control Panel Mode** option and click **Next**. The **Adobe Gamma** dialog box appears.

64

▶ **NOTE**

If the **Adobe Gamma** icon is not in the **Control Panel**, copy the **Adobe Gamma.cpl** file from the **\Adobe Gamma** folder of the Photoshop Elements CD-ROM to the **\Windows\ System32** folder.

6 Load the Monitor's Profile

Assuming that you were successful in locating and installing an ICC color profile for your monitor, the profile name should appear in the **Description** area of Adobe Gamma. If not, load it into Adobe Gamma by clicking the **Load** button, locating the file, and clicking **Open**. You'll find the profile (*monitorname*.icm) in the **Windows_system32\spool\drivers\color** or **\Windows\system32\color** folder. Adobe Gamma immediately applies those settings to your monitor. Now you can tweak what you're seeing using the other settings in the **Adobe Gamma** dialog box. If you don't have an ICC color profile for your monitor already loaded on your computer (because you couldn't find one), Adobe Gamma has to start from scratch rather than allowing you to adjust the profile settings.

In any case, after you're done here, Adobe Gamma will create a separate monitor profile for you. So that you can easily switch between the profile you're creating and the existing profile (in case you ever want to return to your original settings), enter a unique name for the profile in the **Description** box. Preferably, include the model number of your monitor.

7 Set Basic Chromaticity

The particular definition of pure red, green, and blue is called the monitor's chromaticity. If you've installed your monitor's ICC color profile, then Adobe Gamma will read the chromaticity settings from the profile and display **Custom** in the **Phosphors** list ("phosphors" being what Adobe Gamma calls chromaticity). Skip to step 8.

If you haven't installed a profile for the monitor (because you couldn't find one), then you'll need to enter something in the **Phosphors** box. Here are some tips to help you make a selection:

▶ **NOTE**

Although Adobe Gamma allows you to do so, you should never attempt to guess at the chromaticity settings by manually entering a string of numbers.

64

- When your onscreen color is more than just a tiny bit off, but not completely wrong, *and* if you know for certain that your CRT is a Trinitron—especially if it was manufactured by Sony, but also if your manufacturer licenses Sony's technology—select **Trinitron** for your chromaticity setting.

- If your CRT is not a Trinitron, try the sRGB setting, which Adobe Gamma calls **EBU/ITU**. In Adobe Gamma's **Wizard** mode, you can test your **Before** and **After** settings against one another to see whether the results look right to you. Of all the possibilities, **EBU/ITU** is the most likely to yield acceptable results if you have a non-Trinitron CRT.

- If the **EBU/ITU** setting doesn't result in true colors, and neither your monitor manufacturer nor the Internet can help you locate its true chromaticity settings, your best course of action is to cancel Adobe Gamma and make gamma and *white point* adjustments to your video driver's chromaticity settings directly. In the Windows **Control Panel**, double-click the **Display** icon. Click the **Settings** tab and click the **Advanced** button. Click the tab for your video driver (such as NVIDIA GeForce or ATI Radeon), and then adjust the gamma settings for each channel or for all channels simultaneously. The NVIDIA driver panel shown here enables you to load a monitor profile (including chromaticity data and white points) into the video driver software directly (from the **Custom Color Settings** list), overriding Windows' own color management. You might find this to be a blessing or a curse, but in my experience, never anything in-between.

If you decide to adjust the color correction settings of your video driver, make sure that you do so *after* making whatever changes you want to make to the ICC color profile using Adobe Gamma. Because the video driver's color corrections are applied over top of whatever the ICC color profile is telling the monitor to display, you'll want to make video driver adjustments *last*.

▶ **KEY TERM**

White point—A representation on a chromaticity chart of the monitor's version of "pure white." The white point is often expressed in terms of the *temperature* of the light—a measure of the actual heat it produces. Adobe Gamma enables you to set the basic white point in degrees Kelvin, although you can also express it in coordinates if you have them.

▶ **TIPS**

In some cases—especially if your monitor is more than a few years old—the **EBU/ITU** (sRGB) chromaticity setting might look somewhat better than even your monitor's own designated profile settings. You do not risk damage to your monitor if you use chromaticity settings other than those specified by the manufacturer.

If, no matter what choice you make for chromaticity within Adobe Gamma, the color on your monitor always looks wrong, consider upgrading your video card driver software. Whatever your card's manufacturer is, check its manual to see who produces its internal video chipset (most likely, NVIDIA or ATI). You can also look for the chip name on the video card, or try looking in the **Properties** dialog box for your monitor: Double-click the **Display** icon in the **Control Panel**, click the **Advanced** button on the **Settings** tab, click the tab for your video card, and look for a logo such as NVIDIA or ATI. After determining who makes the chipset for your video card, go to that manufacturer's website and download its latest *benchmark* drivers. These drivers use the latest technology and are generally updated far more frequently than the brand-specific drivers for your video card. They are probably better drivers than what you're using now and will probably reset your chromaticity settings to sRGB specifications, or something at least remotely pleasing. Even so, you can tweak the results of using this new driver by changing the color correction settings of the video driver as explained here. If, after all this, your monitor still doesn't look right, it might be time to explore the possibility of replacing it.

8 **Set Brightness and Contrast**

The sample black and white bars in the **Brightness and Contrast** pane are presented as test patterns for your monitor. If you look closely, you'll notice that the black bar is actually made up of jet black and very dark gray boxes, alternating with one another. If you don't notice this, you will after you complete this section of the calibration. The white bar is there to make the test fair because it's easier to distinguish dark gray from black when they're isolated; it's harder when they're adjacent to white.

Use the physical controls on your monitor (not on Adobe Gamma) to set your **contrast** to 100%, or as high as it will register. Next, set the **brightness** control on your monitor to as *low* a setting as possible where you can still distinguish the very dark gray blocks from the black ones. The moment they become indistinguishable, you're *too low*.

9 Set Gamma for Color Channels

In the **Gamma** pane, from the **Desired** drop-down list, choose **Windows Default** (the other choices are **Macintosh Default** and **Custom**). The Windows default is always a good starting point for achieving best results. Then disable the **View Single Gamma Only** check box to see the test squares for all three color channels. With your eyes squinting, for each square, move the slider until the solid block in the center blends as closely as possible with its striped frame.

64 ▶ NOTES

A monitor's gamma affects the brightness of images displayed on that monitor. Because a monitor does not respond in a linear fashion to changes in brightness in an image (its response looks more like a sharp curve), by properly adjusting the gamma value on your monitor (the point where its luminance curve begins to bend), you can create a near 1:1 relationship between the tonal values in an image and their brightness onscreen. In other words, when the monitor gamma is set correctly, the brightness and contrast of the midtones within an image will appear correctly onscreen.

Windows provides a gamma value for your monitor, whose value is set at 2.20. Adobe Gamma enables you to adjust this starting value and also set gamma variations that pertain to the three color channels individually. Your video card driver might include a *separate* gamma setting that pertains to color correction for your monitor; it does not affect the choices you make in Adobe Gamma or the values saved in the resulting profile. The video card gamma is simply an additional adjustment to the profile *result*; typically this gamma is left at a neutral setting of 1.0 so that it does not affect color management.

10 Set White Point

In the **White Point** pane, click the **Measure** button. In the directions panel that opens, click **OK**. Your screen will go black, and then you'll see three gray squares. The cooler of these shades *in terms of temperature* (thus, the bluer shade) is on the left; the warmer shade (the redder one) is on the right. Study the middle shade carefully. Use the left and right arrow keys to rotate through the shades of gray until the middle square appears as *unbiased* or as neutral as possible (not bluish, not reddish). When you've found that shade, press **Enter**. The **Hardware** list in the **Adobe Gamma** dialog box now displays the word **Custom**.

▶ **NOTES**

The **Adjusted** list normally shows the setting, **Same as Hardware**. If your monitor's manufacturer has provided you with coordinates for its white point, in the **White Point** pane choose **Custom** from the **Adjusted** drop-down list. In the dialog box that appears, enter the white-point coordinates provided by the manufacturer and click **OK**. If your manufacturer has specified the white point in terms of temperature, select the appropriate temperature from the **Adjusted** list.

To make an adequate assessment of whether what you see onscreen matches what you see on paper, you might also want to calibrate (align) your printer's print heads. You can find the routine for aligning your print heads in the **Properties** page for your printer, available from the **Printers and Faxes** page of the Windows **Control Panel**.

11 Save Adjusted Profile

Repeat steps 8 through 10 as necessary until your test image looks as true to its printed counterpart as possible. When you're ready to save your settings, click **OK**. The **Save As** dialog box appears. In the **File name** text box, enter a unique name for the ICC color profile you've just created. Click **Save**.

At this point, all your Adobe programs and most of your Windows programs should start displaying images using the settings you've just saved in the new profile. The notable exception here is Paint Shop Pro, which must be told to use the new profile. Choose **File**, **Preferences**, **Color Management**, and then click **Enable Color Management** and select the **Monitor Profile** from those listed.

12 Turn On Color Management

The first step in creating an environment that will ensure photo prints that match what you see onscreen is to install profiles for all your imaging devices such as your monitor and printer. The next step is to adjust the monitor profile settings using Adobe Gamma, a process called *calibrating*. The final step is to let the printer know what gamut (color space) you've been using to view and edit an image and to judge it ready to print. Your digital images are probably already tagged with the gamut used by your digital camera; Photoshop Elements respects this and uses that gamut to translate the image for display, preserving the gamut information in the image file. If an image does not specify a gamut, Color Management enables you to tell Photoshop Elements which one to use.

64

Choose **Edit**, **Color Settings** from the Editor menu. The **Color Settings** dialog box appears. Choose a color management option and click **OK**:

- **No Color Management**—Removes color space (gamut) information from files as they are opened. Translates the image for display using the monitor ICC profile only. Does not embed any gamut in the image file.

- **Always Optimize Colors for the Computer Screen**—Preserves gamut information in the image file (if any), translating the image for display using the sRGB gamut. Embeds sRGB gamut in image files when saving if they do not have gamut information.

- **Always Optimize For Printing**—Preserves gamut information in the image file (if any), translating the image for display using the AdobeRGB gamut. Embeds AdobeRGB gamut in image files when saving if they do not have gamut information.

- **Allow Me to Choose**—Preserves gamut information in the image file (if any), while letting you choose which gamut to use with images with no gamut information.

64 ▶ **NOTES**

If you don't want to turn on color management, you can select a color printer profile for an image just before printing; see **36** Print an Image for help. The profile you select, however, is not saved to the image file; the next time you print the image, you must make that same choice again (assuming that it was the right choice).

You can experiment to see what produces the best results, but you'll typically want to use the sRGB gamut for display. Then when saving the image before printing, embed either the printer's ICC profile or the Adobe RGB profile, which is optimized for printing.

To test your new profiles and the monitor calibration, print your test image from your printer and compare it to what you see on your newly recalibrated monitor. The result should be fairly close to a true match.

65 | **Crop a Portion of an Image**

✔ BEFORE YOU BEGIN	→ SEE ALSO
27 About Editing Images	**32** Change Image Size or Resolution

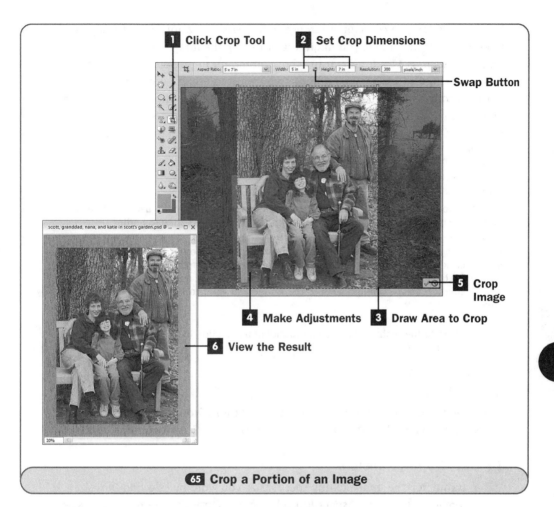

1 Click Crop Tool   **2** Set Crop Dimensions

Swap Button

5 Crop Image

4 Make Adjustments   **3** Draw Area to Crop

6 View the Result

65 Crop a Portion of an Image

To ensure a quality photograph that uses good composition, it's important to properly frame a photograph before you shoot. Whenever possible, you should crop in the lens, when taking the photo. Doing so prevents the loss of quality (resolution) that occurs when you have to manually crop an image after the fact. However, even with careful planning, unwanted objects sometimes appear along the border of otherwise perfect images. In such cases, careful cropping after the fact can help eliminate the unwanted distractions. Cropping, by the way, is a process that cuts away the outer portions of an image that you no longer want to keep. Cropping not only eliminates distractions from your subject, it can also create a stronger composition by concentrating the image on your subject rather than the background.

Using the Editor, you can crop an image to any size you want. However, if you intend to print the image, you might prefer to crop the image to a particular print size, such as 4" × 6". To ensure that you maintain proper quality after cropping, you can also specify the resolution you want to use. If necessary, the Editor automatically generates extra pixels through resampling so that the final image matches the desired resolution. As you crop, a rectangle appears on the image; portions of the image outside this rectangle are discarded when the cropping is complete.

▶ TIPS

With the **Cookie Cutter** tool, you can crop a single layer of an image using a shaped border (such as a heart or an arrow) rather than a rectangular-shaped border.

If you want to crop the image to the same dimensions as another image, open that image, click the **Crop** tool, and then select **Use Photo Ratio** from the **Aspect Ratio** list on the **Options** bar. The dimensions of the current image appear in the **Width**, **Height**, and **Resolution** boxes. Change back to the image you want to crop, and continue to step 3.

You can crop to the rectangular area surrounding a selection by choosing **Image**, **Crop** from the menu bar.

65

1 Click Crop Tool

Open the image you want to crop in the Editor in **Standard Edit** mode and save it in Photoshop (***.psd**) format. Then click the **Crop** tool in the **Toolbox**.

2 Set Crop Dimensions

You can crop the image to any specific size you want by selecting that size beforehand. Open the **Aspect Ratio** list on the **Options** bar and select a size. To flip the dimensions (to specify 4" × 6" for example instead of 6" × 4") click the **Swap** button on the **Options** bar. To retain the photo's original aspect ratio, choose **Use Photo Ratio**. If you can't find a preset that matches the exact size you want to crop the image to, choose **Custom** and enter the dimensions you want to use in the **Width** and **Height** boxes. If you want to draw the exact cropping area yourself, choose **No Restriction**.

Enter the **Resolution** you want to use. For images you intend to print (photo prints), use a resolution setting of 200 to 300 PPI; for images meant to be seen on-screen only (for instance, in web pages), use a resolution of 72 PPI.

3 Draw Area to Crop

Click on the image in the upper-left corner of the area you want to keep. Drag downward and to the right to draw the cropping rectangle. The portions of the image within this rectangle are kept, and portions outside the rectangle (shown in a darkened color) are discarded.

4 Make Adjustments

To move the cropping rectangle around the image, click inside the rectangle and drag. To resize the rectangle while maintaining the same dimensions you specified in step 2, drag a corner handle inward to make the rectangle smaller or outward to make it bigger.

To rotate the rectangle (place the rectangle at an angle), move the mouse pointer a slight distance from any outer edge of the rectangle, until the mouse pointer changes to a curved two-headed arrow. Then drag in a clockwise or counter-clockwise direction to rotate the rectangle.

5 Crop Image

When the cropping rectangle is positioned as desired, click the **Commit** (the check mark) button to crop the image. The outer portions of the image are cropped. If the image contains layers, all the layers are cropped to this same size. To cancel the cropping operation, click the **Cancel** button (the slashed circle) instead.

6 View the Result

After you're satisfied with the image, save the PSD file. Then resave the result in JPEG, PNG, or non-layered TIFF format, leaving your PSD image unflattened so that you can return at a later time and make adjustments if you want.

Cropping this informal portrait of my husband and his family improved its composition. I then added a blue-gray wooden frame using a technique discussed in **107** **Frame a Photograph** (this task is found on the Web at www.samspublishing.com).

65

66   Straighten an Image

✔ BEFORE YOU BEGIN	→ SEE ALSO
27 About Editing Images	65 Crop a Portion of an Image
	86 Repair Minor Tears

Straightening an image is the process of rotating it by just a few degrees. The main reason for straightening an image is to draw the viewer's attention away from distractions such as a sidewalk running downhill, a slanting horizon, a pole that's leaning to one side, and so on. You might also use this technique to deliberately place an image on a slant to make it more interesting for use on a greeting card, Web page, scrapbook page, and so on.

Unfortunately, although the Editor provides you with both the **Image, Rotate, Straighten Image** and an **Image, Rotate, Straighten and Crop Image** command, neither one seems to make the same automatic choices that you would have made. So, to straighten a crooked image, you should use the **Straighten** tool. With the **Straighten** tool, you draw a horizontal or vertical line to mark the alignment of the horizon or the vertical edge.

66

1 Click Straighten Tool

Open the image you want to straighten in the Editor in **Standard Edit** mode and save it in Photoshop (***.psd**) format. Click the **Straighten** tool on the **Toolbox**.

2 Select Layer(s) to Rotate

If the image contains more than one layer, select the layer you want to straighten from the **Layers** palette. If this layer is the background layer, convert it to a regular layer by choosing **Layer, New, Layer From Background**, type a **Name** for the layer, and click **OK**. (If you don't convert the layer, open areas created by the straightening will be filled with the current background color.) To straighten all layers, select **Rotate All Layers** on the **Options** bar.

▶ **TIP**

Suppose that you have a photo in which the subject appears crooked but the background seems straight, or vice versa. Using selection tools, you can separate the elements into different layers and then use these steps to straighten just one layer and leave the other as it is. See 53 **Create a New Image or Layer from a Selection.**

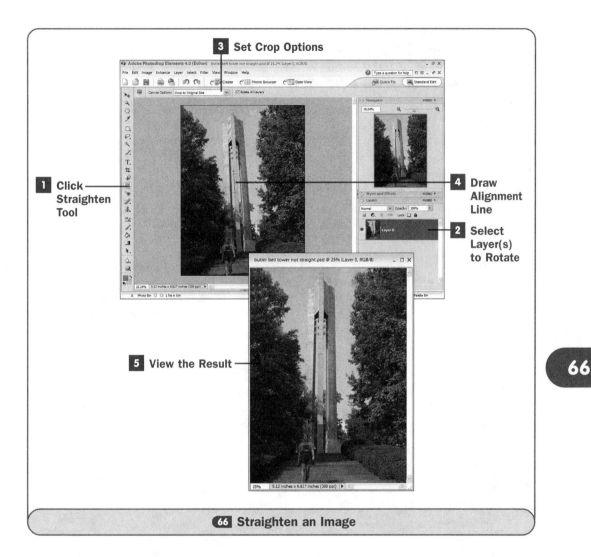

3 Set Crop Options

1 Click Straighten Tool

4 Draw Alignment Line

2 Select Layer(s) to Rotate

5 View the Result

66 Straighten an Image

66

3 Set Crop Options

Normally, when you straighten an image, one pair of opposite corners of the image will extend past the edges of the canvas. From the **Canvas Options** menu on the **Options** bar, select how you want holes created along the sides of the image during the straightening process to be handled:

- **Grow Canvas to Fit**—After straightening, this option changes the size of the image canvas to include all image data so that no data is lost.

- **Crop to Remove Background**—This option crops the image to remove empty areas created by the straightening, causing some data loss.

- **Crop to Original Size**—This option crops the image to its original size, removing data outside that area. Some blank areas will still exist with this option, but the result is less data loss than **Crop to Remove Background**, but more than **Grow Canvas to Fit**.

4 Draw Alignment Line

Drag to draw a line against something in the image that you want to be perfectly horizontal. The line doesn't have to touch anything, but tracing an object you know isn't straight will help you indicate clearly what needs to be straightened. To draw a vertical alignment line instead, press **Ctrl** as you drag. As soon as you release the mouse button, Photoshop Elements uses the line you drew to straighten the image.

5 View the Result

When you're satisfied with the image, save the PSD file. Then resave the result in JPEG, PNG, or non-layered TIFF format, leaving your PSD image unflattened so that you can return at a later time and make adjustments if you want.

After straightening and cropping, this image of a bell tower at a local college had some gaps on either side. I quickly filled the small gap in the lower left corner using the **Clone Stamp** tool, as described in **86** **Repair Minor Tears**. For the larger gap in the upper-right corner, I used the technique described in **87** **Repair Large Holes, Tears, and Missing Portions of a Photo**.

---

67 Correct Red Eye

✔ BEFORE YOU START	→ SEE ALSO
27 About Editing Images	**105** Awaken Tired Eyes (on the Web)

When used properly, a camera flash can help lighten shadows and illuminate an otherwise dark image. Unfortunately, using a flash might sometimes have unintended effects, such as *red eye*. In nonhuman subjects such as dogs or cats, the result might be "glassy eye" rather than red eye. You have several options when dealing with photos that contain red eye. For example, you can have Photoshop Elements automatically remove red eye from photos as you import them into the Organizer catalog (see **3** **Import Media from a Folder, CD-ROM, or DVD** and **4** **Import Images from a Digital Camera**). You can also remove red eye automatically from selected photos already in the catalog, by choosing **Edit**, **Auto Red Eye Fix**. For an equally easy and yet still hands-on approach, you can use the Editor's **Red Eye Removal** tool as explained in this task.

1 Zoom In on Eye

3 Set Options

2 Click Red Eye Removal Tool

Zoom Tool

4 Select the Red Pupil

5 Repeat for Second Eye

67 Correct Red Eye

▶ **KEY TERM**

Red eye—A reddening of the pupil caused by a reflection of the intense light from a camera flash against the retina in the back of the subject's eyes.

▶ **TIPS**

When you're shooting your photograph, you can avoid giving your subjects red eye by separating the flash unit from the camera (if possible), or by telling your subjects to not look directly at the camera.

Some cameras have a red-eye reduction feature, which causes the flash to go off several times. The first series of flashes at lower intensity cause the pupil to contract, thus blocking the reflection, while the final flash at full intensity illuminates the subject for the picture. Just be sure to warn your subject not to move until the second flash goes off.

1 Zoom In on Eye

Open an image in the Editor in either **Quick Fix** or **Standard Edit** mode and save it in Photoshop (***.psd**) format. Zoom in on the first eye you want to correct so that you can see it better. To zoom in, click the **Zoom** tool in the **Toolbox**. Then click on the image to zoom in, or drag a rectangle within the image around the eye you want to see more closely.

2 Click Red Eye Removal Tool

Click the **Red Eye Removal** tool in the **Toolbox**.

3 Set Options

If the *pupil* of the eye you want to correct is larger in area than 50% of the *iris*, change the **Pupil Size** setting on the **Options** bar to the correct ratio. If the **Pupil Size** ratio is way off, the Editor might not remove all the red eye, or it might paint in too much of the iris color, making the iris larger than it should be.

Typically, you won't have to adjust the **Darken Amount** on the **Options** bar. However, if the pupil is not darkened enough after you apply the **Red Eye Removal** tool, you can try the tool again after increasing the **Darken Amount**.

▶ **KEY TERMS**

Pupil—The black center of the eye that adjusts in size based on the amount of ambient light.

Iris—The colored part of the eye; typically brown, blue, or green.

4 Select the Red Pupil

Drag the **Red Eye Removal** tool to select the eye—iris, pupil, and all. You don't have to be terribly precise because the Editor is looking for a large group of contiguous red pixels within the selected area. After you drag, those

67

red pixels are changed to black or the iris color, depending on the **Pupil Size** you've set.

5 Repeat for Second Eye

Scroll the image if necessary so that you can see the second eye. Drag again to select the red area. The red pixels within that area are changed to black.

▶ TIPS

Instead of dragging to select the area to change, you can click anywhere within the red area of the pupil. Red pixels contiguous to the pixel you clicked are changed to black. If one method doesn't work for you, try the other and you might get better results.

Sometimes, when photographing a pet, you'll get red eye that can easily be removed by following these steps. Other times, you'll get yellow glassy eye. To remove it, use the **Magic Wand** to select the glassy area. Feather the selection to soften the effect, then use the **Paint Bucket** to fill the selection with black to restore the pupil that was washed out by the camera flash.

After you're satisfied with the result, make any other changes you want to the PSD image then save it. Resave the result in JPEG, PNG, or non-layered TIFF format, leaving your PSD image with its layers (if any) intact so that you can return at a later time and make adjustments if you want.

68

---

68 | Apply a Quick Fix

✔ BEFORE YOU BEGIN	→ SEE ALSO
27 About Editing Images	**92** Improve Brightness and Contrast
	97 Adjust Hue and Saturation Manually
	99 Sharpen an Image

The strategies for making a particular image more pleasing to the eye are frequently the same for most images. Using the Editor's **Quick Fix** tools, you can make the most common image corrections easily, without messing around with a lot of separate dialog boxes. In the **Quick Fix** pane, you can rotate an image, improve its contrast, remove a color cast, reduce or increase saturation, remove red eye, or sharpen a fuzzy image. Quick Fix might not help you fix every photo, but it can save you from engaging the **Standard Edit** mode in the Editor in an attempt at a more complex solution.

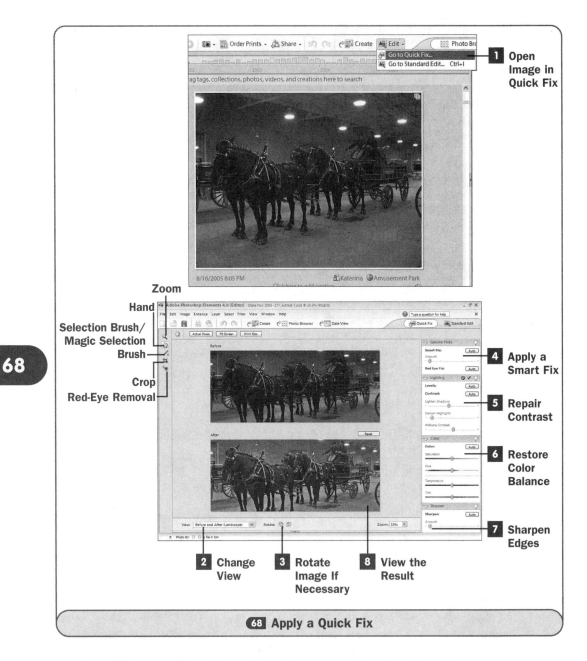

68

1 Open Image in Quick Fix

Zoom

Hand

Selection Brush/
Magic Selection
Brush

Crop

Red-Eye Removal

4 Apply a Smart Fix

5 Repair Contrast

6 Restore Color Balance

7 Sharpen Edges

2 Change View

3 Rotate Image If Necessary

8 View the Result

68 Apply a Quick Fix

Two of the **Quick Fix** tools are similar in purpose: **Auto Levels** and **Auto Contrast**. With both **Auto Levels** and **Auto Contrast**, the darkest darks and the lightest lights are adjusted while the medium tones are not affected. Because of the way **Auto Levels** goes about this process, however, its result might introduce a color cast in some images. **Auto Levels** balances the range of light to dark pixels in each of the three color channels—red, green, and blue. **Auto Contrast** balances the range of light to dark pixels by darkening the darks and lightening the lights in the final image rather than within each color channel. If you're not sure which option to pick, try one, undo it, and then try the other and pick the result that works best for the image you are attempting to fix.

▶ **NOTE**

The automatic commands discussed in this task can also be activated by selecting that command from the **Enhance** menu. For example, selecting **Enhance, Auto Levels** is the same as clicking the **Auto** button in the **Levels** area on the **Quick Fix** pane. (There is, however, no "auto sharpen" menu command, so to sharpen an image automatically, you *must* use **Quick Fix**.)

1 Open Image in Quick Fix

In the Organizer, click the thumbnail of the image you want to change. Then click the **Edit** button on the **Shortcuts** bar and, from the menu, select **Go to Quick Fix** to send the image to the Editor. Save the image in Photoshop (***.psd**) format.

If the image is already open in the Editor, save it in Photoshop (***.psd**) format and then if needed, click the **Quick Fix** button on the **Shortcuts** bar to change to **Quick Fix** mode. If your image has multiple layers, click the layer you want to edit in the **Layers** palette before changing to **Quick Fix** mode. To work on the image as a whole, select **Layer, Flatten Image** before changing to **Quick Fix** mode to reduce your image to a single layer.

2 Change View

In **Quick Fix** mode, only a limited set of tools appear on the left. On the right is the **Quick Fix** pane; you'll make your choices here to adjust the image. You can apply any or all of these options as you see fit. Initially, only the **After** image is shown; to compare your selections to the original image, choose **Before and After (Portrait)** or **Before and After (Landscape)** from the **View** list.

▶ **NOTE**

For help in using the **Zoom** and **Hand** tools, see **31** Zoom In and Out; for help with the selection brush tools, see **48** Paint a Selection; for help with the **Crop** tool, see **65** Crop a Portion of an Image; for help with the **Red-Eye Removal** tool, see **67** Correct Red Eye.

68

3 Rotate Image If Necessary

If needed, click either the **Rotate photo 90° clockwise (right)** or **Rotate photo 90° counterclockwise (left)** button at the bottom of the **Quick Fix** window to rotate the image.

4 Apply a Smart Fix

Instead of applying individual changes to an image's color, contrast, and sharpness, apply a **Smart Fix**. To apply an automatic **Smart Fix**, click the **Smart Fix Auto** button. To adjust how obvious or how drastic you want the **Smart Fix** change to be, drag the **Amount** slider left for less or right for more, then click the **Commit** button (the check mark) to make the change.

5 Repair Contrast

To have the Editor automatically adjust the contrast within each color channel individually, click the **Levels Auto** button. If you prefer to automatically adjust the image's total contrast (rather than the contrast within each color channel), click the **Auto** button next to **Contrast** instead.

You can make manual adjustments to an image's contrast if you prefer. To lighten the darkest pixels, increase the **Lighten Shadows** value. To darken the lightest pixels, increase the **Darken Highlights** value. Finally, to lighten the midtones, drag the **Midtone Contrast** slider to the left. To darken the midtones, drag the slider to the right instead. Then click the **Commit** button (the check mark) to make the change.

6 Restore Color Balance

To normalize the colors throughout the image so that any unnatural color cast is removed or so that any over- or under-saturation is compensated for, click the **Color Auto** button.

You can make manual adjustments to color if you like. To desaturate the image, drag the **Saturation** slider to the left; to add more saturation, drag it to the right. To shift the colors along the color wheel, drag the **Hue** slider to the left (toward teal) or to the right (toward green). To make an image cooler (more bluish), drag the **Temperature** slider to the left; to make the image warmer (more reddish), drag the slider to the right. To add more green to an image (and possibly remove a color cast), drag the **Tint** slider to the left; to add magenta instead, drag the slider to the right. Then click the **Commit** button (the check mark) to make the change.

68

7 Sharpen Edges

To sharpen the image automatically, click the **Sharpen Auto** button. You might also notice, especially in large areas of primarily one shade, an increase in graininess and the possible inclusion of spots. You can click the **Auto** button more than once to increase the contrast along the edges of objects in a photo.

To manually select the amount of sharpening applied to the image, drag the **Amount** slider to the right to strengthen it or to the left to reduce it. Then click the **Commit** button (the check mark) to make the change.

▶ **NOTES**

To sharpen an image, **Quick Fix** increases the contrast along the edges of objects in a photo. To determine where the edges are, **Quick Fix** looks for significant differences in lightness between adjacent pixels and then makes those differences greater. The **Sharpen** option cannot fix a photo that is really fuzzy or out of focus.

At any time, you can undo all changes made to an image using **Quick Fix** by clicking the **Reset** button.

8 View the Result

When you're satisfied with the image, save the PSD file. Then resave the result in JPEG, PNG, or non-layered TIFF format, leaving your PSD image unflattened so that you can return at a later time and make adjustments if you want. To display just the after image, select **After Only** from the **View** list. If you want to return to regular editing, click the **Standard Edit** button.

For this photo I took of a competitive Clydesdale team, I increased the **Temperature** setting and adjusted the **Tint** to remove a bluish cast to the image that was making it look cold. I then lightened the shadows to bring out the details in the black horses and darkened the highlights to make the lights above them less prominent.

68

10

Retouching Photos with Tools

IN THIS CHAPTER:

69 About the Toolbox

70 Create Your Own Brush Tips

71 Select a Color to Work With

72 Draw on a Photo with a Pencil

73 Paint an Area of a Photo with a Brush

74 Paint an Area of a Photo with the Airbrush

75 Fill an Area with a Color or Pattern

76 Fill an Area with a Gradient

77 Draw a Shape

78 Add a Text Caption or Label

79 Add a Backscreen Behind Text

80 Create Metallic Text

81 Create Text That Glows

82 Fill Text with an Image

Sometimes you might have to repair a damaged photograph or reinvigorate one that is old and faded. But often you'll just want to retouch an image that is not too bad but still could be better. The Editor has several tools you can apply to retouch an image. Naturally enough, you'll find many of them on the **Toolbox**: brushes, pens and pencils, and the means to add patterns, shapes, and *gradients* to your images. Each tool comes with an assortment of options that you choose from the **Options** bar. For example, the **Brush** tool lets you select from an assortment of brush sizes and stroke patterns. In this chapter, you'll learn how to use a variety of tools to add shapes and text to your images.

▶ **NOTE**

If you want to apply a filter to a shape or a bit of text, you'll need to convert the shape/text to raster data by choosing **Layer**, **Simplify Layer**.

---

69 | **About the Toolbox**

✔ **BEFORE YOU BEGIN**	→ **SEE ALSO**
Just jump right in!	**71** Select a Color to Work With

The **Toolbox** is the work center of Photoshop Elements. Nearly everything you do begins here. For example, if you want to crop an image, the first thing you do is to select the **Crop** tool from the **Toolbox**. The tools on the **Toolbox** are grouped together by purpose:

- *The viewing and picking tools*, which include the **Move** tool (for picking an object and moving or resizing it), **Zoom** tool (for zooming in or out), **Hand** tool (for scrolling), and **Eyedropper** tool (for choosing a color).

- The *selection tools,* used for selecting portions of an image: the **Rectangular Marquee, Elliptical Marquee, Lasso, Magnetic Lasso, Polygonal Lasso, Magic Wand, Magic Selection Brush**, and **Selection Brush** tools.

- The *type and cropping tools*, including the **Horizontal Type, Vertical Type, Horizontal Type Mask**, and **Vertical Type Mask** tools.

- The *retouching tools*, which are used for improving photographs: **Straighten, Red Eye Removal, Spot Healing Brush, Healing Brush, Clone Stamp, Pattern Stamp, Eraser, Background Eraser, Magic Eraser, Blur, Sharpen, Smudge, Sponge, Dodge**, and **Burn** tools.

- The *painting, drawing, and shape tools*, which you use to paint and draw on an image, fill an area with color, pattern, or a gradient, or to create a vector shape.

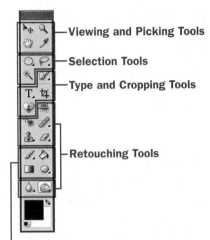

— Viewing and Picking Tools

— Selection Tools

— Type and Cropping Tools

— Retouching Tools

Painting, Drawing, and Shape Tools

*The Editor **Toolbox**.*

▶ **NOTE**

The toolbox shown here has been moved into the workspace by dragging it by its top bar. You can resize it to fit the area you're working in by dragging its edges. To dock the toolbox along the left side of the window again, just drag and drop it there. The size of the tools vary a bit from those shown, depending on your screen resolution. For example, at 800 by 600 screen resolution, the toolbox when docked is displayed in two rows and the buttons are larger than the ones shown here.

To identify a tool, hover the mouse pointer over it, and a screentip appears. Click the tool's name in this screentip, and help for that tool appears. Some tools are grouped under one button; those tools are marked with a small triangle in their lower-right corners. Click and hold such a button, and a menu appears with other tools in that group. Select a tool from this menu to switch to that tool. When you select a tool, it's selected until you choose a different tool. The options for the currently selected tool appear on the **Options** bar near the top of the screen.

▶ **TIP**

You also can select a **Toolbox** item by typing its keyboard shortcut, which appears on the screentip. To cycle through the tools in a slot, repeatedly press its shortcut key. For example, if you repeatedly press **U**, you cycle through a variety of shape-drawing tools.

The **Toolbox** is located on the left side of the Editor window. In **Standard Edit** mode, you can move the **Toolbox** into the work area by dragging it by the bar located at its top. The **Toolbox** expands to two columns when you move it into the work area. Once in the work area, you can resize the **Toolbox** by dragging a corner. At the bottom of the **Toolbox** are swatches that represent the background color and foreground color. You'll learn to set these colors in **71** **Select a Color to Work With.** If you've set the foreground color to a color you'd like to reuse in this image or other images (even after you switch to other colors along the way), you can add it to the **Color Swatches** palette. Move the mouse pointer over an empty area of the palette, and it turns into the **Paint Bucket** tool. Click, and in the dialog box that appears type a **Name** for the color and click **OK**. The color is added to the **Color Swatches** palette.

The **Info** palette (choose **Window, Info** to display it) has a four-square grid that displays color and position information about the pixel that's currently under the tool pointer. You can use this information to identify an image color or to position a tool more precisely. By default, in the upper-left square, color data about the pixel under the mouse pointer is displayed in RGB notation. The upper-right square displays the same color data using Web notation. To display color data using a different notation (such as HSB or grayscale), click the **Eyedropper** icon in either of the top two squares and choose the option you want from the menu that appears. By the way, as you move or resize an object, or draw a line, the amount of change and the angle in which you're drawing appear in the upper-right square, replacing the color data temporarily.

69

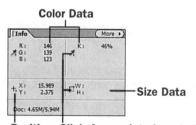

The Info palette.

By default, inches are used as the unit of measurement for the bottom two squares, which display the X/Y coordinates of the cursor and the width/height of any area you might be drawing, such as a selection, shape, or cropping area. To change the unit of measurement in either of the bottom squares, click the **Crosshair** icon and choose the unit of measurement to use from the menu that appears.

Common Tool Options

As I mentioned earlier, when you select a tool, options for that tool appear on the **Options** bar. After you have set options for using a tool, you can return to its original settings. Click the tool icon at the far left end of the **Options** bar, and from the pop-up menu that opens, select **Reset Tool.**

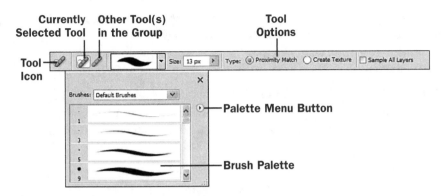

*The **Options** bar.*

The most common options you will find among the Editor's tools are the following:

- **Brush Presets**—Many tools such as the **Brush**, **Clone Stamp**, and the **Eraser** use preset brush tips. To choose a brush tip, open the **Brushes** menu on the **Options** bar to display a palette of brush tips of different sizes and styles. Some brush tips are solid; others have feathered edges. To display a different library of brush tips, open the **Brushes** list on the palette and select the library to use. Here, you'll find special-purpose tips such as those that paint butterflies or maple leaves, or emulate faux finishes.

▶ **NOTE**

For the **Gradient** and **Custom Shape** tools, you change from one library of choices to another by clicking the **Palette Menu** button and choosing the library of gradients or shapes to use from the menu that appears. On the **Brushes** palette shown here, the **Palette Menu** button also displays a menu but its choices do not include brush libraries, but instead other palette options such as saving a brush style, displaying the brushes as small thumbnails, and so on.

- **Size**—This setting controls the size of the brush tip on tools that use a brush. Here, the **Size** is expressed in **pixels**, which means that the relative size of the brush varies depending on the resolution of the image you're drawing on. For instance, a brush tip that's 24 pixels will look larger in a 100 ppi image than it will in a 300 ppi image.

- **Opacity**—Several tools such as the **Brush**, **Clone Stamp**, and **Eraser** use the **Opacity** setting to control the relative transparency of the tool's effect from 100% (in which the tool's effect completely replaces existing pixels) to lesser percentages (in which the tool's effect blends with existing pixels, only partially affecting them).

69

- **Tolerance**—The **Tolerance** setting is used by tools such as the **Magic Wand**, **Paint Bucket**, **Magic Eraser**, and **Background Eraser** to determine how closely other pixels must match the pixel you click before it's affected by the tool. A high **Tolerance** setting will match more pixels than a lower setting.

- **Feather**—The brush tools allow you to soften the edge of the tool's effect by choosing a feathered brush; other tools that work without a brush tip, such as the selection tools, allow you to soften the area selected with the **Feather** setting.

- **Hardness**—This option is available only on a few tools, such as the **Paint Brush** and **Selection Brush**, and it works like feathering to soften the effect of a tool. Hardness, unlike feathering, works from the center out, defining the area of pure effect within the brush tip—the portion of the tip that's completely hard. For example, if you set its **Hardness** to 33%, the **Paint Brush** will paint pure color in the middle third of its tip, with less color fading out to the tip's outer edges. With the **Selection Brush** tool, for example, a **Hardness** of 33% causes the brush to fully select pixels only over the inner third of its tip, partially selecting pixels from this hard core to the tip's outer edge.

- **Anti-Aliased**—For some tools, such as the **Magic Wand**, **Lasso**, and **Magic Eraser**, you can turn on anti-aliasing to smooth curves at the edge of the affected area through the addition of semi-transparent pixels.

- **Sample All Layers/Use All Layers**—By default, tools work only on the current layer, and when matching pixels, sample only those pixels on the current layer. Setting this option enables the tool to sample the true color of a pixel (the result of a blending of colors on all layers).

- **Aligned**—For the tools that copy data (**Clone Stamp**, **Pattern Stamp**, and **Healing Brush**), this option tells the tool to move the spot you're copying *from*, in tandem with the spot you're copying *to*. For example, if you copy data with the **Aligned** option on, and then move left two inches and start copying again, the source spot also moves two inches to the left of the original source point you selected. If this option is turned off, the source snaps back to the original source spot with each stroke, even if you move to the left two inches with each stroke.

- **Contiguous**—For tools that affect large groups of pixels with a single click (**Magic Wand**, **Magic Eraser**, and **Paint Bucket**), this option designates whether pixels must be *neighboring pixels* to the pixel you click in order to be affected.

▶ KEY TERM

Neighboring pixels—Pixels that physically touch each other.

- **Mode**—For tools that copy or paint pixels onto a layer, this setting allows you to blend those pixels with existing pixels in particular ways. See the bonus material for this book on the Web (start at www.samspublishing.com) for a description of the various *blend modes* and how they affect the resulting pixel.

▶ **KEY TERM**

Blend modes—Tool or layer settings that govern the way in which pixels copied or painted by a tool or existing on a top layer are blended with existing pixels.

---

70 **Create Your Own Brush Tips**

✔ **BEFORE YOU BEGIN**

69 About the Toolbox

Certain tools allow you to choose from various brush presets (brush tips). For example, when you use the **Clone Stamp** tool, you can choose not only the size but style of brush you want to use to copy pixels from one part of an image to another. You can create your own brush tips and use them with any tool that uses a brush tip, but they are most useful with the painting tools. To create a brush tip, you start with the contents of a layer or a selection. A grayscale version of that image data is then saved as a brush tip. You can then paint with the brush tip using the **Brush** tool or any other tool that uses a brush tip. For example, you might create a brush tip from a photo of your son, and paint his face around the border of an image to frame the photograph, or you might create a brush tip from some sand, and use it to add texture to a cloning operation.

1 **Select Pattern to Use**

Open an image in the Editor in **Standard Edit** mode. On the **Layers** palette, select the layer that contains the pattern you want to use for your brush tip. If you want to use only a portion of the layer for your brush tip, make that selection now, using any of the selection tools.

▶ **TIPS**

Brush tips are limited to a size of 2500 by 2500 pixels; if needed, use the **Image, Resize, Image Size** command to adjust the resolution of an image so that the data you want to select for the tip meets these size limitations.

You can also create texture patterns and save them for reuse in the library. See **75** Fill an Area with a Color or Pattern.

70

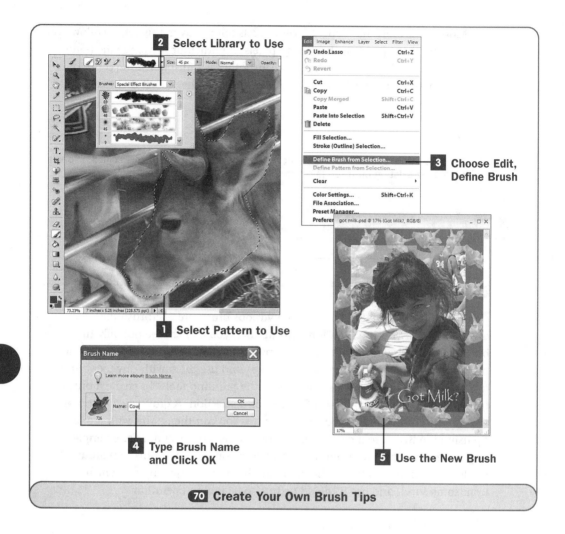

70

70 Create Your Own Brush Tips

2 Select Library to Use

Your new brush tip will be saved with other tips in the current brush library—the set of brush tips currently displayed on the **Brush** palette. Change to a tool that uses a brush tip, such as the **Brushes** tool. Then open the **Brushes** menu on the **Options** bar and choose the library you want to save your new brush tip in. Choose a library that matches the tip's purpose; here, I choose the **Special Effects Brushes** library.

3 Choose Edit, Define Brush

To create the brush tip using the contents of the selection or layer, choose **Edit**, **Define Brush** or **Edit**, **Define Brush From Selection** from the menu.

4 Type Brush Name and Click OK

In the **Brush Name** dialog box that opens, a preview of your selection or layer appears on the left, along with its width in pixels (again, a brush cannot be wider than 2500 pixels). Type a **Name** for the new brush and click **OK**. The brush is added to the brush library you selected in step 2.

5 Use the New Brush

To use your new brush, change to the brush tool you want to use. Then select the library your brush is stored in from the **Brushes** list on the **Options** bar. Set other tool options as needed and use the tool in the normal way. Here, I used my new brush tip to paint the image of a cow on the frame of this image of my daughter enjoying her winner's swig of milk after a day spent at the Indianapolis Motor Speedway.

▶ TIPS

To save the current brush settings, such as those for the **Brush** tool, open the **Brushes** menu on the **Options** bar, select the brush library to which you want to add your brush from the **Brushes** drop-down list, click the **Palette Menu** button (right arrow), and choose **Save Brush**. Type a **Name** and click **OK**.

To delete a brush tip you no longer need, right- click it in the **Brush** palette and choose **Delete Brush** from the context menu.

71

---

71 Select a Color to Work With

✔ BEFORE YOU BEGIN	→ SEE ALSO
69 About the Toolbox	**35** Change Color Mode

At the bottom of the **Toolbox** you'll find the foreground/background color swatches. The *foreground color* is applied with the **Brush**, **Pencil**, and **Paint Bucket** tools; it's also the color that initially appears on the **Options** bar for the **Text** and **Shape** tools (although you can change it to a different color without affecting the foreground color on the **Toolbox**). The *background color* is applied by the **Eraser** when you erase pixels on the background layer. These colors are also used jointly by the **Gradient** tool as well as by some filters such as the **Clouds** filter. By default, the foreground color (the upper swatch) is black and the background color (the lower swatch) is white. You can select a new foreground or background color from the **Color Picker** or the **Color Swatches** palette. You can also pick up the color to use from the image by using the **Eyedropper** tool.

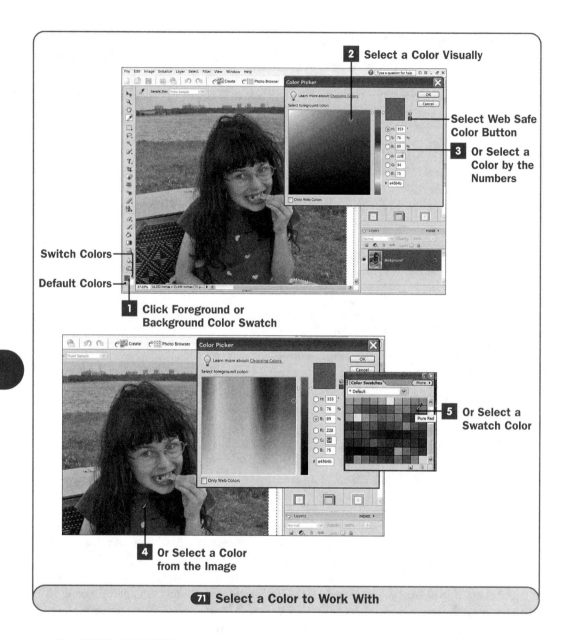

2 Select a Color Visually

Select Web Safe
Color Button

3 Or Select a
Color by the
Numbers

Switch Colors

Default Colors

1 Click Foreground or
Background Color Swatch

5 Or Select a
Swatch Color

4 Or Select a Color
from the Image

71 Select a Color to Work With

▶ **KEY TERMS**

Foreground color—The color that's applied through the **Brush**, **Pencil**, **Paint Bucket**, **Text**, and **Shape** tools.

Background color—The color that's applied when you erase the background layer with the **Eraser** tool.

1 Click Foreground or Background Color Swatch

Select a tool from the **Toolbox** that uses the foreground or background color. Click the foreground color swatch or the background color swatch at the bottom of the **Toolbox**. The **Color Picker** opens.

▶ **NOTE**

To return the foreground and background swatches on the **Toolbox** back to black and white, click the **Default Colors** button or press **D**. To swap the foreground and background colors, click the **Switch Colors** button or press **X**.

2 Select a Color Visually

If needed, click the **H** (hue) radio button. Click in the large color field to choose a color, or drag the vertical color slider. Click the **S** (saturation) radio button and drag the color slider to adjust the amount of saturation (the amount of white) in the selected color. Click the **B** (brightness) radio button and drag the color slider to adjust the lightness (the amount of black) in the selected color.

The new color appears on the right in the upper box; the original color appears in the lower box. You might see an alert cube next to the original color box; this tells you that the chosen color is not a web-safe color (is not one of the 216 colors both Macs and PCs use). To adjust your chosen color so that it is web safe, click the **Select Web Safe Color** button. The Editor then changes your chosen color to a web-safe color.

▶ **NOTES**

To limit the color field to display only web-safe colors so you won't accidentally choose a non-web color, enable the **Only Web Colors** check box in the lower-left corner of the **Color Picker**.

The number of colors in the **Color Picker** is limited by the number of colors allowed in the image, which is based on the color mode the image is using. To change color modes—and the number of colors allowed in an image—see **35** Change Color Mode.

3 Or Select a Color by the Numbers

Instead of clicking the color you want in the large color field, you can specify an exact color by entering its numeric value using one of three color systems:

- **RGB**—Enter the values of red, green, and blue that make up the color you want, using a scale of 0 to 255 for each component. For example, a medium orange is R254, G147, B41.

71

- **HSB**—Enter the color's hue, saturation, and brightness. The hue indicates a color's position on the color wheel; saturation and brightness values indicate a color's percentage of white and black. On this scale, medium orange is H30, S84, B99.

- **HTML**—Enter the HTML color code for the desired color. This is a single value, using six digits preceded by a pound sign. The digits express the RGB values on a hexadecimal scale. The first two digits contain the red value, the second two the green value, and the final two the blue value. In this notation, medium orange is #FE9329.

4 Or Select a Color from the Image

In the **Color Picker**, you can pick up a color from the image rather than selecting that color visually or by the numbers. Simply move the mouse pointer over the image; it changes to an eyedropper. Click anywhere on the image to choose that color.

To finalize your color choice and close the **Color Picker**, click **OK**.

5 Or Select a Swatch Color

Instead of using the **Color Picker** to select a color to work with, you can choose a color from those saved to the **Color Swatches** palette. Choose **Windows**, **Color Swatches** to display the palette. From the list at the top of the palette, select the library of swatches you want to use, such as **Default** or **Web Safe Colors**. Move the mouse pointer over a swatch, and the pointer turns into an **Eyedropper** icon. To set the foreground color, click a swatch; to set the background color, **Ctrl+click** a swatch.

▶ TIPS

To save the current foreground color as a swatch on the **Color Swatches** palette, move the mouse pointer over an empty area of the palette; the pointer turns into the **Paint Bucket** icon. Click, and in the dialog box that appears, type a **Name** for the color and click **OK**. The color is added to the **Color Swatches** palette.

You can pick up a color from the image at any time, without opening the **Color Picker**: Click the **Eyedropper** tool in the **Toolbox** and click the image to set the foreground color; **Alt+click** the image to set the background color. To get an average color within an area, set the **Sample Size** value on the **Options** bar before clicking.

71

---

72 | **Draw on a Photo with a Pencil**

✔ BEFORE YOU BEGIN	→ SEE ALSO
69 About the Toolbox	**73** Paint an Area of a Photo with a Brush
71 Select a Color to Work With	

The **Pencil** and **Brush** tools are close cousins; you can use either to draw on a picture. The main difference is that the **Brush** tool is intended to create often fluffy strokes of color; the **Pencil** is designed to create hard-edged lines. You might use the **Brush** to add a decorative swath of color or pattern to an image, or to paint in missing detail on a badly damaged photo. A typical use of the **Pencil** is to call out various elements of a diagram or photo.

1 Select the Pencil Tool

Open the image you want to modify in the Editor in **Standard Edit** mode and save it in Photoshop (***.psd**) format. In the **Layers** palette, select the layer on which you want to draw. In the **Toolbox**, select the **Pencil** tool.

2 Select Options

Set the foreground color to the color you want to use for the pencil line. See **71** **Select a Color to Work With**. Select a brush tip from the **Brushes** list. Adjust the **Size** of the brush tip in the **Options** bar as well.

You also can select a blend **Mode** and adjust the **Opacity** of the line you will draw.

▶ NOTES

The **Brushes** list includes brush tips that are soft and fuzzy (feathered); when these kinds of brush tips are applied to the **Pencil** tool, the brush shape is retained, but not its softness. After selecting such a brush tip, notice the preview of an unfeathered version of that tip that appears in the **Options** bar so there's no confusion of what you'll get when you use that brush tip with the **Pencil**.

If you enable the **Auto Erase** option, the **Pencil** paints with the background color if you start your stroke over pixels of the foreground color. If you start your stroke over pixels of any other color, the **Pencil** paints with the foreground color. See **71** Select a Color to Work With.

3 Apply the Pencil to the Image

Drag with the **Pencil** tool to draw. To draw a straight line, click to mark the starting point, press **Shift**, and then click to mark the ending point.

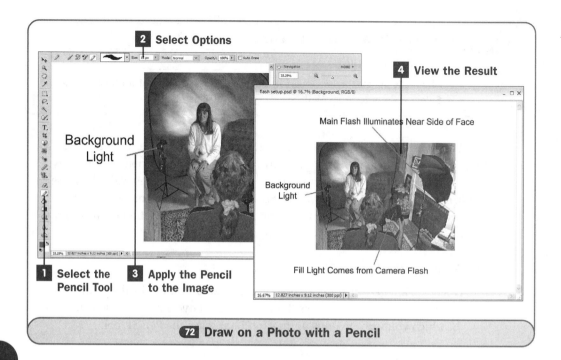

2 Select Options

4 View the Result

Background
Light

Main Flash Illuminates Near Side of Face

Background
Light

Fill Light Comes from Camera Flash

1 Select the
Pencil Tool

3 Apply the Pencil
to the Image

72 Draw on a Photo with a Pencil

4 View the Result

After you're satisfied with the result, make any other changes you want, then save the PSD image. Resave the result in JPEG, PNG, or non-layered TIFF format, leaving your PSD image with its layers (if any) intact so that you can return at a later time and make adjustments if you want.

Here, I used the **Pencil** and **Type** tools to help create some basic callouts for a photo illustrating the flash setup for shooting a portrait at home.

73 | Paint an Area of a Photo with a Brush

✔ BEFORE YOU BEGIN	→ SEE ALSO
69 About the Toolbox	**72** Draw on a Photo with a Pencil
71 Select a Color to Work With	

The **Pencil** draws lines; the **Brush** works in smoother, softer, and more variable strokes. For that and many other reasons, you probably will find the **Brush** a much more versatile tool than the **Pencil**. You can use it to fix someone's hair or darken their eyelashes; or paint a flowery or leafy border around an image.

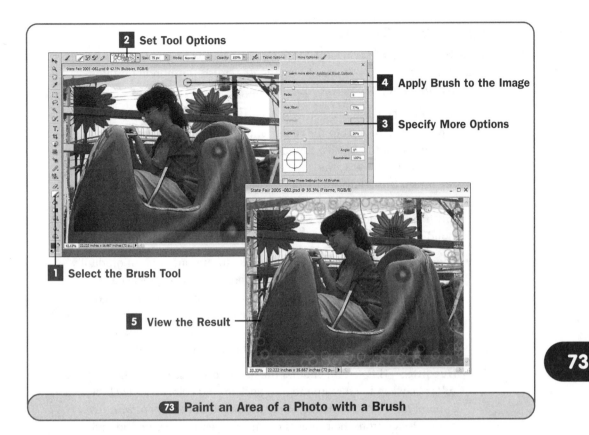

2 Set Tool Options

4 Apply Brush to the Image

3 Specify More Options

1 Select the Brush Tool

5 View the Result

73 Paint an Area of a Photo with a Brush

73

The **Brush** tool offers a set of brush dynamics options through its **More Options** button. These brush settings are not critical, but they are nice to use when you want to have fun making a unique brush that you might even save and use later. (See **69** **About the Toolbox** for details.) Among the dynamics options are settings for the rate at which a brush stroke fades out, and the rate at which patterns repeat themselves or change color.

1 **Select the Brush Tool**

Open an image in the Editor in **Standard Edit** mode and save it in Photoshop (***.psd**) format. In the **Layers** palette, select the layer you want to paint on. Select the **Brush** tool in the **Toolbox**.

2 **Set Tool Options**

Select a brush tip, adjust its **Size**, and set other options such as **Mode** and **Opacity** as desired. Set the foreground color swatch at the bottom of the **Toolbox** to the color you want to apply with the brush.

❸ Specify More Options

To set brush dynamics, click the **More Options** button on the **Options** bar and adjust the desired settings. As you do, the brush thumbnail on the **Options** bar changes to reflect your choices:

- **Spacing**—The distance between deposits of color, measured from the center of one deposit to the center of the next. Spacing is expressed as a percentage of the brush's current size. At 100%, each deposit just touches the next. At 200%, the gap between deposits is equal to the width of the brush; this seems weird, but if you measure the distance between centers of those two deposits, you'll see that it is 2 times the width of the brush. You might use this setting to create a dotted line or a string of cloud puffs.

- **Fade**—This setting enables a brushstroke to run out of paint gradually (the stroke gradually grows more transparent). It is expressed as the number of *steps* (deposits of paint) before the brush runs out of paint. So if you're using a high **Spacing** value and thus are dropping deposits of paint far apart, set **Fade** low if you want to run out of paint quickly. You could use this setting to re-create the look of a real paint brush.

- **Hue Jitter**—This setting enables the brush to switch within the range of colors between the foreground and background colors with each deposit of paint (step). At 100%, the color changes with each step, with the color selected from the range of colors between the foreground and background colors. You could use this setting to paint delicate repairs in a background area on a photo, re-creating the subtle color changes nature makes.

- **Hardness**—Sets the size of the hard center of a brush, the part with pure color. The **Hardness** value is relative to the brush tip size; at 50%, the hard center is half the size of the brush tip. With a feathered brush, **Hardness** is initially set to 0%, so increasing the **Hardness** setting increases the area of pure color.

- **Scatter**—Scatter causes each deposit (step) to be placed "off center" from the line you drag, by the amount you specify. Set this to a high value, and steps are placed within a wide area from the line you drag. With an unusual brush tip pattern, such as stars, balloons, or blades of grass, a high **Scatter** setting lets you create instant pointillism and frivolity.

- **Angle**—This setting governs the tilt of the brush tip by the number of degrees you specify. Its range is –180° to +180°, with a positive setting twisting the brush tip counter-clockwise from straight east. With a

73

round brush tip, this setting is inconsequential. For a wedged tip, however, the **Angle** setting enables you to rotate the brush the way you'd tip the nib of a calligraphy pen, enabling such effects as thin side-to-side strokes and thick downstrokes.

- **Roundness**—Allows you to set how round or flat a brush tip is. At 50%, a brush is half as tall as it is wide.

▶ TIPS

If you're using the **Brush** tool with a pen tablet, you can select specific tool settings that are controlled by the pressure of the pen on the tablet. On the **Options** bar, click the **Tablet Options** button to display a palette of settings. Enable any settings you want to control with the tablet, such as **Size**, **Opacity**, **Hue Jitter**, **Scatter**, and **Roundness**. Then press harder with the pen to increase the chosen settings; press lighter to decrease them. For example, if you enable the **Size** and **Opacity** settings, when you press down with the pen, the brush tip size and opacity gradually increases until it reaches the limit set on the **Options** bar.

The changes you make to the dynamics of any brush tip are *not* permanent; if you choose a different preset from the **Brushes** list, the brush dynamics are reset. To use the same dynamics settings for any new brush tip you choose, enable the **Keep These Settings for All Brushes** check box.

To save a brush tip and all its settings so that you can recall it at any time, see **70** **Create Your Own Brush Tips**.

4 Apply Brush to the Image

Click and drag to paint with the brush. To paint a straight line, press **Shift** and then drag, or click to mark the starting point, press **Shift**, and click to mark the ending point.

5 View the Result

After you're satisfied with the result, make any other changes you want, then save the result in JPEG, PNG, or non-layered TIFF format, leaving your PSD image with its layers (if any) intact so that you can return at a later time and make adjustments if you want.

For this photo, I drew a rectangular selection in the center of the photo and inverted it to select the outer area for a frame. I filled the frame area with a bright blue and used the **Hard Light** blend mode to make the "frame" semi-transparent. To dress up the frame, I chose a brush with a circular tip to pick up the dot motif on the amusement car. I chose a dark blue and a lime green (colors picked up from the photo) as my foreground and background colors, set the brush dynamics to scatter the paint and to jitter between the two colors, and then used my customized brush to paint dots along the frame.

▶ **TIP**

For a special effect, try the **Impressionist Brush**; just drag the brush over an image to remix existing pixels, creating a simulation of an Impressionist painting.

---

74 | **Paint an Area of a Photo with the Airbrush**

✔ BEFORE YOU BEGIN	→ SEE ALSO
69 About the Toolbox **71** Select a Color to Work With	**73** Paint an Area of a Photo with a Brush

---

Without the **Airbrush** option, the **Brush** tool applies paint to an image *as you move the mouse pointer*. With the **Airbrush** option turned on, the **Brush** tool applies paint to an image *as long as you hold the mouse button down, whether you move the mouse or not*. If you hold the brush still, the **Airbrush** continues to flow paint onto the layer until it fills the brush tip and little bit beyond. At that point, the paint flow stops, even if you continue to hold the mouse button down and the keep the brush still. It's also important to note that although the paint will flow outward if you hold the brush still, the paint will not accumulate; in other words, the paint will retain its opacity and will not "increase in thickness" or "build up." You can, of course, accumulate paint over an area by making multiple strokes of the **Airbrush** at low opacity. But you can do that with the **Brush** tool as well.

1 **Select the Brush Tool**

Open an image in the Editor in **Standard Edit** mode and save it in Photoshop (***.psd**) format. In the **Layers** palette, select the layer you want to paint. Select the **Brush** tool from the **Toolbox**.

2 **Enable the Airbrush Option**

Click the **Airbrush** icon on the right side of the **Options** bar.

3 **Set Options**

Select a brush tip, adjust its **Size**, and set other options such as **Mode** and **Opacity** as desired. No single stroke of the **Airbrush** can build up paint beyond the amount specified in the **Opacity** setting; single **Airbrush** strokes are not cumulative within themselves, although multiple passes with a less-than-fully opaque airbrush *do* accumulate paint. Set the foreground color swatch at the bottom of the **Toolbox** to the color you want to apply.

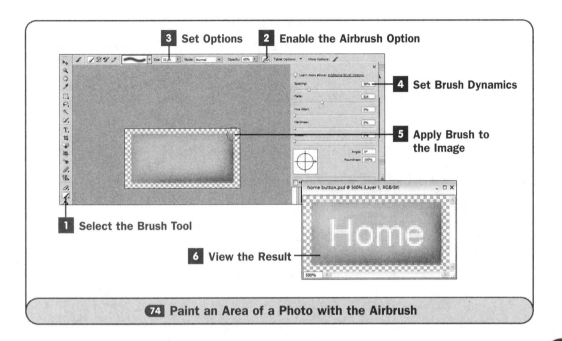

3 Set Options   **2** Enable the Airbrush Option

4 Set Brush Dynamics

5 Apply Brush to the Image

1 Select the Brush Tool

6 View the Result

74 Paint an Area of a Photo with the Airbrush

4 Set Brush Dynamics

To set brush dynamics options, click the **More Options** button on the **Options** bar. Descriptions for the brush dynamics settings appear in **73** **Paint an Area of a Photo with a Brush**.

▶ NOTE

The **Airbrush** option of the **Brush** tool changes the meaning of the **Spacing** dynamics setting. Instead of measuring the distance between deposits, the **Spacing** option for the **Airbrush** controls *how long* to wait between deposits.

5 Apply Brush to the Image

Click and drag to paint with the brush. If you hold the mouse pointer over an area with the mouse button still pressed, paint spills outward from the tip. To paint a straight line, press **Shift** and then drag, or click to mark the starting point, press **Shift**, and click to mark the ending point.

6 View the Result

After you're satisfied with the result, make any other changes you want and save the result in JPEG, PNG, TIFF format, leaving your PSD image with its layers (if any) intact so that you can return at a later time and make adjustments if you want.

74

In this example, I used the **Airbrush** to softly paint shadows on the sides of this web button to make it look more three-dimensional. To make sure that I sprayed only the sides of the button and not the transparent area around it, I locked the transparency on that layer. I then added a layer and used the **Airbrush** to paint a soft white highlight in the upper-left corner of the button. To soften the effect even further, I added a **Gaussian Blur** to the highlight layer.

75	**Fill an Area with a Color or Pattern**

✔ **BEFORE YOU BEGIN**	→ **SEE ALSO**
69 About the Toolbox	**76** Fill an Area with a Gradient

74

Using the **Paint Bucket** is like throwing a bucket of paint at the side of a barn. It fills large areas with a color or *pattern*, and does it with a single click. Actually, the **Paint Bucket** identifies the color of the pixel you click and throws paint on pixels of a similar color. You use the **Tolerance** setting on the **Options** bar to control how similar a pixel must be to "match" the pixel you click. If the **Tolerance** is set low, then pixels must match pretty closely to be changed. If **Tolerance** is set high, the matches won't be that exact. The **Contiguous** setting can also be used to control the **Paint Bucket**'s effects. When you enable this option, the **Paint Bucket** changes only neighboring pixels of similar color to those it has already changed. If this option is disabled, the **Paint Bucket** searches the entire layer for similar colors and changes every instance it finds. The results are unpredictable.

▶ **KEY TERM**

Pattern—A design that repeats at regular intervals, like wallpaper.

1 **Select the Paint Bucket Tool**

Open an image in the Editor in **Standard Edit** mode and save it in Photoshop (***.psd**) format. In the **Layers** palette, select the layer you want to fill. Click the **Paint Bucket** tool on the **Toolbox**.

▶ **TIP**

To prevent transparent pixels from being filled, lock the layer's transparency by selecting the layer in the **Layers** palette and then clicking the **Lock transparent pixels** button at the top of the palette.

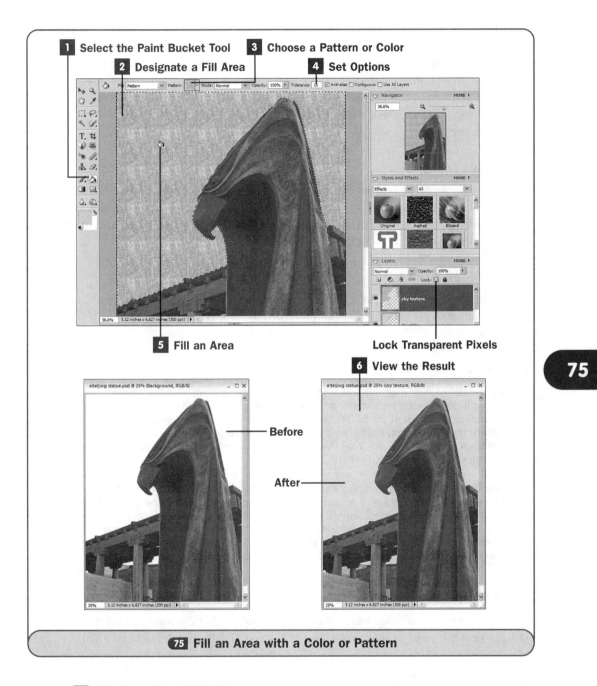

75 Fill an Area with a Color or Pattern

2 Designate a Fill Area

To limit the area that might be filled by the **Paint Bucket**, select a portion of the layer using any selection tool.

3 Choose a Pattern or Color

On the **Options** bar, select **Foreground** or **Pattern** from the **Fill** drop-down list. If you choose **Foreground**, be sure to set the foreground color swatch at the bottom of the **Toolbox** to the color you want to use for the fill. If you choose **Pattern**, open the **Pattern** drop-down list and select the pattern to use for the fill.

4 Set Options

On the **Options** bar, set the **Mode**, **Opacity**, and **Tolerance** you want. The **Tolerance** value controls how similar pixels must be to the one you click in order to also be filled. Enable the **Anti-alias**, **Contiguous**, and **Use All Layers** options as desired; see **69 About the Toolbox**.

5 Fill an Area

In the layer, click a pixel in the area you want to fill. The **Paint Bucket** fills similar pixels with the color or pattern you chose based on the options you set in step 4.

75

▶ NOTES

You can define your own patterns and add them to the pattern libraries. Create a pattern with the tools, filters, effects, or layer styles, or pick one up from an image (make a rectangular selection of the pattern with no feathering). Then choose **Edit**, **Define Pattern from Selection**. Name the pattern and click **OK** to add the pattern to the current library. See **70 Create Your Own Brush Tips** for help in understanding the library and managing items you create.

With the **Pattern Stamp** tool, you can stamp a pattern onto a layer, rather than pouring it on with the **Paint Bucket**. The tool has one unique option, **Impressionist**, which paints the pattern you select using blurry daubs of color, rather than as a sharply textured pattern. The **Healing Brush** tool also uses patterns, not to help you paint patterns all over an image, but rather to help you hide your repair work as you copy pixels from one area to another. See **83 Remove Specks, Spots, and Scratches**.

6 View the Result

After you're satisfied with the result, make any other changes you want and save the result in JPEG, PNG, or non-layered TIFF format, leaving your PSD image with its layers (if any) intact so that you can return at a later time and make adjustments if you want.

This photo of a lovely statue outside a local museum was almost overshadowed by the overly white sky. Fortunately, this deficit was easy to fix: First, I selected the white sky areas using the **Magic Wand**. Then I inserted a new layer and used the **Paint Bucket** to fill the selection with a light gray blue.

By placing the sky color on its own layer, I can better control the effect; for example I lowered the **Opacity** of the sky layer. Because the original sky was so white and textureless, I added a second layer and filled the same selected areas with a **Textured Tile** texture (although there is a **Clouds** texture available, it seemed too rough for my photo). I applied the **Soft Light** blend mode to blend the texture with the sky color and the original photo layers.

76	**Fill an Area with a Gradient**
✔ **BEFORE YOU BEGIN**	→ **SEE ALSO**
69 About the Toolbox	**75** Fill an Area with a Color or Pattern

A *gradient* is a transition from one color to another—often between several colors. You might use a gradient as a backdrop for an image or to fill a frame around an image. The simplest gradient is one that gradually fades in linear fashion from the foreground color to the background color. More complex gradients make the transition outward from the center, at angles, and across multiple colors. There are many preset gradients you can choose from with the **Gradient** tool. If you don't find what you want, click the **Edit** button on the **Options** bar to create your own gradient.

76

▶ KEY TERM

Gradient—A gradual transition between two colors, sometimes by way of a third (or more) color.

1 Select Gradient Tool

Open an image in the Editor in **Standard Edit** mode and save it in Photoshop (***.psd**) format. In the **Layers** palette, select the layer you want to change. To put the gradient on a new layer, create the layer by clicking the **Create a new layer** button on the **Layers** palette. To limit the gradient to a specific area of a layer, make a selection now. To limit the gradient to non-transparent areas of the layer, lock the transparency by clicking the **Lock Transparent Pixels** button on the **Layers** palette.

Because a lot of gradients use the foreground and background colors, set the foreground and background colors to the colors you want to use, as explained in **71** **Select a Color to Work With**. Click the **Gradient** tool on the **Toolbox**.

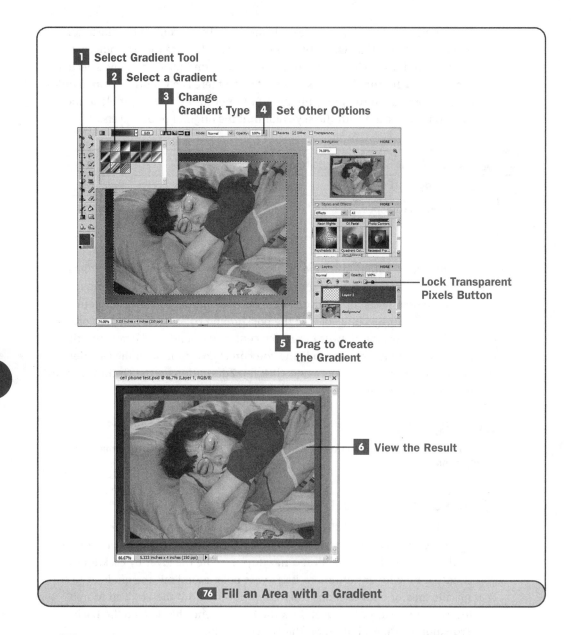

1 Select Gradient Tool

2 Select a Gradient

3 Change Gradient Type   **4** Set Other Options

Lock Transparent Pixels Button

5 Drag to Create the Gradient

6 View the Result

76 Fill an Area with a Gradient

76

2 Select a Gradient

On the **Options** bar, open the **Gradient Picker** drop-down list and select a gradient. To change to a different library of gradient styles, click the **Palette Menu** button (right arrow) on the palette and choose a gradient set from those listed at the bottom of the menu that appears.

3 Change Gradient Type

Make a selection from one of the five gradient styles displayed on the **Options** bar. The gradient styles define how the gradient will fill the area you select:

- **Linear** applies a straight-line gradient from one color to the next.

- **Radial** applies the gradient outward in all directions from the center of the selected area.

- **Angle** applies the gradient in a 360° sweep starting at a designated angle, resulting in an effect that looks like an old air traffic control radar.

- **Reflected** applies the gradient in bands on either side of the center of the selected area.

- **Diamond** applies the gradient in a diamond shape, radiating from the point where you click to begin the gradient.

4 Set Other Options

Set the **Mode** and **Opacity** as desired. You can reverse the order of the colors in the gradient by enabling the **Reverse** option. To reduce a possible banding effect where colors blend when the gradient is printed, enable the **Dither** option. To retain transparent areas of a gradient, enable the **Transparency** option. If you turn this option off (or if you use the gradient on the **Background** layer which does not support transparency), then the transparent areas are filled with the colors from the gradient.

5 Drag to Create the Gradient

Click and drag across the area you want to fill with the gradient in the direction you want the gradient to transition. For example, drag from the upper-left corner of the layer to its lower-right corner to have the gradient's colors transition in that direction. If you made a selection, you can drag outside the area of the selection, but the gradient is applied only to the selected area. If you didn't make a selection in step 1, the gradient is applied to the entire layer (assuming that the transparency for the layer is not locked; if it is, then the gradient is applied to only the non-transparent pixels).

76

▶ **NOTES**

When you drag to create the gradient, keep in mind that the gradient bands of color often appear in the opposite direction. For example, if you drag from upper-left to lower-right to create a **Linear** gradient, the color bands appear in diagonals that bend from the lower-left to the upper-right. The color in the gradient bands, however, changes as it moves from upper-left to lower-right.

To create a gradient with an angle that's an exact multiple of 45 degrees, press and hold **Shift** as you drag to create the gradient.

6 View the Result

After you're satisfied with the gradient, make any other changes you want and save the result in JPEG, PNG, or non-layered TIFF format, leaving your PSD image with its layers (if any) intact so that you can return at a later time and make different adjustments if you want.

To create a frame for this photo of a sleeping child, I made a rectangular selection then inverted it to select the frame area. I then selected a gradient that happened to use colors present in the photo, and filled the selection with the gradient. I expanded the selection to create an inner frame, and on another layer, filled that second selection with a complementary gradient created with the foreground and background colors. Finally, I returned to the layer with the first (outer) gradient, and applied a bevel layer style to give the outer frame more dimension.

77 Draw a Shape

✔ BEFORE YOU BEGIN	SEE ALSO
69 About the Toolbox	**71** Select a Color to Work With

With the **Shape** tool, you can add to an image shapes such as a rectangle, circle, or a line. With the **Custom Shape** tool, you can draw a variety of irregular shapes such as a heart, star, flower, butterfly, or pawprint. You might add a circle, for example, to frame some text, or a star to adorn a favorite photo of your son. Shapes are placed on special shape layers; typically, you'll find only one shape on a layer, although you can draw more than one shape on a shape layer if you like. You might place multiple shapes on the same layer to build a larger shape, or to easily format those shapes the same way. Shapes are vector objects, so they can be easily edited and reedited. For example, you can change the color, size, and rotation of a shape after you've drawn it.

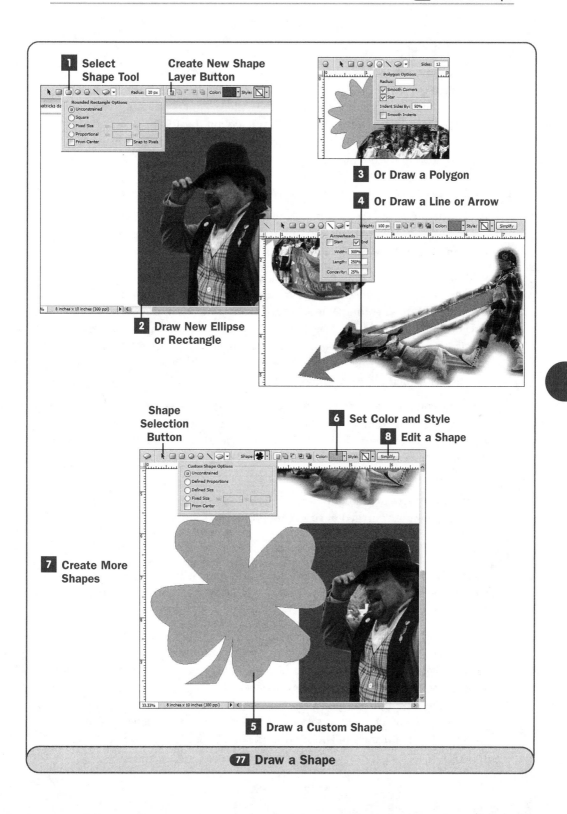

1 Select Shape Tool

Create New Shape Layer Button

3 Or Draw a Polygon

4 Or Draw a Line or Arrow

2 Draw New Ellipse or Rectangle

Shape Selection Button

6 Set Color and Style

8 Edit a Shape

7 Create More Shapes

5 Draw a Custom Shape

77 Draw a Shape

1 Select Shape Tool

Open an image in the Editor in **Standard Edit** mode and save it in Photoshop (***.psd**) format. In the **Layers** palette, select the layer above which you want the object to appear. (The shape will appear on a shape layer above the layer you select.) Click the **Shape** tool on the **Toolbox**. Don't worry about what shape is shown on the button; you'll select the actual shape you want to draw in upcoming steps.

2 Draw New Ellipse or Rectangle

At the left end of the **Options** bar, in the shapes section, click the button for the shape you want to draw: **Rectangle**, **Rounded Rectangle**, or **Ellipse**. Click the **Create New Shape Layer** button on the **Options** bar.

Click the arrow at the right end of the shapes section to display the **Geometry Options** palette, and then select the size you want: **Square** (creates a square with the **Rectangle** or **Rounded Rectangle** tools), **Circle** (creates a circle with the **Ellipse** tool), **Fixed Size** (draws the shape in the exact size you specify in the **Width** and **Height** boxes that appear), **Proportional** (draws the shape using the aspect ratio indicated by the **Width** and **Height** values), or **Unconstrained** (draws a shape in the size you designate by dragging).

On the **Geometry Options** palette, set how you want to draw the shape, choosing as many options that apply: **From Center** (draws the shape from the center out) or **Snap to Pixels** (snaps the edges of the shape to the nearest pixel). On the **Options** bar, adjust the **Radius** to adjust the roundness of corners on a rounded rectangle.

Click on the layer and drag to draw the shape. The shape is placed on its own layer, and is restricted in size or proportion as specified.

3 Or Draw a Polygon

On the **Options** bar, in the shapes section, click the **Polygon** button. Set the number of **Sides** you want in your polygon. Click the **Create New Shape Layer** button.

Click the arrow at the right end of the shapes section to display the **Geometry Options** palette, and set other options: **Radius** (sets the exact size of the polygon by limiting the distance from the center of a polygon to one of its outer points, in inches), **Smooth Corners** (smoothes the corners of the polygon, in most non-star polygons, this option creates a circle), or **Star** (creates a star). If you chose **Star**, set other options as desired: **Indent Sides By** (sets the depth of a star's indentation) and **Smooth Indents** (rounds a star's indents).

77

Click on the layer and drag to draw the polygon. The polygon is restricted in size (radius) and number of sides as specified.

4 Or Draw a Line or Arrow

On the **Options** bar, in the shapes section, select the **Line** button. Set the line thickness (**Weight**). Click the **Create New Shape Layer** button.

If you want to create an arrow, click the arrow at the right end of the shapes section to display the **Geometry Options** palette, and indicate whether you want to add an arrowhead at the **Start** and/or **End** of the line. Set the size of the arrowheads: **Width** (sets the width of arrowhead, as a percentage of the line weight, from 10%–1000%), **Length** (sets the length of the arrowhead, as a proportion of the line weight, from 10%–5000%), and **Concavity** (sets the curvature of the back of the arrowhead, where it touches the line, as a percentage of the arrowhead length; this ranges from 50% to –50%, 0% being flat, and negative values curving back toward the line rather than toward the point).

Click on the layer and drag to draw the line. Press **Shift** as you drag to restrict the angle of the line in 45° increments from the starting point. The line is placed on its own layer, and the line and its arrowheads (if any) are restricted in thickness and size as specified.

77

5 Draw a Custom Shape

On the **Options** bar, in the shapes section, click the **Custom Shape** button. Open the **Shape** list and select a shape from the palette. Some of the shapes have an open center, and create a natural frame around an image, which is a nice effect. To display a different library of shapes, click the **Palette Menu** button (the right arrow) on the **Shapes** palette and select a library from the menu that appears. (See **69** **About the Toolbox** for help in switching from one shape library to another.) On the **Options** bar, click the **Create New Shape Layer** button.

Click the arrow at the right end of the shapes section to display the **Geometry Options** palette, and select the size you want: **Defined Proportions** (draws shape using the proportions defined in its style), **Defined Size** (draws shape in the size defined in its style), **Fixed Size** (draws the shape in the exact size you specify in the **Width** and **Height** boxes), or **Unconstrained** (draws a shape in the size you designate by dragging). To draw the shape from the center out, select **From Center**.

Click on the layer and drag to draw the custom shape. The shape is placed on its own layer and is restricted in size and proportion as specified.

6 Set Color and Style

Select a **Color** and a layer style (**Style**) for the new shape. To remove a layer style applied in error, choose **Layer, Layer Style, Clear Layer Style**.

▶ **NOTE**

Although you can select a **Color** and **Style** for a shape before you draw it, if the current layer is also a shape layer, your selections will change the current shape layer as well. So it's typically better to select a shape color and style *after* it's drawn.

7 Create More Shapes

Repeat steps 1–6 to create new shapes on their own layer. You can modify an existing shape by indicating how you want the new shape to interact with the existing shape: on the **Options** bar, click **Add** to add the area defined by the new shape to the existing shape; click **Subtract** to subtract the new shape's area from the existing shape where they overlap; click **Intersect** to create a shape defined by where the two shapes overlap; or click **Exclude** to combine the two shapes, removing the area where they overlap.

8 Edit a Shape

77

Click the **Shape** tool on the **Toolbox** (if needed), and then on the **Options** bar, in the shapes section, click the **Shape Selection** button. Click a shape in the image; *handles* appear around the perimeter of the shape's *bounding box*. Resize a shape by dragging a handle inward (to make the shape smaller) or outward (to make it bigger). To move the shape, drag it from the center. You can skew or distort an object in the same way you can a layer; see **59 Move, Resize, Skew, or Distort a Layer or Selection**. You can rotate a shape in the same way you rotate a layer; see **60 Rotate the Data in a Layer or Selection**.

To recolor a shape, double-click its layer thumbnail on the **Layers** palette. To apply a filter or effect to the shape, the shape must be simplified first (that is, converted to raster data). Click the **Simplify** button on the **Options** bar.

▶ **KEY TERMS**

Bounding box—A rectangle that describes the boundaries of a drawn object, cropping border, or the data on a layer.

Handles—Small squares that appear along the perimeter of the bounding box surrounding a drawn object, layer or cropping border. By dragging these handles, you can resize the object, layer data, or cropping border.

After you're satisfied with the result, make any other changes you want and save the result in JPEG, PNG, non-layered TIFF format, leaving your PSD image with its *layers* (if any) intact so that you can return at a later time and make adjustments if you want.

In this example, I used a variety of shapes to frame a collage of images taken at a St. Patrick's Day parade.

---

78 | **Add a Text Caption or Label**

→ **SEE ALSO**

79 Add a Backscreen Behind Text
82 Fill Text with an Image

In the Editor, you add a text label or caption to an image using the **Type** tool on the **Toolbox**. When you select the **Type** tool, you can customize how the text will look by selecting the appropriate options such as font, size, and color on the **Options** bar. There are actually four **Type** tools. You use the **Horizontal Type** tool to type horizontal (left to right) text, and the **Vertical Type** tool to type vertical (up and down) text. Even so, because text is a vector object, you can rotate, skew, or distort it after the fact by using the **Move** tool (see **59** **Move, Resize, Skew, or Distort a Layer or Selection**). You can also type text as a selection you can fill, modify, and use just like any other selection, using the **Horizontal Type Mask** and the **Vertical Type Mask** tools. See **82** **Fill Text with an Image**.

78

▶ **NOTE**

The type of text label/caption you'll learn to add in this task is different from a caption you might add through the Organizer: in the Editor, the text caption/label becomes a part of the image itself, while in the Organizer, any caption you add becomes part of the image's EXIF data, but does not appear on the image itself.

1 **Select Type Tool**

Open an image in the Editor in **Standard Edit** mode and save it in Photoshop (***.psd**) format. On the **Layers** palette, select the layer above which you want the text layer to appear. The text layer will be inserted above the layer you choose. Select the **Type** tool on the **Toolbox**.

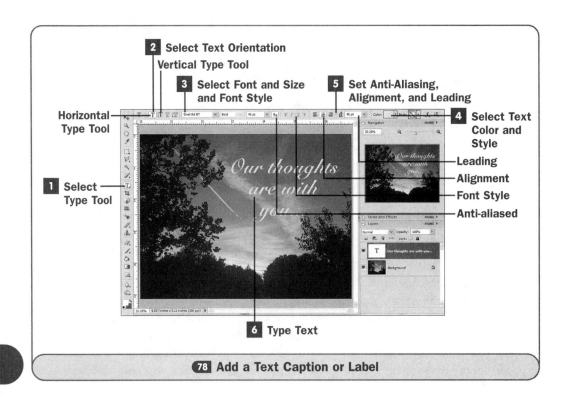

2 Select Text Orientation
Vertical Type Tool

3 Select Font and Size
and Font Style

5 Set Anti-Aliasing,
Alignment, and Leading

Horizontal
Type Tool

4 Select Text
Color and
Style

Leading

Alignment

Font Style

Anti-aliased

1 Select
Type Tool

6 Type Text

78 Add a Text Caption or Label

78

2 Select Text Orientation

In the **Options** bar, click the **Horizontal Type** or **Vertical Type** tool. Because
a lot of formatting options are not available on the **Options** bar until you set
the cursor, click in the image where you want to align the text. *To make formatting the text easier, however, do not type the text until after you select the formatting options you want in the upcoming steps.*

3 Select Font and Size and Font Style

Click the arrow next to the **Font** drop-down list box and select the font you
want to use for your text label or caption. Open the **Font Style** list and select
a font style if desired, such as bold. If the font you've chosen does not offer
the font style you want, you can click the **Faux Bold**, **Faux Italic**, **Underline**,
or **Strikethrough** buttons located to the right of the **Font Style** list. Select or
type a font **Size** (in points).

▶ NOTES

Normally, when choosing fonts to use in a file that you intend to share with other people, you should select a font you know they also have, or risk having your text re-rendered in an alternative font. However, unless you're going to share your actual **PSD** working file, you can use any font you like because the vector text will be converted to raster when you flatten the image to save it in a single layer format such as non-layered TIFF, JPEG, or GIF.

After you type text, you can select portions of text by dragging over it and apply formats such as bold to just those selected characters.

4 Select Text Color and Style

Open the **Color** list and select a color from the **Color Swatch** palette. To pick a color using the **Color Picker**, click the **More Colors** button. The color you choose is added to the swatch palette. You can also apply a layer style **(Style)** to the text layer if desired.

5 Set Anti-Aliasing, Alignment, and Leading

Click the **Anti-aliased** button to soften jagged curves by adding semi-transparent pixels. Choose a text **Alignment**, such as center or left-align. If you plan on typing more than one line of text, adjust the spacing between lines by setting a **Leading** value (in points) or choose **Auto** (to allow Photoshop Elements to adjust the leading based on the text's font size).

78

6 Type Text

Type your text. Press **Enter** to begin a second line of text. Click the **Commit** button (the check mark) to finalize the text, or click **Cancel** (the circle with slash) to abort. The text is added to your image on a new text layer, which is named using the text you wrote. The text layer is marked in the **Layers** palette with a large *T* on its layer thumbnail.

Make additional changes to the image. When you're satisfied with the image, save the PSD file. Then merge the layers together and resave the result in JPEG, PNG, or non-layered TIFF format, leaving your PSD image unflattened so that you can return at a later time and make adjustments if you want.

▶ TIPS

To change text after committing it, click the text layer on the **Layers** palette and then choose a **Type** tool or double-click the text layer's thumbnail. Select the text and then make any desired changes to the settings on the **Options** bar. To change horizontal text to vertical text or vice versa, select the text and click the **Change the Text Orientation** button (at the right end of the **Options** bar). Notice that the **Style** option doesn't appear when you're editing text; to add a layer style to the text, select the style from the **Styles and Effects** palette.

If you do not like the positioning of the text after committing it, select the text layer in the **Layers** palette and click the **Move** tool on the **Toolbox**. A bounding box appears around the text object. Click within this box and drag the text to the desired location on the layer.

If you are adding text to create a copyright for an image, you might want to add the **Emboss** filter and apply the **Hard Light** blend mode to make the copyright text more subtle. Merge all layers and then resave the file in its final format for distribution. To apply the filter, you'll need to convert the layer to raster data (simplify the layer, which makes it uneditable). Luckily Photoshop Elements automatically prompts you to simplify the layer when you add the filter; to simplify a layer manually, choose **Layer, Simplify Layer**.

78

79 **Add a Backscreen Behind Text**	
✔ **BEFORE YOU BEGIN**	→ **SEE ALSO**
78 Add a Text Caption or Label	**100** About Blend Modes (on the Web)

If your text seems to get lost in the detail of your image, you might want to try adding a backscreen behind the text. Typically, a backscreen looks like a portion in the original image, but one that has been lightened, blurred, or changed in some fashion so that text is easier to read against it. In this example, we are going to select a portion of the image under the text and copy that section to a new layer. Then we will modify that layer by adjusting the brightness so that the text can stand out against that portion of the background.

1 Add Text

Open an image in the Editor in **Standard Edit** mode and save it in Photoshop (*.psd) format. On the **Layers** palette, select the layer above which you want the text layer to appear. The text layer is inserted above the layer you choose.

Select the **Type** tool from the **Toolbox**, select the font, size, and other attributes you want, then type your text. See **78** **Add a Text Caption or Label**.

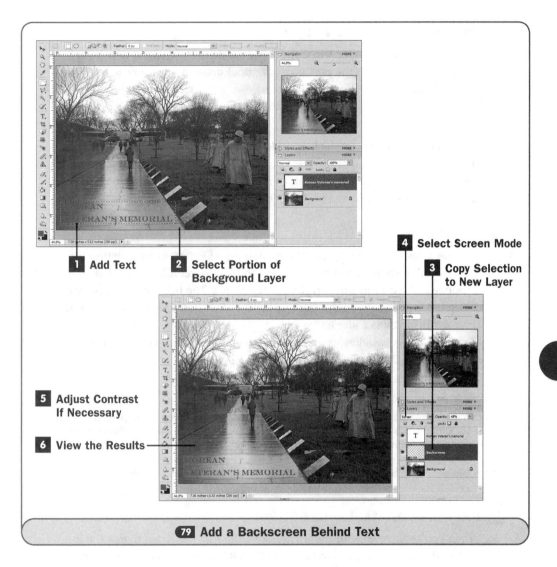

1 Add Text

2 Select Portion of Background Layer

3 Copy Selection to New Layer

4 Select Screen Mode

5 Adjust Contrast If Necessary

6 View the Results

79 Add a Backscreen Behind Text

2 Select Portion of Background Layer

To create the backscreen, in the **Layers** palette, select the **Background** layer.
Use one of the selection tools on the **Toolbox** to select a portion of the
Background layer under the text you typed. The **Rectangular Marquee** tool
works well for selecting a rectangular-shaped area.

▶ TIP

If you need to reposition the backscreen selection, make sure that you still have any
selection tool active (except for the **Selection Brush**). Click the **New Selection** button on
the **Options** bar (if needed), position the mouse pointer within the selection marquee,
and drag it into position.

3 Copy Selection to New Layer

Choose **Layer**, **New**, **Layer Via Copy** from the menu to create a new layer that contains a copy of the portion of the **Background** layer you selected in step 2. Name this new layer **Backscreen**.

4 Select Screen Mode

On the **Layers** palette, set the blend **Mode** of the **Backscreen** layer to **Screen**. This setting should lighten the background, making it easier to see the text. If you want to darken the backscreen to make light text show up better against it, select the **Hard Light** or **Soft Light** blend mode instead.

5 Adjust Contrast If Necessary

In some cases, you can improve the readability of your text by lowering the contrast and increasing the brightness of the **Backscreen** layer. Choose **Enhance**, **Adjust Lighting**, **Brightness/Contrast**. The **Brightness/Contrast** dialog box appears. Drag the **Contrast** slider to the left to lower the contrast. Drag the **Brightness** slider to the right to increase the brightness if needed. Watch the image window as you make adjustments; when your text is clearly readable, click **OK** to apply your changes.

79

▶ TIPS

You can use any tool to adjust the **Backscreen** layer to improve the readability of the text. For example, you can apply a filter such as **Gaussian Blur** to blur the **Backscreen** layer and further reduce the distraction of a busy background.

Add a **Bevel** or **Drop Shadow** layer style to your **Backscreen** layer for a finished look.

6 View the Results

When you're satisfied with the image, save the PSD file. Then merge the layers together and resave the result in JPEG, PNG, or non-layered TIFF format, leaving your PSD image unflattened so that you can return at a later time and make adjustments if you want.

After making the appropriate adjustments to your backscreen layer, the text should be easy to read on your image. Alternative methods you can try include making a selection, creating a new layer, and filling the selection with white, another solid color, or a gradient and then using a blend mode on the **Backscreen** layer such as **Screen** or **Soft Light**. You can try lowering the **Opacity** on this layer as well. Another method to try involves making a selection and creating an adjustment layer (such as **Levels** or **Brightness/Contrast**) which automatically affects just that selection.

Here, I placed a backscreen behind a piece of text to make it more visible against the texture of the sidewalk. I set the blend **Mode** to **Screen** and reduced the **Contrast** to improve the text visibility.

---

80 | Create Metallic Text

✔ BEFORE YOU BEGIN	→ SEE ALSO
78 Add a Text Caption or Label	**81** Create Text That Glows

Sometimes, plain text is just not what you are looking for to set off an image. Photoshop Elements provides several different effects, filters, and layer styles you can use to create metallic text. You'll find these effects and filters on the **Styles and Effects** palette, which you can display if needed by selecting **Window**, **Styles and Effects**. To apply some of the effects and filters, you might have to simplify the text first (convert it to raster data), which means that the text won't be editable after that. Simplifying text is usually done automatically for you after you select the style you want to apply; to simplify text manually, choose **Layer**, **Simplify Layer**. So be sure to make your edits to the text *before* attempting this task.

80

1 Add Text

Open an image in the Editor in **Standard Edit** mode and save it in Photoshop (*.**psd**) format. On the **Layers** palette, select the layer above which you want the text layer to appear. The text layer is inserted above the layer you choose.

Select the **Type** tool from the **Toolbox** and add text to your image. It usually doesn't matter what color you use to create the text; the filters, effects, and layer styles usually replace the color with the metallic finish. You might want to use a font with enough size and body, however, so that you can see that the text is metallic. See **78** **Add a Text Caption or Label** for more information on adding text.

2 Select a Metallic Finish

In the **Styles and Effects** palette, select the metallic finish you want to use. Layer styles leave your text editable, while filters and effects do not. First, select **Layer Styles**, **Filters**, or **Effects** from the first list on the **Styles and Effects** palette. Then choose a category from the second list, such as **text effects**. Here's a listing of metallic finishes you might want to try:

- **Chrome** (sketch filter)
- **Brushed Metal** (text effect)

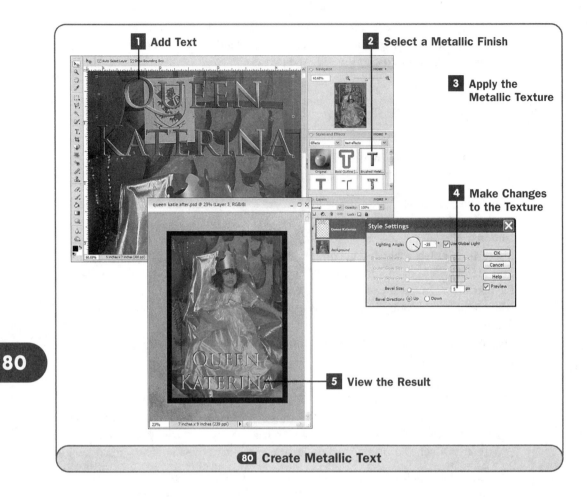

1 Add Text

2 Select a Metallic Finish

3 Apply the Metallic Texture

4 Make Changes to the Texture

5 View the Result

80 Create Metallic Text

- **Gold Sprinkles** (textures effect)
- **Rusted Metal** (textures effect)
- **Brushed Metal** (patterns layer style)
- **Copper** (patterns layer style)
- **Chrome Fat** (complex layer style)
- **Diamond Plate** (patterns/complex layer style)
- **Molten Gold** (complex layer style)
- **Rivet** (complex layer style)
- **Wow Chrome** (Wow Chrome layer style)—A collection of five different chrome layer styles

3 Apply the Metallic Texture

To apply the two textures effects (**Gold Sprinkles** and **Rusted Metal**), you must select the text first by clicking it with the **Magic Wand** tool; otherwise, the effect will be applied to the entire layer.

To apply the chosen metallic texture, in the **Styles and Effects** palette, double-click the thumbnail of the filter, effect, or layer style you want to apply. If prompted to flatten the image or to simplify the layer, click **OK** to continue.

4 Make Changes to the Texture

If you applied an effect or layer style, you can customize the metallic texture somewhat. In the **Layers** palette, double-click the **f** icon next to that layer's name. The **Style Settings** dialog box appears. Change options as desired (some options are not available with every texture.)

Adjust the **Lighting Angle** by typing a value in the field or twisting the **Lighting Angle** knob. To ensure that the text is given the same lighting angle as all other 3D effects in the image, enable the **Use Global Light** check box. Adjust the amount of shadow with the **Shadow Distance** value. Change the amount of glow with the **Outer Glow Size** and **Inner Glow Size** values. Adjust the bevel size by dragging the **Bevel Size** slider or by typing a value. The **Bevel Direction** option designates whether the appearance of the metal bevel is raised (**Up**) or lowered (**Down**). Click **OK**.

You can remove an effect or layer style from your text by right-clicking the layer in the **Layers** palette and selecting the **Clear Layer Style** option from the context menu that appears.

80

▶ TIP

To create your own style of gold text, apply one of the chrome or silvery metallic textures, then group it with a **Hue/Saturation** adjustment layer (by choosing **Layer, New Adjustment Layer, Hue/Saturation** and enabling the **Group With Previous Layer** option) that you use to colorize the text with a **Hue** of **59**, **Saturation** of **58**, and **Lightness** of **–26**, and enabling the **Colorize** option. For bronze text, try a **Hue** of **31**, **Saturation** of **58**, and a **Lightness** of **18**.

5 View the Result

When you're satisfied with the image, save the PSD file. Then merge the layers together and resave the result in JPEG, PNG, or non-layered TIFF format, leaving your PSD image unflattened so that you can return at a later time and make adjustments if you want.

In this example, I applied the **Brushed Metal** text effect, then recolored it with a **Hue/Saturation** adjustment layer so it would look golden. For the text to more closely match the color of the gold in the girl's crown and the throne, I used the **Colorize** settings of **Hue 43**, **Saturation 58**, and **Lightness 28**. I decided the text looked better at the bottom of the photo, so I moved it there and added a backscreen rectangle of light blue behind it to make it more readable. Next, I cropped the photo to remove some of the busy background. I expanded the canvas and created a gold frame by applying the **Gold Sprinkles** layer style to a new layer. I then made a selection around the photo and filled with it with black to create an inner mat.

---

81 **Create Text That Glows**

✔ **BEFORE YOU BEGIN**	→ **SEE ALSO**
51 Save and Reload a Selection	**80** Create Metallic Text
78 Add a Text Caption or Label	**82** Fill Text with an Image

---

80

When I think of the term *glowing*, I infer from it the concept of emitting light. The best way I know to suggest that something gives off light is to show something that the light is reflecting off. Surprisingly, the Editor's **Outer Glows** layer styles are not too convincing. Its **Wow Neon** layer styles are better at achieving a convincing glow effect, but what I prefer is an effect that looks like one of those shadow-box neon signs, where light is emitted from the *back* of the letter blocks and bounces off the back plate, illuminating the area *around* the letters. This task shows a homemade version of that glowing text style.

1 Add Text

Open an image in the Editor in **Standard Edit** mode and save it in Photoshop (***.psd**) format. On the **Layers** palette, select the layer above which you want the text layer to appear. The text layer is inserted above the layer you choose.

Select the **Type** tool from the **Toolbox** and add text to your image. Choose a well-saturated color with a brightness of about 50 to 60, since the brightness of your final text will increase significantly with this technique. Choose a large fat font or add bold to make the glowing text effect more apparent. See **78** Add a Text Caption or Label.

2 Simplify the Text Layer

When the text looks exactly the way you want, select **Layer**, **Simplify Layer** to convert the layer to raster data. Name this new layer **Base**.

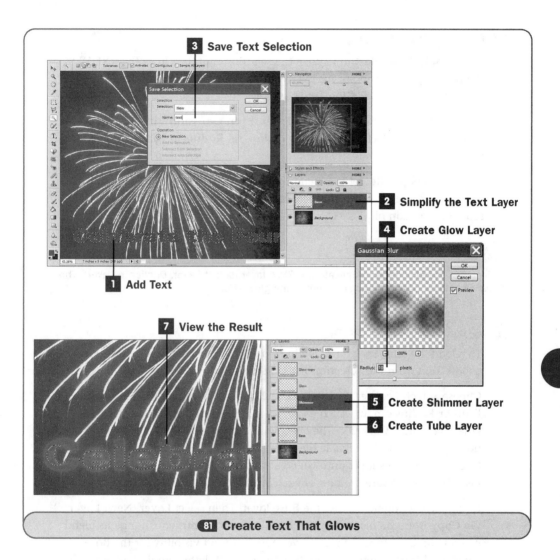

81 Create Text That Glows

3 Save Text Selection

In the **Layers** palette, choose the **Base** layer. From the **Toolbox**, click the **Magic Wand** tool, disable the **Contiguous** option on the **Options** bar, and click the text to select the individual letters.

You'll be using this selection pattern more than once in this task, so choose **Select, Save Selection** to save it. In the **Save Selection** dialog box, enter **Text** as the selection's name and click **OK**. See **51** **Save and Reload a Selection**.

4 Create Glow Layer

Choose **Select**, **Deselect** to remove the selection marquee from the text. With the **Base** layer still chosen, select **Layer**, **Duplicate Layer** to make a copy of it. Name the new layer **Glow** and click **OK**.

With the **Glow** layer chosen, select **Filter**, **Blur**, **Gaussian Blur**. For the blur effect to be effective in creating a glow, set **Radius** to **10.0** or higher. Click **OK**.

In the **Layers** palette, set the blend mode for the **Glow** layer to **Screen**. If you like what you see, *you can stop here* and save your results. The next steps reproduce a neon glow effect.

▶ **NOTE**

To increase the glow effect, duplicate the **Glow** layer (select **Layer, Duplicate Layer**). The **Glow copy** layer will dramatically brighten the glow effect.

5 Create Shimmer Layer

To reload the selection you saved in step 3, choose **Select**, **Load Selection**, choose **Text** from the **Selection** list, and click **OK**.

Choose **Select**, **Feather**. For text above 72 points in size, enter a large **Feather Radius** amount such as **20**; for 72 points and smaller, enter a smaller feather value. Click **OK**. The effect you're going for is to reduce the selection to a series of blobs inside the letters, as shown. The area you select will be copied to a new layer and will create an inner glow like the inside of a neon bulb, so be sure the part of each letter you want to glow is selected.

In the **Layers** palette, choose the **Base** layer. Then select **Layer**, **New**, **Layer via Copy** from the menu bar. Rename the layer **Shimmer**. Change its blend mode to **Screen**. To see what you've made, turn off visibility for the **Base**, **Glow**, and **Glow copy** layers for a moment. Each letter should look very faint, like a ghost of the text layer.

6 Create Tube Layer

On a neon sign, the inner neon tube is always visible, even if the sign glows brightly. In this step, you'll create the neon tube. In the **Layers** palette, make the layers visible. With the **Base** layer chosen, load the **Text** selection again. Then choose **Select**, **Modify**, **Contract** from the menu bar, and enter a value about one-fourth the amount you entered in step 5. Click **OK**. You'll end up with a selection that's shaped like the text, but smaller.

81

Choose **Select**, **Modify**, **Feather** and enter a small value such as **2**. Click **OK**. The feathering will soften the edges of the selection, softening the effect. You'll use this selection to create the neon tube inside your glowing text.

With the **Base** layer still chosen, select **Layer**, **New**, **Layer via Copy**. Name the new layer **Tube**. Then set its blend mode to **Difference**. Restore the visibility of all layers. Now your letters have a glowing rim and a second tier of glow on the inside.

7 View the Result

When you're satisfied with the image, save the PSD file. Then merge the layers together and resave the result in JPEG, PNG, or non-layered TIFF format, leaving your PSD image unflattened so that you can return at a later time and make adjustments if you want.

▶ TIP

One of my favorite twists on this technique is to pick one letter and eliminate the selection for that letter before creating the **Shimmer** layer, thus making it look like the light has burned out on one of the letters.

82

82 | Fill Text with an Image

✔ BEFORE YOU BEGIN	→ SEE ALSO
78 Add a Text Caption or Label	**80** Create Metallic Text
	81 Create Text That Glows

You can make your text more interesting by filling it with another image rather than a color. When you do this, the image is visible only inside the letters of the text—in effect, framing the image. To create this magic, you use either the **Horizontal** or **Vertical Type Mask** tool to create a type-shaped selection. You can do anything you want with this text selection, including making modifications to it using any of the selection tools (such as the **Selection Brush**), filling it with a gradient or pattern using the **Paint Bucket** or **Gradient** tools, and even saving it for reuse.

You can fill a text selection using one of two methods: First, you could paste all or part of an image into the selection. The problem with the first method is that you have little control over what portion of the image shows up within the text "frame"; and manipulating the image so that the exact portion you want to see shows through is difficult because you can't see the image as you make your adjustments (see **52** About Copying, Cutting, and Pasting Data Within a Selection).

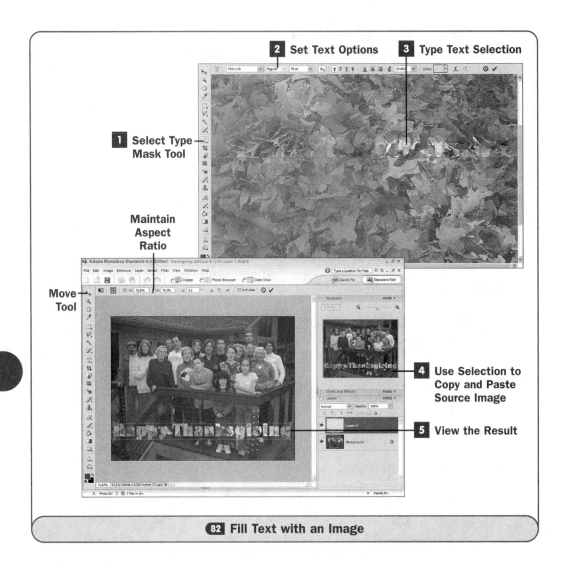

2 Set Text Options   **3** Type Text Selection

1 Select Type Mask Tool

Maintain Aspect Ratio

Move Tool

4 Use Selection to Copy and Paste Source Image

5 View the Result

82 Fill Text with an Image

As explained in this task, the second method you can use to fill a text selection is to maneuver the selection itself over the image and copy exactly the data you want. If the image doesn't fill the selection adequately no matter where you move it, you can change the selection text's size or font to find a better fit.

1 **Select Type Mask Tool**

In the Editor, in **Standard Edit** mode, open the source image you want to use for the interior of your text. On the **Layers** palette, select the layer that contains the data you want to appear within your text. Click the **Horizontal Type Mask** tool or the **Vertical Type Mask** tool on the **Toolbox**.

▶ **TIP**

For my source image, I typically pick something that's dense with texture or color, because you're probably not going to be able to make out a lot of individual detail within the text.

2 **Set Text Options**

On the **Options** bar, select a fairly wide **Font** and a large **Size**. Set other options as desired, such as **Anti-aliased** (which helps soften any jagged curves in the text selection).

3 **Type Text Selection**

Click on the image in the area you want to use to fill your text and type the text. A red mask appears over your image, and the text is revealed as you type. This red screen (the mask) helps you see how the image below will fill the text.

Edit the text if needed; because this is a selection and not actual text, you won't be able to go back later and make changes to it after you commit (although you will be able to reposition the selection; see the following **Note**). When you have created a text selection that's the size and shape you need, click the **Commit** button (check mark) on the **Options** bar.

▶ **NOTE**

If the text-shaped selection is not positioned to select the exact area of the image you want to use, move the selection after committing it by clicking any selection tool (but not the **Selection Brush**), enabling the **New Selection** option on the **Options** bar, and dragging the selection marquee.

4 **Use Selection to Copy and Paste Source Image**

Select **Edit**, **Copy** to copy the data within the text selection. Select **Edit**, **Copy Merged** instead if you want to select all visible pixels within the selection and not just those on the current layer.

Open the image in which you want the text to appear and save it in Photoshop (***.psd**) format. On the **Layers** palette, select the layer above which you want the filled text to appear. Select **Edit**, **Paste**. The filled text appears on its own layer within the image, above the layer you selected.

82

▶ **TIP**

You can move and resize the filled text if needed; see **59** Move, Resize, Skew, or Distort a Layer or Selection. If you're resizing, be sure to enable the **Maintain Aspect Ratio** option. You can also rotate the filled text layer if you like; see **60** Rotate the Data in a Layer or Selection.

5 **View the Result**

When you're satisfied with the image, save the PSD file. Then merge the layers together and resave the result in JPEG, PNG, or non-layered TIFF format, leaving your PSD image unflattened so that you can return at a later time and make adjustments if you want.

In this example, I started with a photograph of some fall leaves. I used the **Horizontal Type Mask** tool to copy the leaves in a text shape into an image of my family enjoying a nice Thanksgiving. I then used the **Move** tool to resize the text and to position it in the lower portion of the photo.

82

11

Repairing and Improving Photographs

IN THIS CHAPTER:

83 Remove Specks, Spots, and Scratches

84 Repair Minor Tears

85 Repair Large Holes, Tears, and Missing Portions of a Photo

86 Restore Color and Tone to an Old Photograph

87 Restore Quality to a Scanned Photograph

88 Remove Unwanted Objects from an Image

When people suffer a disaster, what are some of the first things they try to protect or recover? Family pictures. No doubt more than once you've seen heartbreaking stories on the news of people searching through the wreckage of their homes, looking for pictures that were dear to them. Even without natural disasters, the pictures from your past face a formidable hazard: old age. Even if you store them carefully in albums, your cherished images tend to fade, bend, and decay.

Recognizing this, the makers of Photoshop Elements have packed up an extensive kit of tools to help restore old photographs. In this chapter, you'll learn how to remove scratches and specks and to repair tears, stains, and even holes. You'll also learn how to quickly restore color and contrast to an old photograph, and to repair any loss of quality when you scanned in the photograph. When you're finished, you might look at the results and decide the old homestead never looked better and that Uncle Ben was a surprisingly handsome guy.

83 Remove Specks, Spots, and Scratches

✔ BEFORE YOU START	→ SEE ALSO
69 About the Toolbox	**84** Repair Minor Tears

This small photo has been around since the 1940s and has had plenty of opportunity to acquire small specks, dust spots, and scratches. Such a picture is a good candidate for a progressive approach: Start with a tool such as the **Dust & Scratches** filter to remove thin, short scratches and scattered dust spots in a small area. Then, move up to the **Healing Brush** or the **Spot Healing Brush** to remove longer and wider scratches. The **Healing Brush** works like the **Clone Stamp**, copying pixels from another area of a photo to make a repair. Unlike the **Clone Stamp**, the **Healing Brush** *blends* copied pixels with existing pixels, creating a softer, less visible, repair—this makes the **Healing Brush** perfect for repairing large areas of a photograph in which detail is not critical, such as a background area. The **Spot Healing Brush** is great for repairing small, isolated spots or scratches, because it copies pixels from the outer edges of the brush tip to the area under the tip to make its repair.

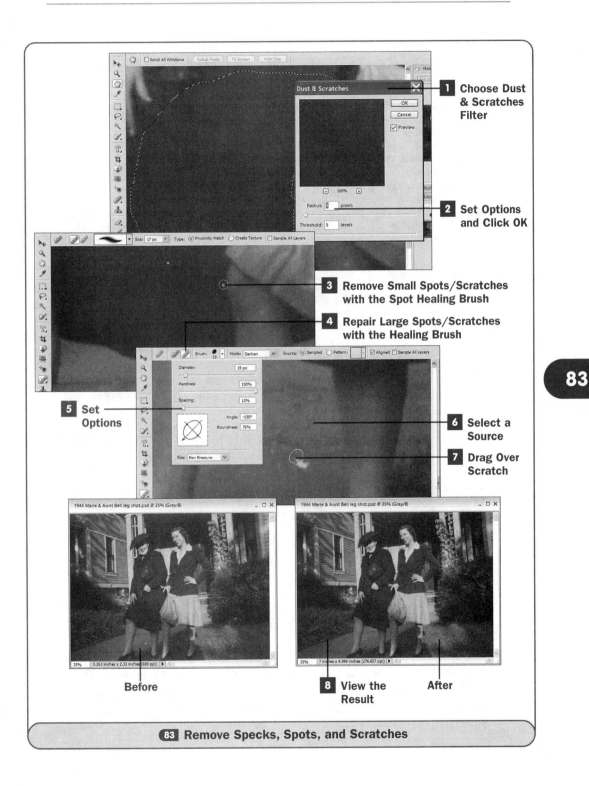

1 Choose Dust & Scratches Filter

2 Set Options and Click OK

3 Remove Small Spots/Scratches with the Spot Healing Brush

4 Repair Large Spots/Scratches with the Healing Brush

5 Set Options

6 Select a Source

7 Drag Over Scratch

Before

8 View the Result

After

83 Remove Specks, Spots, and Scratches

▶ **NOTE**

Dust specks, scratches, and other "age spots" aren't the only kinds of damage a picture can suffer. Digital cameras and cell phone cameras might add *noise* to an image, if you take a long exposure in low light, overextend the digital zoom, or use an ISO setting above 100. Noise can also appear in scans of printed newspaper or magazine photos or in still images captured from video. You can use one of three noise filters to eliminate these specks from an image: The **Median** filter changes pixels to the same average brightness as their neighbors, making it a good choice to remove general, high-contrast noise. The **Despeckle** filter blurs pixels to smooth out areas of low contrast, leaving areas of high contrast (which are typically the edges of objects in a photo) untouched, making it good at removing low-contrast noise in a large area while preserving your edges. The **Reduce Noise** filter, like the **Median** filter, changes the brightness of pixels that are much brighter than their neighbors; the filter also evens out color by averaging the hue of each pixel with that of its neighbors. And like **Despeckle**, the **Reduce Noise** filter preserves the contrast along edges in your photo.

▶ **KEY TERM**

Noise—A random pattern of pixels over the entire surface of an image, giving it a grainy texture.

83

1 **Choose Dust & Scratches Filter**

Open an image in the Editor in **Standard Edit** mode and save it in Photoshop (***.psd**) format. Zoom in on an area of dust spots—it's easier to work with an enlarged view.

To limit the effect of the filter (and prevent it from removing detail you want to keep), use any of the selection tools to select an area that contains thin scratches or dust spots. Choose **Filter**, **Noise**, **Dust & Scratches**. The **Dust & Scratches** dialog box appears.

2 **Set Options and Click OK**

The **Dust & Scratches** filter searches for pixels that contrast greatly with their neighbors and reduces this contrast to remove high-contrast dust spots and very small scratches. The larger the **Radius**, the larger the area examined for brightness differences, and the larger the spots the filter can remove. Ideally, you want to set the **Radius** to roughly the same size as the scratches or spots you're trying to get rid of.

If **Threshold** is set to a low value, the spot or scratch must contrast a lot with neighboring pixels before it will be removed. As you raise the **Threshold** little by little, you'll remove more spots at the risk of possibly losing some detail in the selected area. When you find the right balance between the settings, click **OK** to apply them.

▶ TIP

Repeat steps 1 and 2 to remove the next set of spots and scratches. To reapply the last filter you used, with the exact same settings, press **Ctrl+F**, or choose that filter from the very top of the **Filter** menu, where it will continue to appear until you use a different filter.

3 Remove Small Spots/Scratches with the Spot Healing Brush

The **Dust & Scratches** filter does a wonderful job of removing tiny spots, especially when they are grouped together, but you must be careful to apply the filter to a small area or you'll lose detail. To remove spots that are isolated or larger than a small dot, use the **Spot Healing Brush**.

You don't have to make a selection first; the effect is controlled by the size of your brush tip. Zoom in so that you can see the spot you want to remove, and then select the **Spot Healing Brush** on the **Toolbox**. On the **Options** bar, select a brush tip and adjust its **Size** to something slightly larger than the size of the spot you want to repair. Set the **Type** option to **Proximity Match**. This option analyzes the pixels around the edges of the brush to create a patch for the repair. Click the spot to remove it.

83

▶ TIP

If the area the spot is in has a definite texture, you can replicate that texture to a degree by enabling the **Create Texture** option on the **Options** bar. This option analyzes all the pixels under the brush tip for both color and tone, and then uses that sampling to create a similar pattern.

4 Repair Large Spots/Scratches with the Healing Brush

To remove wider spots or longer scratches, select the **Healing Brush** tool. You'll use the tool to copy pixels from an undamaged area of the image, in a manner similar to the **Clone Stamp** tool. The **Healing Brush**, however, blends these copied pixels with existing pixels at the site, creating a more invisible repair than you could achieve by using the **Clone Stamp** tool.

5 Set Options

On the **Options** bar, open the **Brush** palette and adjust the brush **Diameter** to the size of the scratch or spot you're trying to repair. For a scratch, try reducing the **Roundness** setting to flatten the brush tip and adjusting the tip **Angle** to match the angle of the scratch. Enable the **Sampled** option. Because the scratch is lighter than the pixels you'll be copying from an undamaged area of the image, select **Darken** from the blend **Mode** list. Set any other options as desired, such as **Aligned**. See 59 **About the Toolbox**.

6 Select a Source

Press **Alt** and click the image to establish the source for the repair. Be sure to select a source area from an undamaged part of the image. I typically click very near the scratch so that the cloned pixels will match the repair area closely.

7 Drag Over Scratch

Drag the brush over the scratch to remove it. The source point (the crosshair) moves along with you, showing you exactly which pixels are being copied. If you did not enable the **Aligned** option, then as you begin each stroke, the source point (the crosshair) moves back to the original source point (the original point you clicked in step 6). If you *did* enable the **Aligned** option, the source point when you begin a new stroke is placed relative to the original source point and the place where you click to begin the stroke. In other words, assume that you selected a source point and then clicked to begin the first stroke just to the left of that point (the source is located on the right). If the **Aligned** option is enabled, then when you begin a second stroke, the source point is located just to the right of that stroke.

Pixels are copied from the source and blended with existing pixels, completing the repair. Because you selected the **Darken** blend mode, the cloned pixels replace the source pixels completely if they are darker than the scratch. Repeat steps 4 to 7 to repair any remaining scratches.

8 View the Result

After removing the scratches and spots on your photo, make any other changes you want and save the PSD file. Then resave the file in JPEG, PNG, or non-layered TIFF format, leaving your PSD image with its layers (if any) intact so that you can return at a later time and make adjustments if you want.

After less than five minutes, and with the help of the **Dust & Scratches** filter, **Spot Healing Brush**, and the **Healing Brush**, I have easily removed the majority of the specks, spots, and faint scratches on this old photo.

---

84   Repair Minor Tears

✔ BEFORE YOU BEGIN	→ SEE ALSO
69 About the Toolbox	**83** Remove Specks, Spots, and Scratches
	85 Repair Large Holes, Tears, and Missing Portions of a Photo

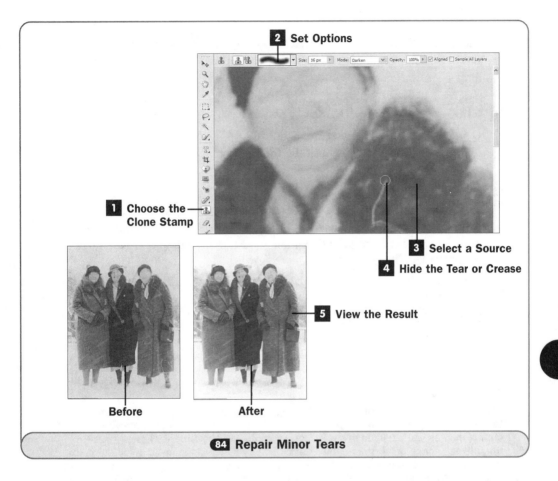

2 Set Options

1 Choose the Clone Stamp

3 Select a Source

4 Hide the Tear or Crease

5 View the Result

Before

After

84 Repair Minor Tears

Even cute pictures from the past are vulnerable to damage. Sometimes the damage is minor but annoying, such as a thin crease, small tear, scratch, spot, or stain. As you learned in **83** **Remove Specks, Spots, and Scratches**, you can use the **Dust & Scratches** filter to remove tiny specks grouped in the same area, the **Spot Healing Brush** to remove small spots and scratches by blending them with surrounding pixels, and the **Healing Brush** to remove larger scratches and specks.

Sometimes the damage to the image is too much for the **Healing Brush** to correct. Although the **Healing Brush** works in a manner similar to the **Clone Stamp**, it *blends* copied pixels with those in the area you're repairing, and sometimes, blending is not what you want. For example, if you're repairing a tear that's fairly white, the **Healing Brush** blends the copied pixels (taken from an intact part of the picture) with the whiteness of the tear, creating an almost ghost-like effect. The same thing happens if you use the **Healing Brush** to repair a large hole; the whiteness of the hole will interfere with the cover-up job you're trying to achieve. In this task, you'll learn how to use the **Clone Stamp** to clone missing data back into a photo. In **85** **Repair Large Holes, Tears, and Missing Portions of a Photo**, you'll learn an alternative technique that's quick and effective at filling in missing information.

1 Choose the Clone Stamp

Open an image in the Editor in **Standard Edit** mode and save it in Photoshop (***.psd**) format. Select the **Clone Stamp** tool from the **Toolbox**.

2 Set Options

Select a soft brush tip and set the **Size** just a bit larger than the flaw you want to repair. Because tears and creases are lighter than surrounding pixels, select the **Darken** blend **Mode**. Enable the **Aligned** option, and set **Opacity** to 100% to fully replace the tear.

3 Select a Source

Press and hold the **Alt** key. Click in the image near the crease or tear to specify the source point—the "good pixels" you want the tool to clone to fix the flaw.

84

▶ TIPS

The source point (the crosshair) moves along with you as you drag the **Clone Stamp** tool, showing you exactly which pixels are being copied. If you do not enable the **Aligned** option, then as you begin each stroke, the source point (the crosshair) moves back to the original source point (the original source point you click in step 3). If you *do* enable the **Aligned** option, then the source point when you begin a new stroke is placed relative to the original source point and the place where you click to begin the stroke. In other words, assume that you select a source point and then click to begin the first stroke just to the left of that point (the source is located on the right). If the **Aligned** option is enabled, then when you begin a second stroke, no matter where you click, the source point is located just to the right of that stroke.

The disadvantage in using the **Clone Stamp** tool is that it copies flaws along with good pixels. This is why selecting your source point is important. As a rule, select the source as physically close to the flaw as you can. As the tear or crease changes direction, adjust the source point as well (by pressing **Alt** and clicking the image again) so that you can continue to match objects perfectly, without picking up any flaws near the tear you're repairing.

4 Hide the Tear or Crease

Click at the beginning of the tear or crease and drag slowly down the crease. The pixels you sampled in step 3 are copied over the flaw as you drag. As you work, the source point (marked by a crosshair) moves with the brush tip.

5 View the Result

This photo of three elderly aunts braving a snow storm was apparently stored
in someone's pocket. It has many creases, spots, specks, and a few water
stains. It took a little while to repair the damage, but as you can see, the
result is a great improvement. After making the repairs, I adjusted the contrast to bring the portrait back to life.

85	**Repair Large Holes, Tears, and Missing Portions of a Photo**
✔ **BEFORE YOU BEGIN**	→ **SEE ALSO**
54 Create a New Image Layer	**84** Repair Minor Tears
57 Erase Part of a Layer	

Photoshop Elements has retouching tools that can take care of most of the small
defects in an old photo. They will even take care of some of the larger ones. But
once in a while, a picture might be missing a corner or have holes in it from
being mounted on a bulletin board. Repairing this kind of damage has the same
purpose as using the **Clone Stamp** or the **Healing Brush** to repair smaller areas:
The goal is to replace the bad section of a photo with a good section of the photo.
However, when you must repair a large damaged area, using the **Clone Stamp** or
Healing Brush to copy data is not only tedious (you have to move the source
often to hide what you're doing) but often leads to poor results despite your best
efforts. In this task, I show you a slick approach to filling in big gaps in your
photo.

1 Copy Bottom Layer

Open an image in the Editor in **Standard Edit** mode and save it in
Photoshop (*.**psd**) format. On the **Layers** palette, drag the layer onto the
Create a New Layer button or select **Layer**, **Duplicate** to create a duplicate
of the original **Background** layer. Rename this new layer **Shifted**.

▶ TIP

If the good information you want to use to repair the hole or tear is located in another
image, open that image and adjust its size and resolution to match the image you want
to repair. See **32** Change Image Size or Resolution. Then, instead of duplicating the
Background layer as instructed in step 1, choose **Select**, **All** to select the entire good
image, and then choose **Edit**, **Copy** to copy the good image. Change to the image you
want to repair and choose **Edit**, **Paste** to paste the image with the good data onto a
new layer. Rename this new layer **Shifted**.

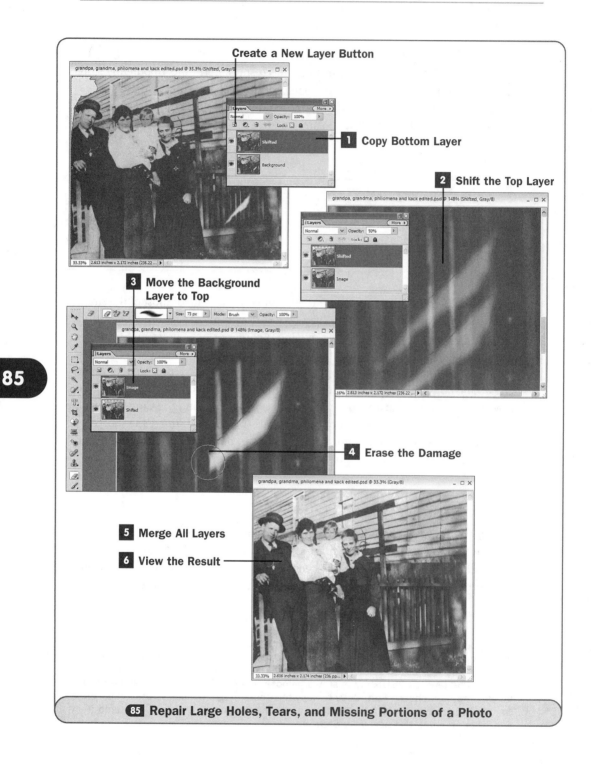

85 Repair Large Holes, Tears, and Missing Portions of a Photo

2 Shift the Top Layer

On the **Layers** palette, change the **Opacity** of the **Shifted** layer to **50%**. This setting lets you see the **Background** layer as you shift the top layer. You're going to use good pieces of the **Shifted** layer to cover the holes and tears in the **Background** layer.

Click the **Move** tool on the **Toolbox**. Click the **Shifted** layer in the image and slowly move it left, right, up, or down until its good portion covers up the area on the **Background** layer that you want to fill in.

3 Move the Background Layer to Top

In the **Layers** palette, reset the **Opacity** of the **Shifted** layer to 100%. Convert the **Background** layer to a regular layer (a process also known as "simplifying") by choosing the **Background** layer in the **Layers** palette and choosing **Layer**, **New**, **Layer from Background**. Name the converted layer **Image**. Simplifying the background layer allows you to move its position in the layer stack.

Click the newly created **Image** layer in the **Layers** palette and drag it above the **Shifted** layer. The **Shifted** layer is now on the bottom, with the **Image** layer on top. Notice that the hole in the original image is noticeable once again.

85

4 Erase the Damage

On the **Layers** palette, select the **Image** layer. In the **Toolbox**, select the **Eraser** tool. In the **Options** bar, set the **Mode** option to **Brush**, select a soft-edged brush, and adjust its **Size** to fit the size of the hole or tear. Set **Opacity** to **100%**.

Start brushing over the damaged area, erasing the top image layer to reveal the undamaged area of the **Shifted** layer under it.

5 Merge All Layers

If the shifted data happens to line up with another hole or tear, you can repeat step 4 to repair that damage as well. If not, you'll need to merge the layers, and then repeat steps 1 to 4 to repair any other damaged areas. To merge the layers, choose **Layer**, **Flatten Image**.

6 View the Result

After you've made all necessary repairs to the holes and tears, make any other changes you want, such as removing small spots and creases. Save the PSD file, and then resave the file in JPEG, PNG, or non-layered TIFF format, leaving your PSD image with its layers (if any) intact so that you can return at a later time and make different adjustments if you want.

This old photo of my grandparents, great-grandmother, and aunt (as a baby) has been through a lot, as you can see. There was a tear in the middle and in one corner; small specks and spots adorned various areas, and it had lost its tone. To repair the damage, I borrowed a good spot in the fence and, following the steps in this task, repaired it. I repeated the process to fix the missing section in the upper-left corner. After merging all layers, I adjusted the contrast and used the **Spot Healing Brush** on the specks. The result, as you can see, is much improved.

86	Restore Color and Tone to an Old Photograph

✔ BEFORE YOU BEGIN	→ SEE ALSO
89 About an Image's Histogram	90 Improve Brightness and Contrast
	91 Improve a Dull, Flat Photo
	95 Adjust Hue and Saturation Manually

85

The colors in this picture are a clue to the picture's age. As photos age, their colors fade at different rates, causing not only a loss in saturation, but a color shift as well. The Editor has several automatic tools on the **Enhance** menu to correct the color balance and tone of photos like this one, but they aren't always as precise as you might like. In the case of this picture, using **Enhance**, **Auto Levels** or **Enhance**, **Auto Color Correction** was like using a sledgehammer when the situation called for a scalpel.

In this task, I'll explain how to manually adjust the color saturation and tones in your image to improve its overall appeal. In most old photos, the overall tone is medium and the contrast is not as sharp as it should be; when you display a histogram for the image, the graph doesn't meet either end of the scale. The first step in restoring an old photograph is to find the brightest and darkest points in the picture and place them at each end of the histogram to balance the overall tone. You'll accomplish that task with the **Levels** dialog box. To help you make precise adjustments, you'll display the **Info** palette and use its information to help you locate the lightest and darkest pixels in the image so that the various levels of brightness can be evenly distributed throughout the image. This process also helps to balance the color in an image, removing any color cast. Finally, to restore your old photo to its former brilliance, you'll increase the saturation as needed.

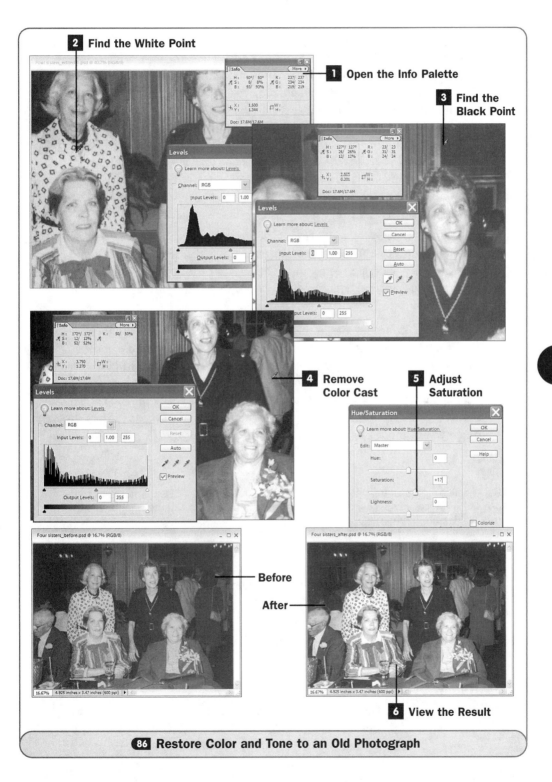

2 Find the White Point

1 Open the Info Palette

3 Find the Black Point

4 Remove Color Cast

5 Adjust Saturation

Before

After

6 View the Result

86 Restore Color and Tone to an Old Photograph

1 Open the Info Palette

Open an image in the Editor in **Standard Edit** mode and save it in Photoshop (***.psd**) format. Open the **Info** palette by choosing **Window, Info** from the menu bar. The **Info** palette provides data about whichever pixel is currently under the mouse pointer; you'll use this information to select the darkest and lightest points in the image. To make the **Info** palette show the HSB (hue, saturation, and brightness) values you'll need to complete this task, click the **Eyedropper** icon in the first pane and select **HSB Color** from the context menu.

2 Find the White Point

Choose **Enhance, Adjust Lighting, Levels** from the menu bar. The **Levels** dialog box appears. To locate the lightest point in the image, press **Alt** and click the white slider just below the right end of the histogram. The image changes to display the lightest points. Memorize the general area of one of these points.

Select the white eyedropper in the **Levels** dialog box. Move the dropper over the area you identified earlier as containing the lightest spot. Look for the highest **B:** reading in the **Info** palette. When you find the lightest pixel, click it. The picture brightens considerably because the **Levels** dialog box uses the white point you just specified to adjust its histogram. The point you clicked becomes "absolute white" in the image, and the brightness of the rest of the pixels in the image are adjusted to accommodate this shift.

86

▶ **TIP**

When selecting the whitest point in the image, ignore reflections. Extreme bright spots like these are called *specular highlights* and should not be considered when finding the true white point in an image.

3 Find the Black Point

Press **Alt** and click the slider below the left end of the histogram in the **Levels** dialog box, and make note of the darkest points in the image. Select the black eyedropper in the **Levels** dialog box. As you move the mouse pointer over the image, look for the lowest **B:** value on the **Info** palette. When you find the darkest point in the image, click it.

4 Remove Color Cast

Assuming there's something in your photograph that should look medium gray (but it's not shown in its true color right now), you can use the gray eyedropper in the **Levels** dialog box to remove any color cast in the image.

Otherwise, remove any color cast by choosing **Enhance**, **Adjust Color**, **Remove Color Cast** and clicking a point in the image that should be true white or true black.

Click the gray eyedropper in the **Levels** dialog box. Click a pixel in the image that you think should look medium gray—for example, concrete or stone, a light shadow on a white wall, or a gray hair. The colors in the image shift; assuming that you've clicked a pixel that should be medium gray, any color cast is removed. (If you select an incorrect pixel, the colors still shift, but in that case, you'll actually *create* a color cast.) Click **OK** to close the **Levels** dialog box and accept the changes.

5 Adjust Saturation

Choose **Enhance**, **Adjust Color**, **Hue/Saturation** from the menu bar to display the **Hue/Saturation** dialog box. Drag the **Saturation** slider to the right to increase the intensity of the colors in a faded image. (For more information about the **Hue/Saturation** dialog box, see **95** **Adjust Hue and Saturation Manually**.) Click **OK** to save your changes.

▶ TIPS

Sometimes the color in a photograph fades unevenly. You can increase the saturation in selected parts of an image using the **Sponge** tool. Click the **Sponge** tool on the **Toolbox**, set the **Mode** to **Saturate**, adjust the **Flow** as desired, and then drag the tool over the area you want to saturate.

You can also increase the saturation in an old photo by duplicating the image on another layer and setting the duplicate layer's blend mode to **Multiply**.

6 View the Result

When you're satisfied with the color and tone of the image, make any other changes you want and save the PSD file. Then resave the file in JPEG, PNG, or non-layered TIFF format, leaving your PSD image with its layers (if any) intact so that you can return at a later time and make adjustments if you want.

After improving the contrast and saturation in this old photo and removing a color cast that seemed to make everything greenish, the final result is a much improved treasure.

87 **Restore Quality to a Scanned Photograph**

✔ BEFORE YOU BEGIN	→ SEE ALSO
5 Import and Separate Multiple Scanned Images	**83** Remove Specks, Spots, and Scratches
	90 Improve Brightness and Contrast
	97 Sharpen an Image

Even if the original photograph is sharp and vibrant, these subtle qualities some-times can be lost when you scan the picture. To improve your chances of getting a good scan, you might want to scan at double the image resolution you're going to need for printing—600 PPI. After making the adjustments shown in this task, you can resize the image downward as a last step, a process that increases the quality of the scan by making the pixels in an image even smaller.

The worst type of photo to scan is a halftone photograph common to newspapers and some magazines. In fact, scanning any type of printed material often results in a poor-quality digital image. If your scanner has a **Descreen** option, turn it on when scanning such photos; it can help remove the *moiré pattern* that often occurs. If your scanner does not have a **Descreen** option, you can use the filters in Photoshop Elements to remove a moiré pattern.

87

▶ KEY TERM

Moiré pattern—The pattern that appears when one regular geometric pattern—such as a grid made up of dots—overlays another or similar pattern when placed slightly askew. For example, two window screens placed on top of each other at an angle form a moiré effect.

1 Remove Moiré Pattern and Noise

Open an image in the Editor in **Standard Edit** mode and save it in Photoshop (***.psd**) format. If your scan is of a halftone image, it might have a moiré pattern. Even if a scan is of a regular photograph, the scanning process might have introduced some noise that's more easily seen when the image is zoomed in.

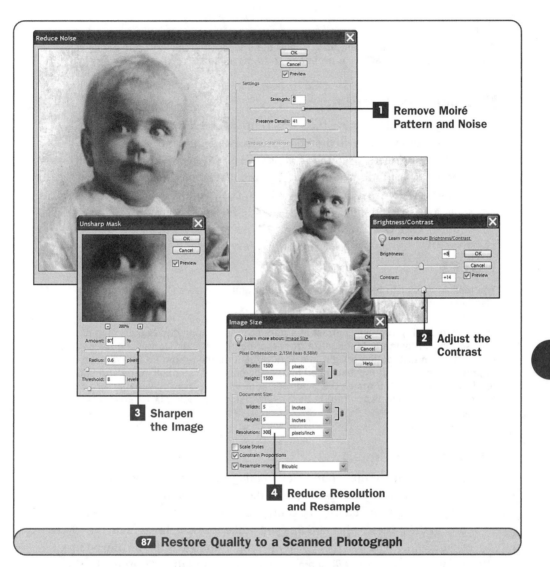

1 Remove Moiré Pattern and Noise

2 Adjust the Contrast

3 Sharpen the Image

4 Reduce Resolution and Resample

87 Restore Quality to a Scanned Photograph

In **83** **Remove Specks, Spots, and Scratches**, you learned about the various filters Photoshop Elements provides for removing noise from an image. Because it combines the best of both the **Despeckle** and **Median** filters, the **Reduce Noise** filter is often a very good choice: choose **Filter, Noise, Reduce Noise**. Increase the **Preserve Details** setting to preserve as much sharpness along the edges of objects in the photo as you can; at the same time, increase the **Strength** until you notice that a sufficient amount of noise has been reduced, without losing the natural texture of elements such as skin or fabric. For color scans, adjust **Reduce Color Noise** as needed to remove the color dotted noise. When you're satisfied, click **OK**.

▶ **TIP**

For persistent noise, you might have to blur the image while preserving the edge contrast (sharpness). See **98** **Blur an Image to Remove Noise.**

2 **Adjust the Contrast**

Next, you should improve the scan's contrast and tone. There are various ways you can do that, but the easiest method is to use the **Brightness/Contrast** command, described in **90** **Improve Brightness and Contrast.** Select **Enhance, Adjust Lighting, Brightness/Contrast.** The **Brightness/Contrast** dialog box appears. Drag the **Brightness** or **Contrast** slider to the right to increase it, or drag to the left to decrease it. When you're satisfied, click **OK.**

▶ **NOTES**

The techniques illustrated in **86** **Restore Color and Tone to an Old Photograph** might also help restore contrast and saturation to your scan.

One way to quickly improve contrast in a dark scan is to apply the **Equalize** filter. Choose **Filter, Adjustments, Equalize** from the menu. The filter works automatically to create an even distribution of light and dark pixels throughout the image. You can also improve the contrast in most scanned images by dragging the outer white and black level markers inward to match the outer edges of the histogram (these markers are located just below the histogram) in the **Levels** dialog box. See **91** **Improve a Dull, Flat Photo.**

3 **Sharpen the Image**

When making multiple changes to an image, it's generally recommended that you not do any sharpening until the final step because sharpening is really a process that adjusts the contrast between pixels. If you sharpen too early in the process, other changes you make can sometimes undo the effects of sharpening. The best tool for sharpening an image is the **Unsharp Mask,** explained in detail in **97** **Sharpen an Image.** Select **Filter, Sharpen, Unsharp Mask.** The **Unsharp Mask** dialog box opens. Adjust the **Radius** to set the size of the area around each pixel to be examined for contrast, and set the **Threshold** to a value that tells the filter what level of contrast must exist before a pixel is changed. Finally, set the **Amount** to the amount of contrast by which you want to increase qualifying pixels. When you're happy with the results, click **OK.**

4 Reduce Resolution and Resample

If you scanned the image at 600 PPI or higher, you can reduce the resolution without changing the image's print size. Although you might think the fatter pixels that would result would also leave you with a less clear image, for many scanned images—especially those scanned from newspapers—the resampling process that takes place when you reduce the resolution can also average out the contrasting areas that cause moiré patterns. The result is an image that looks clearer *to your own eyes*, which is where it really counts anyway.

Save the PSD file and then resave the file in JPEG, PNG, or non-layered TIFF format, leaving your PSD image with its layers (if any) intact so that you can return at a later time and make adjustments if you want. Starting with a flattened image speeds up the process of resampling, while preserving the resolution of your original scan.

Choose **Image, Resize, Image Size** from the menu. The **Image Size** dialog box appears. Enable the **Resample Image** option, and from the drop-down list beside it, choose **Bicubic Sharper**, which is the resampling mode most preferred for downsizing. Next, type a value that's half the image's current resolution in the **Resolution** box. To finalize your choices, click **OK**. See **32 Change Image Size or Resolution**.

▶ **NOTE**

Scanning your original photo at very high resolution—especially higher than what you intend to print—and then resizing downward and resampling, is not a solution for every photograph, but it *does* work for any image in which the scanning process generates geometric patterns that don't belong to the image. If you don't have to remove moiré patterns from a scan, you can leave the image in its higher resolution and skip step 4.

88

---

88 | **Remove Unwanted Objects from an Image**

✔ BEFORE YOU BEGIN	→ SEE ALSO
69 About the Toolbox	**84** Repair Minor Tears

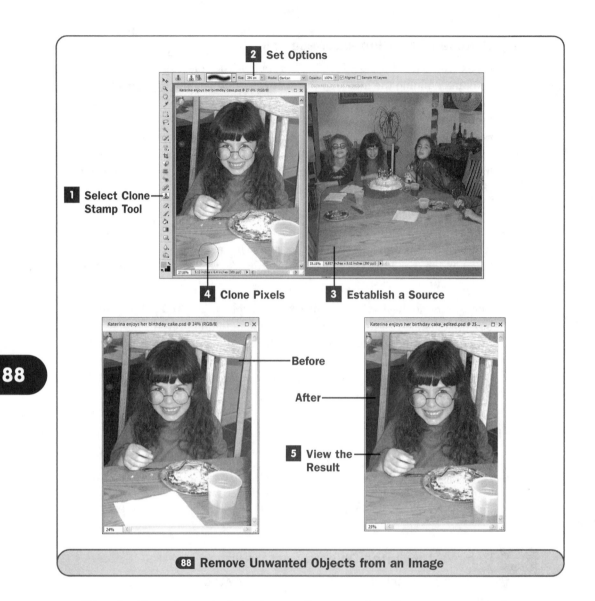

2 Set Options

1 Select Clone Stamp Tool

4 Clone Pixels

3 Establish a Source

Before

After

5 View the Result

88 Remove Unwanted Objects from an Image

Using the **Clone Stamp** tool, you can easily remove from an image unwanted objects such as telephone poles, wires, trash cans, a thumb that wandered in front of the lens, or a few stray hairs blown in the wind simply by copying over these distractions with pixels located somewhere else in the image (or in another image). To use the **Clone Stamp**, you first indicate the source area, and then you drag to paint with pixels copied from the source. Be sure to "cover your tracks" and avoid creating a noticeable pattern as you copy. The best ways to do that are to lower the **Opacity** of the **Clone Stamp** tool, to select a blend mode so that the pixels you clone blend with existing pixels, to paint with single clicks or very short strokes, to use a large brush to avoid copying multiple times to the same area (but a small-enough brush that you don't copy things you don't want), and to vary the source area from which you're copying by re-establishing a new source point every so often. The source you select for the **Clone Stamp** can be located within a different image, on a different layer, or on the same layer. For example, you might clone some hair from one side of a photo to repair a small rip or a bad hair day. Or, you might clone a squirrel from one photo onto the head of your brother in another photo to create a comic image.

▶ TIPS

You might also be able to remove objects from an image in the same way you repair tears and holes. See **85** **Repair Large Holes, Tears, and Missing Portions of a Photo.**

You can remove small objects with the **Spot Healing Brush** or **Healing Brush** by covering them up with pixels copied from the surrounding area. See **83** **Remove Specks, Spots, and Scratches.**

1 Select Clone Stamp Tool

Open an image in the Editor in **Standard Edit** mode, and save it in Photoshop (*.psd) format. Click the **Clone Stamp** tool on the **Toolbox**.

2 Set Options

On the **Options** bar, select a brush tip and brush **Size** and enable the **Aligned** check box. Set other options as desired. See **69** **About the Toolbox.**

3 Establish a Source

If you're cloning a region from another image, open that image in the Editor. On the **Layers** palette, choose the layer containing the data you want to copy. If the image has multiple layers, enable the **Sample All Layers** option to copy data from all visible layers.

Finally, press **Alt** and click on the image layer to establish the source point. Be careful not to click too close to objects you don't want to clone.

▶ TIPS

If you're cloning data from one image into another, it might be easier if you tile the images so that you can see them both at the same time, but you don't have to. The source point is maintained as you clone, even if you can't see the source image. To tile all the open images, choose **Window**, **Images**, **Tile** from the menu.

To hide your clone tracks (if you're cloning a texture such as skin rather than a specific object such as a nose), change the source often by pressing **Alt** and clicking a different source point.

88

4 Clone Pixels

If needed, change to the image to which you want to copy the source data. On the **Layers** palette, change to the layer on which you want to copy the data.

To begin copying pixels, click on the layer or drag with short strokes to sample pixels from the source and paint them under the brush tip. Note that a crosshatch pointer shows you the location of the source point, and that it moves as your painting point moves. Don't confuse one point with the other. Repeat until the repair has been made or until the undesirable object has been painted over.

5 View the Result

After you're satisfied with the result, make any other changes you want and save the PSD file. Then resave the file in JPEG, PNG, or non-layered TIFF format, leaving your PSD image with its layers (if any) intact so that you can return at a later time and make adjustments if you want.

I liked this photo of my daughter's seventh birthday, but the more I looked at it, the more distracting the large white napkin in the foreground became. And no matter how I cropped the photo, that napkin still seemed to draw attention to itself. So, I cloned a bit of the same table from another photo taken at that same time and with the same lighting conditions, over top of the napkin, essentially removing the napkin from the photo. I used the **Clone Stamp** and not the **Healing Brush**, even though it does a very nice job of cloning, because the **Healing Brush** also *blends* the cloned pixels with the existing pixels. If I had used the **Healing Brush**, it would have blended the table pixels with the white napkin pixels, creating a "ghostly napkin" effect.

88

12

Correcting Brightness, Contrast, Color, and Sharpness

IN THIS CHAPTER:

89 About an Image's Histogram

90 Improve Brightness and Contrast

91 Improve a Dull, Flat Photo

92 Lighten a Subject on a Snowy Background

93 Lighten or Darken Part of an Image

94 Correct Color, Contrast, and Saturation in One Step

95 Adjust Hue and Saturation Manually

96 About Sharpness

97 Sharpen an Image

98 Blur an Image to Remove Noise

99 Blur a Background to Create Depth of Field

This chapter is about how you can address the attributes of a photograph that affect its perceived quality. One of the easiest problems to overcome is poor exposure. Your picture might be overexposed (too light) or underexposed (too dark). It might have too little contrast (flat) or too much contrast (harsh shadows). Color balance is another characteristic that can ruin a good photo, and when it's off, you'll know it because the colors will just look "wrong." Perhaps someone's skin tone looks too red or too green, or perhaps Uncle John's favorite blue sweater is just not the color you remember it to be. Removing a color cast (a bias towards one color, such as red) will fix all the colors in an image, making the photo instantly "right."

Sharpness is the final critical factor in creating a great photograph. Digitally, sharpness is increased or decreased by changing the level of contrast along the edges of objects. Unfortunately, you will not be able to sharpen an out-of-focus image and make it look right, but if an image is only slightly off, you can gently sharpen it and improve its appearance. You can also blur portions of an image, which you might do in order to get a subject to stand out more against a busy background. In this chapter, you'll learn how to improve the brightness, color, and sharpness of your images.

89 About an Image's Histogram

→ **SEE ALSO**

91 Improve a Dull, Flat Photo

One of the most important tools you can use to uncover what's right or wrong with an image is its *histogram*, a chart that describes the progression of tones (brightness) and color throughout an image. An image's histogram appears on the **Histogram** palette (choose **Window**, **Histogram** to display it), and it basically looks like a wave. Suppose that you wanted to study the distribution of red throughout an image. Keeping in mind that each pixel is actually a blend of red, green, and blue, if you chose the **Red** histogram, all the pixels with no red at all (0) would be counted, and their number represented along the left side of the histogram; if there were lots of pixels in an image with no red at all, the left side of the histogram "hill" would be high. All pixels whose red component was 255 (the most red a pixel can have) would also be counted and that value represented along the right side of the chart; all the pixels with intermediate amounts of red would be represented within the middle of the chart. So, you now have a chart that shows the number of dark reds on the left and bright reds on the right. Combine this with a chart of relative greens and relative blues, and the chart now gives you a complete picture of the distribution of all the colors in the available spectrum, throughout your image.

▶ KEY TERM

Histogram—A chart that depicts the relative distribution of pixels in an image that share the same characteristics, such as lightness, saturation, hue, or presence in a particular color channel (red, green, or blue). Use it to determine whether particular colors or brightness values disproportionately predominate, diminishing picture quality.

What do you learn from looking at such a chart? When you know there's something wrong with the appearance of a photograph but you just can't put your finger on what or why, the histogram helps you discover what's wrong. For instance, old color photographs—especially Polaroid prints—tend to look dreary and muted. After you've scanned one, the histogram of its color channels will probably reveal a dip in its green levels on the right end. Optically, red and green combine to produce yellow; and on a Polaroid print, yellow is the ink that tends to fade the soonest (cyan next, whereas magenta always seems to outlast the other two inks). A histogram of the same photo's brightness channel will probably also reveal deep chasms along both the left and right sides, indicating an image with neither sharp brights nor deep darks. Shifting the weight of these plots to restore balance to the green channel and to fill in the side gaps on the brightness channel can restore most, if not all, the original print's luster and brilliance. With Photoshop Elements's **Levels** command, you can restore an image by directly tinkering with its histogram; for example, if the chart formed a hill with gaps on both sides, you could drag the left and right sides of the hill so that they touched the edges of the chart. The result would be a redistribution of the chosen value (such as brightness) throughout all pixels, restoring their natural range from brightest brights to darkest darks.

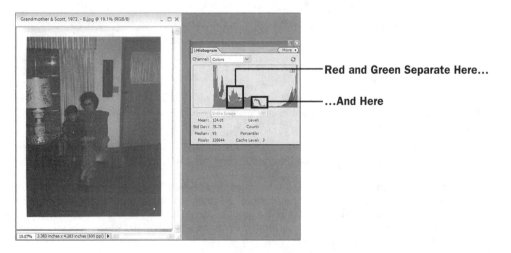

*An old Polaroid print whose yellows have faded, and the **Histogram** palette that documents its color shift.*

▶ **NOTE**

Although yellows tend to fade first in old Polaroid prints, the cyan inks fade first in old Kodak prints, leaving the reds, pinks, and yellows.

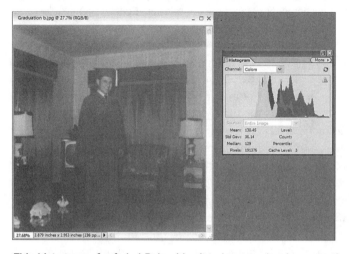

This histogram of a faded Polaroid print shows a classic separation between the channels.

89

There is, however, one tricky point to histogram adjustment, and it involves neither the left side nor the right side, but the *middle*, because in a chart showing brightness distribution, the middle represents the *midtones*. If the midtones of an image are not right, important details such as the texture of a face or the shape of a hand might be lost. Midtones represent colors that are neither light (bright) nor dark (shadows). Adjusting the middle values involves moving the *gamma* point, and that in turn, can end up shifting the dark and the light values in the image as well.

▶ **KEY TERMS**

Midtones—Pixels with a luminance value near the middle of those allowed—a value of about 128. The midtones in an image are an object's true color, without shadows or highlights (reflected light).

Gamma—The relationship between the input voltage of a monitor, printer, or scanner, and the intensity of the resulting output. In a perfect world, such devices would have a gamma of 1.0, and a medium-bright pixel in an image would display or print as medium bright. With gamma set at 1.0, the relationship between input voltage and output would be plotted as a straight line rising from left to right. Instead, your monitor and printer's output (scanners are usually okay) is a definite curve, which you can flatten to more of a straight line through a gamma correction to an image. When the gamma is off, it mostly affects how the midtones of an image are displayed.

No single adjustment is more effective at restoring midtones to an image than repositioning the gamma point. When an image is first scanned in or imported from a digital camera, the Editor assumes a gamma for that image of 1.0. This value represents the bias that the Editor is applying to the image it's processing now; keep in mind that your camera might already have applied its own bias when it originally shot the photo. The adjustments you make to an image's gamma in the **Levels** dialog box affect the way the Editor reinterprets the image.

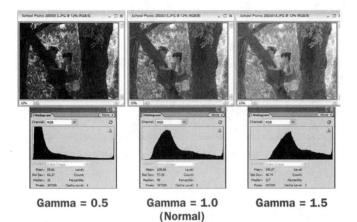

| Gamma = 0.5 | Gamma = 1.0 (Normal) | Gamma = 1.5 |

In the middle is the original image. On the left is a copy with gamma decreased; on the right is a copy with gamma increased.

89

With the **Levels** command, you can make the adjustments that restore the balance and continuity to a scene that your mind told you it had when you first received the impulse to take a picture of it. You can make the lights lighter and the darks darker, and in so doing, vastly improve the contrast of an image while losing none of the detail. Yet these types of changes are not at all the same as turning up or down the contrast and brightness knobs. Those other one-touch changes affect the whole picture equally and proportionally in all places. And as the histogram will demonstrate to you, they don't actually restore or create balance. Because everything is adjusted equally, these controls simply move the *imbalance* of an optical factor from one point to another, less noticeable point.

Reduced to its technical underpinnings, *contrast* can be defined as the differentiation between light and dark elements. Thus, arguably, images with the sharpest possible contrasts would use only black and white pixels. The Editor would plot the histogram for such an image with high cliffs on the left and right, and a chasm in-between. More realistic images with very extreme light and dark contrasts would have relatively high peaks on the left and right, with a dip in the middle, suggesting a relative absence of midtones. To make such a pronounced image more pleasing to the eye, one type of histogram adjustment you might attempt is to blunt the peaks and fill up some of the valley. With histogram adjustment, you experiment with altering the image by tinkering with the geometry of the graph.

"Twin peaks" help illustrate the clear and natural contrast between midtones and highlights in this photo.

Astonishingly, a photograph that's mainly a portrait of a person's face reveals its own signature through its histogram: from left to right, a blue peak, followed by a green one, and then a red one. This is true for faces with any skin tone, dark or light; with lighter tones, the trio of peaks simply appears further to the right. African skin tones register on the histogram with their green peaks slightly to the right of the middle; Norwegian and other light skin tones register slightly to the left of the middle. In any case, the green peak falls between the other two. Knowing this, one way you can correct an apparent discoloration in someone's portrait is to examine the histograms of other well-balanced portraits of the same person and adjust the graphs of the red, green, and blue channels of the discolored photo so that the peaks fall mainly within the same areas.

89

*The **Colors** channel in the **Histogram** palette reveals the telltale signature of human flesh tones in direct sunlight: a blue peak, followed by green, followed by red. In indoor light or cloudy skies, the green and blue peaks can exchange with one another.*

Using the **Levels** command and the **Histogram** palette in conjunction with one another, you can learn why your composition works the way it does. For example, would you believe the smaller rose in this picture is *green*? From the computer's vantage point, what appears to be a red rose is actually comprised of strong, dark blue-green tones according to the **Colors** channel of the **Histogram** palette. Why? Because blues and greens combine to form an optical opposite of red, and opposites are used in combination with pure colors to *darken* them. So, the dark parts of the rose are less saturated as a result. But notice that it's the bright reds that stand out on the right side of the histogram, as it appears in the **Red** channel of the histogram in the **Levels** dialog box. It's this standing out that gives the entire rose its red appearance. If the red and green peaks were closer together on the right side of the graph, the little rose might look more like the big yellow rose at the top of the image. In **91 Improve a Dull, Flat Photo**, you'll see how to use the **Levels** dialog box.

*With the **Levels** command, you can see whether brights and darks within a selection are pinched together or spread apart.*

With the **Histogram** palette, you can view the current statistics for any open image—specifically, from any chosen layer in that image or from the current selection for a layer in that image. To display the palette, select **Window**, **Histogram** from the Editor's main menu. If it's convenient, you can keep this palette open at all times, either docked in the Palette bin or free-floating. You don't have to do anything more; from that point on, the palette shows the graph of your choice for whatever is currently selected.

You can use the **Histogram** palette to display information for the three color channels (red, green, and blue), either separately or as a whole. Open the

Channels drop-down list at the top of the **Histogram** palette and choose **Red**, **Green**, or **Blue**. The histogram curve changes to reflect the distribution of pixels in just that color channel. To get a clearer idea of how colors interact with one another, choose **Colors** from the **Channels** list. In this display, each color component is shown with its own natively colored curve. The histogram shows *cyan* where the blue and green curves intersect, *yellow* where the green and red curves intersect, *magenta* where the red and blue curves intersect, and *gray* where all three curves intersect with each other.

The histogram for the **Luminosity** channel displays an *evaluation* of the relative brightness of pixels in the image. There's a subtle difference between the **Luminosity** channel and the **RGB** channel of the **Histogram** palette: Commonly considered the primary histogram, **RGB** displays relative values of the Brightness (**B**) component of all the pixels in the image; whereas **Luminosity** is a result of a formula that evaluates the other two components of a pixel—Hue (**H**) and Saturation (**S**). Think of the **Luminosity** channel as representing the *richness* of color, as opposed to its brightness or *whiteness*. Don't confuse **Luminosity** with *luminance*, which is a term often used elsewhere to mean brightness and, in some color models, is used in place of Brightness (**B**).

89

As you make a change to all or part of an image using a tool such as the **Brightness/Contrast** dialog box (covered in **90** **Improve Brightness and Contrast**), when the **Preview** option is enabled, the **Histogram** palette shows you the extent of the change you're making *as you're making it*. For the currently displayed channel (except for **Colors**), the palette shows a gray curve with a bright peak, representing the current state of the image, along with a black curve representing the state of the image *if and when* you apply the changes. You can watch the black curve move away from the gray curve as you use the slider.

---

90 | **Improve Brightness and Contrast**

✔ BEFORE YOU BEGIN	→ SEE ALSO
89 About an Image's Histogram	**91** Improve a Dull, Flat Photo

---

If you grew up using a television set that had an old style of operating control called *knobs*, you'll recall there were two such gadgets, generally labeled *Brightness* and *Contrast*. And if you ever played with these knobs as a child—and survived with your wrists unscathed—you remember that Brightness made your picture *whiter* while Contrast made the blacks and whites in your picture stand out.

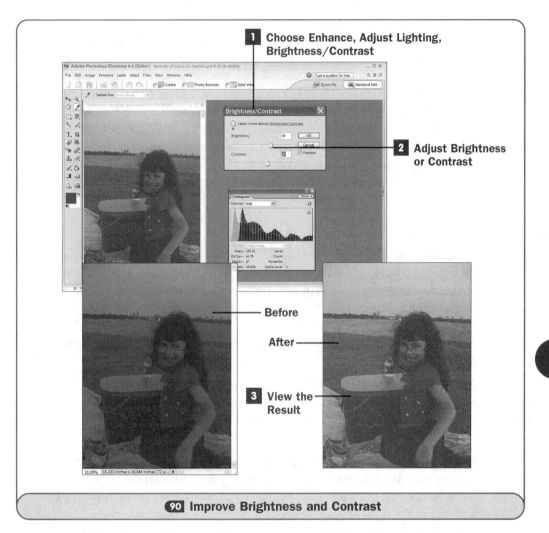

1 Choose Enhance, Adjust Lighting, Brightness/Contrast

2 Adjust Brightness or Contrast

Before

After

3 View the Result

90 Improve Brightness and Contrast

90

▶ **NOTE**

With the **Brightness/Contrast** command, brightness is added to an image (or to a layer or selection) by adding equal amounts to, or subtracting from, the **Brightness** component of *every pixel in the image*. So, although you might be restoring the natural brightness level of the midtones, natural darks might be washed out. By comparison, a contrast adjustment mathematically redistributes brightness across the entire image, flattening the image's histogram and reducing its peaks. However, the same danger of losing bright and dark values remains valid with contrast adjustment, except on both sides of the histogram instead of one.

With all due respect to Philco-Ford, Admiral, Magnavox, and the other great manufacturers of the past century, I'm going to show you here how to use Photoshop Elements's equivalent of the Brightness and Contrast knobs. And then

I'm going to rap you on the wrists if you use them too much. Actually, I'm not kidding this time: Although it does help in some circumstances to restore a more natural appearance to an image, the **Brightness/Contrast** command, when used too liberally, can result in a washed-out look (too bright), a washed-*down* look (too dark), or an underexposed look (too much contrast). More importantly, because pixels cannot have a brightness value of greater than 255 or less than 0, when you brighten or darken pixels *too much*, you lose the distinguishing contrasts between the brightest or darkest pixels among them. Then when you try to get those contrasts back with a **Levels** adjustment, you can't. With the technique demonstrated here, you can use the **Brightness/Contrast** command effectively and safely, without losing information in your image.

90

1 Choose Enhance, Adjust Lighting, Brightness/Contrast

Open the image you want to adjust in the Editor in **Standard Edit** mode and save it in Photoshop (*.**psd**) format. To display the **Histogram** palette if it is not already showing, select **Window**, **Histogram**. From the palette's **Channel** drop-down list, choose **RGB**. If there is more than one layer in the image, choose the layer you want to adjust in the **Layers** palette. If you want to limit your adjustment to a region of the image, use a selection tool to select that region.

Choose **Enhance**, **Adjust Lighting**, **Brightness/Contrast** from the menu bar. The **Brightness/Contrast** dialog box opens. Enable the **Preview** check box so that you can see the results of the adjustments you're making in the actual image.

In this example, the photo was taken at dusk without a flash. Although it does capture the moment, it's the worst time of day to take a digital photo for many cameras. If the flash had been turned on, the subject would have been well lit, but the sky would no longer be a dreamy blue but a dreary clay color. My goal here, for now, is to make the subject matter clearly visible while losing as little of the original color scheme as possible.

2 Adjust Brightness or Contrast

To add brightness to all the pixels in the designated region, slide the **Brightness** slider to the right, or enter a positive value in the **Brightness** text box. To reduce brightness in all the pixels in the designated region, slide the **Brightness** slider to the left, or enter a negative value in the **Brightness** text box.

▶ **NOTE**

As you increase contrast for an image, you might notice that the black curve in the **Histogram** palette has "teeth" in it—specifically, evenly spaced vertical stripes. This is natural, and is an accurate depiction of the brightness values in an adjusted image. For the sake of argument, suppose that there were only 10 levels of brightness in a given image, ranging in value from 10 to 20. After the adjustment, suppose that they now ranged in value from 5 to 25. Because all pixels were adjusted—none are left behind—*there are still only 10 levels of brightness*. They've just been broken up, such that there are pixels with brightness of 5, 7, 9, and so on, but none with 6, 8, 10, and so on. Notice in the example how the contrast-adjusted image looks spotty, noisy, and unsmooth. What your eyes see is verified by the "teeth" in the contrast-adjusted histogram.

▶ **TIP**

If you press the **Alt** key on your keyboard, the **Cancel** button changes to read **Reset**. Click that button to erase your changes to the image, leaving the dialog box open so that you can try again.

To add contrast between pixels in the designated region (making light pixels lighter and darks darker), slide the **Contrast** slider to the right, or enter a positive value in the **Contrast** text box. To reduce contrast between pixels in the designated region (bringing all brightness values together toward a middle gray tone), slide the **Contrast** slider to the left, or enter a negative value in the **Contrast** text box.

As you make adjustments, notice the instant change to the **Histogram** palette. The gray curve with the bright tip represents the image's existing histogram; the black curve represents the adjusted state as you see it in the preview. With a brightness change, the entire "mountain" of the graph shifts to the left or right. With a contrast change, the entire "mountain" is flattened, as if eroded by a rising tide. While you're making these changes, watch the **Histogram** palette, being mindful of two things:

- Don't adjust the image so much that pixels on either or both sides of the histogram fall off the edge. When that happens, you're losing vital information which, when saved, cannot be retrieved.

- In the interest of restoring one of the image's qualities to a natural or pleasing appearance—for example, distinguishing a little girl from her picnic basket—don't introduce negative qualities on the opposite end of the scale, such as a washed-out tone for the grass, or water that appears to glow as if it were emanating from a nuclear facility.

To finalize your adjustments, click **OK**.

90

3 View the Result

When you're satisfied with the result, make any other changes you want and save the PSD file. Then resave the result in JPEG, PNG, or non-layered TIFF format, leaving your PSD image with its layers intact so that you can return at a later time to make new adjustments.

In the example, after adding +**30** to brightness and +**20** to contrast, the range of color now looks more natural. But the image has far to go before it's fixed. In the adjustment, I did lose some of the distinguishing bright values along the right side of the histogram, although not many.

---

91 | Improve a Dull, Flat Photo

✔ BEFORE YOU BEGIN	→ SEE ALSO
89 About an Image's Histogram	86 Restore Color and Tone to an Old Photograph
	90 Improve Brightness and Contrast

90

Perhaps the real revolution in computing has finally been realized with the introduction of color photocopying systems into the average home. Today, the everyday individual has it within her grasp to duplicate photographs and documents with astounding resolution and brilliance. But scanning a printed image is by no means a perfect science. In the act of copying a color photograph, so many translations of color tables and formulas take place that the initial product often ends up washed out, as if it had been left out in the sun for several weeks.

In this task, we'll restore some of a faded, scanned photograph's natural brilliance and contrast by narrowing the range of its input levels. A similar feat of restoration is demonstrated in 86 **Restore Color and Tone to an Old Photograph**, although the parts of the **Levels** dialog box we'll use here focus primarily on regulating the three primary color channels. When a photograph fades—as the one in this example did—not only does it take on a decided color cast, it loses its darkest darks. With the **Levels** command, this task demonstrates bringing those natural darks back, one channel at a time, paying attention to the histogram all the while, and relying on what you know about *what color things should be* to help you out.

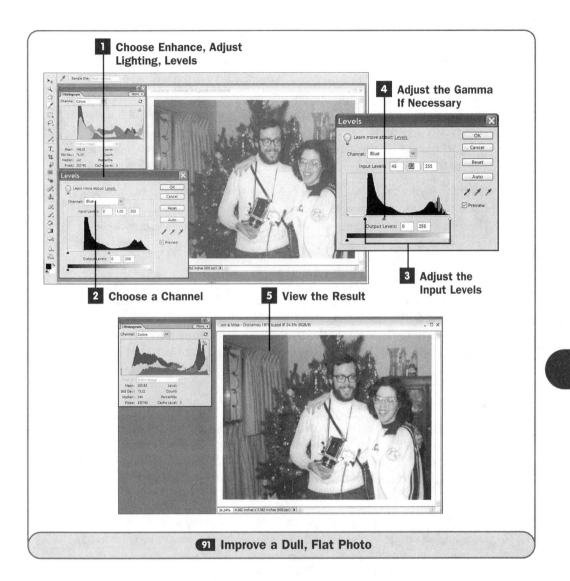

1 Choose Enhance, Adjust Lighting, Levels

4 Adjust the Gamma If Necessary

2 Choose a Channel

5 View the Result

3 Adjust the Input Levels

91

▶ TIP

The scanner drivers shipped with many flatbed scanners tend to use their own automatic levels correction when scanning faded photos, especially black-and-whites. More often than not, these drivers tend to overestimate their own corrections and perform too much contrast adjustment. Rather than wrestle with undoing in the Editor the errors that your scanner driver caused, try turning *off* the automatic correction feature *before* you proceed with the scan, and then make the right corrections yourself with the **Levels** command. See **5** **Import and Separate Multiple Scanned Images** for more about bringing images into the Editor or the Organizer from a scanner.

1 Choose Enhance, Adjust Lighting, Levels

Open the image you want to adjust in the Editor in **Standard Edit** mode and save it in Photoshop (***.psd**) format. To display the **Histogram** palette if it is not already showing, select **Window, Histogram**. From the **Channel** drop-down list, choose **Colors**. If there is more than one layer in the image, choose the layer you want to adjust from the **Layers** palette. If you want to limit your adjustment to a region of the image, use a selection tool to select that region.

From the menu bar, select **Enhance, Adjust Lighting, Levels**. The **Levels** dialog box opens to display a histogram of the picture. Enable the **Preview** check box so that you can see the result of the adjustments you make in the actual image.

2 Choose a Channel

From the **Channel** drop-down list, choose whether you want to adjust the **RGB** channel (the combined brightness of all three color channels) or the color value of the **Red**, **Green**, or **Blue** channel independently. For a grayscale image (especially a grayscale TIFF), this setting will read **Gray** and will have been made for you.

3 Adjust the Input Levels

The histogram shown in the **Levels** dialog box represents a brightness scale, showing all *possible* brightness values in the image for the chosen channel, for all possible values between 0 and 255. A clear indication that an image can be lightened is when few or no pixels are registered in the rightmost region of the histogram.

The *white point* of an image represents the pixel or region of pixels that should be the brightest region, and therefore perhaps should be corrected to become pure white. The **Levels** dialog box begins by representing the theoretical white point as the white up-pointing arrow on the scale just below the histogram, on the far right side. To try brightening the image, slide the white point to the left, toward the right tail end of the charted pixels in the histogram. The white point on the histogram is like one side of a fence. Wherever you set it, all pixels represented on the histogram that are currently plotted at the white point *or higher* will be altered to the maximum brightness level represented in the second box above the graph marked **Input Levels**. Then all the other pixels' brightness values from that point toward the left side are rescaled upward, rendering them brighter in the process. The **Histogram** palette shows the effects of this change the moment your preview

91

of the image changes. No distinctions or contrasts between pixels are lost *unless* pixels on the histogram fall to the right of the white point.

▶ KEY TERM

Black and white points—Pixels in a photo that should be pure white or pure black. By identifying these pixels, you can correct the color balance and tone throughout an image.

The *black point* on the histogram is on the other side of the scale. When the **Levels** dialog box first appears, the black point (the black up-pointing arrow on the scale just below the histogram, on the far left side) is set at 0. To darken the image, slide the black pointer to the right. Wherever you set it, all pixels represented on the histogram that are currently plotted at the black point *or lower* will be altered to the minimum brightness level represented in the first box above the graph marked **Input Levels**. Then all the other pixels' brightness from that point toward the right side will be rescaled downward, rendering them darker in the process. No contrasts will be lost unless pixels on the histogram fall to the left of the black point.

By moving the white and black points, you're "fencing in" your photograph, ensuring that there is a black and a white *somewhere*. For most images, this is what you want.

91

▶ NOTES

Suppose that you are preparing an image for printing on a commercial press. You've been told that the press cannot reproduce detail in highlights where the amount of ink required is thinner than 5% of the maximum. You can use the white **Output Levels** slider to set the brightest point to 242—which, when rounded off, is 5% less than the maximum of 255. This setting ensures that the press will reproduce all your highlight detail. You can make a similar adjustment to allow for press characteristics in printing shadow detail.

You can use the eyedroppers in the **Levels** dialog box to select black, white, and neutral gray points. Click the black eyedropper in the dialog box and then click a point in the image to identify that point as the blackest. Click the white eyedropper and then click in the image to identify that point as the whitest point in the image. The adjustment that **Levels** makes creates a new brightness curve between the two points you select. For more about using eyedroppers to set black, gray, and white points, see **86** Restore Color and Tone to an Old Photograph.

4 Adjust the Gamma If Necessary

The gray pointer in the middle of the scale represents the degree of bias in determining how to rescale the brightness values of pixels between the black and white pointers. As you move the black or white pointer, notice that the gray pointer also moves, registering the same gamma bias applied to the relocated scale. A gamma of 1.0 implies no bias toward either brights or darks. To make more room for bright pixels—brightening the overall image and increasing the gamma—slide the gray pointer to the *left*, toward the dark side. This *reduces* the interval between the black and gray pointers, indicating less room for darks and more for brights. To make room for dark pixels—darkening the image and decreasing the gamma—slide the gray pointer to the *right*.

▶ **NOTE**

Adjusting the gamma will give you weird results if you don't adjust the white and black points first. The gamma describes an important geometric point on a curve. The white and black points are at opposite ends of this curve. Adjusting the gamma is almost pointless if you intend to adjust the white and black points later, which will move the curve.

For this example, noting how red this photo had become, I started off by making adjustments to the **Blue** channel. I moved its black point to **45**, at the left cusp of the curve. I then tried several gamma settings before settling on a startlingly high **2.2** (up from the presumed normal setting of **1.00**). In judging whether these settings were right, I kept an eye on the **Histogram** palette, which shows the increased spread in brightness in comparison to the other two channels. I also took note of my wife's collar. (Yes, that's my wife, circa 1975. No, that's my brother-in-law.) I knew she was supposed to be wearing a white pullover jacket with patriotic blue and red trim. What I tried to do was bring back as much blue as possible without making the pine tree behind them look like a blue spruce.

91

5 View the Result

When you're satisfied with the result, make any other changes you want and save the PSD file. Then resave the result in JPEG, PNG, or non-layered TIFF format, leaving your PSD image with its layers intact so that you can return at a later time to make new adjustments.

For this example, after restoring the **Blue** channel, I proceeded to the **Red** channel, raising its black point to **92** and its gamma to **1.50**. For the **Green** channel, I raised its black point to **46** and its gamma to **1.91**. Those numbers, in and of themselves, probably seem pointless on the surface; but take a look at the **Histogram** palette for the result figure. The three color channels now begin and end at basically the same point on the graph, and their peaks and valleys are more in sync with one another. The numbers I just rattled at you were the ones that put this histogram in sync. Now the pine tree is green, the blue jeans are blue, the silver garland isn't wine-colored, Mike's hair is...*there*, and my wife is a striking brunette.

92   Lighten a Subject on a Snowy Background

✔ BEFORE YOU BEGIN	→ SEE ALSO
89 About an Image's Histogram	**90** Improve Brightness and Contrast
91 Improve a Dull, Flat Photo	

Typically, the sheer brightness of snow changes the way your camera handles light from darker objects—and on a snowy day, almost everything is darker than snow. Digital cameras are especially sensitive to bright light reflecting off snow, bleaching out the rest of the scene and causing subjects in the foreground, including people, to appear muted and dark. Furthermore, because many digital cameras tend to normalize their light input on-the-fly, even though the snow is the brightest thing in the image, the camera makes it gray, making your foreground subjects even darker to compensate.

In remedying an image that suffers from this problem, you could start by invoking the **Levels** command, but you know already that your bright whites are going to command the right edge of the graph for the **RGB** channel. Besides, you might not want to change your *snow* at all, especially if it's bright enough. The technique you're about to see helps you easily separate your foreground subject from your background snow (which is, after all, mostly the same shade), so that you can restore the foreground despite the snow.

92

▶ NOTE

If your digital camera includes a scene mode such as **Snow** or **Beach**, use it when taking a photo with a bright background, and your subject will not appear so dark in the resulting photograph.

1   Duplicate the Background Layer

Open the image you want to adjust in the Editor in **Standard Edit** mode and save it in Photoshop (***.psd**) format. To display the **Histogram** palette if it is not already showing, select **Window, Histogram**. From the **Channel** drop-down list, choose **Luminosity**.

In the **Layers** palette, choose the **Background** layer. From the menu bar, select **Layer, Duplicate Layer**. Name the new layer **Threshold**.

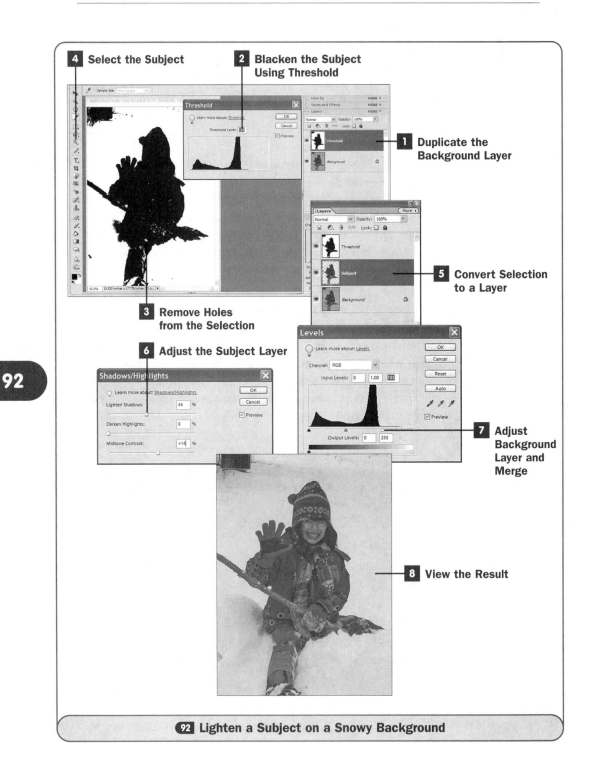

92

92 Lighten a Subject on a Snowy Background

2 Blacken the Subject Using Threshold

With the **Threshold** layer chosen, from the menu bar, select **Filter**, **Adjustments**, **Threshold**. In the **Threshold** dialog box, adjust the **Threshold Level** setting until the black area just covers your subject. You'll probably also blacken *some* of the shadows your subject is casting on the snow; don't worry, that's okay. Click **OK**.

3 Remove Holes from the Selection

Your subject should now be black and the background white, but that's only temporary. At this moment, your selection probably includes some specks of snow on your subject—especially if she's recently been in a snowball fight. These beads of snow will produce holes in your black subject area. The simplest way to remove them is using the **Brush** tool. In the **Toolbox**, click the **Brush** tool, and then click the **Default Colors** button in-between the foreground color and background color boxes. Choose a five-pixel-wide brush tip from the **Options** bar and apply that brush tip to the small holes in the black image. Choose a larger brush tip and sweep away the larger areas of dustier snow from the subject.

4 Select the Subject

From the **Toolbox**, click the **Magic Wand** tool. In the image, use the tool to select the subject. In this example, the selection included the girl, the big stick she was holding, and a portion of the shadow behind her back. It did not include the shadow of the air conditioning unit in the upper-left corner. Use of the **Magic Wand** tool is explained in **47** **Select Areas of Similar Color**.

5 Convert Selection to a Layer

In the **Layers** palette, change to the **Background** layer, and select **Layer**, **New**, **Layer via Copy** from the menu bar. Right-click **Layer 1** in the **Layers** palette, and from the context menu, select **Rename Layer**. In the dialog box, type **Subject** and click **OK**. Your subject is now isolated on its own layer, where you can make adjustments that bring out its own details without disturbing the snowy background. You can also adjust the snowy background by brightening it significantly, without in turn over-brightening the subject.

You no longer need the **Threshold** layer. In the **Layers** palette, choose the **Threshold** layer and select **Layer**, **Delete Layer** from the menu bar. Click **Yes** to confirm. For now, your image looks exactly as it did before.

92

6 **Adjust the Subject Layer**

In the **Layers** palette, choose the **Subject** layer. From the menu bar, select **Enhance, Adjust Lighting, Shadows/Highlights**. The **Shadows/Highlights** dialog box appears. You might have to reposition it to get a clear view of both your image and the **Histogram** palette.

With the **Histogram** palette open and visible, it's easy to get a clear read of what the **Shadows/Highlights** command does, and what your limits are with regard to safely using it. Sliding the **Lighten Shadows** setting forward clearly bunches up the histogram from the left side against the right edge. You gain brightness, but at the expense of contrast, so be careful not to trade off too much. Similarly, sliding the **Darken Highlights** setting forward bunches up the histogram from the right side against the left edge.

Sliding the **Midtone Contrast** to the left bunches up tones in the histogram toward the middle of the chart, whereas sliding it to the right splits tones into two humps. The simple rules of shaping a histogram (don't push tones off the edges; evenly distribute them whenever possible; don't segment tones into two equal humps like a camel's back) and the rules of adjusting an image (don't overcorrect for brightness; balance your lights, darks, and midtones whenever possible; don't sacrifice your midtones for darks and lights) correspond to one another. You'll be surprised how many corrections you can make "flying on instrumentation alone"—trusting the histogram to tell you how far to go, and when you're in danger of going too far.

For this example, the highlights were dark enough already. I needed to lighten the shadowy areas to give the picture more punch—especially to bring Katerina's bright red glove toward you (because vivid colors tend to convey the illusion of dimension better). I adjusted **Lighten Shadows** significantly higher, and then added a little to **Midtone Contrast** to compensate.

To finalize your adjustments, click **OK**.

7 **Adjust Background Layer and Merge**

On the **Layers** palette, choose the **Background** layer. From the menu bar, select **Enhance, Adjust Lighting, Levels**. Using the method described in **91** Improve a Dull, Flat Photo, reduce the white point until you've restored your snowy whites. Your subject will be unaffected. With this method, I significantly lowered the white point from 255 all the way down to 186 without losing any information about the crisp, clear, fresh snow.

8 View the Result

When you're satisfied with the result, make any other changes you want and save the PSD file. Resave the image in JPEG, PNG, or non-layered TIFF format, leaving your PSD image with its layers intact so that you can return at a later time to make new adjustments.

My original photo suffered from a phenomenon common to digital cameras: The brightness of the snow overwhelmed the light detectors, even when the camera was set for bright outdoors. As a result, Katerina's colors were muted and dull. I made **Shadows/Highlights** adjustments to brighten her clothes, but had my image been one undivided layer, the same changes I made to her clothes and skin tones would have made the snow pink. By separating the snow from the foreground, I was able to shield the snow from the changes I made to the color channels, and then applied color-safe changes to the snow.

93 Lighten or Darken Part of an Image

✔ BEFORE YOU BEGIN	→ SEE ALSO
89 About an Image's Histogram	**90** Improve Brightness and Contrast
	91 Improve a Dull, Flat Photo

93

To make a photographic print, the classic development technique is to project an image of the negative onto sensitized printing paper. To lighten an area, the developer can *dodge* it by placing an object, usually a small paddle, in the projected light. To darken an area, he would *burn* it by forming a sort of donut hole with his hands and directing extra exposure light to the target area.

The **Dodge** and **Burn** tool icons in Photoshop Elements depict these traditional tools. Their jobs are, in essence, to lighten a spot and to blacken a spot, respectively. But they don't do this by painting white and black; you could do that with a **Brush** tool. Instead, the **Burn** tool reduces the brightness of whatever it touches, while the **Dodge** tool increases brightness. It's like taking the portion of the image you touch and moving its **Luminosity** values on the histogram down (**Burn**) or up (**Dodge**). Along the way, both contrast and saturation in the areas you touch is generally reduced with both tools. Because you apply these tools to your image using an adjustable brush tip, you can pinpoint your changes to a few pixels or make changes to broader areas of the image. The effect much more closely resembles the old darkroom technique.

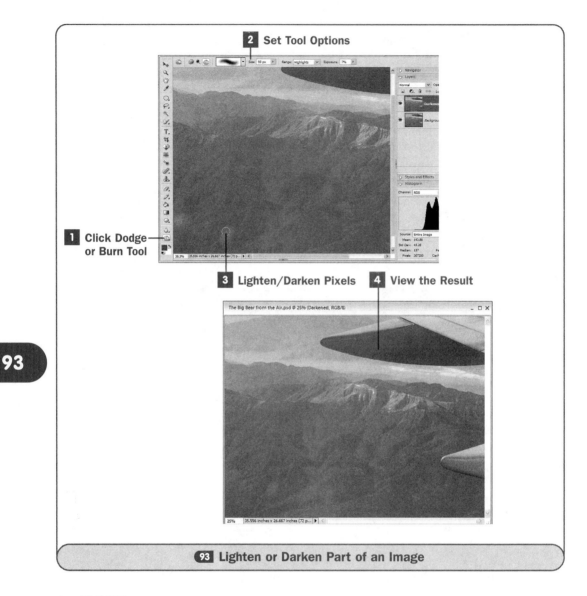

93

93 Lighten or Darken Part of an Image

▶ **NOTE**

Both the **Dodge** and **Burn** tools have the side effect of desaturating what they touch. But they're not to be confused with another tool specifically designed for desaturation (or resaturation): the **Sponge** tool. The **Sponge** could conceivably darken an area by compounding its native color. And when desaturating a spot, the **Sponge** doesn't lighten it; instead, it removes the colored hue, shifting it more toward grayscale.

1 Click Dodge or Burn Tool

Open the image you want to adjust in the Editor in **Standard Edit** mode and save it in Photoshop (***.psd**) format. If there's more than one layer in the image, from the **Layers** palette, choose the layer containing the contents you want to modify. To protect parts of the image, select the region containing the spot you want to correct.

In the **Toolbox**, click the **Dodge** tool if you want to lighten an area; click the **Burn** tool if you want to darken an area.

2 Set Tool Options

The **Options** bar offers several options that control the brush you'll use to apply the burn to the image. Open the brush presets drop-down list and select the type of brush you want to use. One with a feathered edge works best with these tools; hard-edged brushes can result in unnatural effects. In the **Size** text box, enter a brush size in pixels or select one using the slider. You can check the relative size by passing the tool over the picture without clicking; a circle shows the brush area that will be used.

From the **Range** drop-down list, select whether to alter shadows, midrange tones, or highlights. This is an extremely important setting because it enables you to further protect those elements of your image that don't need correcting. For instance, you might not want to indiscriminately darken *everything* the **Burn** tool touches, so you might consider setting its **Range** to **Midtones**. Likewise, using the **Dodge** tool, you might not want to lighten the lightest tones, but only the **Shadows**. Choose the **Range** you want to change.

The **Exposure** scale enables you to set the strength of the effect. In general, stick to the standard **Exposure** setting of 50% or less. That way, you can make multiple passes that change the picture in small increments.

93

3 Lighten/Darken Pixels

Begin applying the tool by clicking and holding the mouse button where you want to start. For a pen tablet, position the pointer by hovering the pen, and then tap and hold the pen where you want the stroke to begin.

To draw a freehand stroke, continue holding the button down as you drag the mouse. The mark you draw will follow your pointer. As you continue applying the tool to an area, its effects are cumulative—which means you can continue applying the **Dodge** tool to the same area within the same stroke, and it will continue to lighten the area. The tool's effect within the same stroke are limited, however, to the extent of the **Exposure** setting.

To draw a straight horizontal or vertical line, press **Shift** now and continue dragging the mouse. The Editor senses whether you intend for the line to move up, right, left, or down, by the general direction in which you're moving the mouse—it doesn't have to be exact.

▶ **TIP**

To change brush tips for the **Burn** or **Dodge** tool at any time, right-click the image. The **Brush Presets** palette appears. Choose a new tip from the **Brushes** list, and then click the **X** button to dismiss the palette.

To draw a straight line between points, release the mouse button. For a pen tablet, lift the pen. Move the pointer to where you want the end of the line (or, to be geometrically accurate, the *line segment*) to appear. Press **Shift** and click this point. The line will be an application of the tool over the distance between the start and end points, relative to the tool's current **Exposure** setting. You can continue drawing from here—either a freehand mark or another straight line segment.

4 **View the Result**

93

When you're satisfied with the result, make any other changes you want and save the PSD file. Then resave the result in JPEG, PNG, or non-layer TIFF format, leaving your PSD image with its layers intact so that you can return at a later time to make new adjustments.

This sample image is a natural candidate for dodging and burning. The key problem with taking aerial shots from a commercial aircraft is never really having control of how clean the window is, or how much glare you'll have to put up with. There are a number of possible ways to correct this image, one of which is to restore some of the natural shadows in select areas using the **Burn** tool. The advantage of this method over a **Levels** adjustment, for this image, is that you're able to apply small changes to the areas that need it. For example, I used the **Burn** tool to darken the water droplets and remove them from the left side of the image, and to deepen the shadows in the mountain top. I also used the **Dodge** tool to lighten the snow and the top edge of the mountain to make it more of a focus for the image.

94 **Correct Color, Contrast, and Saturation in One Step**

✔ BEFORE YOU BEGIN	→ SEE ALSO
Just jump right in!	**95** Adjust Hue and Saturation Manually

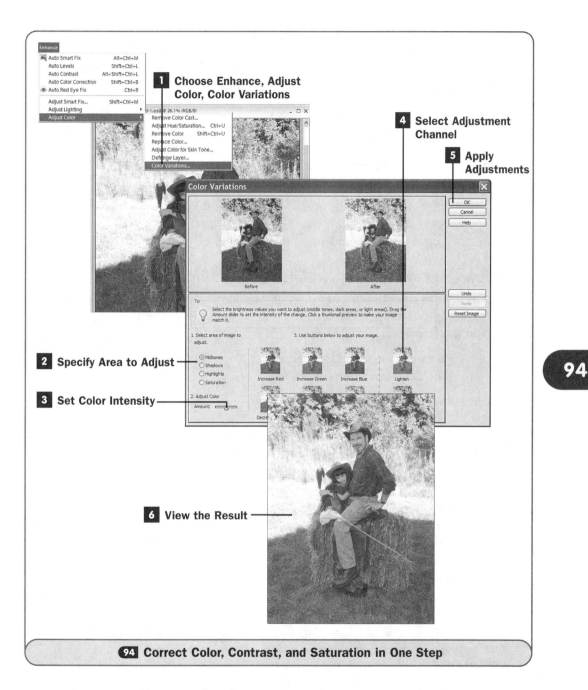

1 Choose Enhance, Adjust Color, Color Variations

4 Select Adjustment Channel

5 Apply Adjustments

2 Specify Area to Adjust

3 Set Color Intensity

6 View the Result

94 Correct Color, Contrast, and Saturation in One Step

You can quickly correct the color, contrast, and saturation in a photo using the **Color Variations** command. With this command, you select the color correction for the image by simply clicking a thumbnail variation of the image. For example, if you want to reduce the red in your image, you click the **Decrease Red** thumbnail.

You can adjust the color variations within your image for the **Midtones**, **Shadows**, and **Highlights** tonal areas. The **Shadows** adjustments affect all the darker areas in the image. The **Highlights** adjustments affect the lighter areas, and the **Midtones** adjustments affect the middle values in the image.

You can also control the saturation of the colors in the image by selecting the **Saturation** option. Then you can click either the **Less Saturation** thumbnail to decrease saturation (making the color more muted) or the **More Saturation** thumbnail to increase it (making the color more vivid).

As you make changes to the color, contrast, and saturation of the image, the before and after previews display at the top of the **Color Variations** dialog box. These views of your image enable you to see your progress. At any time, you can restart the process by clicking the **Reset Image** button.

1 **Choose Enhance, Adjust Color, Color Variations**

Open the image you want to correct in the Editor in **Standard Edit** mode and save it in Photoshop (***.psd**) format. In the **Layers** palette, choose the layer you want to correct.

From the menu bar, select **Enhance**, **Adjust Color**, **Color Variations** from the menu. The **Color Variations** dialog box appears.

2 **Specify Area to Adjust**

Select the radio button that corresponds to the tonal area of the image you want to adjust. For example, to adjust the middle range of colors, select the **Midtone** radio button.

3 **Set Color Intensity**

Set the color intensity for the adjustment by dragging the **Adjust Color Amount** slider to the left to decrease the intensity or to the right to increase it. As you drag the slider, you will see the color intensity adjusted for the thumbnail images.

▶ **TIP**

If you select the **Saturation** option, buttons appear to adjust the saturation. Click the **Less Saturation** button to reduce the saturation or the **More Saturation** button to increase it.

4 **Select Adjustment Channel**

Click the thumbnail image that corresponds to the type of color adjustment you want to make. For the **Midtones**, **Shadows**, and **Highlights** adjustment areas, the top row of thumbnails is devoted to *increases*, the bottom row to *decreases*. The group of adjustments on the left is devoted to individual color channels (red, green, and blue); on the right, **Lighten** and **Darken** apply changes to all three channels simultaneously. When you click a thumbnail, the changes are applied to the image in the right preview widow at the top of the dialog box. In addition, the thumbnail images at the bottom of the dialog box update to reflect the changes you just applied.

Repeat steps 2 through 4 to make adjustments for other areas of the image. As the adjustments are made to the image, you can view the result in the **After** preview window on the top-right of the **Color Variations** dialog box.

▶ **TIPS**

If you do not like the corrections selected, click the **Reset Image** button to switch back to the original version of the image.

To quickly correct an image in which a person's skin tone is off (typically because of a color cast), choose **Enhance, Adjust Color, Adjust Color for Skin Tone**. After the dialog box appears, click any area of someone's skin whose color seems wrong to you, and the colors in the image are instantly adjusted. If the result is still "off," you can adjust the **Tan** and **Blush** values. You can also adjust the **Ambient Light** temperature to change the skin tone—push the slider toward blue to cool a picture and remove a warm orange or reddish color cast; push it toward red to remove a cool blue or greenish color cast. Click **OK**. This adjustment, however, does not correct saturation or brightness problems; it only removes a color cast.

94

5 **Apply Adjustments**

When you have made the desired adjustments, click the **OK** button to close the dialog box and apply the color variation selections to the image.

6 **View the Result**

When you close the dialog box, Photoshop Elements applies the selections to your image. This process might take a few seconds. When you're satisfied with the results, make any other changes you want and save the PSD file. Resave the result in JPEG, PNG, or non-layered TIFF format, leaving your PSD image with its layers (if any) intact so that you can return at a later time and make different adjustments if you want.

For this example, we didn't exactly pick the best location or time of day to shoot this photo. It was mid-morning on the West side of the house; as a result, we appeared in shadow. To compensate for this, I needed to bring back some of the richer colors that match the leafy greens in the background. So I added a few "shots" of green, if you will, and quite a bit of red—almost too much, but the slightly rustic look that resulted is in keeping with our costumes.

95   Adjust Hue and Saturation Manually

✔ BEFORE YOU BEGIN	→ SEE ALSO
Just jump right in!	**94** Correct Color, Contrast, and Saturation in One Step

A pixel's color value is defined by three components: hue, *saturation*, and lightness (or *luminance*, or *luminosity*). A pixel's hue represents its location on the color wheel, which is the entire spectrum of colors in the computer's gamut or colorspace. Saturation defines the relative power of that hue within a pixel—quantifying, for instance, the range between a clear red (full saturation) to a colorless gray (no saturation). Lightness defines the amount of white in a pixel, from black (no light) to white (all light) to somewhere in-between (light pink). To make individual adjustments to these components of pixels within a given region, use the **Adjust Hue/Saturation** command. For example, many images taken with digital cameras seem to lack saturation. A boost of saturation by even a few degrees can revive an otherwise dull image, infusing it with excitement and drama.

By reducing the saturation in a color image, you can create a black-and-white photo—often with better results than simply converting the image to grayscale. By adjusting the hue of a selected object, you can change its color from red to green, for example. By reducing the lightness of an image's background, you can make it fade into the distance—placing more importance on the subject of your image.

▶ **KEY TERM**

Saturation—The amount of a particular hue present in a pixel. A fully saturated red pixel is bright red; a less saturated red pixel has more gray and its reddish tone is more subtle.

1 Choose Enhance, Adjust Color, Adjust Hue/Saturation

Open the image you want to correct in the Editor in **Standard Edit** mode and save it in Photoshop (**.psd*) format. In the **Layers** palette, choose the layer you want to adjust. To restrict your adjustment to a given region of the chosen layer, use a selection tool to select that region.

From the menu bar, select **Enhance**, **Adjust Color**, **Adjust Hue/Saturation** to display the **Hue/Saturation** dialog box. Enable the **Preview** check box to see examples of your choices in the image before making them final.

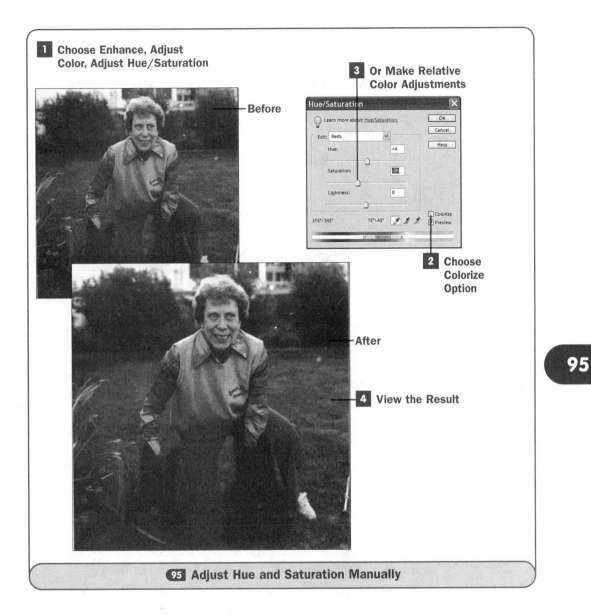

1 Choose Enhance, Adjust Color, Adjust Hue/Saturation

3 Or Make Relative Color Adjustments

Before

2 Choose Colorize Option

After

4 View the Result

95

95 Adjust Hue and Saturation Manually

2 Choose Colorize Option

This dialog box has two purposes: The *second* of these purposes is to give you a way to apply a single hue to the designated region. *Colorizing* a region in this way eliminates all the area's original color information, replacing it with the values designated by the **Hue** and **Saturation** settings. To colorize the designated region and *replace* color values rather than simply *adjust* them, enable the **Colorize** check box. When you do this, the meanings of the sliders change. The **Hue** slider represents an angle on the color wheel between **0°** and **360°**, theoretically encompassing all the colors of the rainbow. **Saturation** is a percentage representing how much of the chosen **Hue** to apply to the region, while **Lightness** remains a relative setting between **–100** and **+100**, governing how much white is added or removed. (Technically, sliding **Lightness** in either direction should remove saturation, but in this case, the **Saturation** slider remains stable.)

If you're colorizing the designated region, make your adjustment choices from these sliders and click **OK** to exit the dialog box and skip to step 4. Otherwise, continue to step 3.

▶ **TIP**

Whereas the **Adjust Hue/Saturation** command applies changes to all or part of a layer, you can create an adjustment layer that applies a saturation adjustment to several underlying layers in an image. See **56** **Create an Adjustment Layer** for details.

3 Or Make Relative Color Adjustments

With the **Colorize** option disabled, the purpose of the **Hue/Saturation** dialog box is to make *relative* adjustments to one, two, or all three of the color channels in the designated region.

From the **Edit** drop-down list, select the color channels you want to adjust. The **Master** option refers to all three (red, green, and blue) in combination. The primary channels (**Reds**, **Greens**, and **Blues**) are represented on this list, as well as the secondary colors (**Yellows**, **Cyans**, and **Magentas**). **Yellows** refers to the red and green channel, **Cyans** to the green and blue channel, and **Magentas** to the blue and red channel.

At this point, the **Hue** slider represents an angle of adjustment between **–180°** and **+180°**. When you adjust this setting, the **Hue** component values of all pixels in the selected region are adjusted by that amount on the color wheel. For example, a yellow pixel when increased 180 degrees becomes blue.

The **Saturation** slider represents a percentage of adjustment between **–100** and **+100**. Any non-zero setting represents a degree of increase or decrease of color in the chosen channels. Drag the **Saturation** slider to the right to increase the saturation of the designated region or to the left to decrease the saturation.

The **Lightness** slider represents a percentage of adjustment between **–100** and **+100**. Any non-zero setting represents a degree of increase or decrease of *whiteness* in the chosen channels. Drag the **Lightness** slider to the right to increase the lightness of the selected color range or to the left to decrease the lightness. If you've chosen **Blues**, for instance, setting **Lightness** above zero adds *white* to the blues in the selected region.

Click the **OK** button to close the dialog box and apply the adjustments to your image.

4 View the Result

When you're satisfied with the results, make any other changes you want and save the PSD file. Resave the result in JPEG, PNG, or non-layered TIFF format, leaving your PSD image with its layers (if any) intact so that you can return at a later time and make adjustments if you want.

This example featured a scanned photograph that was damaged from exposure to sunlight for several years, probably clinging to the front door of the refrigerator. My first objective was to restore some of the warm skin tones to Aunt Betty's face. I did this by choosing the **Reds** channel, moving the **Hue** setting to +4 to restore some of the yellows that had faded (yellows always fade first from exposure to sunlight), and set **Saturation** to –20 to help balance her skin tones.

Next, I restored the radiant sunlight on the edges of Betty's sweater and hair by choosing the **Yellows** channel, setting **Hue** to +9, **Saturation** to a relatively high +41, and **Lightness** to a quite high +63. Now the subject matter looks bright and in the center of the picture once again. I used the **Magentas** channel as an opportunity to bring back contrast to Betty's face because the print was using magenta tones in the shadows. With the **Magentas** channel chosen, I set **Hue** to +11 (taking it more toward the red), **Saturation** to +9, and **Lightness** way down to –25. Now Betty's face truly is in the center of the picture.

These adjustments were far from enough to fix the overall picture. I tried to add saturation to the **Greens** channel, for instance, but the problem with this faded print is that too much of the grass and shrubbery color is made up of elements from the **Blues** channel. I'll need to make spot adjustments to the garden, perhaps with the **Color Replacement** tool. And nothing I do with the **Hue/Saturation** dialog box will help me restore contrast to Betty's two jet-black Scottie dogs. And now, I have Betty's warm, radiant face smiling at me again, and that's a very good start. Look for this image in the Color Gallery.

95

▶ TIP

It is extremely difficult to demonstrate in black-and-white what the color adjustment does for this photo—when you put the two side by side *in monochrome*, there's almost no difference. In a way, that's what you want. This shows that we've retained the natural brightness values while adjusting the color fade.

96 About Sharpness

✔ BEFORE YOU BEGIN	→ SEE ALSO
Just jump right in!	**97** Sharpen an Image
	98 Blur an Image to Remove Noise
	99 Blur a Background to Create Depth of Field

96

Unfortunately, when you take photographs with either a standard film camera or a digital camera, the camera does not always capture a picture as sharp as what you are able to see with your eyes. The sharpness of the picture can be affected by multiple conditions, such as poor lighting, poor visibility, or even the fact that your digital camera is set to capture images at a lower resolution. The sharpness of a photo can also be diminished when you scan a photo into your computer. Fortunately, you can improve the sharpness of an image with Photoshop Elements.

Photoshop Elements provides several filters you can use to improve the sharpness of your image. You can apply the filter to the entire layer of the image or to just a selected portion of the layer. Each of the following filters uses a slightly different method of increasing the contrast of adjacent pixels to make the image appear sharper:

- **Sharpen**—Use this filter to increase the distinction between contrasting regions of an image by eliminating the appearance of blending along the edges of those regions. Think of the **Sharpen** filter as the *opposite* of anti-aliasing. To apply the **Sharpen** filter to your selection, select **Filter, Sharpen, Sharpen**.

- **Sharpen Edges**—Use this filter to sharpen the edges of objects within your selection or layer. This filter sharpens the edges by finding regions where there is a significant change in the colors between adjoining pixels. Those regions appear sharper by increasing the contrast between the pixels while the other areas in the image remain untouched. To apply the **Sharpen Edges** filter to your selection, select **Filter, Sharpen, Sharpen Edges**.

- **Sharpen More**—Use this filter when you want to create a stronger focus and more clarity to the selection than what is provided by the **Sharpen** filter. To apply the **Sharpen More** filter to your selection, select **Filter, Sharpen, Sharpen More**.

▶ **TIP**

You can use the **Sharpen** tool, available from the **Toolbox**, to sharpen specific portions of your image. With this tool, you paint the areas of the image you want to sharpen. This tool works well when you want to sharpen only a small portion of the image.

- **Unsharp Mask**—Although its name can be misleading, this filter actually enables you to create the most professional sharpening effect of all the sharpen filters. With the **Unsharp Mask** filter, you can adjust the contrast of the edge detail in your image to emphasize the edge by creating darker and lighter lines on each side of the edge. When you use this filter, you specify the amount of contrast used to compare the pixels that surround the edges by adjusting the **Threshold** level. You can specify the exact region around each pixel to compare by adjusting the **Radius** setting. You apply the **Unsharp Mask** filter by selecting **Filter, Sharpen, Unsharp Mask**. See **97 Sharpen an Image** for more information on using the **Unsharp Mask** filter to sharpen an image.

▶ **NOTE**

Why is the filter called "unsharp mask" if it sharpens content? As preposterous as it might sound, the way this filter works begins with the act of *blurring*. In the computer's memory, the filter creates a duplicate of the selected layer or region that you'll never see, and then blurs that duplicate. Mathematically, the product of the data from the duplicate is subtracted from the data from the visible image. The theory is that the remainder of the *mostly* blurred region combined with a *partly* blurred version of that same region will yield a cleaner, clearer, and sharper rendering of that region. Don't knock it; it works.

97 | **Sharpen an Image**

✔ BEFORE YOU BEGIN	SEE ALSO
Just jump right in!	**50** Smooth and Soften a Selection
	62 Mask an Image Layer
	98 Blur an Image to Remove Noise
	99 Blur a Background to Create Depth of Field

97

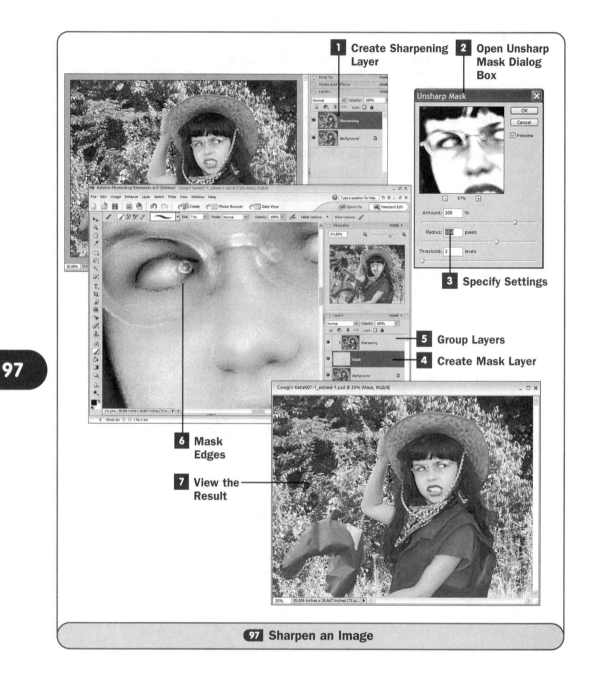

1 Create Sharpening Layer

2 Open Unsharp Mask Dialog Box

3 Specify Settings

4 Create Mask Layer

5 Group Layers

6 Mask Edges

7 View the Result

97 Sharpen an Image

Virtually every image you create will have a particular point on which you want the viewer to focus. This focal point is often referred to as the *subject* of the image. When the subject of your photo stands out sharply from the background, it helps the viewer to maintain the illusion of depth and focus. One tool that works well for sharpening an image is the **Unsharp Mask** filter. When you apply this filter to your image, it locates the pixels in the image that differ from the surrounding pixels and increases the contrast between those pixels. When you use this filter, you control the sharpening effect by specifying the amount of contrast, the number of pixels to sharpen around the edges, and the **Threshold**, or how different the target pixels need to be from the surrounding pixels.

You can apply the **Unsharp Mask** to an entire layer or to a selection. Keep in mind that everything within the selection will be affected by the filter. If you don't select a portion of the image, the entire active layer is sharpened. You might want to sharpen only the subject of the image, leaving its surrounding elements as they are so that the subject stands out even more. To accomplish this, select that subject using one of the selection tools and then apply the **Unsharp Mask** filter. If you want to have more control over how the **Unsharp Mask** filter affects the final image, you can use an *edge mask* to apply the filter as explained in this task. In creating an edge mask, you sharpen an image so that the edges of its subject matter are well pronounced. You can then mask the image so that only the edges you select are actually visible to the viewer.

▶ NOTE

Although Photoshop Elements allows you to create masking effects, you cannot create and save masks as you can with other photo editing software packages such as Adobe Photoshop. Masking works well for hiding portions of an image you don't want to be visible. See **62** Mask an Image Layer for more information on masking portions of an image.

▶ KEY TERM

Edge mask—A selection that encompasses only the edge pixels in an image, thus preventing unwanted sharpening to everything else.

1 Create Sharpening Layer

Open the image you want to adjust in the Editor in **Standard Edit** mode and save it in Photoshop (***.psd**) format. If it's not already showing, display the **Layers** palette by selecting **Window, Layers**. In the **Layers** palette, click to select the **Background** layer and choose **Layer, Duplicate Layer** from the menu bar to duplicate the background layer. On the **Duplicate Layer** dialog box, specify a name for the duplicate layer, such as **Sharpening**. The layer you are creating is where you will apply the **Unsharp Mask** filter. You want to create a separate sharpening layer so that you can mask out the edges you want visible in the image.

2 Open Unsharp Mask Dialog Box

With the **Sharpening** layer chosen in the **Layers** palette, select **Filter**, **Sharpen**, **Unsharp Mask**. The **Unsharp Mask** dialog box opens. Enable the **Preview** check box.

▶ TIPS

Don't worry about oversharpening the background. You are going to use a mask to display only the desired sharpened edges of the subject.

Use the – and + buttons to change the size of the image that displays in the preview window.

If you plan to print the image, you'll want the sharpening effects to be more dramatic. Images from printers are not as sharp as they appear on the screen.

3 Specify Settings

In the **Amount** field, specify a value representing the amount by which you want to increase the contrast between the pixels. For these purposes, you'll want to choose a much higher value than you'd want for a layer you actually intend to keep, such as **200%** or higher.

In the **Radius** field, specify a value that indicates how many pixels around the vicinity of each pixel play a role in adjusting the color to appear sharper. The larger the number, the wider the band of pixels that are evaluated when sharpening each one.

The **Unsharp Mask** filter adjusts every pixel to some extent based on its evaluation of the color values of its neighboring pixels. The **Radius** setting determines how many neighboring pixels to evaluate for each pixel being evaluated. **Threshold** is a relative setting designating how much of a brightness difference between neighboring pixels constitutes a *meaningful* difference—in other words, how much contrast is a contrast that *matters*. Material contrasts are the ones that are enhanced, so a lower **Threshold** setting means that more contrasts (by lesser differences) are enhanced.

For the purposes of this task, you want to turn up the contrast along the edges of objects as much as possible. This generally means you should set **Radius** to a high value (above **50**) and **Threshold** to a low value to compensate, such as **2**. Take a good look at the preview and remember that you're looking for edges to be *overemphasized*. Click the **OK** button to finalize your choices.

97

4 Create Mask Layer

In the **Layers** palette, click the **Background** layer and then choose **Layer**, **New**, **Layer** from the menu bar to create a new blank layer. Name this layer **Mask** because it is the layer where you will mask the sharpened edges of the image. You are going to create a mask that includes just the sharper edges of the image.

5 Group Layers

In the **Layers** palette, choose the **Sharpening** layer. Select **Layer**, **Group with Previous** from the menu bar to group the **Sharpen** layer with your new **Mask** layer. The **Mask** layer is indented under the **Sharpening** layer on the **Layers** palette to indicate that the **Mask** layer is masking the contents of the **Sharpening** layer (controlling what portion of the **Sharpening** layer shows through).

▶ **TIP**

If you don't want some of the edges to appear as sharp, you can reduce the **Opacity** setting for the **Brush** tool in the **Options** bar before painting those edges.

97

Notice that the sharpening effects are no longer visible—now the image looks as it did in step 1. When you group layers, the top layer (in this case, the **Sharpening** layer) shows through only where there is *content* in the bottom layer (in this case, the as-yet empty **Mask** layer). When you paint on the **Mask** layer in the next step, however, you will allow only selected areas of the **Sharpening** layer to appear.

6 Mask Edges

The next thing to do is to add content to the **Mask** layer where you want the edges of the image to appear sharpened. To accomplish this, you use the **Brush** tool.

In the **Layers** palette, choose the **Mask** layer, and then select the **Brush** tool from the **Toolbox**. On the **Options** bar, select a soft brush style and a brush size that matches the width of the edge you want to sharpen. Make sure that the **Opacity** setting is **100%**, and that **Mode** is set to **Normal**. It actually does not matter what you use for your foreground color, although you might want to choose black simply because your marks become more visible in the thumbnail for the **Mask** layer in the **Layers** palette.

In the image, paint along the edges of the subject where you want to sharpen. As you paint, the sharpened edges from the **Sharpen** layer will become visible.

▶ **NOTE**

Because this task involves the use of the **Unsharp Mask** filter as well as *masks* (a principal feature of Photoshop CS2), you might be wondering what the connection is. Despite their labels, they're two different types of masks entirely. It would be less confusing, I admit, if they had different names.

To remove part of a sharpened edge, select the **Mask** layer and, using an eraser tool, remove the portion you do not want visible. You can also use any of the selection tools to delete part of the mask. For example, you can use the **Lasso** tool to select part of the mask, and then press the **Delete** key to remove the selection.

7 View Results

When you're satisfied with the result, make any other changes you want and save the PSD file. Then resave the result in JPEG, PNG, or non-layered TIFF format, leaving your PSD image with its layers intact so that you can return at a later time to make changes or additions.

The **Unsharp Mask** filter makes a number of positive corrections to the sharpness of a layer, along with a wide array of really wild and unwanted changes. But with masking, you can paint directly on top of those areas that reflect the **Unsharp Mask** changes you do want, and leave behind those areas of changes you don't want.

You should never put too much faith in the autofocus of your digital camera. Luckily, I took several shots of Katie on her hay-horse during her birthday, but I wanted to try to save this shot, for which the autofocus centered in on the background foliage and not the subject. Separating the unsharp mask layer from the background layer, and then using the mask to bring in just the distinctions between Katie—or Katie's hat—and her background, enabled me to remove most of the shimmering halo between the foreground subject and the greenery in the background. Later, I could blur the greenery to help create the illusion of depth of field.

98 Blur an Image to Remove Noise

✔ BEFORE YOU BEGIN	→ SEE ALSO
96 About Sharpness	**97** Sharpen an Image

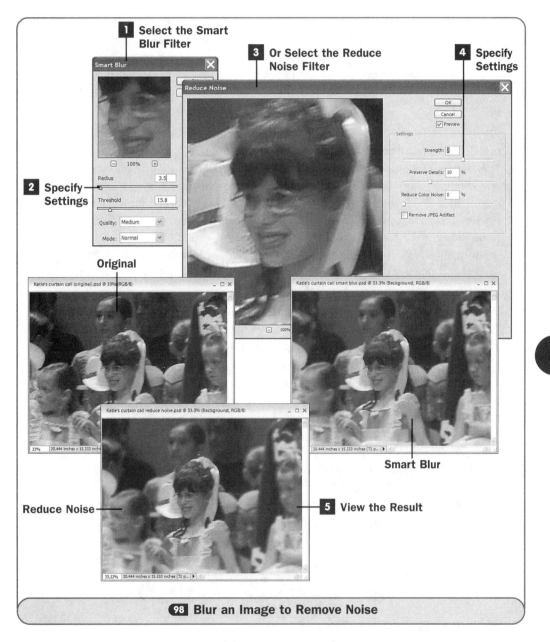

98 Blur an Image to Remove Noise

If you have a grainy-looking image such as an old photograph you scanned in, you can blur portions of it to remove the graininess (noise). You might also need to remove noise caused by taking a digital image with too little light. Unfortunately, removing noise by blurring pixels often removes any sharpness the image may have had. You can, of course, opt to blur selected areas of an image, creating the *perception* of sharpening the subject of the image by blurring the surrounding background. But this approach won't solve the problem of any graininess that remains in the subject itself. You can approach this problem by blurring a copy of the image, and then erasing the blurred edges to reveal the sharp edges in the original layer beneath. See **97 Sharpen an Image** for a task that uses this approach.

When you blur an image or portion of the image, the pixels along color edges are blended with one another—sometimes using averaging—to create a softer edge. This averaging and blending of colors creates smoother transitions between different colored sections of the image, thus eliminating the appearance of tiny spots, often called noise, from the image. With the **Blur** filter, noise is eliminated from the photo by averaging the color values of the pixels where transitions occur to create hard lines or shaded areas. The **Blur More** filter performs the same steps as the **Blur** filter, but the effect is much stronger. Neither filter is really the best to use when removing noise, however, because you'll lose sharpness in your image. You can use the **Blur** tool if you like, to selectively blur areas of an image, but to remove noise from an image requires an all-over blur, and such an approach would be tedious at best.

98

To remove noise effectively while retaining sharpness, you have two choices: **Smart Blur** or **Reduce Noise**. You can try both and compare the results. The **Smart Blur** dialog box enables you to specify custom **Radius** and **Threshold** settings. By specifying a **Radius** value, you indicate how far to search for pixels that don't match. You indicate the **Threshold** value to specify how different the pixels must be before they are blurred. This filter also enables you to select the blur quality and indicate the blur mode. The **Reduce Noise** filter works by combining the best of the **Despeckle** and **Median** filters (see **83 Remove Specks, Spots, and Scratches**). Like the **Median** filter, the **Reduce Noise** filter looks for pixels that contrast a lot with the ones around it and then reduces that contrast. Like the **Despeckle** filter, the **Median** filter preserves the contrast only along an object's edges. With this filter, you indicate the relative strength of the blur and the amount of detail you want to preserve. You can also reduce color noise (pixels whose colors vary greatly from those around them) and JPEG artifacts, which can creep in with noise when you save an image in a low-quality JPEG format.

1 Select the Smart Blur Filter

Open the image you want to adjust in the Editor in **Standard Edit** mode and save it in Photoshop (***.psd**) format. If it's not already showing, display the **Layers** palette by selecting **Window, Layers**. In the **Layers** palette, click the layer you want to sharpen by blurring its graininess and select **Filter, Blur, Smart Blur**.

▶ **NOTE**

See **97** Sharpen an Image for a technique that describes how to apply the filter to a duplicate layer and then reveal the sharp edges in the original layer using a clipping mask. If your original image doesn't have sharp edges worth protecting, you can apply the blur filter to the original layer and use the technique described in the task to generate sharp edges on a duplicate layer.

2 **Specify Settings**

In the **Smart Blur** dialog box, specify the settings for blurring your image. You can view a sample of how the image will be blurred in the preview window at the top of the dialog box. In the **Radius** field, specify a value that indicates the number of pixels around each pixel that the **Smart Blur** filter will search for dissimilar pixels to blur.

▶ **TIPS**

Use the − and + buttons to adjust the zoom size of the preview window. As you point to the preview, the mouse pointer becomes the **Hand** tool. Use this tool to drag the image to see another portion.

Click and hold the preview window to toggle the effect off, and release to turn it back on. This trick enables you to compare the look of the image before and after the effect is applied.

In the **Threshold** field, specify a value between **0** and **100** that indicates, relatively, how different the pixels must be in tonal difference before they are blurred. The higher the **Threshold** level, the more pixels are blurred in your image.

In the **Quality** drop-down list box, specify the desired blur quality for the image. You can select from **Low**, **Medium**, or **High** quality. The higher the quality setting, the longer it takes to apply the filter, although a **Quality** setting of **High** produces the smoothest results. However, the higher the **Quality** setting, the more likely you will have banding when you print or view the image.

The **Mode** list box presents the different modes the filter uses to create the blur. The default selection, **Normal**, blurs the entire selection. Select **Edge Only** if you want to create pure white edges on a pure black background, like sketches made with a thin stylus on a blackboard. Select **Overlay Edge** to combine this white edge with the existing image contents for a special effect that divides contrasting regions of the image by a thin white boundary.

When the preview appears as you intend, click **OK**.

3 Or Select the Reduce Noise Filter

In the **Layers** palette, click the layer you want to sharpen by blurring its graininess and select **Filter**, **Noise**, **Reduce Noise**.

4 Specify Settings

In the Reduce Noise dialog box, start by lowering the Preserve Details value so that you can see the effect. This value controls how much contrast a pixel must have with its neighbor before its brightness is lowered to bring it more in line with the "neighborhood average." Slowly increase this value to preserve your edges, lower it as needed to reduce noise even more. Strength controls how much a pixel's brightness can be changed.

To change pixel colors in a manner similar to the way Strength affects the brightness of discordant pixels, adjust the Reduce Color Noise value. To remove artifacts caused by low JPEG quality, enable the Remove JPEG Artifact option. Click OK.

5 View the Result

98

When you're satisfied with the result, make any other changes you want and save the PSD file. Then resave the result in JPEG, PNG, or non-layered TIFF format, leaving your PSD image with its layers intact so that you can return at a later time to make changes or additions.

This example features a digital photo of a ballet curtain call that suffers from many of the same problems faced by digital video photographers: It was taken at high digital zoom, using no tripod. So, the shakiness of the photographer's hand (mine), coupled with noise introduced by the digital zoom, resulted in a nice moment confounded by the problems of modern technology.

Neither sharpening nor blurring restores focus to an image, but it can restore some sense of *composition*...or, at least, cover up some of my mistakes. This example actually shows two types of blurs at work: Along the edge of the photo, I used the **Elliptical Marquee** tool to create a feathered, vignette-shaped selection around my daughter, inverted the selection, and then applied a mild **Gaussian Blur** (see **99** **Blur a Background to Create Depth of Field**). For the **Background** layer, I used the **Smart Blur** filter described here. I set **Radius** to a low value of **3.5** to preserve the shading of Katerina's face and to prevent posterization. I then set **Threshold** to **15.8**, which was a nice balance between blurring and losing her face altogether (higher) and returning to the original spottiness (lower).

The result shows how **Smart Blur** reconstructed an even tone to the subject of the image, thus restoring the illusion of sharpness; the **Gaussian Blur** technique compounded the illusion by taking the viewer's focus away from the edges and corners, without disrespecting the other fine performers in the production.

The second example shows the same technique but using the **Reduce Noise** filter instead. I think that the **Smart Blur** filter did a slightly better job at removing noise while preserving edges in this particular image, but you can judge for yourself.

99 Blur a Background to Create Depth of Field

✔ BEFORE YOU BEGIN	→ SEE ALSO
96 About Sharpness	**97** Sharpen an Image
	98 Blur an Image to Remove Noise

One good method to make the subject of your image stand out is to blur the background of the image. When you do this, you can draw more attention to the actual subject and eliminate distractions. For example, you might have a picture of your child playing with other children. You can blur all the other children in the photo so that your child stands out. By blurring the background of the image, you create depth of field. Suddenly, all the other surrounding distractions in the image fade into the distance, and the viewer's eyes can concentrate on the subject, the situation, and the moment.

99

The best tool for blurring the background of your image is the **Gaussian Blur** filter. When you select this filter, you can create a hazy effect by controlling the level of blurring with the **Radius** value. The higher the **Radius** value, the hazier your selection appears. The **Radius** value indicates the range of the scan, in pixels, from each pixel in the currently selected region or layer. If any pixels within that range are dissimilar, the filter will blur them.

Because you want to blur only the background of the image, you must preserve the subject. One way to accomplish this is to create a duplicate copy of the **Background** layer and apply the **Gaussian Blur** filter to the **Background** layer only. Then switch to the unblurred copied layer and use the **Eraser** tool to erase the background portion of the layer, revealing the blurred **Background** layer.

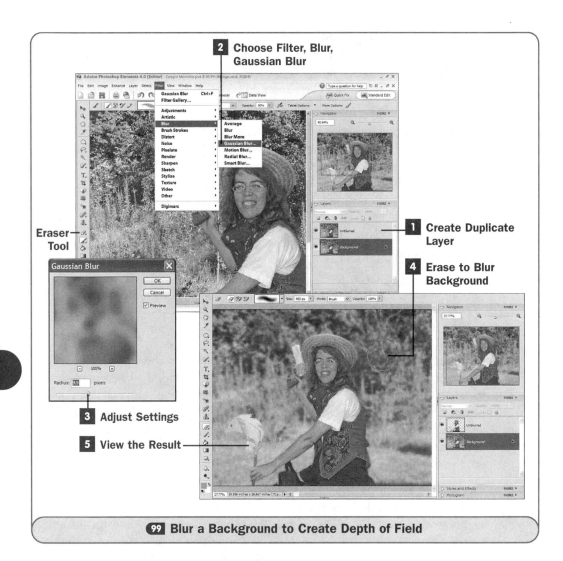

99 Blur a Background to Create Depth of Field

1 Create Duplicate Layer

Open the image you want to adjust in the Editor in **Standard Edit** mode and save it in Photoshop (***.psd**) format. If it's not already showing, display the **Layers** palette by selecting **Window, Layers**. In the **Layers** palette, select the **Background** layer and then choose **Layer, Duplicate Layer** from the menu bar to duplicate the selected layer. Rename this layer **Unblurred**.

2 Choose Filter, Blur, Gaussian Blur

In the **Layers** palette, select the **Background** layer once again, and choose **Filter, Blur, Gaussian Blur**. In the **Gaussian Blur** dialog box, enable the **Preview** check box.

3 Adjust Settings

Select a **Radius** value representing the extent of how much each pixel in the region is blurred, measured in terms of pixel length. For this technique, you'll want to set **Radius** just high enough (8 pixels or above) that you almost cannot make out the contents of the current layer.

Click **OK** to close the dialog box and apply the blur settings to the **Background** layer. You will not be able to see the effects of the blurring in the image window because the blurred **Background** layer is beneath the non-blurred copied layer.

4 Erase to Blur Background

Click the **Eraser** tool on the **Toolbox**. On the **Options** bar, set the **Opacity** of the tool to **100%**, and from the **Presets** list, choose a wide, soft brush tip you can easily work with. If **Opacity** is less than 100%, the copied layer will not be completely erased.

In the **Layers** palette, select the **Unblurred** layer. Use the **Eraser** tool to erase the background areas and reveal the blurred image underneath.

▶ TIPS

You can also use the selection tools to select the part of the layer you want to blur and then delete the selection. See **57** **Erase Part of a Layer** for more information on removing contents from layers.

If you want to erase content from the **Unblurred** layer that's directly adjacent to your subject matter, you might want to use the **Background Eraser** tool. Use this tool to carefully follow outside the border separating your subject matter from its surroundings. The Editor judges where the areas of color contrast are and automatically erases the outside half of those contrast zones. Use the **Background Eraser** to get right up close, and then finish the job for the rest of the image with the **Eraser** tool (see **88** **Remove Unwanted Objects from an Image**).

5 View the Result

When you're satisfied with the result, make any other changes you want and save the PSD file. Then resave the result in JPEG, PNG, or TIFF format, leaving your PSD image with its layers intact so that you can return at a later time to make changes or additions.

It's Mommy's turn on the horse now, and with this shot, I thought the background was simply too distracting. I don't mind the rugged, natural, wild west look of the backdrop, but I don't want it competing with my wife. (I don't want *anything* competing with my wife.) So I duplicated and blurred the **Background** layer, and used a very wide and soft eraser brush tip on the

99

Unblurred layer to reveal the blurred background underneath. It's worth noting that I never created a mask layer for this technique: The erased portion of the blurred duplicate layer reveals the background behind it without the aid of a mask. So unlike the Lone Ranger, both this picture and its subject matter look better without a mask.

99

PART IV

Chapters on the Web

IN THIS PART:

CHAPTER 13   Blending Pixels Together   Web:1

CHAPTER 14   Improving Portraits   Web:11

CHAPTER 15   Creative Photographs   Web:29

Visit www.samspublishing.com/bookstore/register.asp, register your book, and download additional information to enhance your Photoshop Elements experience.

Index

A

Accented Edges command (Filter menu), Web:74, Web:79

Action Menu button, 67

Actual Pixels button, 67, 149

actual print sizes, resolution, 7

Actual Size option, 173

Adaptive algorithm, 165

Add New Address link, 201

Add Noise filter, Web:46-48

Add to Selection button, 224

Add to Selection operation, 232

Add To tool, 261

Adjust Color command (Enhance menu), Web:18

Adjust Color for Skin Tone command (Enhance menu), 401

Adjust Color Intensity slider, 400

Adjust Date and Time command (Edit menu), 72

Adjust Hue/Saturation command (Enhance menu), 402, Web:18, Web:54

Adjust Lighting command (Enhance menu), 370, 384, 388, Web:48

Adjustment command (Filter menu), 393

adjustment layers, 217
  creating, 251-254
  masks, 270-273

Adjustments command (Filter menu), 206

Adobe Gamma, color profile, 281

Adobe Gamma icon, 287

Adobe Photoshop Services, 197

Adobe RGB option, 174

Advanced Blending option, Web:41

AE Lock option, Web:39

aging photos, Web:52-58

airbrushes, painting area of photo, 324-326

albums, scrapbook pages, Web:36

Aligned option, 360

All command (Select menu), 216, 361

All Missing Files command (File menu), 52, 154

All Version Sets command (Find menu), 99

Allow Photos to Resize option, 66

Allow Videos to Resize option, 66

alpha transparency, 137-138

Amount slider, 305

Anchor pad, 160

anchor points, 160

Angle gradient style, 331

Anti-aliased button, 339

anti-aliasing, 312

   defined, 227

   text, 9, 137

archival inks, photo longevity, 6

artifacts, 136-137, 153, 166

Artistic command (Filter menu), Web:73

As a Copy option, 140-143

Attach to Email command (File menu), 194

audio

   captions, 54

   files, photo well display, 34

   locating files, 96

      captions, 106-108

      catalog, 96-99

      dates, 108-111

      history, 112-114

      metadata, 102-103

      same markers, 99-101

      similar filenames, 104-105

Auto button, 303

Auto Color Correction command (Enhance menu), 364

Auto Contrast option, 302

Auto Levels command (Enhance menu), 303, 364

Auto Levels option, 302

Auto Red Eye Fix command (Edit menu), 130, 298

Auto Select Layer option, 237, 265

Auto Smart Fix command (Edit menu), 130, 280

Automatically Fix Red Eyes option, 42, 46

Automatically Tile Windows button, 119-120

B

Back button, 32

Back to All Photos button, 33, 98

Background Brush tool, 261

Background Color option, 129

Background Contents drop-down list, 129

Background Copy layer, 206-207

Background Eraser tool, 256-258, Web:81, Web:85

Background layers, 160, 207, 391, 417

   creating image layers, 245

   repairing large areas, 361

backgrounds

   blurring to create depth of field, 417-420

   colors, 16, 237

      creating images, 126

      tools, 315

   fake water, Web:49

   layers, 237

      creating images, 126

      increase canvas area, 158

      replacing, 259-263

   retouching photos, 316

   selection, 129

   sharpening, 410

   subject on snowy background, 391-395

Backscreen layers, 342

backscreening text, 340-343

Backup command (File menu), 54

backups

   catalogs, 57-60

   Organizer, 54-57

Base layers, 347

Baseline ("Standard") option, 137

Baseline Optimized option, 137

Behind mode, Web:3

Bevel Direction option, 345

Bevel Size slider, 345

Bicubic resampling, 152

Bicubic Sharper resampling, 152

Bicubic Smoother resampling, 152-154

Bilinear resampling, 152

Bitmap mode, 167

bitmaps

   color mode, 129, 163

   converting to, 167

bits, 164

Black & White forces, 165

black-and-white photos, changing from color, Web:58-61

black points, 389

Blank File command (File menu), 128, Web:36

blemishes, removal, Web:15-17

blend modes, 240, 313, Web:2-10

color layers, 167

Hard Light, 323

layers, 18

soft, 342

Blizzard effect, Web:48

Bloat tool, Web:43

blue channels, 404-405

Blur command (Filter menu), 414, Web:12, Web:15

Blur filter, 414

Blur More command (Filter menu), Web:15

Blur More filter, 414, Web:16

Blur More icon, Web:15

Blur tool, 308, 414

blurred layers, opacity settings, Web:14

blurring, 407

background to create depth of field, 417-420

images, 413-417

Border command (Select menu), 224, Web:34

Border option, 175

bounding boxes, 173, 237, 336

handles, 269

scrapbook pages, Web:37

brightness

adjustment layers, 251

blurring

background to create depth of field, 417-420

images, 413-417

color saturation correction, 399-401

faded scanned photos, 386-390

histogram, 376-382

hue and saturation manual correction, 402-405

improving, 382-386

monitor adjustment, 290

portion of image adjustment, 395-398

sharpness, 406-412

subject on snowy background, 391-395

Brightness and Contrast pane, 289

Brightness slider, 342, 370, 384

Brightness/Contrast command (Enhance menu), 370, 383-384

Brush Presets palette, 398

brush pressure, Web:44

Brush Strokes command (Filter menu), Web:66

Brush Strokes filters, Web:51

Brush tool, 8, 270, 308, 311, 321, 393-395

airbrush area of photo, 324-326

blend modes, Web:3

drawing on photo, 319-320

foreground color, 315

painting area of photo, 320-323

Brushed Metal finish, 343-344

brushes

presets, 257

tips, 313-315

Burn command (File menu), 58

Burn tool, 308, 395, Web:24-28

Burn/Backup wizard, 54-55, 58-59

By Caption or Note command (Find menu), 106-107

By Details (Metadata) command (Find menu), 102

By Filename command (Find menu), 104-105

By History command (Find menu), 112

By Media Type command (Find menu), 99

By Searching command (File menu), 38

byte order, 139

C

Calendar command (Edit menu), 110

calibrating monitors, 128

cameras, digital

file formats, 5

JPEG format, 137

storage capabilities, 5

canvas, 158

increasing area, 158-161

reducing size, 160

Canvas Size command (Image menu), 160, Web:32

captions, 31, 36, 146

attaching to images, 87-89

locating files, 106-108

text, 171

Cascade Windows button, 119

Catalog command (File menu), 55

catalogs, 31

backups, 57-60

digital image management, 5

finding items, 96

locating files, 96-99

Organizer, 30

processing files, 154

properties, 31

CD-R, digital image management, 5

CD-ROMs, storage, 96

Center Image option, 174

Change Caption button, 87

Change the Text Orientation button, 340

Choose border color box, 175

Choose Color button, 80

chromaticity, monitors, 283-284

Chrome Fat finish, 344

Chrome finish, 343

Circle tool, 334

circular areas, selection, 208-210

Clear Amount, Diffuse Glow filter, Web:55

Clear Date Range command (Find menu), 74, 98

Clear Layer Style option, 345

Clear mode, Web:3

Clipping Mask layers, 274-276

clipping masks, 217, 244, 273

Clone Stamp tool, 298, 308-313, Web:28

blemish removal, Web:15-17

blend modes, Web:3

eyeglasses glare removal, Web:26

minor tear repair, 359-361

removing unwanted objects, 372-374

cloning images, source point, 373

Close button, Editor, 118

Clouds filter, background color, 315

CMYK (cyan, magenta, yellow, and black), 11

collections, 74

creating, 81-84

markers, 30, 64, 146

locating files, 96

organizing, 36

collective purposes, 74

Color Auto button, 304

Color Dodge blend mode, Web:6

Color Management command (File menu), 291

Color Mode drop-down list, 129

Color Picker, 161

Color Replacement tool, 405, Web:84

Color Settings command (Edit menu), 292

Color Swatches command (Window menu), 318

Color Swatches palette, 124, 318

Color Variations command (Enhance menu), 399, Web:18

Colored Pencil filter, 21

colorizing, 403

colors

backgrounds, 16, 126, 237

contrast and saturation corrections, 399-401

histograms, 376-382

installing profile, 284-292

intensity, 400

layers

blend modes, 167

fills, 249-251

management, 280-282

monitor chromaticity, 283-284

printers, 282-283

mode

changing, 161-168

creating image, 126

selection, 129

photos, changing from black and white, Web:58-61

restoring to old photos, 364-367

retouching photos

airbrush area of photo, 324-326

Brush tool, painting area of photo, 320-323

drawing with pencil, 319-320

fill with gradient, 329-332

filling photo area, 326-329

selection, 315-318

similar selections, 214-216

value, 165

Colors channel, 380

commands

  Edit button, 33

  Edit menu

    Adjust Date and Time, 72

    Auto Red Eye Fix, 130, 298

    Auto Smart Fix, 130

    Color Settings, 292

    Contact Book, 190

    Copy, 234-235

    Copy Merged, 234-236

    Define Brush, 314

    Define Brush From Selection, 314, 328

    Delete, 238

    Edit with, 118

    Paste, 262, 351

    Paste Into Selection, 234

    Preferences, 27, 45

    Rotate 90° Left, 130

    Rotate 90° Right, 130

    Stack, 70

    Stroke (Outline) Selection, 224

    Update Thumbnail, 118

    Version Set, 133

  Enhance menu

    Adjust Color, Web:18

    Adjust Lighting, 370, Web:48

    Auto Color Correction, 364

    Auto Levels, 303, 364

File menu

  Attach to Email, 194

  Backup, 54

  Burn, 58

  Catalog, 55

  File Info, 144

  Get Photos, 38

  Import, 47

  New, Web:36

  Order Prints, 186

  Page Setup, 170

  Place, 237

  Print, 172

  Print Multiple Photos, 177, 181

  Process Multiple Files, 156

  Reconnect, 52, 154

  Rename, 51

  Restore, 55

  Save, 142

  Save As, 134, 142

  Save for Web, 134

  Watch Folders, 38

Filter menu

  Adjustments, 206, 393

  Artistic, Web:73

  Blur, Web:12, Web:15

  Brush Strokes, Web:66

  Distort, Web:14, Web:44

  Noise, 356

  Pixelate, Web:46

  Sharpen, 406, Web:23

  Sketch, Web:37, Web:78

  Stylize, Web:48

  Texture, Web:56

Find menu

  All Version Sets, 99

  By Caption or Note, 106

  By Details (Metadata), 102

  By Filename, 104-105

  By History, 112

  By Media Type, 99

  Clear Date Range, 74, 98

  Items by Visual Similarity with Selected Photo(s), 99

  Items Not in any Collection, 99

  Items with Unknown Date or Time, 99

  Untagged Items, 99

Image menu

  Crop, 294

  Divide Scanned Photos, 50

  Magic Extractor, 261

  Mode, Web:12

  Resize, 152, 160

  Rotate, Web:51

  Transform, 266, Web:51

Layer menu

  Delete Layer, 207, 393

  Duplicate, 361

  Duplicate Layer, 206-207, Web:12

  Flatten Image, 15, 303

  Group with Previous, 276

  Layer from Background, 363

  Merge Down, 276

  Merge Layers, 15

  Merge Visible, Web:33

New, 160, 234

New Adjustment Layer, Web:60

New Fill Layer, Web:32

Simplify Layer, Web:37, Web:44

Modify menu, Smooth, 225, 228

More menu, Place in Palette Bin, 122

Select menu

All, 216

Deselect, 20

Feather, Web:57

Grow, 223

Inverse, Web:34, Web:57

Load Selection, Web:57

Modify, 221

Reselect, 20

Save Selection, Web:57

Similar, 223

View menu

Grid, 125

Menu Types, 34

Rulers, 124, Web:34

Selection, 20

Snap to Grid, 125, Web:86

Window menu

Color Swatches, 318

Histogram, 376

Images, 120, 373

Info, 310

Layers, 409

Navigator, 149

Order Prints, 185

Organize Bin, 101

Photo Bin, 119

Properties, 87, 145-146

Reset Palette Locations, 124

Styles and Effects, 343

Commit button, 266, 339

Complete option, 146

Composition layer, Web:72

Constrain Proportions check box, 152

Constrain Proportions option, 158

Contact Book, 185, 190

Contact Book command (Edit menu), 190

contact sheets, printing, 177-181

contacts, emailing photos, 190-191

Contract command (Select menu), 221, 348, Web:57

contracting selections, 221-224

contrast, 379

adjustment layers, 251

blurring

background to create depth of field, 417-420

images, 413-417

color saturation corrections, 399-401

faded scanned photos, 386-390

hue and saturation manual correction, 402-405

improving, 382-386

monitor adjustment, 290

portion of image adjustment, 395-398

scanned photo quality restoration, 370

sharpness, 406-412

subject on snowy background, 391-395

Contrast slider, 342, 370

Control Panel Mode option, 287

Convert Files to option, 158

Convert Photos to JPEGs option, 195

Cookie Cutter tool, 273, 294, Web:37

Copper finish, 344

Copy command (Edit menu), 234-235

Copy Merged command (Edit menu), 234-236

copying, data in selections, 234-238

Copyright Info URL box, 146

Copyright Notice text box, 146

copyright notices, 145

Copyright Status drop-down list, 146

copyrights, 146, 157

corrections, photos, 280

color management, 280-284

cropping portion of image, 293-295

installing color profile, 284-292

Quick Fix tools, 301-305

red eye, 298-301

straightening, 296-298

Create a new layer button, Web:12

Create Adjustment Layer button, 249, 253

Create button, 31, 120

Create Event button, 111

Create New Layer button, 17, 246

Create New Shape Layer button, 334-335

Create Slide Show button, 68

Create Texture option, 357

creating images, 126-129

Creation Wizard, 186

creations

    backups, 58

    making, 89, 92-93

    Organizer, catalog, 30

    searches by filenames, 104

Creations Wizard, 76, 89, 92-93

Crop command (Image menu), 294

Crop to Fit option, 183

Crop to Fit Print Proportions option, 173

Crop tool, 294, 303, 308

cropping

    images, 183

    portion of images, 293-295

    tools, 308

cross-hairs, 125

Crystallize filter, 21

current display, 32

Custom Shape tool, 129, 334-337, Web:33

Custom Size option, 173

Cutout command (Filter menu), Web:84

Cutout filter, Web:84

cutting, data in selections, 234-238

cyan, magenta, yellow, and black (CMYK), 11

Cylindrical Mapping option, Web:41

D

Daily Note, 108

damages

    color restore, 364-367

    minor tears, 359-364

Darken Amounts option, 300

Darken blend mode, 358

Darken Highlights setting, 394

data. *See also* text

    layers, 24

    masks, 272

    rotating in layers, 267-269

    selections, 234-238

Date View, 31, 64, 108

Date View button, 31, 110, 120

dates

    changing, 70-73

    locating files, 96, 108-111

Decrease Red button, Web:23

Default Colors button, 317, 393, Web:54

Define Brush command (Edit menu), 314

Define Brush From Selection command (Edit menu), 314, 328

Defringe button, 262

Delete Brush command (Brushes menu), 315

Delete command (Edit menu), 238

Delete Layer button, 17

Delete Layer command (Layer menu), 207, 393

deleting, portions of layers, 254-259

depth of field

    blurring background, 417-420

    panorama, Web:39

desaturation

    Dodge and Burn tools, 396

    photos, 396

Descreen option, 368

Description category, Organizer, 146

Description page, 146

Deselect command (Select menu), 20, 348

Despeckle filter, 356, 369, 414

dialog boxes

    Accented Edges, 74

    Add Noise, 46

    Add Photos, 179, 182

    Adjust Date and Time, 72

    Adobe Gamma, 287

    Adobe Photo Downloader, 45

    Adobe Photoshop Services Kodak EasyShare, 200

    Attach Selected Items to E-mail, 194

    Attach to E-mail, 194

    Bitmap, 167

    Brightness/Contrast, 342, 370

    Brush Name, 315

    Canvas Size, 85, 160

    Color Picker, 165-166

    Color Settings, 292

    Color Table, 165

    Color Variations, 22, 400

    Contact Book, 190

    Contract Selection, 57, 224

Create Category, 78-80

Create Collection Group, 82

Create Sub-Category, 78

Create Tag, 80

Display Properties, 286

Duplicate Layer, 409

Dust & Scratches, 356

Expand Selection, 224

Face Tagging, 86

Feather Selection, 57, 228-229

File Info, 96, 145-146

Find by Caption or Note, 106

Find By Details (Metadata), 102

Find by Filename, 104

Forced Color, 165

Full Screen View Options, 65

Gaussian Blur, 12, 418

Get Photos by Searching for Folders, 38

Get Photos from Camera or Card Reader, 45

Get Photos from Files and Folders, 41

Getting Photos, 39, 42

Grain, 56

Hue/Saturation, 60, 367, 402

Image Size, 152, 371

Import Attached Tags, 39, 43

Indexed Color, 135, 165

Items Not Imported, 39

JPEG Options, 137

Levels, 253, 379

Liquefy, 44-45

Load Selection, 57, 232

Magic Extractor, 259

Missing Files Check Before Backup, 54

Motion Blur, 48

New, 36, 128

New Contact, 190

New Group, 191

New Layer, 57, 274

New Order Prints Target, 185

Open, 143

Option, 144

Page Setup, 170-172

Pattern Fill, 57

Photomerge, 39

Pointillize, 46

Preferences, 25, 45, 118

Print, 175

Print Photos, 179

Print Preview, 12, 171-172

Print Selected Photos, 177, 181

Print Space, 178

Printer, 283

Process Multiple Files, 156

Properties, 173, 286

Reconnect Missing Files, 52

Replace Color, 84

Save As, 41, 50

Save for Web, 135

Save Selection, 57, 231-232

Send to Mobile Phone, 194

Set Date and Time, 73

Shadows/Highlights, 394

Smart Blur, 414

Smooth Selection, 58, 228

Style Settings, 32, 345

Threshold, 206, 393

Tiff Options, 139

Time Zone Adjust, 73

Unsharp Mask, 23, 67

Diamond gradient style, 331

Diamond Plate finish, 344

Diffuse Glow command (Filter menu), 14, 54

Diffuse Glow filter, 14, 54-55

diffusing errors, 167

Diffusion Dither option, 168

Diffusion option, 166

digital cameras
    file formats, 5
    JPEG formats, 137
    storage capabilities, 5

digital images
    file formats, 5
    pixels, 6
    resolution, 5
    storage media, 5

digital photography, 4-5

Digital Vibrance option, 287

Discard Layers and Save a Copy option, 139

Distort command
    Filter menu, Web:14, Web:44
    Image menu, 266

distorting layers, 263-267

distortion filters, Web:44

dither patterns, 166

dithering, 136

Divide Scanned Photos command (Image menu), 50

Document Name property, 157

Document Size Width box, 153

Dodge tool, 204, 308, 395
eyeglass glare removal, Web:24-28
sharpening eyes, Web:20-24
whitening teeth, Web:18-20

DPI, printer output, 7

drawings
Andy Warhol technique, Web:80-81, Web:84-87
changing photo effect, Web:75, Web:78-80
pencil on photo, 319-320
selections, freehand, 210-214
shapes, 332-337
tools, 308

drivers, scanners, 387

Duplicate command (Layer menu), 361

Duplicate Layer command (Layer menu), 206-207, Web:12

Dust & Scratches command (Filter menu), 356, Web:73

Dust & Scratches filter, 356-358

DVD-R, digital image management, 5

DVDs, storage, 96

E

E-mail button, 194

E-mail Settings command (Edit menu), 195

Edge Contrast option, 212

edge masks, 409

Edge Simplicity slider, Web:84

Edit and Enhance Photos option, 119

Edit button, 33, 119

Edit Contacts button, 195

Edit menu commands
Adjust Date and Time, 72
Auto Red Eye Fix, 130, 298
Auto Smart Fix, 130
Color Settings, 292
Contact Book, 190
Copy, 234-235
Copy Merged, 234-236
Define Brush, 314
Define Brush From Selection, 314, 328
Delete, 238
Edit with, 118
Paste, 262, 351, 361
Paste Into Selection, 234
Preferences, 27, 45, 77
Rotate 90° Left, 130
Rotate 90° Right, 130
Stack, 70
Stroke (Outline) Selection, 224
Update Thumbnail, 118
Version Set, 133

Edit with command (Edit menu), 118

editing
additional programs, 118
images, 130-133
blemish removal, Web:15-17
creating soft focus effect, Web:12-15
eyeglass glare removal, Web:24-28

sharpening eyes, Web:20-24
whitening teeth, Web:18-20
using multiple layers, 244
adjustment layers, 251-254
creating new image layer, 244-247
erasing, 254-259
fills, 249-251
masks, 270-276
moving, 263-267
replacing background, 259-263
rotating data, 267-269

Editor, 3, 118-120
captions, 337
creating images, 128-129
editing images, 130-133
grids, 124-126
information display, 144-146
modes, 118
Options bar, 121
Palette Bin, 122-124
printing images, online services, 185
rulers, 124-126
Shortcuts bar, 120
similar photo changes, 140
tool options, 311-313
Toolbox, 121

effects
creating images, 129
soft focus, Web:12-15

visual
aging photos, Web:52-58
Andy Warhol technique, Web:80-81, Web:84-87

changes to black and white, Web:58-61

creating weather, Web:46-49

drawing effect, Web:75, Web:78-80

melting images, Web:42-45

oil painting effect, Web:61, Web:64-68

water reflection simulation, Web:49-52

watercolor effect, Web:69, Web:72-74

Ellipse tool, 334

elliptical areas, selection, 208-210

Elliptical Marquee tool, 208, 308, 416

email

clients, 187

images, 187-188

contacts, 190-191

sharing photos, 191, 194-196

Emboss filter, 340

Enhance menu commands

Adjust Color, Web:18

Adjust Lighting, 370, Web:48

Auto Color Correction, 364

Auto Levels, 303, 364

Equalize command (Filter menu), 370

Equalize filter, scanned photo quality restoration, 370

Eraser tool, 256, Web:14

erasers, Background Eraser, 257-258

erasing, portions of layers, 254-259

errors

diffusion, 166-167

messages, saving to text files, 158

event banners, 108

Exchangeable Image File. See EXIF

EXIF (Exchangeable Image File), 96-97, 146. See also metadata

locating files, 102-103

Photoshop support, 140

scanning images, 97

Exif Print option, 178, 181

Exit button, 68

Expand menu (Select menu), 221

expanding selections, 221-224

Export Clipboard option, 236

Export to Clipboard option, 240

exposure

brightness improvement, 382-386

contrast improvement, 382-386

portion of image adjustment, 395-398

scanned photos, input levels, 386-390

subject on snowy background, 391-395

Exposure scale, 397

Eyedropper icon, 310, 318

Eyedropper tool, 166, 308

eyedroppers, 389

eyes

glasses glare removal, Web:24-28

sharpening, Web:20-24

F

faded photos, input levels, 386-390

fake water, Web:49

Fast Save compression, 138

Faux Bold button, 338

Faux Italic button, 338

Feather command (Select menu), 228, 348, Web:57

Feather value, 229

feathering, 225-228

defined, 227

photo edges, 20

selections, 207

File Info command (File menu), 144

File menu commands

Attach to Email, 194

Backup, 54

Burn, 58

Catalog, 55

File Info, 144

Get Photos, 38

Import, 47

New, 128, 160, Web:36

Order Prints, 186

Page Setup, 170

Place, 237

Print, 172

Print Multiple Photos, 177, 181

Process Multiple Files, 156

Reconnect, 52, 154

Rename, 51

Restore, 55

Save, 142

Save As, 134, 142

Save for Web, 134

Watch Folders, 38

File Size option, 138

filenames, locating files, 104-105

files

captions, 106-108

dates, 72, 108-111, 146

images, 72

locating files, 96

Windows Explorer, 74

formatting, 5, 104

history, 112-114

importing, 36-51

locating, 96

catalog, 96-99

same markers, 99-101

metadata, 102-103

similar filenames, 104-105

Files command (Edit menu), 51

Fill Page with First Photo option, 183

fills

Gradient tool, 329-332

layers, 16, 249-251, 270-273

Paint Bucket tool, 326-329

text with image, 349-352

film, detail recording, 5

Film Grain filter, Web:54

Filter command (Filter menu), 206

Filter menu commands

Adjustments, 206, 393

Artistic, Web:73

Blur, 414, Web:12, Web:15

Brush Strokes, Web:66

Distort, Web:14, Web:44

Noise, 356, 369, 416

Pixelate, Web:46

Sharpen, 406, Web:23

Sketch, Web:37, Web:78

Stylize, Web:48

Texture, Web:56

filters. *See also* individual filter names

aging photos, Web:54

creating images, 129

Find bars, Organizer, 33

Find by Caption or Note dialog box, 106

Find By Details (Metadata) dialog box, 102

Find by Filename dialog box, 104

Find Faces for Tagging button, 86

Find menu commands

All Version Sets, 99

By Caption or Note, 106-107

By Details (Metadata), 102

By Filename, 104-105

By History, 112

By Media Type, 99

Clear Date Range, 74, 98

Items by Visual Similarity with Selected Photo(s), 99

Items Not in any Collection, 99

Items with Unknown Date or Time, 99

Untagged Items, 99

finding items, 96

captions, 106-108

catalog, 96-99

dates, 108-111

history, 112-114

metadata, 102-103

same markers, 99-101

similar filenames, 104-105

Fit On Screen button, 149

Fit to Page option, 173

Fixed Size tool, 334

Flatten Image command (Layer menu), 15, 303, 363

Flatten Set command (Edit menu), 133

Flatten Stack command (Edit menu), 70

Flip Layer Vertical command (Image menu), Web:51

floating palettes, 122

fonts, type, 338

Forced Color dialog box, 165

Foreground Brush tool, 261

Foreground Color swatch, Web:32

foregrounds

colors

gradient patterns, 250

tools, 315

retouching photos, 316

Format drop-down list, 142

formatting

locating files, 104

saving

images, 134

selection, 231

TIFF, 5

Forward button, 33

frames

increasing canvas area around, 158-161

photos, Web:30-34

freckles, removal, Web:15-17

Free Transform command (Image menu), Web:51

free-floating palettes, 149

freehand drawings, selections, 210-214

Frequency option, 212

From Camera or Card Reader command (File menu), 45

From Files and Folders command (File menu), 41

full-screen photo reviews, reviewing images, 64-68

G

gammas, 378

   brightness adjustment, 389

   monitors, 290

   white and black points, 390

gamuts, 281

Gaussian Blur command (Filter menu), 418, Web:12

Gaussian Blur filter, 417

   blemish removal, Web:15-17

   soft focus effect, Web:12-15

Gaussian Blur icon, Web:12

General command (Edit menu), 27, 98, 236

Geometry Options palette, 334

Get Photos button, 41, 45

Get Photos command (File menu), 38, 41, 45

GIF files

   format, 134-135

   Organizer, 39

glare, removal from eyeglasses, Web:24-28

Glass command (Filter menu), Web:65

Glass filter, 129, Web:44

Glow Amount, Diffuse Glow filter, Web:55

glowing text, 346-349

Go to Quick Fix command (Edit button), 33

Go to Standard Edit command (Edit button), 33

Go to Standard Edit option, 119

Gold Sprinkles finish, 344

gradient maps, adjustment layers, 251

Gradient tool, 249, 272, 275, 311

   background color, 315

   blend modes, Web:3

   filling photo area, 329-332

gradients, 16, 308

   fill area of photo, 329-332

   layer fills, 249-251

Grain command (Filter menu), Web:56

Graininess values, Web:14

grainy photos, blurring images, 413-417

graphic images. See images

Graphic Pen command (Filter menu), Web:79

graphics, Editor, 118-120. See also photos; images

   grids, 124-126

   Options bar, 121

   Palette Bin, 122-124

   rulers, 124-126

   Shortcuts bar, 120

   Toolbox, 121

graphics editors, 3, 31

grayscale

   color mode selection, 129, 163

   converting to, 167

   increasing mode to RGB, 163

Grayscale command (Image menu), 216, Web:60

green channel, 404-405

greeting cards, scrapbook pages, Web:36

Grid command

   Edit menu, 126

   View menu, 125

grids, Editor, 124-126

Group with Previous command (Layer menu), 276, 411

groups

   images, processing, 154-158

   palettes, 122

Grow command (Select menu), 223

Growing Thumbnail option, 138

H

Hand tool, 149, 262

handles, 269, 336

hard disks, digital image management, 5

Hard Light blend mode, 323, 340

Healing Brush tool, 308, 312, 328

   blemish removal, Web:15-17

   removing small objects, 373

   scratch removal, 354-358

height, adjusting, 128

hidden tags, 77

hidden tools, Toolbox, 121

Histogram command (Window menu), 376, 381, 384

Histogram palette, 123-124, 376-377

histograms, 376-382

histories, locating files, 112-114

History tab (Properties pane), 72

holes, repairing large areas, 361-364

Horizontal tool, 249, Web:38

Horizontal Type Mask tool, 308, 350-352

Horizontal Type tool, 308, 337

How To palette, 122

HSB color, 318

HTML

   color, 318

   Photo Gallery, 197

Hue slider, 404

hues

   adjustment layers, 251

   saturation, manual correction, 402-405

I

IBM PC option, 139

ICC

   color profiles, 146

   printer profiles, 171

ICC Profile option, Save dialog box, 143

ICM (Image Color Management), 281

icons, photo well, 35

Ignore Palettes option, 149

Image Color Management (ICM), 281

Image Compression option, 139

Image Effects layer styles, 23

Image from Clipboard command (File menu), 241

Image layer, 276

Image menu commands

   Crop, 294

   Divide Scanned Photos, 50

   Magic Extractor, 261

   Mode, 163, 216, Web:12

   Resize, 152, 160, 313, 371

   Rotate, 267, 296, Web:51

   Transform, 266, Web:51

Image Size command (Image menu), 152, 313

images. *See also* photos; graphics

   attaching markers, 84-86

   brightness

      blurring, 413-420

      color saturation corrections, 399-401

      faded scanned photo, 386-390

      hue and saturation manual correction, 402-405

      improving, 382-386

      portion of images, 395-398

      sharpness, 406-412

      subject on snowy background, 391-395

   captions, adding, 87-89

   collections creation, 81-84

colors, changing modes, 161-168

contrast

   blurring, 413-420

   color saturation corrections, 399-401

   faded scanned photo, 386-390

   hue and saturation, manual correction, 402-405

   improving, 382-386

   portion of images, 395-398

   sharpness, 406-412

   subject on snowy background, 391-395

creating, 126-129

creating from selections, 240-242

creations, making, 89-93

cropping portion, 293-295

date and time change, 70-73

digital. *See* digital images

editing, 130-133

   blemish removal, Web:15-17

   creating soft focus effect, Web:12-15

   eyeglass glare removal, Web:24-28

   sharpening eyes, Web:20-24

   whitening teeth, Web:18-20

Editor, 3, 118-120

   grids, 124-126

   Options bar, 121

   Palette Bin, 122-124

   rulers, 124-126

   Shortcuts bar, 120

   Toolbox, 121

emailing, 187-188

contacts, 190-191

sharing photos, 191, 194-196

filling text, 349-352

flattening, 15

group processing, 154-158

histograms, 376-382

increasing canvas area, 158-161

information display, 144-146

layers

adjustment, 251-254

creating new, 244-247

erasing portions, 254-259

fills, 249-251

masks, 270-276

moving, 263-267

replacing back-grounds, 259-263

rotating data, 267-269

locating, 96

captions, 106-108

catalog, 96-99

dates, 108-111

history, 112-114

metadata, 102-103

same markers, 99-101

similar filenames, 104-105

melting, Web:42-45

organization, 74-77

Organizer, 3

printing, 11-13, 171-175

Quick Fix tools, 301-305

red eye correction, 298-301

resolution, changing, 150-154

reviewing, 64-68

saving, 133-144

saving selections for reusing, 231-233

selections, 204-208

sharing, online services, 197-202

sizing, 150-154

stacking, 68-70

straightening, 296-298

tag creation, 78-81

thumbnails, 34

version sets, 68

zooming, 147-149

Images command (Window menu), 120, 373

Import button, 190

Import command (File menu), 47

Import Folders button, 39

Imported On command (Find menu), 112

importing

contacts, 190

dates, 72, 146

media files, 36-51

Organizer, 31

Impressionist Brush, 324

improving photos

large areas, 361-364

minor tears, 359-361

removing scratches, 354-358

removing unwanted objects, 372-374

restoring colors, 364-367

scanned photo quality restore, 368-371

Include All Subfolders option, 156

Include Captions option, 66

Include in the Organizer option, 140-142

Include Metadata option, 138

Include Transparency option, 138

Increase Blue button, Web:18

Indexed Color mode, 164, 168

Indexed color modes, 163

Indicate Foreground button, 221

Info command (Window menu), 310, 366

Info palette, 124-126

color fading correction, 366

sizing, 123

information, images, 144-146

Ink Outlines command (Filter menu), Web:78

input levels, faded photos, 386-390

Instant Tag button, 84

Interlaced option, 136

interlacing, 138

Interleaved option, 139

interleaving, 138

Internet

emailing images, 187-188

contacts, 190-191

sharing photos, 191, 194-196

online services

printing, 183-186

sharing photos, 197-202

uploading digital images, 6

Intersect with Selection button, 224

Inverse command (Select menu), 20, Web:34, Web:57

Invert Image option, 175

inverting images, adjustment layers, 252

iris, 300

Items by Visual Similarity with Selected Photo(s) command (Find menu), 99

Items Not in any Collection command (Find menu), 99

Items with Unknown Date or Time command (Find menu), 99

J–K

JP2 Compatible option, 138

JP2 format (JPEG 2000 format), 231

saving images, 137

saving selections, 231

JPEG 2000 format (JP2 format), 231

saving images, 137

selection saving, 231

JPEG format, 134

digital cameras, 137

photograph detail, 5

saving images, 136

saving to preserve quality, 13

Keep as Layers option, Web:41

keyboard shortcuts, Toolbox items, 309

Keywords category, 146

Kodak EasyShare Gallery, 197

Kodak EasyShare website, 200

Kodak Picture Maker, 30

L

labels, 156, 337-340

Labels pane, 156-157

Lasso tool, 212, 308, Web:37

Layer from Background command (Layer menu), 245, 254

Layer menu commands

Delete Layer, 207, 393

Duplicate, 361

Duplicate Layer, 207, 257, 391, Web:12

Flatten Image, 15, 303, 363

Group with Previous, 276

Layer from Background, 363

Merge Down, 276

Merge Layers, 15

Merge Visible, Web:33

New, 160, 234

New Adjustment Layer, Web:60

New Fill Layer, Web:32

Simplify Layer, Web:37, Web:44

Layer via Copy command (Layer menu), 241, Web:26

Layer via Cut command (Layer menu), 241

layers, 142, 244

adjustment, 217

backgrounds, 237

creating images, 126

increasing canvas area, 158

layers, 245

replacing, 259-263

blend modes, 18

colors, blend modes, 167

creating

adjustment, 251-254

from selection, 240-242

new image layer, 244-247

data, 24

duplicating contents, 246

erasing portions, 254-259

fills, 16, 249-251

masks, 270-276

merging, 15

moving, 263-267

rotating data, 267-269

selecting, 19

selections, distinguishing boundaries, 204-208

styles, 17, 244

creating images, 129

scaling, 23

Layers as Frames option, 135

Layers command (Window menu), 409

Layers option, Save dialog box, 142

Layers palette, 122, 206, Web:14-16

layout printing options, 179

Less Saturation button, 400

Less Saturation thumbnail, 400

levels, adjustment layers, 251

Levels Auto button, 304

Levels command (Enhance menu), 366, 388

libraries, patterns, 328

Lighten button, Web:18, Web:23

Lighten Shadows setting, 394

Lightness slider, 404

Limits option, Background Eraser tool, 258

Line button, 335

Linear gradient style, 331

Link icon, 18

Link Layers button, 18

Link with Layer option, 250

Liquefy command (Filter menu), Web:44

Liquefy filter, 129, Web:42-45

Liquefy tools, melting images, Web:42-45

Load Selection command (Select menu), Web:57

loading, saved selections, 232-233

Local options, 164

locating files, 96

captions, 106-108

catalog, 96-99

dates, 108-111

history, 112-114

metadata, 102-103

same markers, 99-101

similar filenames, 104-105

locations, palettes, 123

Lock All button, 17

Lock icon, 17

Lock Transparent Pixels button, 17, 326

log files, 158

Lossless compression, 138

low-resolution images

excluding from contact sheet, 179, 182

printing, 171

luminance, 382, 402

luminosity, 395, 402

Luminosity channel, 382

LZW option, 139

M

Macintosh option, 139

Magentas channel, 405

Magic Eraser tool, 256-258, 308, 312

Magic Extractor command (Image menu), 261

Magic Extractor tool, 256

Magic Selection Brush tool, 217, 220, 308

Magic Wand tool, 204, 214-217, 308, Web:34

Magnetic Lasso tool, 204, 212, 216, Web:85

Maintain Aspect Ratio button, 265

Maintain Aspect Ratio option, 352

management, digital images, 5

markers

attaching, 84-86

collection, 64

locating files, 99-101

tags. See tags

Marquee Selection tools, 208

Mask layer, Web:34

masks, 412

clipping, 217, 244, 273

defined, 270

edge, 409

fill layers, 16

layers, 270-276

saved selections, 231

Master options, 164

Match Location command (Window menu), 120

Match Zoom command (Window menu), 120

Matte drop-down list, 166

Maximize button, Editor, 118

Maximize mode, 120

Maximize Mode button, 118

Measure button, 290

measurements, ruler changes, 126

media files

collections. See collections

importing, 36-51

Median filter, 356, 369, 414

melting images, Web:42-45

memory cards, 5, 43

Menu Types command (View menu), 34

Merge Down command (Layer menu), 276

Merge Layers command (Layer menu), 15

Merge Visible command (Layer menu), Web:33

merging layers, 15

metadata. See also EXIF

images, 144-146

locating files, 102-103

Metadata button, 145

Metadata tab, 146

metallic text, 343-346

Method area, 168

midtones, 290, 378, 394

Minimize button, Editor, 118

Missing File command (File menu), 52

mistakes, undos, 27

Mode command (Image menu), 163, 216, Web:12

modes

blend, 313

color changing, 161-168

modified dates, 72, 146

Modify command (Select menu), 221, 348

Modify menu commands, Smooth, 225, 228

modifying selections

adding areas similar to current selections, 221-224

smoothing, 225-229

softening, 225-229

moiré patterns, 368

Molten Gold finish, 344

monitors

calibrating, 128

color management, 283-284

gamma value, 290

Month button, 110

More menu commands, Place in Palette Bin, 122

More Options button, 321

More Saturation button, 400

More Saturation thumbnail, 400

Move Files option, 5

Move tool, 237-238, Web:38

movies, locating, 96

captions, 106-108

catalog, 96-99

dates, 108-111

history, 112-114

metadata, 102-103

same markers, 99-101

similar filenames, 104-105

moving layers, 263-267

Multi-window mode, 119-120

Multi-window Mode button, 120

multiple images, viewing, 119

multiple layers, 244

adjustment layers, 251-254

creating new image layer, 244-247

erasing portions, 254-259

fills, 249-251

masks, 270-276

moving, 263-267

replacing background, 259-263

rotating data, 267-269

N

Navigator command (Window menu), 149

Navigator palette, 124, 149

Nearest Neighbor resampling, 153

neighboring pixels, 207, 312

neutral gray points, 389

New Adjustment Layer command (Layer menu), Web:60

New button, 80, 128

New command, 160, Web:36

New Contact button, 190

New Fill Layer command (Layer menu), Web:32

New Group button, 191

New Layer icon, 17

New Selection button, 208, 341

New Size pane, 160

noise

pixels, 356

reducing in grainy photo, 413-417

removing from digital pictures, 356

restoring scanned photo quality, 368-371

Noise command (Filter menu), 356, 369, 416

Noise option, 167

non-anti-aliased text, 9

notes, adding to images, 87-89

O

objects, removing with Clone Stamp tool, 372-374

Ocean Ripple filter, Web:44

offline storage, 96

oil paintings, changing photo, Web:61, Web:64-68

old photos, repairing

color restore, 364-367

large areas, 361-364

minor tears, 359-361

scratch removal, 354-358

online services

printing images, 183-186

sharing photos, 197-202

opacity layers, 16

Opacity settings

blend modes, Web:3

blurred layers, Web:14

optical discs, digital image management, 5

optical illusions
   aging photos, Web:52-58
   Andy Warhol technique, Web:80-81, Web:84-87
   changes to black and white, Web:58-61
   creating weather, Web:46-49
   drawing effect, Web:75, Web:78-80
   melting images, Web:42-45
   oil painting effect, Web:61, Web:64-68
   water reflection simulation, Web:49-52
   watercolor effect, Web:69, Web:72-74
options, Toolbox, 310-313
Options bar, 35-47, 121, 308
Order Online button, 186
Order Prints button, 177, 181, 186
Order Prints command
   File menu, 186
   Window menu, 185
Order Prints palette, 185
organization, images, 74-77
Organize Bin, 77
   collections, 82-83
   markers, 84-86
   Organizer, 33-34
   tags, 78-81
Organize Bin command (Window menu), 101
Organizer, 3
   basics, 30-31
      Find bar, 33
      Options bar, 35-47, 50-60
      Organize Bin, 33-34

photo well, 34-35
   Shortcuts bar, 32-33
   Timeline, 33
   work area, 31-32
captions, 87-89, 337
catalog, 30
collections, creating, 81-84
creations, making, 89-93
cropping images, 183
data and time change, 70-73
digital image management, 5
editing
   images, 130
   in other programs, 118
importing images, 31
markers, attaching to images, 84-86
organizing images, 74-77
printing images, online services, 185
Properties pane, 146
reviewing images, 64-68
stacking images, 68-70
tags, creating, 78-81
Outer Glows layer styles, 346
Output Levels slider, 389
Overlay Color list, 220

P

packages, printing pictures, 179-183
Page Duration list, 65
Page Setup command (File menu), 170

Paint Brush tool, 312, Web:38
Paint Bucket icon, 318
Paint Bucket tool, 249, Web:34, Web:46, Web:85
   blend modes, Web:3
   filling photo area, 326-329
   foreground color, 315
paintings
   airbrush area of photo, 324-326
   Andy Warhol technique, Web:80-81, Web:84-87
   brushing area of photo, 320-323
   changing photo to oil painting, Web:61, Web:64-68
   selections, 217, 220-221
   tools, 308
   watercolor effect, Web:69, Web:72-74
Palette Bin, Editor, 122-124
Palette Menu button, 311, 330
Palette option, 164
palettes, 122-124. *See also* individual palettes
   colors, 164
   free-floating, 149
Panorama option, Web:39
panoramas, creating, Web:39-42
Parent Collection Group list, 83
Paste command (Edit menu), 262, 351, 361
Paste Into Selection command (Edit menu), 234
pasting data in selections, 234-238
Pattern command (Layer menu), Web:57

Pattern Dither option, 168

Pattern option, 167

Pattern Stamp tool, 308, 312, 328

   blend modes, Web:3

   scrapbook page creation, Web:37

patterns, 326

   filling photo area, 326-329

   layer fills, 249-251

   libraries, 328

   scrapbook page creation, Web:37

Pen Pressure option, 213

Pencil tool, 8, 270

   blend modes, Web:3

   drawing on photo, 319-320

   foreground color, 315

pencils, drawing on photo, 319-320

Per Channel option, 139

Perceptual algorithm, 165

Photo Bin, thumbnails, changing to new image, 118

Photo Bin button, 119

Photo Bin command (Window menu), 119

Photo Browser, 64

Photo Browser Arrangement list, 35, 84

Photo Browser button, 31, 120

Photo Browser view, 31

Photo Compare mode, 67

Photo Downloader, 43

Photo Mail option, 187

Photo Review mode, 67

Photo Review toolbar, 67

photography, digital, 4-5

Photomerge Panorama command (File menu), Web:39

photos. *See also* images; graphics

   attaching markers, 84-86

   brightness

      blurring, 413-420

      color saturation corrections, 399-401

      faded scanned photo, 386-390

      hue and saturation, manual correction, 402-405

      improving, 382-386

      portions of images, 395-398

      sharpness, 406-412

      subject on snowy background, 391-395

   captions, adding, 87-89

   collection creation, 81-84

   contrast

      blurring, 413-420

      color saturation corrections, 399-401

      faded scanned photo, 386-390

      hue and saturation, manual correction, 402-405

      improving, 382-386

      portions of images, 395-398

      sharpness, 406-412

      subject on snowy background, 391-395

   corrections, 280

      color management, 280-284

      cropping portion of image, 293-295

      installing color profile, 284-292

      Quick Fix tools, 301-305

      red eye, 298-301

      straightening, 296-298

   creations, making, 89, 92-93

   date and time change, 70-73

   digital. *See* digital images

   emailing, 187-188

      contacts, 190-191

      sharing photos, 191, 194-196

   filters, adjustment layers, 252

   histograms, 376-382

   organization, 74-77

   removing unwanted objects, 372-374

   repairing

      color restore, 364-367

      large areas, 361-364

      minor tears, 359-361

      scratch removal, 354-358

   retouching, 308

      airbrush area of photo, 324-326

      backscreening text, 340-343

      Brush tool painting area of photo, 320-323

      color selection, 315-318

      creating brush tips, 313-315

      drawing shape, 332-337

      drawing with pencil, 319-320

      fill with gradient, 329-332

filling photo area, 326-329

filling text with image, 349-352

glowing text, 346-349

labels, 337-340

metallic text, 343-346

text captions, 337-340

Toolbox, 308-313

reviews, 64-68

scanned, restore quality, 368-371

sharing, online services, 197-202

stacking, 68-70

tag creation, 78-81

visual impact improvement

aging photos, Web:52-58

Andy Warhol technique, Web:80-81, Web:84-87

changes to black and white, Web:58-61

creating weather, Web:46-49

drawing effect, Web:75, Web:78-80

framing photo, Web:30-34

melting images, Web:42-45

oil painting effect, Web:61, Web:64-68

panoramas, Web:39-42

scrapbook pages, Web:36-38

water reflection simulation, Web:49-52

watercolor effect, Web:69, Web:72-74

wells, Organizer, 34-35

Photoshop RAW format, saving images, 139

picking tools, 308

pictures. See graphics; images; photos

PIM, Photoshop support, 140

Pixel Order, 139

Pixelate command (Filter menu), Web:46

pixels, 311

blend modes, Web:2-10

image size, 150-154

matching original, 223

neighboring, 312

noise, 356

resampling, 150

selecting, 216

transparent, 326

Place command (File menu), 237

Place in Palette Bin command (More menu), 122

Place in Palette Bin option, 123

PNG files, Organizer, 39

PNG format, 134, 138

Pointillize command (Filter menu), Web:46

Pointillize filter, Web:46

Polygon button, 334

Polygonal Lasso tool, 212, 308

portraits, 52

blemish removal, Web:15-17

creating soft focus effect, Web:12-15

eyeglass glare removal, Web:24-28

sharpening eyes, Web:20-24

whitening teeth, Web:18-20

postcards, scrapbook pages, Web:36

posterize, adjustment layers, 253

Posterize command (Filter menu), 206

Posterize filter, 206, Web:84

PPI, monitors, 7

Preferences command (Edit menu), 27, 45, 77

Preserve Exact Colors option, 166

Preset drop-down list, 128

presets, brush tips, 313-315

Presets list, brushes, 257

Primaries option, 165

primary channels, 404

Print button, 171-172

Print command (File menu), 172

Print Crop Marks check box, 175

PRINT Image Matching (P.I.M.) option, 178, 181

Print Multiple Photos command (File menu), 177, 181

Print Selected Area option, 173

Print Size button, 149, 152

Print Size drop-down list, 173

Print Size list, 173

Print This Confirmation button, 201

Printed On command (Find menu), 112

Printer Color Management option, 174

Printer Profile list, 174

printers

color management, 282-283

profile, 174

printing, 170-171

contact sheet, 177-181

image size, 12

images, 153, 171-175

online services, 183-186

picture package, 179-183

Process Files From list, 156

Process Multiple Files command (File menu), 156

processing, image groups, 154-158

Progressive option, 137-138

properties

catalogs, 31

media files, 54

Properties command (Window menu), 87, 145-146

Properties pane, 36, 72, 87, 145-147

Proportional tool, 334

PSD format

saving images, 134

saving selections, 231

Pucker tool, Web:43

Pupil Size setting, 300

pupils, 300

Q–R

Quick Fix mode, 24, 131

editing images, 130

Editor, 118

Quick Fix tools, 280, 301-305

Radial gradient style, 331

rain, creating, Web:46-49

raster data, 244, 308

RAW format

digital cameras, 137

saving images, 139

Reconnect button, 52

Reconnect command (File menu), 52, 154

Reconstruct tool, Web:44

Rectangle tool, 334

rectangular areas, selection, 208-210

Rectangular Marquee tool, 208, 308, 341

red channel, 404

red eye

correcting, 298-301

reducing, 300

removing, 46

Red Eye Removal tool, 298-300, 303, 308

Reduce Noise command (Filter menu), 369, 416

Reduce Noise filter, 356, 369, 414

Reflected gradient style, 331

Reflection tool, Web:43-44

Remember my password option, 200

Remove Color Cast command (Enhance menu), 367

Remove Color command (Enhance menu), Web:60

Remove From Selection tool, 261

Remove Photo from Stack command (Edit menu), 70

Remove Selected Items button, 179, 182

Rename command (File menu), 51

Rename Files check box, 157

Rendering Intent list, 174

repairs

photos

color restore, 364-367

large areas, 361-364

minor tears, 359-361

scratch removal, 354-358

removing unwanted objects, 372-374

scanned photos, restore quality, 368-371

Repeat Slide Show option, 66-67

Replace Color command (Enhance menu), Web:84

Replace mode, Web:3

Resample Image option, 152-153, 371

resampling, 8, 150

disabling, 153

resizing images, 158

Unsharp mask, 154

rescaling, 153

Reselect command (Select menu), 20

Reset Image button, 400-401

Reset Palette Locations command (Window menu), 124

Reset tool, 310

Resize command (Image menu), 152, 160, 313, 371

Resize Images option, 158

Resize Window to Fit option, 149

resizing

brush tips, 313

images, 158

Toolbox, 309

resolution, 293

adjusting, 129

creating images, 126

data, 234

digital images, 5

images

changing, 150-154

print size influence, 12

low

excluding from contact sheet, 179, 182

printing images, 171

Restore command (File menu), 55

Restore Default Settings command, 25

retouching photos

airbrush area of photo, 324-326

backscreening text, 340-343

Brush tool, painting area of photo, 320-323

color

restore, 364-367

selection, 315-318

creating brush tips, 313-315

drawing

shapes, 332-337

with pencil, 319-320

fills

gradient, 329-332

photo area, 326-329

text with image, 349-352

glowing text, 346-349

images, 156

labels, 337-340

large areas, 361-364

metallic text, 343-346

minor tears, 359-361

removing unwanted objects, 372-374

scanned, restore quality, 368-371

scratch removal, 354-358

text captions, 337-340

Toolbox, 308-313

tools, 308

Reveal Photos in Stack command (Edit menu), 70

Reveal Photos in Version Set command (Edit menu), 133

Revert to Original command (Edit menu), 133

reviewing images, 64-68

RGB, 163, 317

color model, 10

mode selection, 129

RGB Color command (Image menu), 216

richness, color, 382

Rivet finish, 344

Rotate 90° Left command (Edit menu), 130

Rotate 90° Right command (Edit menu), 130

Rotate command (Image menu), 267, 296, Web:51

Rotate Image tool, Web:41

Rotate Left button, 67

Rotate Right button, 67

rotating data, layers, 267-269

Rounded Rectangle tool, 334, Web:56

rulers

changing unit of measure, 126

Editor, 124-126

Rulers command (View menu), 124, Web:34

Rusted Metal finish, 344

S

Sample All Layers option, 258

Sampling: Background Swatch button, Web:84

Sampling: Continuous button, Web:84

Sampling: Once button, Web:84

Sams Publishing website, 247

saturation

adjustment layers, 251

contrast and color corrections, 399-401

hue, manual correction, 402-405

Saturation slider, 304, 404

Save As command (File menu), 134, 142

Save Brush command (Brushes menu), 315

Save button, 142

Save command (File menu), 142

Save for Web command (File menu), 134

Save Image Pyramid option, 139

Save in Version Set with Original option, 140, 143

Save Selection command (Select menu), 224, Web:57

Save Transparency option, 139

saving

images, 133-144

selections

for reusing, 231-233

modifying, 232

Saving Files command (Edit menu), 25, 144, 282

scales, adjusting, 173

Scale Effects command (Layer menu), 23

Scale Styles option, 152

Scaled Print Size frame, 173

scaling layer styles, 23

scanned photos

input levels, 386-390

restore quality, 368-371

Scanner command (Edit menu), 25

scanners, drivers, 387

scanning, EXIF (Exchangeable Image File), 97

scrapbook pages, photo visual impact, Web:36-38

scratches, removing, 354-358

screentips, tool identification, 309

scrollbars, view hidden areas, 149

secondary colors, 404

Select a Frame list, 183

Select Image tool, Web:41

Select menu commands

All, 216, 361

Deselect, 20, 348

Feather, 228, 348, Web:57

Grow, 223

Inverse, 20, Web:34, Web:57

Load Selection, 232, 348, Web:57

Modify, 221, 348

Reselect, 20

Save Selection, 224, 231, 347, Web:57

Similar, 223

Select Type of Print drop-down list, 178

Select Web Safe Color button, 317

Selection Brush tool, 19, 217, 308, 312

Selection command (View menu), 20

Selection tools, 125, 204, 308. *See also* selections

selections, 204

circular area, 208-210

creating image, 240-242

data modifying, 234-238

distinguishing boundaries, 204-208

drawing freehand, 210-214

format saved, 231

modifying

adding areas to similar current selections, 221-224

smoothing, 225-229

softening, 225-229

painting, 217, 220-221

points, deleting, 213

rectangular area, 208-210

saving

for reusing, 231-233

modifying, 232

similar color areas, 214-216

tracing edges, 210-214

sending photos, email, 187-188

contacts, 190-191

sharing photos, 191, 194-196

Sepia layer, Web:54

serial numbers, 157

Set As Default button, 286

Set as Top Photo command (Edit menu), 70, 133

Set Vanishing Point tool, Web:41

Shadows/Highlights command (Enhance menu), 394

Shape Selection button, 336

Shape tool, 272, 332-337

shapes

drawing, 332-337

tools, 308

Share button, 194

Sharing command (Edit menu), 195

sharing photos, email, 187-191, 194-196

Sharpen command (Filter menu), 406, Web:23

Sharpen Edges command (Filter menu), 406

Sharpen More command (Filter menu), 406

Sharpen tool, 308

Sharpening layers, 411

sharpness, 406-412

Shear filter, Web:44

Shift Pixels tool, Web:43-44

Shortcuts bar, 33, 120

Organizer, 32-33

Print button, 171-172

tooltips, 33

Show Bounding Box option, 173, 265

Show Closely Matching Sets for Searches option, 98

Show Filmstrip option, 66

Show Hidden Photos option, 103

Show in Photo Browser button, 111

Show in Photo Review button, 111

Show or Hide Properties button, 72, 87, 146

Show Printer Preferences button, 178

shrinking selections, 221-224

Similar command (Select menu), 223

Simple Inner thumbnail, Web:32

Simple Sharp Inner thumbnail, Web:32

Simplify Layer command (Layer menu), 308, Web:37, Web:44

Single Photo view, 87-89

Single Photo View button, 89

sizing

   images, 150-154

   palettes, 123

   zoom amount, 149

Sketch command (Filter menu), Web:37, Web:78

Skew button, 266

Skew command (Image menu), 266

skewing layers, 263-267

Slide Show Editor, 92

slideshows, automatically playing, 66

Smart Blur command (Filter menu), 414

Smart Blur filter, 415

Smart Fix Auto button, 304

Smooth command

   Modify menu, 225, 228

   Select menu, Web:58

smoothing, defined, 227

Smoothing Brush tool, 262

smoothing selections, 225-229

Smudge tool, 308, Web:44

Snap to Grid command (View menu), 125, Web:86

Snap to Image option, Web:41

Snap to Origin button, 250

snow, creating, Web:46-49

soft focus effects, Web:12-15

Soft Light blend mode, 342

softening selections, 225-229

Solarize filter, 21

Solid Color command (Layer menu), Web:32, Web:72

sources, blend modes, Web:2

spacebar, Hand tool, 149

specular highlights, 366

Sponge tool, 308, 367, 396, Web:27

Spot Healing Brush

   blemish removal, Web:15-17

   eyeglasses glare removal, Web:27

   removing small objects, 373

Spot Healing Brush tool, 308, 354-358

spots, repairing, 359-364

Sprayed Strokes filter, Web:51

Sprayer Strokes command (Filter menu), Web:66

Square tool, 334

Stack command (Edit menu), 70

Stack Selected Photos command (Edit menu), 70

stacking images, 68-70

stacks, 133

Stained Glass filter, 21

stains, repairing, 359-364

Standard Edit mode, 119, 128, 131

   editing images, 130

   Editor, 118

Start Automatic Sequencing button, 110

Start Playing Automatically option, 66

Starting serial text box, 157

Stationery & Layouts Wizard, 196

Stitch Assist option, Web:39

storage

   digital images, 5

   offline, 96

Straighten and Crop Image command (Image menu), 296

Straighten Image command (Image menu), 296

Straighten tool, 296, 308

straightening images, 296-298

Strikethrough button, 338

Stroke (Outline) Selection command (Edit menu), 224

Strokes Frame thumbnail, Web:80

styles, layers, 17, 244

   creating images, 129

   scaling, 23

Styles and Effects command (Window menu), 343

Styles and Effects palette, 122, 208, 343, Web:48, Web:57

Stylize command (Filter menu), Web:48

stylus pressure, Web:44

subjects, snowy background, 391-395

Subtract from Selection button, 224

Subtract from Selection mode, 216

Swap button, 294

Switch Colors button, 317

Sync Pan and Zoom button, 67

System (Mac OS) option, Palette list, 164

System (Windows) option, Palette list, 164

T

Tablet Options button, 323

tags, 64, 74

creating, 78-81

digital image management, 5

image organization, 30

locating files, 96

organizing imported files, 36

Tags and Collections command (Edit menu), 77, 81

targets, blend modes, Web:2

tears

removing

large areas, 361-364

minor, 359-361

repairing large areas, 361-364

teeth, whitening, Web:18-20

Temperature slider, 304

text. *See also* data

anti-aliased, 9

backscreening, 340-343

captions, 171, 337-340

attaching to images, 87-89

photo review, 66

filling with image, 349-352

glowing, 346-349

labels, 337-340

metallic, 343-346

non-anti-aliased, 9

selections, 233

tools, 308

Text tool, 272

Texture command (Filter menu), Web:56

Texture layer, Web:56

threshold, adjustment layers, 252

Threshold command (Filter menu), 206, 393

Threshold filter, 206

Threshold layers, 393

Thumbnail Size slider, 36

thumbnails, 5, 34

changing to new image, 118

collapsed version sets, 133

file dates, 76

imported images, 38

updating, 118

TIFF format, 5, 134

digital cameras, 137

saving images, 138

saving selections, 231

Tile command (Window menu), 373

time, changing, 70-73

Timeline, Organizer, 33

Tolerance levels, eraser tools, 256

Tolerance option, Background Eraser tool, 258

Tolerance settings, 214

tones

histograms, 376-382

restoring old photos, 364-367

Toolbox, 308-310

Editor, 121

options, 310-313

retouching photos, 308

Zoom tool, 147

tools. *See also* individual tool names

retouching photos, 308

tips, Shortcuts bar, 33

Toolbox, hidden tools, 121

Torn Edges command (Filter menu), Web:37

Torn Edges filter, Web:37

tracing selections, 210-214

Transfer Printing frame, 175

Transform command (Image menu), 266, Web:51

Transparency option, 166

Transparent option, background color selection, 129

transparent pixels, 326

Turbulence tool, Web:43-45

Turbulent Jitter, Web:44

TWAIN, 50

Twirl Clockwise tool, Web:43

Twirl Counter-Clockwise tool, Web:43

type. *See also* text
backscreening, 340-343
captions, 337-340
filling with image, 349-352
glowing, 346-349
labels, 337-340
metallic, 343-346
tools, 308

Type tool
backscreening text, 340-343
captions and labels, 337-340
glowing text, 346-349
metallic text, 343-346

U

Unconstrained tool, 334
Underline button, 338
Underpainting filter, Web:64
Underpainting layer, Web:64
Undo button, 22
Undo History palette, 27, 124
undos, 27
Uniform option, Palette list, 164
Units & Rulers command (Edit menu), 126
Unsharp mask, resampling, 154
Unsharp Mask command (Filter menu), 370, Web:23
Unsharp Mask filter, 408, 412
unstack images, 70
Unstack Photos command (Edit menu), 70

Untagged Items command (Find menu), 99
Update Thumbnail command (Edit menu), 118
uploading digital images to Internet, 6
Use Lower Case Extension option, Save dialog box, 144

V

Version Set command (Edit menu), 133
version sets, 68, 132
collapsed thumbnails, 133
red-eye fix, 46
Vertical Type Mask tool, 249, 308, 349-352
Vertical Type tool, 308, 337, Web:38
View and Organize Photos button, 31
View menu commands
Grid, 125
Menu Types, 34
Rulers, 124, Web:34
Selection, 20
Snap to Grid, 125, Web:86
View Photos in Order button, 186
View Photos link, 201
viewing tools, 308
vignette frames, creating, Web:56
vintage looks, Web:52
virtual drives, 43
viruses, 196

Visible icon, 16
visual impact, improving
aging photos, Web:52-58
Andy Warhol technique, Web:80-81, Web:84-87
changes to black and white, Web:58-61
creating weather, Web:46-49
drawing effect, Web:75, Web:78-80
framing photo, Web:30-34
melting images, Web:42-45
oil painting effect, Web:61, Web:64-68
panoramas, Web:39-42
scrapbook pages, Web:36-38
water reflection simulation, Web:49-52
watercolor effect, Web:69, Web:72-74

W

Warhol, Andy, photo technique, Web:80-81, Web:84-87
Warp tool, Web:43
Watch Folders command (File menu), 38
Water Paper command (Filter menu), Web:78
water reflections, Web:49-52
Watercolor command (Filter menu), Web:73
Watercolor filter, Web:72-73
watercolors, changing photo, Web:69, Web:72-74
Watermark option, 156

watermarks, 156

Wave filter, 129, Web:44

weather, creating effect, Web:46-49

Web forces, 166

Web option, Palette list, 164

web pages, image formats, 134

websites

Kodak EasyShare, 200

Sams Publishing, 247

White option, background color selection, 129

White Point pane, 290

white points, 289, 388-389

whitening teeth, Web:18-20

WIA (Windows Image Acquisition), 50

width, adjusting, 128

Window menu commands

Color Swatches, 318

Histogram, 376, 381, 384

Images, 120, 373

Info, 310, 366

Layers, 409

Navigator, 149

Order Prints, 185

Organize Bin, 101

Photo Bin, 119

Properties, 87, 145-146

Reset Palette Locations, 124

Styles and Effects, 343

Windows Explorer, file dates, 74

Windows Image Acquisition (WIA), 50

work areas, Organizer, 31-32

Wow Chrome finish, 344

Wow Neon layer styles, 346

wrinkles, removing, Web:15-17

Write E-mail captions to catalog option, 188

X–Y–Z

Year button, 110

Yellows channel, 405

zero origins, 125

ZIP option, 139

Zoom All Windows option, 149

Zoom In button, 147-149

Zoom Out button, 147-149

Zoom slider, 149

Zoom tool, 147-149, 262, 303, 308

melting images, Web:44

red eye removal, 300

zooming, 67, 120, 147-149

Key Terms

Don't let unfamiliar terms discourage you from learning all you can about Photoshop Elements 4. If you don't completely understand what one of these words means, flip to the indicated page, read the full definition there, and find techniques related to that term.

Adjustment layer *A special layer that allows you to make a specific color or contrast adjustment to the layers underneath it.* **Page 251**

Alpha transparency *Variable transparency—from fully transparent to partially transparent, which enables you to gradually fade the pixels along the edge of an image against a Web page background.* **133**

Anti-aliasing *The addition of semi-transparent pixels along the curved edge of a shape or selection to help smooth curves.* **3**

Artifacts *Unwanted blocks of color typically introduced in a digital photo by too much compression.* **133**

Background Eraser *A tool that erases pixels (makes transparent) that match the pixel under its crosshair as you drag.* **254**

Background layer *The lowest layer in an image; it cannot be moved in the layer stack until it is converted to a regular layer.* **3**

Black and white points *Pixels in a photo that should be pure white or pure black. By identifying these pixels, you can correct the color balance and tone throughout an image.* **386**

Blend modes *Tool or layer settings that govern the way in which pixels copied or painted by a tool or existing on a top layer are blended with existing pixels.* **308**

Bounding box *A rectangle that describes the boundaries of a drawn object, cropping border, or selection.* **332**

Canvas *The working area of an image, as defined by the image's outer dimensions.* **158**

Captions *A text or audio description of a media file.* **30**

Clipping mask *Controls what portions of any upper layers grouped with the mask appear in the final image.* **273**

Collection *A marker associated with an ordered group of media files that share the same context or purpose.* **74**

Color management *The process of coordinating the color gamut of your monitor with that of your scanner and printer so that the same colors are reproduced throughout your system.* **280**

Color mode *Determines the number of colors an image can contain.* **126**

Contact sheet *A printout of a group of images, in miniature thumbnails, along with identifying labels.* **175**

Creations *Greeting cards, calendars, Web galleries, slideshows, and other things you can make with the images in the catalog.* **3**

Distort *To stretch a corner of a layer in any one direction.* **Page 263**

Dithering *A technique for simulating a color whose value does not appear in an image's palette by mixing pixels of the two closest available shades.* **133**

DPI (dots per inch) *Used to describe printer output. The higher the DPI, the more detail in a printed image.* **3**

Edge mask *A selection that encompasses only the edge pixels in an image, thus preventing unwanted sharpening to everything else.* **408**

Effect *A combination of filters and other image manipulations applied together automatically.* **3**

Email client *A program that sends and receives email. Popular email clients/programs include Outlook and Outlook Express.* **187**

Eraser *A tool that erases (makes transparent) the pixels under its brush.* **254**

Error diffusion *Any of several mathematical techniques that attempt to compensate for large differences (errors) between the color of an original pixel and its replacement in a resampled image.* **161**

EXIF (Exchangeable Image File) *Data attached to a photo file that contains the key settings the camera used when the photo was shot.* **96**

Feathering *The addition of partly selected pixels along the edge of a selection, often to help blend a relocated selection into its surroundings.* **225**

File Date *The date on which an image was taken or scanned into the system.* **70**

Filter *A series of computer instructions that modify the pixels in an image.* **3**

Gamma *The measure of the contrast of an image or imaging device, such as a monitor.* **376**

Gamut *A palette comprised of all the individual colors that can be reproduced by a device.* **280**

Gradient *A gradual transition between two colors, sometimes by way of a third (or more) color.* **329**

Handles *Small squares that appear along the perimeter of the bounding box surrounding a drawn object, cropping border, or selection marquee.* **332**

Histogram *A chart that depicts the relative distribution of pixels in an image that share the same characteristics, such as lightness, saturation, hue, or presence in a particular color channel (red, green, or blue).* **376**